P U N I S H M E N T
A N D
REHABILITATION
S E C O N D   E D I T I O N

Jeffrie G. Murphy

Arizona State University

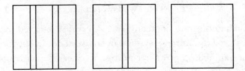

Wadsworth Publishing Company
Belmont, California
A Division of Wadsworth, Inc.

To Jim and Lee Canacakos

Philosophy Editor: Kenneth King

Production Editor: Vicki Friedberg

Design and Cover: Andrew H. Ogus

Print Buyer: Karen Hunt

Copy Editor: Susan Thornton

Cover Illustration: Dennis Nolan

Printed in the United States of America

1 2 3 4 5 6 7 8 9 10—89 88 87 86 85

ISBN 0-534-04614-2

Library of Congress Cataloging in Publication Data
Main entry under title:

Punishment and rehabilitation.

Bibliography: p.
   1. Punishment—Addresses, essays, lectures.
2. Rehabilitation of criminals—Addresses, essays,
lectures. 3. Capital punishment—Addresses, essays,
lectures. I. Murphy, Jeffrie G.
HV8693.P84   1985   364.6   84-21920
ISBN 0-534-04614-2

CONTENTS

PREFACE

The first edition of *Punishment and Rehabilitation,* compiled in 1972, has been in print since 1973, and its extensive classroom use has been very gratifying. When I first prepared the book in 1972, the rehabilitative ideal—the idea that punishment should be supplemented, or perhaps even replaced, with therapy—dominated discussion. This ideal had gifted advocates and gifted critics, and the resulting debate was both lively and profound. This debate is, of course, still with us; thus it remains a central part of this second edition.

In the law of crime and punishment, however, 1972 was a crucial year, a year that placed another issue at the center of philosophical and legal discussion. For several years prior, executions had been delayed all over America as state officials and death row inmates awaited the Supreme Court's decision on the question of whether capital punishment, the punishment of death, represented "cruel and unusual" (and thus constitutionally impermissible) punishment. In a 1972 case, *Furman v. Georgia,* the court issued what was to be the first in a long and complicated series of opinions on this difficult matter. The death penalty became the "in" topic in the philosophy of punishment.

The first edition of *Punishment and Rehabilitation* contained no essays dealing primarily with capital punishment, an issue of central legal and philosophical importance and one that arouses intense student interest. This is such a serious gap that I find I can no longer use the first edition in my own courses without providing supplementary readings on the topic. This second edition has been updated to rectify this shortcoming and so provides both legal and philosophical materials on the issue of capital punishment.

In preparing this new edition, I was glad to have the opportunity to make a few other changes. The discussion of rehabilitation and other possible alternatives to punishment has become more sophisticated since 1973, and I have, therefore, added three new articles to enrich that discussion. I have also added two new articles on the justification of punishment

I'd like also to call the reader's attention to a change in format. In addition to the introduction for the entire collection, I have added special introductions for each part. These introductions are substantive and should not be ignored by the reader. In some cases I was able to summarize material from my own essays that were included in the first edition. This allowed me to add more recent essays to this collection.

Finally, let me express some thanks and issue a request: I have received numerous communications over the past few years from both teachers and students who have used the earlier edition. I have received good suggestions from many of these people and have incorporated some of them into the present edition. I am grateful to those who took the time to write to me. I am also grateful for the helpful ideas offered by series editor Richard Wasserstrom, University of California at Santa Cruz, and for the thoughtful review provided by David Cohen, University of California at Berkeley. So that I can continue to improve this book and for my own benefit and the benefit of my students, I welcome your comments and suggestions.

Jeffrie G. Murphy
Department of Philosophy
Arizona State University
Tempe, Arizona

Introduction

The topic of punishment fascinates people, learned and unlearned alike, to a degree that is rare for any topic that may even in part be called "philosophical." The fiction of crime and punishment, whether that of Dostoevski or Collins or Agatha Christie, is perennially popular. Public debate on topics related to punishment (for example, the legalization of marijuana, the death penalty, the insanity defense) is closely followed by the media. Important and far-reaching developments in tax and real estate law stimulate no comparable popular interest—although most of us pay taxes and own or rent homes, and comparatively few of us will ever experience a serious threat of criminal punishment, much less the actual infliction of such punishment.

The intense interest, then, is perhaps perplexing, and many fanciful explanations for it have been given. Some psychiatrists say that our fascination with punishment is a vicarious satisfaction of certain unconscious mental states, such as the desire to inflict punishment (or at least hurt) on others or the fear that we ourselves may come to suffer a kind of punishment. Philosophers of an existentialist persuasion may claim that we see (and envy) the criminal as a paradigm of a completely free person, autonomous from the chains of social obligation. Others who are inclined to be somewhat more flattering to human nature may explain our interest in punishment on conscious grounds that are perfectly rational: the prudential fear that we may become victims of crime and the moral desire to reduce suffering and injustice in the world by means that do not themselves contribute unnecessarily to suffering and injustice. And theologians see, in punishment, an earthly example of the cosmic drama of sin and redemption.

No doubt there is some truth in all of these claims, at least as explanations of why crime and punishment capture the popular imagination. But a different question is why the topic captures the *philosophical* imagination. Why has this topic, unlike other popular issues (for instance, sex), produced a genuinely astounding volume of writings from philosophers from at least the time of Plato on down through articles in the most recent philosophical journals? I think that there are several explanations for this, and it is worth mentioning them at the outset. I shall focus on six that are, though related, reasonably distinct.

1. *The Intersection of Law and Morals.* In the criminal law, we find a body of evolved and codified thought directed toward issues at the heart of morality: excuse and justification, responsibility, duty and obligation, good and evil, right and wrong. As a result, frequently a study of the legal use of a certain concept, *excuse,* say, will illuminate the moral use of that concept. Such a study of a legal concept is never final in moral analysis, and it does not always even illuminate. But it sometimes does; and moral philosophers need all the help they can get, from whatever quarter.

   Just as a study of the law can sometimes illuminate moral thinking, so too can moral thinking illuminate legal matters. How, for example, is anyone ever to come to terms with constitutional concepts such as *cruel and unusual punishment* or *due process of law* without an ability to think, in morally sophisticated ways, about the nature of suffering and injustice? And of course it goes without saying that all existing systems of criminal law are at numerous points vulnerable to a variety of moral criticisms. A moral person cares about what happens to people (what they are stopped from doing, when they are hurt, and so on), and the criminal law is an example of an institution that functions directly by making things happen to people, for better or for worse. The moral person wants it to be for better.

2. *The Moral Centrality of the Topic of Punishment.* The concept of punishment stands at the core of moral thinking; as a result, its analysis necessarily affects (and in turn is affected by) a great many other moral concepts: blame, praise, reward, responsibility, mercy, forgiveness, justice, charity, obligation, and rights, just to name some. Also its analysis affects, and is affected by, the analysis of what might be called the *moral feelings:* resentment, indignation, remorse, guilt, shame, for example. It is not a topic that one can discuss without making clear one's commitments on most of the other major issues of moral philosophy. And, in turn, one's major moral commitments will entail consequences for one's attitude toward punishment; witness the division, in the theory of punishment, between utilitarians (with their moral stress on the avoidance of suffering) and Kantians (with their moral stress on the avoidance of injustice). I am not sure that there is any topic in moral philosophy that does not ramify in this way. Punishment, however, is a very clear and dramatic example of one that does.

3. *Metaphysical Involvement.* Another reason why the topic of punishment and the family of moral concepts surrounding it are of philosophical interest is their obvious involvement with issues of metaphysics. For it is impossible to discuss, for example, the nature of a just system of responsibility and excuse without coming to terms with the mind-body problem, the problem of free will and determinism, and issues in the analysis of human action. It is also very difficult to generate and make exciting certain metaphysical issues (free will and determinism is a good example here) without noting the moral and legal perplexities from which these issues tend to grow. In examining what people think about punishment one also learns what they think

about the nature of persons: what it is to be a person and what sort of status a person is to enjoy. From *Oedipus Rex* we learn, not just the Greek view on punishment, but also and necessarily something of their view on human beings and the place of human beings in the universe.

4. *Political Philosophy*. It could be persuasively argued that the central problem of political philosophy is in coming to terms with the nature and justification of coercion. Punishment is state coercion in its most obvious (and perhaps most brutal) form. And thus any political philosophy that addresses itself to the core of its discipline must come to terms with the issue of punishment in order either to praise it with Kant and Hegel, tolerate it with Bentham and Mill, or oppose it with Marx and Kropotkin. It is not to be avoided.

5. *Philosophy and Empirical Science*. Another exciting aspect of the topic of punishment is the way in which, unlike a great many topics in philosophy, it intersects and is relevant to discoveries in empirical science. Philosophical theories are not themselves empirical, and philosophers are not in general occupationally qualified to assess the confirmation of empirical claims. Philosophical theories can, however, presuppose certain empirical claims for their truth or intelligibility. Thus philosophers cannot always safely ignore empirical work, since such work may undercut the presuppositions of their own theories. They have an obligation, therefore, to keep themselves informed of relevant work in the scientific community.

Theories of punishment represent a clear example of philosophical theories with empirical presuppositions. The utilitarian deterrence theory, for example, presupposes that people rationally calculate consequences before engaging in crime. One who seeks to evaluate this theory cannot simply ignore the claim often made by psychiatrists that criminality is rarely deliberative but is usually impulsive. And could the retributive theory of punishment, with its stress on doing the just thing, remain intact if the Marxist analysis of criminality as growing out of poverty and unjust exploitation were accepted as true? Philosophy here has something to learn from science.

But science has something to learn from philosophy as well. Psychiatrists and social scientists are frequently arguing for reform in the criminal law, even the complete abandonment of punishment, on grounds that lie outside their scientific competence, for example, B. F. Skinner's claim that the concepts of autonomy, dignity, and responsibility have been refuted by science, or Karl Menninger's claim that justice is unscientific. The philosopher has an important job in pointing out these confusions, in making sure that empirical scientists are accepted as authorities only on claims that are empirical and not on their amateur philosophical speculations.

6. *Practical Urgency*. In respect to practical urgency the philosophical and the popular interest intersect. Many philosophers want their work to be socially useful, and the issues of punishment and responsibility seem to provide an area in which philosophical work can have practical social utility. Everybody wants to do something about the criminal law. Law and order hard-liners want to make it even more terrifying. Some want to eliminate it for a variety of reasons all the way from the Christian's "we are all guilty" to the psychiatrist's "nobody is guilty." The most interesting new challenge comes from behavioral science. From all sides we are bombarded with a variety of scientific challenges to criminal responsibility: criminals are mentally ill; criminals suffer from brain pathology; criminals have chromosome abnormalities; criminals are labeled *deviants* for certain social purposes; criminals are simply people who need their patterns of reinforcement changed. Very often these claims are coup-

led with the claims that determinism has at last been established; that the concepts of responsibility, freedom, and dignity have been shown to be superstitions; and that we can at last move away from punishment into a land of benevolent scientific therapy where deviants will simply be rewired or programmed in order to make them socially acceptable. What are we to make of such claims? Do they really represent an opportunity to free our system of criminal justice from superstitious obscurantism and move it into the clear and bright world of science? Or are they perhaps instead claims based on a pseudoscientific set of illusions, illusions with potentially degrading or even totalitarian implications?

The present anthology presents a variety of essays that, taken together, should provide the reader with an organizing framework within which thought about the above issues can rationally be structured. To get a more detailed idea of the nature and importance of the essays selected, the reader should consult the introductions at the beginning of each section.

PART I

THE JUSTIFICATION OF PUNISHMENT

The core punishments of the criminal law (deprivation of liberty or life) represent very serious assaults on the fundamental rights of persons, stigmatize and humiliate those persons, and typically cause those persons great personal unhappiness. Even when punishments are not actually inflicted on individuals, the possibility that they might be inflicted may be sufficient to generate enough fear in those individuals to cause them to refrain from acting in ways they otherwise would have found desirable: a coercive curtailment of liberty.

Given the radically intrusive nature of criminal punishment, it is natural that persons committed to the values of individual rights and a free society would seek for morally and politically acceptable alternatives to punishment and would regard punishment as justified, as a last resort, only if no less intrusive alternatives (such as "a good talking to") seem likely to work. Adapting constitutional language from a somewhat different context, one might seek to discover whether criminal punishment, as a mechanism that encumbers fundamental rights of persons, is indeed the least restrictive means that could be employed to accomplish whatever compelling goals or interests the state currently seeks to accomplish through punishment. If one truly values the rights of persons, then surely one will want to demand of the state that it not threaten such rights in the pursuit of goals that are of a trivial or controversial social importance.

General philosophical theories of punishment may be thought of as answers to the question of what goal the state should aim at if it must employ the practice of punishment. Two such goals have most often been cited:

1. *Deterrence:* The state punishes Jones in order to give Jones an incentive for not engaging in criminal conduct again in the future (this is called *special deterrence*), or the state punishes Jones as an example to others so that they will have incentives for not engaging in criminal conduct (this is called *general deterrence*). Punishment is here justified by its crime control consequences, and thus the deterrence rationale is also linked to another, namely, *incapacitation:* Jones's punishment is designed to keep Jones out of circulation and therefore no longer be able to prey on others.
2. *Retribution:* The state punishes Jones in order that Jones will be given his or her just deserts and will "pay a debt" for the wrong done to other members of the community by a criminal action. (This is very rough, since one of the problems with the retributive outlook on punishment is to explain just what it means. More careful attempts to define retribution occur in several of the readings.)

In the first essay, Stanley I. Benn provides a comprehensive overview of punishment as a philosophical problem. He analyzes the concept of punishment, discusses various classical theories of its justification, considers questions of personal responsibility for conduct, and closes with a brief examination of a therapeutic response to crime. This essay can best be viewed as providing a general introduction to the readings that follow.

The next selections are concerned with the justification of punishment. The selection from Kant is a classical defense of a *retributive* theory. According to this theory, punishment is justified primarily by backward-looking considerations: The criminal, having engaged in wrongful conduct in the past, *deserves* punishment. It would be unjust for a criminal not to receive it. In receiving punishment, the criminal pays a kind of *debt* to fellow citizens—to those other members of the community who have made the sacrifice of obedience that is required for any just legal system to work. Since all persons benefit from the operation of a just legal system, and since such systems require general obedience in order to work, it is only fair or just that all persons so benefiting make the sacrifice (obedience or self-restraint) required and thereby do their part. Those who do not, must pay in some other way (receive punishment) because it would not be fair to those who have been obedient if the criminal were allowed to profit from wrongdoing. (In this view a certain kind of "profit"—not bearing the burden of self-restraint—is intrinsic to criminal wrongdoing.) Hegel, who elaborated this Kantian retributive theory, argued that criminals, who as rational persons could see that even they derived benefits from participation in a community of law, could be regarded as *rationally willing* (though not empirically desiring) their punishment. This being so, they deserve it in the sense that they have a *right* to it. Though the claim that a criminal has a right to be punished seems initially counterintuitive, Herbert Morris in his "Persons and Punishment" attempts to show that the claim contains an important moral insight. In his "A Paternalistic Theory of Punishment," Morris goes beyond a purely retributive outlook on punishment, arguing that punishment is acceptable only if tied to the moral improvement of the criminal.

Bentham, in his classic statement of the *utilitarian* theory of punishment, predicates his entire discussion upon the assumption that the retributive theory outlined above is nothing but a combination of obscurantist nonsense and primitive vindictiveness. Punishment, he argues, is to be justified solely by an appeal to forward-looking considerations. The only important questions are the following: Will punishing this person bring about more good than bad consequences for society as a whole? That is, will it deter, incapacitate, or reform? If so, will this result in benefits sufficient to outweigh the misery that punishment will cause? If the answer is *no,* then we should not punish even if, in some obscure sense, the criminal "deserves" it; for this would be productive of no useful consequences. And, in a utilitarian view, consequences are all that matter in morality.[1] But what if the person is *innocent,* that is, clearly does *not* deserve punishment? It might still produce good consequences if we did punish that individual to make a scapegoat as an example to others. That this could be the case is surely a contingent possibility. And yet it seems clearly wrong (unjust) to punish such a person no matter how good the consequences, and so there may be some virtue in the retributivist's insistence on desert after all. John Rawls, in his essay, tries to combine the best features of both the retributive and utilitarian outlooks, formulating the utilitarian theory so that punishment of the innocent will not be allowed.

The final essay, by Jeffrie G. Murphy, returns attention to the issues raised by Herbert Morris. In "Marxism and Retribution," is is argued that the retributive theory, though morally correct when applied to just societies, may be incorrect in application to most actual societies: societies that might be regarded as class-divided, inegalitarian, and distributively unjust. The topic of punishment is not simply a topic in moral philosophy but must be seen in the context of social and political philosophy as well.[2]

One final note: Theories of punishment always begin with the assumption that a society's penal code has been properly designed: that conduct criminalized is conduct that *should* be criminalized. (If a certain course of conduct should never have been criminalized in the first place, then of course it should not ultimately be punished.) The question of what to criminalize—the question of rationale for specific criminal offenses—is very difficult. Indeed, the question of whether we should even have a criminal law at all is more difficult and controversial than might at first appear. (Why not allow all wrongdoing so long as *compensation* is paid to victims for ary resulting harm?) It is regrettable that limitations of space do not allow material on this topic in the present volume, but fortunately the editor can disinterestedly recommend a good starting reading in the area: Chapter 3 of *The Philosophy of Law: An Introduction to Jurisprudence* by Jeffrie G. Murphy and Jules L. Coleman, Totowa, N.J.: Rowman and Allanheld, 1984.

---

1. The move toward a therapeutic response to crime can be seen as, at least in part, an outgrowth of a utilitarian outlook. If one is going to evaluate punishment solely in terms of its social consequences—its capacity to reduce crime—one might quite reasonably reach the conclusion that therapy would do a better job of bringing about these consequences. Even a retributivist, however, could become sympathetic to a therapeutic approach to crime if convinced that criminals were so mentally abnormal that they could not fairly be held responsible. A person with such a belief about criminals would find it difficult to regard them as fully *deserving* their punishment.

2. For further exploration of this theme see Jeffrie G. Murphy, "Retributivism, Moral Education, and the Liberal State" in *Criminal Justice Ethics,* 1985.

Punishment

Stanley I. Benn

The word "punishment" is used in varying contexts. The punishment meted out by the state to a criminal or by a parent to his children is not the same as the punishment boxers give or receive. The latter, however, is punishment only in a metaphorical sense, for it lacks several of the features necessary to a standard case of punishment. Characteristically, punishment is unpleasant. It is inflicted on an offender because of an offense he has committed; it is deliberately imposed, not just the natural consequence of a person's action (like a hang-over), and the unpleasantness is essential to it, not an accidental accompaniment to some other treatment (like the pain of the dentist's drill). It is imposed by an agent authorized by the system of rules against which an offense has been committed; a lynching is not a standard case of punishment. Philosophers who have written on punishment have usually had in mind punishment in the standard sense rather than in any extended or metaphorical sense.

The philosopher's interest in punishment is mainly connected with questions of justification. It is, prima facie, wrong to deliberately inflict suffering or deprivation on an-

---

other person, yet punishment consists in doing precisely this. What conditions, the philosopher asks, would justify it? Or, more generally, what kind of consideration would count toward a justification? For instance, if a person had already committed a crime, that would clearly be relevant to the question of whether he ought to be punished (although it might not be conclusive). What if he were only expected to commit a crime in the future? Or, again, is it relevant to the question of whether this man should be punished to say that punishing him would deter others? And assuming that criminals ought to be punished, how should we set about deciding appropriate penalties?

It is not, of course, the business of the moral or social philosopher to provide a justification for any particular act or system of punishment or even of the institution of punishment in general. Philosophers are not necessarily apologists for their society and age. They are interested in the procedures and modes of argument that we are committed to by our fundamental conceptions of morality and in criteria of criticism and justification rather than in inquiries into whether actual institutions satisfy them.

Philosophers, it is true, have not always made this distinction; they have often worked on the understanding that a philosophical argument could be seriously shaken by showing that it leads to conclusions inconsistent with some widely approved institution or moral rule. Moreover, for many philosophers, if such a rule or institution seemed to imply a principle inconsistent with other moral principles accepted by the society, there must necessarily be some broader principle, which a philosopher could discover and by which the conflict could be resolved. Applied to the case of punishment, this would mean that a philosopher must reconcile the apparently conflicting principles that wrongdoers should be punished and that it is wrong to deliberately make another man suffer. But this is surely a misconception of the nature of philosophy. There is no point, after all, in asking whether and how punishment can be justified if one assumes in advance that it can. For justification a number of contingent facts are required that the philosopher as such is not qualified to provide. His task is to analyze what is being asked for and so to point out what kinds of facts and arguments are admissible to the discussion.

Justification of Punishment

The question of justification arises at two levels. One can take for granted the principle that wrongdoers should be punished and ask whether a particular case of punishment was justified. At this level the philosopher is concerned with the criteria in a general system which any particular act of punishment must satisfy. One can, however, question the very idea of punishment as an institution which involves deliberately inflicting pain or deprivation. This raises the philosophical question of how one justifies a set of rules or an institution like a penal system. Corresponding to these two levels of justification are two broadly opposed approaches to punishment, the retributivist and the utilitarian. Each, in fact, has been taken to offer an answer to the problems at both levels, but the persuasive force of retributivism is mainly in its answers to problems of the first type, and of utilitarianism to questions of the second type. Characteristically, the retributivist stresses guilt and desert, looking back to the crime to justify punishment and denying that the consequences of punishment, beneficial or otherwise, have any relevance to justification. The utilitarian, on the other hand, insists that punishment can be justified only if it has beneficent consequences that outweigh the intrinsic evil of inflicting suffering on human beings.

Retributivist Theories

{The most thoroughgoing retributivists, exemplified by Kant, maintain that the punishment of crime is right in itself, that it is fitting that the guilty should suffer, and that justice, or the moral order, requires the institution of punishment} This, however, is not to justify punishment but, rather, to deny that it needs any justification. To say that something is right or good in itself means that it does not need to be justified in terms of the value or rightness of anything else. Its intrinsic value is appreciated immediately or intuitively. But since at least some people do doubt that punishment is right, an appeal to intuition is necessarily unsatisfactory. Again, to say "it is fitting" or "justice demands" that the guilty should suffer is only to reaffirm that punishment is right, not to give grounds for thinking so.

Some retributivists, while admitting that punishment is, prima facie, evil, maintain that it is nevertheless better that the wicked should be punished than that they should prosper more than the virtuous and, perhaps, at their expense. In this view, the function of criminal law is to punish wickedness or immorality in order to maintain a kind of cosmic distributive justice. However, it is not self-evident that wickedness should be punished any more than it is self-evident that legal guilt should be. Archbishop Temple, himself a retributivist, declared that he had no "intuition that it is good that the wicked should suffer." Nor is it clear that virtue must be rewarded or that universal justice requires the kind of human rectification that this sort of retributivism envisages. Of course, in a universe in which the wicked prospered, there might be no incentive to virtue, but this is essentially a utilitarian mode of argument. Again, evil motives and a bad character are necessary conditions of wickedness but not of legal guilt and criminal liability. The state's function is to punish breaches of those rules which in the public interest ought to be upheld; it is a matter of indifference in law (but not in morals) that some men who observe the rules do so from the unworthy motive of fear and others break them from laudable motives of principle. Conversely, it is at least doubtful whether the criminal law should provide penalties for offenses against morality except where the public interest is at stake—e.g., whether it should extend to cases of lying other than, say, false pretenses and perjury.

Though immorality is neither a necessary nor a sufficient condition for punishment, the relation between law and morals is nevertheless a close one, and what punishment is to the one, blame is to the other. Both regulate social intercourse, and in any given society the aims and ideals upheld by the law will usually correspond, more or less, with those upheld by the dominant morality. Moreover, in the family and the school punishment is often used to reinforce moral condemnation as part of the process of moral education. Some writers who regard punishment as moral retribution couple this idea with the argument that the point of punishment is to be found in what Lord Justice Denning has called "the emphatic denunciation by the community of a crime." In this view, punishment reinforces the community's respect for its legal and moral standards, which criminal acts would tend to undermine if they were not solemnly denounced.

There is, however, no intrinsic reason why denunciation should take precisely the form of inflicting suffering on criminals, unless, perhaps, one accepts Ewing's view that punishment has the advantage of impressing both on the criminal and on everyone else that a breach of law and morals is so serious that society must do something to prevent it. That, however, is surely to justify punishment by its utility in maintaining respect for the law. Rashdall refers to "the enormous importance of the criminal law in promoting the moral education of the public mind," but Rashdall was a utilitarian who justified punishment by reference to "the production of good effects on conscious beings."

For Hegel punishment is necessary to annul the wrong done by the criminal. By this he means something more than restitution or compensation, neither of which is, strictly speaking, punishment. It is, rather, that the criminal has upset the balance of the moral order, which can be restored only by his being made to suffer. Or, in terms of the dialectic, crime is a negation of right and as such a nullity; punishment negates the negation, thus reaffirming the right. But in what sense can punishment be said to restore the balance or annul the wrong, unless it is taken for granted that criminals deserve to be punished? This is precisely the point in question.

Utilitarian Theories

The utilitarian position is exemplified in Bentham's remark that "all punishment is a mischief. . . . If it ought at all to be admitted, it ought only to be admitted in as far as it promises to exclude some greater evil." By reforming the criminal, by deterring him or others from similar offenses in the future, or by directly preventing further offenses by imprisonment, deportation, or execution, the good that comes out of punishment may outweigh (so the utilitarian argues) the intrinsic evil of suffering deliberately inflicted. Without such effects, or if the suffering inflicted exceeded the suffering avoided, the institution would be unjustified.

The critics of utilitarianism claim that if people generally could be persuaded that an innocent man was guilty, utilitarianism would justify punishing him since as a warning to others he would be just as useful as a genuine offender. Again, offenders might be deterred by threatening to punish their wives and children, particularly, if as is so often the case with political terrorists and resistance fighters, it were difficult to catch the offenders themselves. Or, again, if punishment could be justified as a way of reforming criminals, it would seem better to punish them before, rather than after, they committed their crimes. Retributivists claim that utilitarians are in danger of losing sight of two conditions which are necessary to the very idea of punishment—namely, that an offense should have been committed and that punishment shall be of the offender himself, who alone can be said to deserve it. "Punishment is punishment," wrote F. H. Bradley, "only when it is deserved"; punishment for any other reason is "a crying injustice."

The dilemma of utilitarianism, then, at least in its crude form, is that it justifies punishing innocent people provided that such punishment causes less suffering than might otherwise be caused by the would-be criminals it deters. Some utilitarians argue that in the end the deception would break down, that it could not be used systematically, or that the long-term consequences would be bad for society. But these answers are unsatisfactory because they depend on assumptions of purely contingent consequences. Our revulsion against punishing innocent men seems to go deeper than that. In any case, these answers will not meet the case for punishing hostages, which can certainly be done systematically and requires no deception or secrecy.

Punishment and Principles of Justice

To meet the above criticisms, a crude utilitarianism would have to be supplemented by other moral principles—namely, that differences in treatment must be justified by relevant differences in circumstance or condition, where "relevance" is defined in the light of general rules, and that every human being should be treated with at least a minimum of respect as a source of claims and not as a mere instrument for the promotion of the interests of others. It can be argued that punishment of the innocent or of hostages is an abuse not because it necessarily makes for more unhappiness than it prevents but because it treats innocent men in a way that is appropriate only for the guilty and makes an arbitrary difference in treatment between them and other innocent men. Moreover, a legal system is designed to guide conduct by laying down rules and attaching penalties to those who choose to break them. It is acceptable, in the words of J. D. Mabbott, only because "the criminal makes the essential choice; he 'brings it on himself.'" Otherwise, punishment would not be consistent with the principle of respect for persons. The hostage, on the other hand, has no chance to settle his own fate; he is used as a mere lever for manipulating other people's conduct, and his own interest is subordinate to that of the other members of society. Punishment of the innocent ignores, in short, fundamental procedural rules of justice and morality without which utilitarianism would make little sense, for unless everyone is worthy of equal consideration as a source of claims, whose interest is to count in assessing the utility of a course of action? Whom are we entitled to treat as simply a tool for advancing other men's interests—as Aristotle's "slave by nature"—and what would count as a reason for considering other men before him?

This has bearing, too, on the reasons for accepting as excuses such defenses as duress, unavoidable accident, or ignorance of fact—conditions under which an offender can claim that he could not help doing what he did. Bentham argued that to punish anyone under such conditions would be pointless and, therefore, mischievous, because the threat of penalties could not possibly deter anyone in the future who was similarly placed. Now, it is true that nothing would be lost if such people escaped punishment, provided they could be distinguished from cheats trying to take advantage of such excuses and provided enough offenders without such excuses could be detected to furnish examples for others. The principle of "strict liability," which exists in some legal systems for certain offenses, has been defended on the utilitarian ground that it is impossible to tell a genuine excuse from a pretense. It is questionable, however, whether a person who would otherwise be treated as innocent ought to be treated as guilty because someone else might otherwise escape a merited penalty. Punishing the man who commits an offense through ignorance or accident, because it is too difficult to tell whether he really did it on purpose or because we have to make an example of *someone,* is very like punishing the innocent as a warning to the guilty. The utilitarian case for these excuses is unsatisfactory inasmuch as it makes them subject to such qualifications.

A better ground for such excuses is that punishment is morally acceptable only if it is the consequence of an act freely chosen by the criminal, which it would not be under these conditions. A man acting in ignorance or by accident cannot be said to bring his punishment on himself. Punishment, seen as a way of influencing conduct, cannot be justified if there has been no real possibility of choice. Moreover, the punishment of involuntary offenses introduces into men's lives the possibility of disasters which they can neither foresee nor avert.

Utilitarianism, then, must be supplemented by principles of justice if it is not to clash with other moral principles that are usually considered fundamental. It has, however, the merit, as an approach to the justification of punishment, that it provides a clear procedure for determining whether the institution is acceptable in general terms. This the retributivist approach cannot do because it denies the relevance of weighing advantages and disadvantages, which is what we ultimately must do in moral criticism of rules and institutions. Consequently, a retributivist justification of punishment as an institution usually turns out to be a denial of the necessity for justification, a veiled reference to the beneficial results of punishment (a utilitarianism in disguise), or an appeal to religious authority.

When it is a question of justifying a particular case of punishment, however, the retributivist is in a far stronger position. There would be no point in having a general rule if on every occasion that it had to be applied one had to consider whether the advantages in this particular case warranted acting in accordance with it. Moreover, the point of punishment as deterrent would be quite lost were there no general expectation, based on the general operation of the rule, that guilty men would be punished. Assuming, then, that a penal system can be justified in utilitarian terms, any offense is at least prima facie an occasion for a penalty. Equally, without an offense there is no question of a penalty. The retributivist contention that punishment is justified if, and only if, it is deserved is really applicable, therefore, to the justification of particular instances of punishment, the institution as such being taken for granted.

Severity of Punishment

The clash between the utilitarian and retributivist approaches to punishment also arises in considering the criteria by which appropriate punishments are assessed. The retributivist insists that the punishment must fit the crime; the utilitarian relates the penalty to the general aims of the system, to the prevention of further crime, and, perhaps, to the reform of the criminal.

The most extreme form of retributivism is the law of retaliation: "an eye for an eye." This alone, Kant claimed, could provide a just measure of the penalty, since it was the crime itself and nothing else that settled it. However, to try to apply it literally might be monstrously cruel, or, as Kant recognized, it might be absurd. Thieves can be deprived of their property and murderers hanged, but what penalty is appropriate to the dope-peddler, the blackmailer, and the smuggler?

There is not much sense, either, in trying to construct a table of equivalents so that the amount of suffering inflicted by the criminal could be meted out to him in some other form. How can such a table be drawn up? How many years must a blackmailer spend in jail to experience suffering equal to his victim's? Is it possible, in any case, to make comparisons of suffering between persons? Of course, we do assess the gravity of an offense and try to ensure that the punishment for a trivial offense is less severe than for a serious one. But this is possible only because we take for granted an existing scale of penalties and grade new offenses accordingly. Such grading does not imply an intrinsic relation between the crime and the penalty apart from that established by the scale. Some retributivists admit this but claim nevertheless that the penalties prescribed by the law ought to reflect the moral heinousness of the offense. The most serious offenses against morals deserve the most severe penalties. This, however, only shifts the question a step back, for what makes one moral offense more serious than another?

Utilitarians have tended to concentrate on deterrence, turning away from the actual criminal act except as one of a class of actions that might be prevented by punishing the particular instance severely enough (but only just enough) to make the action unattractive to the offender and to possible future offenders. Unfortunately, there are always people who cannot be deterred or reformed. Beyond a certain point the additional suffering one would have to inflict on all offenders to reduce their number might be so great as to exceed the amount of suffering thereby averted. The aim of the utilitarian, then, would presumably be to select the penalty at which the aggregate of suffering caused by crimes actually committed and punishments actually inflicted would be the smallest possible.

The utilitarian approach has often been criticized as justifying severe penalties for trivial offenses and vice versa. To eliminate parking offenses might need heavier penalties than to eliminate blackmail, which would be monstrous. But this criticism misses the point of the utilitarian case. There would, indeed, be no objection to threatening the severest penalty for any offense providing the threat never had to be carried out. Punishment is only an unfortunate consequence of the fact that the threats, which are the true operative elements in the system, are partially ineffective and would be wholly ineffective if they were not carried out when they failed to deter. In fixing penalties, the utilitarian's problem is not, therefore, to minimize the number of offenses, irrespective of the punishment inflicted, but to minimize the total amount of suffering from both sources. If we call parking offenses trivial, we mean that each one causes relatively little suffering; therefore, we are prepared to put up with a large number of them rather than incur the cost of making offenders suffer heavy penalties. Blackmail, on the other hand, causes so much suffering that if heavier penalties would yield even a small reduction in the number of offenses, there might be a net gain even though offenders would suffer more than they did before. In this way a utilitarian might agree with the retributivist that severe penalties ought to be restricted to serious offenses, but he would argue that we call an offense serious precisely because it causes a great deal of suffering. For the retributivist only serious crimes *deserve* severe penalties; for the utilitarian only serious crimes are worth averting at the cost of severe penalties.

The utilitarian approach to this matter does not supply a procedure for sentencing particular criminals (any more than a justification for punishment as an institution would be a case for any particular application of it). Arguing from expected consequences, one might establish a kind of standard penalty for each class of offense. Officials drafting new rules might consider whether a proposed maximum penalty would keep offenses down to manageable proportions, or people concerned about road accidents might argue that heavier penalties for motoring offenses would make drivers more careful. Deciding the sentence in a particular case, however, is clearly a different matter. The maximum penalty is a limiting factor, but questions like the degree of responsibility, provocation, and the offender's previous record are all relevant. However, one might reasonably ask why, as a matter of principle, they should be relevant.

Punishment and Responsibility

The problem of responsibility arises in relation to punishment as it does in relation to blame in moral theory. The principle, discussed already, that a man ought not to be punished for doing what he cannot help creates difficulties when extended to actions which a man could not help doing because of his own state of mind instead of external or contingent factors, like duress or ignorance of fact. An insane man, as defined, say, by the M'Naghten rules (that is, one who did not know what he was doing or did not know that what he was doing was wrong), cannot be said to choose his act because he cannot know it for what it is. But sometimes a man may know that what he is doing is wrong yet still be unable to stop himself from doing it. He may be subject, for instance, to an irresistible temptation or provocation. But how is that to be understood? A temptation is not irresistible merely because a particular man has yielded to it or even because he might have been expected to yield to it. However, a temptation may be so strong that we might expect any ordinary person to yield to it (even though a few people may in fact resist it), or, as one might say, it might be "more than human nature can stand." In that sense it may be "irresistible."

Some people, of course, find it much more difficult than others to resist temptation. Some, like kleptomaniacs, are "impelled" to act in the sense that deliberation neither plays, nor could play, any part in what they do. Such people might be distinguished from plain wrongdoers by the fact that nothing—not blame, punishment, praise, or rational argument—seems to affect their disposition to break the rules. Or, again, their actions may lack any point, or if they can be said to have any point, it is only in relation to a set of aims and standards of achievement so distorted and eccentric that they are intelligible only to a psychiatrist. The kleptomaniac who steals nylon stockings for which he has no possible use (according to ordinary standards of utility) might properly be said to be unable to help stealing them. Far more difficult is the case of the psychopath, who seems to have no wish to resist temptation or, rather, who knows that some of the things he wants to do are wrong in the sense that other people disapprove of them but on whom this knowledge enforces no internal restraint beyond prompting a degree of caution. Criminals of this type would once have been described as "wicked" but are now often described as incapable of self-control. To say, however, that they are not responsible for their acts creates the odd situation that anyone is liable to punishment who usually resists temptation but sometimes fails, whereas the man who never resists is not liable at all.

The determinist has a short way with these difficulties. Since everyone's actions are the response of his character to a given set of circumstances, how can anyone ever be held responsible for his actions? We do what we must, given what we are, and what we are is the end of a causal chain going back to before we were born. If one knew a person well enough, one might predict that under given conditions he would commit a crime.

Is this compatible with saying that he can choose whether to do so, or is his belief in his freedom to choose simply an illusion? Can the result of a genuine choice be predicted?

To say that something is predictable is not, however, the same as saying it is unavoidable. We can forecast a man's actions just because we know the kind of choices that he regularly makes. The more we know of his dispositions and his preferences, the more likely we are to be right. But that does not mean that he never acts voluntarily or that he never makes a real choice but only thinks he does. If all choices are illusions, what would a real choice be like? A man's behavior may be predictable because he can be relied upon to do what is reasonable, but to act with good reason is the very reverse of being subject to an inner compulsion. An essential difference between voluntary and involuntary action is that it makes sense to speak of the motives, aims, and reasons for the former but only of the causes of the latter. It is only when a person's behavior seems pointless or when explanations in terms of aims do not seem sufficient that we look for the kind of cause which would justify saying that he could not help himself. Of course, a complete account of voluntary and rational behavior must refer to causes as necessary conditions for action, but such causes would not constitute a sufficient explanation. An account of the electronic activity in the brain would not provide a sufficient explanation of a move in a game of chess unless the move was so completely and absurdly irrelevant that it had to be accounted for simply as the result of a nervous twitch. In that case, however, it would not really be a move in the game at all, not an action, indeed, but something that happens to the player. The weakness of the determinist position, insofar as it purports to undermine the notion of responsibility, is that it treats such abnormalities as the explanatory model for the normal.

It is arguable, in any case, that the concept of responsibility *requires* that human behavior be causally accountable rather than the reverse. As Hume pointed out in *An Enquiry Concerning Human Understanding,*

> [Where actions] . . . proceed not from some *cause* in the character and disposition of the person who performed them, they can neither redound to his honour, if good; nor infamy, if evil. . . . The person is not answerable for them; and as they proceeded from nothing in him that is durable and constant, and leave nothing of that nature behind them, it is impossible [that] he can, upon their account, become the object of punishment or vengeance.

In Hume's view universal causality is consistent with the concept of choice and is a necessary condition for responsibility and, therefore, for blame and punishment.

Strictly speaking, all that is necessary for a theory of punishment is that human conduct should be capable of being modified by threats. For some people—for instance, compulsive lawbreakers like kleptomaniacs—that is not the case. Others, however, commit crimes believing they can escape punishment; still others, in a spirit of rebellion, indifference, or, more rarely, of martyrdom, prefer to do what they want and risk the consequences rather than conform. Why they prefer it—what conditions account for their being the men they are—is irrelevant. To say "they prefer it" is to say they might have chosen to do otherwise but did not, and that is all that is necessary for the concept "responsibility." To ask whether they were free to prefer otherwise, being what they were, is to ask whether they could choose to choose, and it is not clear that this really means anything. The experience of punishment may provide a reason for choosing differently next time, but to have a reason for choosing is not to be without a choice and, therefore, without responsibility.

Extenuation

Though a criminal may be held responsible for his actions, there may nevertheless be circumstances which, so it is said, diminish responsibility or extenuate guilt. Temptation or provocation, though not irresistible, may have been very great. The offender may have had a good character, and there may be no reason to expect any future lapse.

In some cases mitigation of sentence on such grounds can be readily justified in utilitarian terms. Little is to be gained by punishing the obviously exceptional lapse; a very small penalty might be enough to dissuade other respectable people who might otherwise be tempted to imitate it and for whom the shame of being treated as a criminal, whatever the penalty, is usually deterrent enough.

However, it is not easy to show, at least in utilitarian terms, that mitigation is reasonable in all the instances in which it is commonly thought appropriate. Nor does everyone agree on what are extenuating circumstances. It is not self-evident that whoever is sorely (but not irresistibly) tempted should be treated more leniently than people who have done the same thing but under less temptation. A strong temptation might be withstood if there were sufficient counterinducement. Leniency might weaken the resolve of others in the future. Some people treat crimes of passion leniently; others would say that the temptation is so commonly felt that if people were not discouraged from taking the law into their own hands by treating offenses of this kind severely, such offenses would rapidly multiply. Again, some people would accept a plea of drunkenness as an extenuation of an offense, whereas others would consider it an aggravation.

It is doubtful whether our ideas on this aspect of punishment depend on utilitarian considerations. Nor is there any reason to suppose that any system of utilitarian argument could show them to be consistent and rational. It was suggested earlier that though the criteria of morality and law, of blame and punishment, are not identical, they influence one another. If we blame people less for yielding to strong temptation, we also feel they deserve a less severe punishment. But this only shifts the question a step back. Why should temptation mitigate blame?

A possible answer might be that at least some temptations can be pleaded as partial justifications. Thus, a man who pleads that he killed someone to shorten his suffering or a woman who kills her deformed baby is appealing to another moral principle to excuse the act. Similarly, a man who kills his wife's lover might claim that his victim was violating his rights. These are not complete justifications, as a plea of self-defense would be, but they are excuses which count, as it were, against the initial presumption of guilt and so incline us to look at the offense more sympathetically and more leniently, whatever the advantages of severity in terms of deterrence, prevention, or reform. There is nothing irrational in striking a balance of desert.

But differences of opinion about a criminal's deserts often turn not on the way such a balance is struck but on the extent to which his judges (or their critics) are able to comprehend his action. Anyone who could imagine himself tempted in similar circumstances would probably be more sympathetic than someone who could not and who would therefore see no reason for being indulgent. On the other hand, anyone who suspected that he himself might yield to such a temptation and who flinched from the possibility might react to it with very great severity indeed.

Punishment and Reform

There is no reason to suppose, then, that the sentencing practice of the courts will display rational and consistent principles; furthermore, any attempt to set up criteria of rational judgment on strictly utilitarian principles is likely to cut across deeply rooted moral convictions. Accordingly, some criminologists and psychiatrists, like Eliot Slater and Bernard Glueck, and some penal reformers, like Barbara Wootton, have swung away from the general conceptions of punishment and desert. Instead of asking what penalty is warranted by the crime, whether the agent was fully responsible for his action, whether circumstances exonerate him wholly or in part, they prefer to ask what kind of treatment is most likely to rehabilitate him, subject, of course, to the example it might set for others.

This comes very close to repudiating altogether the concept of punishment as a deliberate infliction of suffering, which the criminal deserves, consequent to a voluntary breach of law. First, the treatment most likely to rehabilitate him need not be unpleasant (though if it is to instill a measure of discipline, it very well may be). And, second, avoiding the question of moral responsibility, the reformer also avoids the question of what the criminal deserves, because the reformer's prime concern is with the treatment he needs. Criminals would no more deserve punishment than the sick deserve medicine. Indeed, for such writers as Samuel Butler and the American lawyer Clarence Darrow, criminality is a kind of sickness to be treated rather than a wrong to be punished.

Attractive as this approach may seem on humanitarian grounds, it has at least one serious consequence. The concepts of responsibility and desert cannot be discarded without some loss. For it is not a necessary condition of medical treatment that a patient must have shown symptoms of a disease; those exposed to smallpox are vaccinated before they develop a fever. Without the principle that punishment must be deserved, there would be no obstacle to subjecting people likely to become criminals to corresponding forms of penal prophylaxis. Moreover, if we substitute for punishment the idea of rehabilitative treatment, there is nothing against sentencing a person of bad character to a severe course of treatment for the most trivial offense if his character would be better for it in the end. This would clearly be incompatible with the usually accepted principle that trivial offenses should not carry severe penalties.

Reformism of this kind is open to attack from another quarter. The point has been made by Hegel and Bosanquet, among others, that retributive punishment is a kind of tribute to the moral personality of the criminal. It is precisely as a morally responsible agent, recognized as capable of making reasoned choices and accepting the consequences, that the criminal is punishable. Bosanquet goes so far as to say that punishment is "his right, of which he must not be defrauded." It is to be distinguished, argued Bradley, from the discipline or correction appropriately administered to animals and children. Punishment "is inflicted because of wrong-doing, as desert, the latter is applied as means of improvement." Since rational adults are neither animals nor children, no one has the right to treat them as if they were. It might be similarly argued that lunatics are under tutelage because they are incapable of looking after their own interests and cannot be expected to respect those of other people. The sane criminal, on the contrary, can be made to pay for his antisocial choices in order to demonstrate to him and, through him, to others that crime does not pay, but it diminishes his stature as a rational adult to deny that he is responsible for ordering his own life and to impose upon him ends of another person's choosing.

Nevertheless, retributivists have often been much concerned with moral reformation. They have insisted, however, that this was something the criminal must do for himself. Because it was associated with shame and rejection, punishment could bring the criminal up short and force him to reconsider his life in the light of society's condemnation of his actions. But the remorse which was a necessary condition for self-reformation was entirely dependent on the criminal's recognition that his punishment was deserved. Without that there could be no inward reformation, no reassertion of moral standards, but only a sense of resentment and injustice. Accordingly, punishment can yield the benefits of reform only if it is thought of, above everything else, as retributive—as the appropriate desert of a responsible guilty agent. It is this which distinguishes the retributive approach to moral reformation from the kind of utilitarianism which turns its back on desert and responsibility and is concerned only with the needs of rehabilitation.

It is, of course, an open question whether punishment ever does produce the kind of self-reformation the Hegelians had in mind or whether it does so more often than it produces a moral decay. Indeed, our knowledge of the facts of criminal behavior is probably far too scanty and uncertain for us to know how relevant much of the philosophical discussion of punishment really is. We cannot say for sure that a penal system is justified because it tends to reform criminals. Nor do we know, for that matter, whether the deterrent view of punishment is applicable to all kinds of crime. Many people commit offenses without seeming to take any account of consequences before they act, and they repeat the same offenses again and again in spite of punishment. Perhaps those who do not, would not repeat them even without punishment. Perhaps there would be no more cases of certain classes of crime than there are already; perhaps the only people to commit them are those who also do not take account of consequences before they act. It seems likely that some potential offenders are deterred from evading taxes or from smuggling by the threat of punishment, but is there any certain evidence that the threat of punishment deters anyone who would otherwise commit rape or arson? Utilitarians tend to assume that punishment as an institution can be justified by its beneficial consequences, but the argument depends on certain a priori assumptions about criminal (or would-be criminal) behavior that may be greatly overintellectualized. However, even though research should prove the usual utilitarian justifications for punishment groundless, that does not mean that some other, nonutilitarian justification is better. The proper procedure may well be to ask, with the utilitarian, whether the consequences are by and large beneficial; it is equally possible that punishment as an institution might fail that test. A theory of punishment that led to the conclusion that all punishment was wrong need be no more necessarily mistaken than a theory that led to a similar conclusion as regards, say, slavery, which, after all, was accepted as uncritically in Aristotle's day as punishment is today.

The Right to Punish

Immanuel Kant

The right to punish contained in the penal law [*das Strafrecht*] is the right that the magistrate has to inflict pain on a subject in consequence of his having committed a crime. It follows that the suzerain of the state cannot himself be punished; we can only remove ourselves from his jurisdiction. A transgression of the public law that makes him who commits it unfit to be a citizen is called either simply a crime (*crimen*) or a public crime (*crimen publicum*). [If, however, we call it a public crime, then we can use the term "crime" generically to include both private and public crimes.] The first (a private crime) is brought before a civil court, and the second (a public crime), before a criminal court. Embezzlement, that is, misappropriation of money or wares entrusted in commerce, and fraud in buying and selling, if perpetrated before the eyes of the party who suffers, are private crimes. On the other hand, counterfeiting money or bills of exchange, theft, robbery, and similar acts are public crimes, because through them the commonwealth and not just a single individual is exposed to danger. These crimes may be divided into those of a base character (*indolis abjectae*) and those of a violent character (*indolis violentae*).

Judicial punishment (*poena forensis*) is entirely distinct from natural punishment

---

From pp. 99–106 of *The Metaphysical Elements of Justice (Metaphysische Anfangsgründe der Rechtslehre*, Part I of the 1797 *Metaphysik der Sitten*), translated by John Ladd, Indianapolis, 1965. Copyright © 1965 by The Bobbs-Merrill Company. Reprinted with permission of the publisher. Immanuel Kant, author of *Critique of Pure Reason* and other philosophical masterpieces, is one of the most important thinkers in Western civilization.

(*poena naturalis*). In natural punishment, vice punishes itself, and this fact is not taken into consideration by the legislator. Judicial punishment can never be used merely as a means to promote some other good for the criminal himself or for civil society, but instead it must in all cases be imposed on him only on the ground that he has committed a crime; for a human being can never be manipulated merely as a means to the purposes of someone else and can never be confused with the objects of the Law of things [*Sachenrecht*]. His innate personality [that is, his right as a person] protects him against such treatment, even though he may indeed be condemned to lose his civil personality. He must first be found to be deserving of punishment before any consideration is given to the utility of this punishment for himself or for his fellow citizens. The law concerning punishment is a categorical imperative, and woe to him who rummages around in the winding paths of a theory of happiness looking for some advantage to be gained by releasing the criminal from punishment or by reducing the amount of it — in keeping with the Pharisaic motto: "It is better that one man should die than that the whole people should perish." If legal justice perishes, then it is no longer worth while for men to remain alive on this earth. If this is so, what should one think of the proposal to permit a criminal who has been condemned to death to remain alive, if, after consenting to allow dangerous experiments to be made on him, he happily survives such experiments and if doctors thereby obtain new information that benefits the community? Any court of justice would repudiate such a proposal with scorn if it were suggested by a medical college, for [legal] justice ceases to be justice if it can be bought for a price.

What kind and what degree of punishment does public legal justice adopt as its principle and standard? None other than the principle of equality (illustrated by the pointer on the scales of justice), that is, the principle of not treating one side more favorably than the other. Accordingly, any undeserved evil that you inflict on someone else among the people is one that you do to yourself. If you vilify him, you vilify yourself; if you steal from him, you steal from yourself; if you kill him, you kill yourself. Only the Law of retribution (*jus talionis*) can determine exactly the kind and degree of punishment; it must be well understood, however, that this determination [must be made] in the chambers of a court of justice (and not in your private judgment). All other standards fluctuate back and forth and, because extraneous considerations are mixed with them, they cannot be compatible with the principle of pure and strict legal justice.

Now, it might seem that the existence of class distinctions would not allow for the [application of the] retributive principle of returning like for like. Nevertheless, even though these class distinctions may not make it possible to apply this principle to the letter, it can still always remain applicable in its effects if regard is had to the special sensibilities of the higher classes. Thus, for example, the imposition of a fine for a verbal injury has no proportionality to the original injury, for someone who has a good deal of money can easily afford to make insults whenever he wishes. On the other hand, the humiliation of the pride of such an offender comes much closer to equaling an injury done to the honor of the person offended; thus the judgment and Law might require the offender, not only to make a public apology to the offended person, but also at the same time to kiss his hand, even though he be socially inferior. Similarly, if a man of a higher class has violently attacked an innocent citizen who is socially inferior to him, he may be condemned, not only to apologize, but to undergo solitary and painful confinement, because by this means, in addition to the discomfort suffered, the pride of the offender will be painfully affected, and thus his humiliation will compensate for the offense as like for like.

But what is meant by the statement: "If you steal from him, you steal from your-self"? Inasmuch as someone steals, he makes the ownership of everyone else insecure, and hence he robs himself (in accordance with the Law of retribution) of the security of any possible ownership. He has nothing and can also acquire nothing, but he still wants to live, and this is not possible unless others provide him with nourishment. But, because the state will not support him gratis, he must let the state have his labor at any kind of work it may wish to use him for (convict labor), and so he becomes a slave, either for a certain period of time or indefinitely, as the case may be.

If, however, he has committed a murder, he must die. In this case, there is no substi-tute that will satisfy the requirements of legal justice. There is no sameness of kind between death and remaining alive even under the most miserable conditions, and consequently there is also no equality between the crime and the retribution unless the criminal is judicially condemned and put to death. But the death of the criminal must be kept entirely free of any maltreatment that would make an abomination of the humanity residing in the person suffering it. Even if a civil society were to dissolve itself by common agreement of all its members (for example, if the people inhabiting an island decided to separate and disperse themselves around the world), the last mur-derer remaining in prison must first be executed, so that everyone will duly receive what his actions are worth and so that the bloodguilt thereof will not be fixed on the people because they failed to insist on carrying out the punishment; for if they fail to do so, they may be regarded as accomplices in this public violation of legal justice.

Furthermore, it is possible for punishment to be equal in accordance with the strict Law of retribution only if the judge pronounces the death sentence. This is clear be-cause only in this way will the death sentence be pronounced on all criminals in propor-tion to their inner viciousness (even if the crime involved is not murder, but some other crime against the state that can be expiated only by death). . . .

It may also be pointed out that no one has ever heard of anyone condemned to death on account of murder who complained that he was getting too much [punishment] and therefore was being treated unjustly; everyone would laugh in his face if he were to make such a statement. Indeed, otherwise we would have to assume that, although the treatment accorded the criminal is not unjust according to the law, the legislative authority still is not authorized to decree this kind of punishment and that, if it does so, it comes into contradiction with itself.

Anyone who is a murderer—that is, has committed a murder, commanded one, or taken part in one—must suffer death. That is what [legal] justice as the Idea of the judicial authority wills in accordance with universal laws that are grounded a priori. . . .

In opposition to this view, the Marquis of Beccaria,[1] moved by sympathetic senti-

---

1. [Cesare Bonesana, Marquis di Beccaria (1738–1794), Italian publicist. His *Dei delitti e delle pene* (1764) *(On Crimes and Punishments,* trans. Henry Paolucci, "The Library of Liberal Arts," No. 107 [New York: The Liberal Arts Press, 1963]) was widely read and had great influence on the reform of the penal codes of various European states.]

mentality and an affectation of humanitarianism, has asserted that all capital punishment is illegitimate. He argues that it could not be contained in the original civil contract, inasmuch as this would imply that every one of the people has agreed to forfeit his life if he murders another (of the people); but such an agreement would be impossible, for no one can dispose of his own life.

No one suffers punishment because he has willed the punishment, but because he has willed a punishable action. If what happens to someone is also willed by him, it cannot be a punishment. Accordingly, it is impossible to will to be punished. To say, "I will to be punished if I murder someone," can mean nothing more than, "I submit myself along with everyone else to those laws which, if there are any criminals among the people, will naturally include penal laws." In my role as colegislator making the penal law, I cannot be the same person who, as subject, is punished by the law; for, as a subject who is also a criminal, I cannot have a voice in legislation. (The legislator is holy.) When, therefore, I enact a penal law against myself as a criminal it is the pure juridical legislative reason (*homo noumenon*) in me that submits myself to the penal law as a person capable of committing a crime, that is, as another person (*homo phaenomenon*) along with all the others in the civil union who submit themselves to this law. In other words, it is not the people (considered as individuals) who dictate the death penalty, but the court (public legal justice); that is, someone other than the criminal. The social contract does not include the promise to permit oneself to be punished and thus to dispose of oneself and of one's life, because, if the only ground that authorizes the punishment of an evildoer were a promise that expresses his willingness to be punished, then it would have to be left up to him to find himself liable to punishment, and the criminal would be his own judge. The chief error contained in this sophistry (πρωτονψευδοζ) consists in the confusion of the criminal's own judgment (which one must necessarily attribute to his reason) that he must forfeit his life with a resolution of the Will to take his own life. The result is that the execution of the Law and the adjudication thereof are represented as united in the same person. . . .

Persons and Punishment

Herbert Morris

They acted and looked . . . at us, and around in our house, in a
way that had about it the feeling — at least for me — that we were
not people. In their eyesight we were just things, that was all.

—*Malcolm X*

؟ (We have no right to treat a man like a dog.)
— *Governor Maddox of Georgia*

Alfredo Traps in Durrenmatt's tale discovers that he has brought off, all by
himself, a murder involving considerable ingenuity. The mock prosecutor in the
tale demands the death penalty "as reward for a crime that merits admiration,
astonishment, and respect." Traps is deeply moved; indeed, he is exhilarated, and the
whole of his life becomes more heroic, and, ironically, more precious. His defense
attorney proceeds to argue that Traps was not only innocent but incapable of guilt, "a
victim of the age." This defense Traps disavows with indignation and anger. He makes
claim to the murder as his and demands the prescribed punishment—death.

The themes to be found in this macabre tale do not often find their way into philosophical discussions of punishment. These discussions deal with large and significant

Reprinted from *The Monist*, 52, No. 4 (October 1968), pp. 475–501, with the permission of the
author and The Open Court Publishing Company, LaSalle, Illinois. Herbert Morris is Professor of
Philosophy and Professor of Law at the University of California, Los Angeles. He is the editor of
Freedom and Responsibility, Stanford, 1961, and the author of a number of articles that have appeared in philosophical and legal journals on a variety of topics in moral philosophy, the philosophy of law, and the philosophy of mind. A collection of his essays, *On Guilt and Innocence*, was
published in 1976 by University of California Press.

questions of whether or not we ever have the right to punish, and if we do, under what conditions, to what degree, and in what manner. There is a tradition, of course, not notable for its present vitality, that is closely linked with motifs in Durrenmatt's tale of crime and punishment. Its adherents have urged that justice requires a person be punished if he is guilty. Sometimes—though rarely—these philosophers have expressed themselves in terms of the criminal's *right to be punished*. Reaction to the claim that there is such a right has been astonishment combined, perhaps, with a touch of contempt for the perversity of the suggestion. A strange right that no one would ever wish to claim! With that flourish the subject is buried and the right disposed of. In this paper the subject is resurrected.

My aim is to argue for four propositions concerning rights that will certainly strike some as not only false but preposterous: first, that we have a right to punishment; second, that this right derives from a fundamental human right to be treated as a person; third, that this fundamental right is a natural, inalienable, and absolute right; and, fourth, that the denial of this right implies the denial of all moral rights and duties. Showing the truth of one, let alone all, of these large and questionable claims is a tall order. The attempt, or, more properly speaking, the first steps in an attempt, follow.

1. When someone claims that there is a right to be free, we can easily imagine situations in which the right is infringed and easily imagine situations in which there is a point to asserting or claiming the right. With the right to be punished, matters are otherwise. The immediate reaction to the claim that there is such a right is puzzlement. And the reasons for this are apparent. People do not normally value pain and suffering. Punishment is associated with pain and suffering. When we think about punishment we naturally think of the strong desire most persons have to avoid it, to accept, for example, acquittal of a criminal charge with relief and eagerly, if convicted, to hope for pardon or probation. Adding, of course, to the paradoxical character of the claim of such a right is difficulty in imagining circumstances in which it would be denied one. When would one rightly demand punishment and meet with any threat of the claim being denied?

So our first task is to see when the claim of such a right would have a point. I want to approach this task by setting out two complex types of institutions both of which are designed to maintain some degree of social control. In the one a central concept is punishment for wrongdoing and in the other the central concepts are control of dangerous individuals and treatment of disease.

Let us first turn attention to the institutions in which punishment is involved. The institutions I describe will resemble those we ordinarily think of as institutions of punishment; they will have, however, additional features we associate with a system of just punishment.

Let us suppose that men are constituted roughly as they now are, with a rough equivalence in strength and abilities, a capacity to be injured by each other and to make judgments that such injury is undesirable, a limited strength of will, and a capacity to reason and to conform conduct to rules. Applying to the conduct of these men are a group of rules, ones I shall label "primary," which closely resemble the core rules of our criminal law, rules that prohibit violence and deception and compliance with which provides benefits for all persons. These benefits consist in noninterference by others with what each person values, such matters as continuanc f life and bodily security.

The rules define a sphere for each person, then, which is immune from interference by others. Making possible this mutual benefit is the assumption by individuals of a burden. The burden consists in the exercise of self-restraint by individuals over inclinations that would, if satisfied, directly interfere or create a substantial risk of interference with others in proscribed ways. If a person fails to exercise self-restraint even though he might have and gives in to such inclinations, he renounces a burden which others have voluntarily assumed and thus gains an advantage which others, who have restrained themselves, do not possess. This system, then, is one in which the rules establish a mutuality of benefit and burden and in which the benefits of noninterference are conditional upon the assumption of burdens.

Connecting punishment with the violation of these primary rules, and making public the provision for punishment, is both reasonable and just. First, it is only reasonable that those who voluntarily comply with the rules be provided some assurance that they will not be assuming burdens which others are unprepared to assume. Their disposition to comply voluntarily will diminish as they learn that others are with impunity renouncing burdens they are assuming. Second, fairness dictates that a system in which benefits and burdens are equally distributed have a mechanism designed to prevent a maldistribution in the benefits and burdens. Thus, sanctions are attached to noncompliance with the primary rules so as to induce compliance with the primary rules among those who may be disinclined to obey. In this way the likelihood of an unfair distribution is diminished.

Third, it is just to punish those who have violated the rules and caused the unfair distribution of benefits and burdens. A person who violates the rules has something others have—the benefits of the system—but by renouncing what others have assumed, the burdens of self-restraint, he has acquired an unfair advantage. Matters are not even until this advantage is in some way erased. Another way of putting it is that he owes something to others, for he has something that does not rightfully belong to him. Justice—that is, punishing such individuals—restores the equilibrium of benefits and burdens by taking from the individual what he owes, that is, exacting the debt. It is important to see that the equilibrium may be restored in another way. Forgiveness— with its legal analogue of a pardon—while not the righting of an unfair distribution by making one pay his debt is, nevertheless, a restoring of the equilibrium by forgiving the debt. Forgiveness may be viewed, at least in some types of cases, as a gift after the fact, erasing a debt, which had the gift been given before the fact, would not have created a debt. But the practice of pardoning has to proceed sensitively, for it may endanger, in a way the practice of justice does not, the maintenance of an equilibrium of benefits and burdens. If all are indiscriminately pardoned less incentive is provided individuals to restrain their inclinations, thus increasing the incidence of persons taking what they do not deserve.

There are also in this system we are considering a variety of operative principles compliance with which provides some guarantee that the system of punishment does not itself promote an unfair distribution of benefits and burdens. For one thing, provision is made for a variety of defenses, each one of which can be said to have as its object diminishing the chances of forcibly depriving a person of benefits others have if that person has not derived an unfair advantage. A person has not derived an unfair advantage if he could not have restrained himself or if it is unreasonable to expect him to behave otherwise than he did. Sometimes the rules preclude punishment of classes of persons such as children. Sometimes they provide a defense if on a particular occasion a person lacked the capacity to conform his conduct to the rules. Thus, someone who in an epileptic seizure strikes another is excused. Punishment in these cases would be punishment of the innocent, punishment of those who do not voluntarily renounce a burden others have assumed. Punishment in such cases, then, would not equalize but rather cause an unfair distribution in benefits and burdens.

Along with principles providing defenses there are requirements that the rules be prospective and relatively clear so that persons have a fair opportunity to comply with the rules. There are, also, rules governing, among other matters, the burden of proof, who shall bear it and what it shall be, the prohibition on double jeopardy, and the privilege against self-incrimination. Justice requires conviction of the guilty, and requires their punishment, but in setting out to fulfill the demands of justice we may, of course, because we are not omniscient, cause injustice by convicting and punishing the innocent. The resolution arrived at in the system I am describing consists in weighing as the greater evil the punishment of the innocent. The primary function of the system of rules was to provide individuals with a sphere of interest immune from interference. Given this goal, it is determined to be a greater evil for society to interfere unjustifiably with an individual by depriving him of good than for the society to fail to punish those that have unjustifiably interfered.

Finally, because the primary rules are designed to benefit all and because the punishments prescribed for their violation are publicized and the defenses respected, there is some plausibility in the exaggerated claim that in choosing to do an act violative of the rules an individual has chosen to be punished. This way of putting matters brings to our attention the extent to which, when the system is as I have described it, the criminal "has brought the punishment upon himself" in contrast to those cases where it would be misleading to say "he has brought it upon himself," cases, for example, where one does not know the rules or is punished in the absence of fault.

To summarize, then: first, there is a group of rules guiding the behavior of individuals in the community which establish spheres of interest immune from interference by others; second, provision is made for what is generally regarded as a deprivation of some thing of value if the rules are violated; third, the deprivations visited upon any person are justified by that person's having violated the rules; fourth, the deprivation, in this just system of punishment, is linked to rules that fairly distribute benefits and burdens and to procedures that strike some balance between not punishing the guilty and punishing the innocent, a class defined as those who have not voluntarily done acts violative of the law, in which it is evident that the evil of punishing the innocent is regarded as greater than the nonpunishment of the guilty.

At the core of many actual legal systems one finds, of course, rules and procedures of the kind I have sketched. It is obvious, though, that any ongoing legal system differs in significant respects from what I have presented here, containing "pockets of injustice."

I want now to sketch an extreme version of a set of institutions of a fundamentally different kind, institutions proceeding on a conception of man which appears to be basically at odds with that operative within a system of punishment.

Rules are promulgated in this system that prohibit certain types of injuries and harms.

In this world we are now to imagine when an individual harms another his conduct is to be regarded as a symptom of some pathological condition in the way a running nose is a symptom of a cold. Actions diverging from some conception of the normal are viewed as manifestations of a disease in the way in which we might today regard the arm and leg movements of an epileptic during a seizure. Actions conforming to what is normal are assimilated to the normal and healthy functioning of bodily organs. What a person does, then, is assimilated, on this conception, to what we believe today, or at least most of us believe today, a person undergoes. We draw a distinction between the operation of the kidney and raising an arm on request. This distinction between mere events or happenings and human actions is erased in our imagined system.[1]

There is, however, bound to be something strange in this erasing of a recognized distinction, for, as with metaphysical suggestions generally, and I take this to be one, the distinction may be reintroduced but given a different description, for example, "happenings with X type of causes" and "happenings with Y type of causes." Responses of different kinds, today legitimated by our distinction between happenings and actions, may be legitimated by this new manner of description. And so there may be isomorphism between a system recognizing the distinction and one erasing it. Still, when this distinction is erased certain tendencies of thought and responses might naturally arise that would tend to affect unfavorably values respected by a system of punishment.

Let us elaborate on this assimilation of conduct of a certain kind to symptoms of a

---

1. "When a man is suffering from an infectious disease, he is a danger to the community, and it is necessary to restrict his liberty of movement. But no one associates any idea of guilt with such a situation. On the contrary, he is an object of commiseration to his friends. Such steps as science recommends are taken to cure him of his disease, and he submits as a rule without reluctance to the curtailment of liberty involved meanwhile. The same method in spirit ought to be shown in the treatment of what is called 'crime.'"

Bertrand Russell, *Roads to Freedom* (London: George Allen and Unwin Ltd., 1918), p. 135.

"We do not hold people responsible for their reflexes—for example, for coughing in church. We hold them responsible for their operant behavior—for example, for whispering in church or remaining in church while coughing. But there are variables which are responsible for whispering as well as coughing, and these may be just as inexorable. When we recognize this, we are likely to drop the notion of responsibility altogether and with it the doctrine of free will as an inner causal agent."

B. F. Skinner, *Science and Human Behavior* (1953), pp. 115–116.

"Basically, criminality is but a symptom of insanity, using the term in its widest generic sense to express unacceptable social behavior based on unconscious motivation flowing from a disturbed instinctive and emotional life, whether this appears in frank psychoses, or in less obvious form in neuroses and unrecognized psychoses. . . . If criminals are products of early environmental influences in the same sense that psychotics and neurotics are, then it should be possible to reach them psychotherapeutically."

Benjamin Karpman, "Criminal Psychodynamics," *Journal of Criminal Law and Criminology,* 47 (1956), p. 9.

"We, the agents of society, must move to end the game of tit-for-tat and blow-for-blow in which the offender has foolishly and futilely engaged himself and us. We are not driven, as he is, to wild and impulsive actions. With knowledge comes power, and with power there is no need for the frightened vengeance of the old penology. In its place should go a quiet, dignified, therapeutic program for the rehabilitation of the disorganized one, if possible, the protection of society during the treatment period, and his guided return to useful citizenship, as soon as this can be effected."

Karl Menninger, "Therapy, Not Punishment," *Harper's Magazine* (August 1959), pp. 63–64.

disease. First, there is something abnormal in both the case of conduct, such as killing another, and a symptom of a disease such as an irregular heart beat. Second, there are causes for this abnormality in action such that once we know of them we can explain the abnormality as we now can explain the symptoms of many physical diseases. The abnormality is looked upon as a happening with a causal explanation rather than an action for which there were reasons. Third, the causes that account for the abnormality interfere with the normal functioning of the body, or, in the case of killing, with what is regarded as a normal functioning of an individual. Fourth, the abnormality is in some way a part of the individual, necessarily involving his body. A well going dry might satisfy our three foregoing conditions of disease symptoms, but it is hardly a disease or the symptom of one. Finally, and most obscure, the abnormality arises in some way from within the individual. If Jones is hit with a mallet by Smith, Jones may reel about and fall on James who may be injured. But this abnormal conduct of Jones is not regarded as a symptom of disease. Smith, not Jones, is suffering from some pathological condition.

With this view of man the institutions of social control respond, not with punishment, but with either preventive detention, in case of "carriers," or therapy in the case of those manifesting pathological symptoms. The logic of sickness implies the logic of therapy. And therapy and punishment differ widely in their implications. In bringing out some of these differences I want again to draw attention to the important fact that while the distinctions we now draw are erased in the therapy world, they may, in fact, be reintroduced but under different descriptions. To the extent they are, we really have a punishment system combined with a therapy system. I am concerned now, however, with what the implications would be were the world indeed one of therapy and not a disguised world of punishment and therapy, for I want to suggest tendencies of thought that arise when one is immersed in the ideology of disease and therapy.

First, punishment is the imposition upon a person who is believed to be at fault of something commonly believed to be a deprivation where that deprivation is justified by the person's guilty behavior. It is associated with resentment, for the guilty are those who have done what they had no right to do by failing to exercise restraint when they might have and where others have. Therapy is not a response to a person who is at fault. We respond to an individual, not because of what he has done, but because of some condition from which he is suffering. If he is no longer suffering from the condition, treatment no longer has a point. Punishment, then, focuses on the past; therapy on the present. Therapy is normally associated with compassion for what one undergoes, not resentment for what one has illegitimately done.

Second, with therapy, unlike punishment, we do not seek to deprive the person of something acknowledged as a good, but seek rather to help and to benefit the individual who is suffering by ministering to his illness in the hope that the person can be cured. The good we attempt to do is not a reward for desert. The individual suffering has not merited by his disease the good we seek to bestow upon him but has, because he is a creature that has the capacity to feel pain, a claim upon our sympathies and help.

Third, we saw with punishment that its justification was related to maintaining and restoring a fair distribution of benefits and burdens. Infliction of the prescribed punishment carries the implication, then, that one has "paid one's debt" to society, for the punishment is the taking from the person of something commonly recognized as valuable. It is this conception of "a debt owed" that may permit, as I suggested earlier, under certain conditions, the nonpunishment of the guilty, for operative within a system of punishment may be a concept analogous to forgiveness, namely pardoning. Who it is that we may pardon and under what conditions—contrition with its elements of self-punishment no doubt plays a role—I shall not go into though it is clearly a matter of the greatest practical and theoretical interest. What is clear is that the conceptions of "paying a debt" or "having a debt forgiven" or pardoning have no place in a system of therapy.

Fourth, with punishment there is an attempt at some equivalence between the advantage gained by the wrongdoer—partly based upon the seriousness of the interest invaded, partly on the state of mind with which the wrongful act was performed—and the punishment meted out. Thus, we can understand a prohibition on "cruel and unusual punishments" so that disproportionate pain and suffering are avoided. With therapy attempts at proportionality make no sense. It is perfectly plausible giving someone who kills a pill and treating for a lifetime within an institution one who has broken a dish and manifested accident proneness. We have the concept of "painful treatment." We do not have the concept of "cruel treatment." Because treatment is regarded as a benefit, though it may involve pain, it is natural that less restraint is exercised in bestowing it, than in inflicting punishment. Further, protests with respect to treatment are likely to be assimilated to the complaints of one whose leg must be amputated in order for him to live, and, thus, largely disregarded. To be sure, there is operative in the therapy world some conception of the "cure being worse than the disease," but if the disease is manifested in conduct harmful to others, and if being a normal operating human being is valued highly, there will naturally be considerable pressure to find the cure acceptable.

Fifth, the rules in our system of punishment governing conduct of individuals were rules violation of which involved either direct interference with others or the creation of a substantial risk of such interference. One could imagine adding to this system of primary rules other rules proscribing preparation to do acts violative of the primary rules and even rules proscribing thoughts. Objection to such suggestions would have many sources but a principal one would consist in its involving the infliction of punishment on too great a number of persons who would not, because of a change of mind, have violated the primary rules. Though we are interested in diminishing violations of the primary rules, we are not prepared to punish too many individuals who would never have violated the rules in order to achieve this aim. In a system motivated solely by a preventive and curative ideology there would be less reason to wait until symptoms manifest themselves in socially harmful conduct. It is understandable that we should wish at the earliest possible stage to arrest the development of the disease. In the punishment system, because we are dealing with deprivations, it is understandable that we should forbear from imposing them until we are quite sure of guilt. In the therapy system, dealing as it does with benefits, there is less reason for forbearance from treatment at an early stage.

Sixth, a variety of procedural safeguards we associate with punishment have less significance in a therapy system. To the degree objections to double jeopardy and self-incrimination are based on a wish to decrease the chances of the innocent being convicted and punished, a therapy system, unconcerned with this problem, would disregard such safeguards. When one is out to help people there is also little sense in urging that the burden of proof be on those providing the help. And there is less point to imposing the burden of proving that the conduct was pathological beyond a reasonable doubt. Further, a jury system, which, within a system of justice, serves to make accommodations to the individual situation and to introduce a human element, would play no role or a minor one in a world where expertise is required in making determinations of disease and treatment.

In our system of punishment an attempt was made to maximize each individual's freedom of choice by first of all delimiting by rules certain spheres of conduct immune from interference by others. The punishment associated with these primary rules paid deference to an individual's free choice by connecting punishment to a freely chosen act violative of the rules, thus giving some plausibility to the claim, as we saw, that what a person received by way of punishment he himself had chosen. With the world of disease and therapy all this changes and the individual's free choice ceases to be a determinative factor in how others respond to him. All those principles of our own legal system that minimize the chances of punishment of those who have not chosen to do acts violative of the rules tend to lose their point in the therapy system, for how we respond in a therapy system to a person is not conditioned upon what he has chosen but rather on what symptoms he has manifested or may manifest and what the best therapy for the disease is that is suggested by the symptoms.

Now, it is clear, I think, that were we confronted with the alternatives I have sketched, between a system of just punishment and a thoroughgoing system of treatment, a system, that is, that did not reintroduce concepts appropriate to punishment, we could see the point in claiming that a person has a right to be punished, meaning by this that a person has a right to all those institutions and practices linked to punishment. For these would provide him with, among other things, a far greater ability to predict what would happen to him on the occurrence of certain events than the therapy system. There is the inestimable value to each of us of having the responses of others to us determined over a wide range of our lives by what we choose rather than what they choose. A person has a right to institutions that respect his choices. Our punishment system does; our therapy system does not.

Apart from those aspects of our therapy model which would relate to serious limitations on personal liberty, there are clearly objections of a more profound kind to the mode of thinking I have associated with the therapy model.

First, human beings pride themselves in having capacities that animals do not. A common way, for example, of arousing shame in a child is to compare the child's conduct to that of an animal. In a system where all actions are assimilated to happenings we are assimilated to creatures—indeed, it is more extreme than this—whom we have always thought possessed of less than we. Fundamental to our practice of praise and order of attainment is that one who can do more—one who is capable of more and one who does more—is more worthy of respect and admiration. And we have thought of ourselves as capable where animals are not of making, of creating, among other things, ourselves. The conception of man I have outlined would provide us with a status that today, when our conduct is assimilated to it in moral criticism, we consider properly evocative of shame.

Second, if all human conduct is viewed as something men undergo, thrown into question would be the appropriateness of that extensive range of peculiarly human satisfactions that derive from a sense of achievement. For these satisfactions we shall have to substitute those mild satisfactions attendant upon a healthy well-functioning body. Contentment is our lot if we are fortunate; intense satisfaction at achievement is entirely inappropriate.

Third, in the therapy world nothing is earned and what we receive comes to us through compassion, or through a desire to control us. Resentment is out of place. We can take credit for nothing but must always regard ourselves—if there are selves left to regard once actions disappear—as fortunate recipients of benefits or unfortunate carriers of disease who must be controlled. We know that within our own world human beings who have been so regarded and who come to accept this view of themselves come to look upon themselves as worthless. When what we do is met with resentment, we are indirectly paid something of a compliment.

Fourth, attention should also be drawn to a peculiar evil that may be attendant upon regarding a man's actions as symptoms of disease. The logic of cure will push us toward forms of therapy that inevitably involve changes in the person made against his will. The evil in this would be most apparent in those cases where the agent, whose action is determined to be a manifestation of some disease, does not regard his action in this way. He believes that what he has done is, in fact, "right" but his conception of "normality" is not the therapeutically accepted one. When we treat an illness we normally treat a condition that the person is not responsible for. He is "suffering" from some disease and we treat the condition, relieving the person of something preventing his normal functioning. When we begin treating persons for actions that have been chosen, we do not lift from the person something that is interfering with his normal functioning but we change the person so that he functions in a way regarded as normal by the current therapeutic community. We have to change him and his judgments of value. In doing this we display a lack of respect for the moral status of individuals, that is, a lack of respect for the reasoning and choices of individuals. They are but animals who must be conditioned. I think we can understand and, indeed, sympathize with a man's preferring death to being forcibly turned into what he is not.

Finally, perhaps most frightening of all would be the derogation in status of all protests to treatment. If someone believes that he has done something right, and if he protests being treated and changed, the protest will itself be regarded as a sign of some pathological condition, for who would not wish to be cured of an affliction? What this leads to are questions of an important kind about the effect of this conception of man upon what we now understand by reasoning. Here what a person takes to be a reasoned defense of an act is treated, as the action was, on the model of a happening of a pathological kind. Not just a person's acts are taken from him but also his attempt at a reasoned justification for the acts. In a system of punishment a person who has committed a crime may argue that what he did was right. We make him pay the price and we respect his right to retain the judgment he has made. A conception of pathology precludes this form of respect.

It might be objected to the foregoing that all I have shown—if that—is that if the only alternatives open to us are a *just* system of punishment or the mad world of being treated like sick or healthy animals, we do in fact have a right to a system of punishment of this kind. But this hardly shows that we have a right *simpliciter* to punishment as we do, say, to be free. Indeed, it does not even show a right to a just system of punishment, for surely we can, without too much difficulty, imagine situations in which the alternatives to punishment are not this mad world but a world in which we are still treated as persons and there is, for example, not the pain and suffering attendant upon punishment. One such world is one in which there are rules but responses to their violation is not the deprivation of some good but forgiveness. Still another type of world would be one in which violation of the rules were responded to by merely comparing the conduct of the person to something commonly regarded as low or filthy, and thus, producing by this mode of moral criticism, feelings of shame rather than feelings of guilt.

I am prepared to allow that these objections have a point. While granting force to the above objections I want to offer a few additional comments with respect to each of them. First, any existent legal system permits the punishment of individuals under circumstances where the conditions I have set forth for a just system have not been satisfied. A glaring example of this would be criminal strict liability which is to be found in our own legal system. Nevertheless, I think it would be difficult to present any system we should regard as a system of punishment that would not still have a great advantage over our imagined therapy system. The system of punishment we imagine may more and more approximate a system of sheer terror in which human beings are treated as animals to be intimidated and prodded. To the degree that the system is of this character it is, in my judgment, not simply an unjust system but one that diverges from what we normally understand by a system of punishment. At least some deference to the choice of individuals is built into the idea of punishment. So there would be some truth in saying we have a right to any system of punishment if the only alternative to it was therapy.

Second, people may imagine systems in which there are rules and in which the response to their violation is not punishment but pardoning, the legal analogue of forgiveness. Surely this is a system to which we would claim a right as against one in which we are made to suffer for violating the rules. There are several comments that need to be made about this. It may be, of course, that a high incidence of pardoning would increase the incidence of rule violations. Further, the difficulty with suggesting pardoning as a general response is that pardoning presupposes the very responses that it is suggested it supplant. A system of deprivations, or a practice of deprivations on the happening of certain actions, underlies the practice of pardoning and forgiving, for it is only where we possess the idea of a wrong to be made up or of a debt owed to others, ideas we acquire within a world in which there have been deprivations for wrong acts, that we have the idea of pardoning for the wrong or forgiving the debt.

Finally, if we look at the responses I suggested would give rise to feelings of shame, we may rightly be troubled with the appropriateness of this response in any community in which each person assumes burdens so that each may derive benefits. In such situations might it not be that individuals have a right to a system of punishment so that each person could be assured that inequities in the distribution of benefits and burdens are unlikely to occur and if they do, procedures exist for correcting them? Further, it may well be that, everything considered, we should prefer the pain and suffering of a system of punishment to a world in which we only experience shame on the doing of wrong acts, for with guilt there are relatively simple ways of ridding ourselves of the feeling we have, that is, gaining forgiveness or taking the punishment, but with shame we have to bear it until we no longer are the person who has behaved in the shameful way. Thus, I suggest that we have, wherever there is a distribution of benefits and burdens of the kind I have described, a right to a system of punishment.

I want also to make clear in concluding this section that I have argued, though very indirectly, not just for a right to a system of punishment, but for a right to be punished once there is in existence such a system. Thus, a man has the right to be punished rather than treated if he is guilty of some offense. And, indeed, one can imagine a case in which, even in the face of an offer of a pardon, a man claims and ought to have acknowledged his right to be punished.

2. The primary reason for preferring the system of punishment as against the system of therapy might have been expressed in terms of the one system treating one as a person and the other not. In invoking the right to be punished, one justifies one's claim by reference to a more fundamental right. I want now to turn attention to this fundamental right and attempt to shed light—it will have to be little, for the topic is immense—on what is meant by "treating an individual as a person."

When we talk of not treating a human being as a person or "showing no respect for one as a person" what we imply by our words is a contrast between the manner in which one acceptably responds to human beings and the manner in which one acceptably responds to animals and inanimate objects. When we treat a human being merely as an animal or some inanimate object our responses to the human being are determined, not by his choices, but ours in disregard of or with indifference to his. And when we "look upon" a person as less than a person or not a person, we consider the person as incapable of a rational choice. In cases of not treating a human being as a person we interfere with a person in such a way that what is done, even if the person is involved in the doing, is done not by the person but by the user of the person. In extreme cases there may even be an elision of a causal chain so that we might say that X killed Z even though Y's hand was the hand that held the weapon, for Y's hand may have been entirely in X's control. The one agent is in some way treating the other as a mere link in a causal chain. There is, of course, a wide range of cases in which a person is used to accomplish the aim of another and in which the person used is less than fully free. A person may be grabbed against his will and used as a shield. A person may be drugged or hypnotized and then employed for certain ends. A person may be deceived into doing other than he intends doing. A person may be ordered to do something and threatened with harm if he does not and coerced into doing what he does not want to. There is still another range of cases in which individuals are not used, but in which decisions by others are made that affect them in circumstances where they have the capacity for choice and where they are not being treated as persons.

But it is particularly important to look at coercion, for I have claimed that a just system of punishment treats human beings as persons; and it is not immediately apparent how ordering someone to do something and threatening harm differs essentially from having rules supported by threats of harm in case of noncompliance.

There are affinities between coercion and other cases of not treating someone as a person, for it is not the coerced person's choices but the coercer's that are responsible for what is done. But unlike other indisputable cases of not treating one as a person, for example using someone as a shield, there is some choice involved in coercion. And if this is so, why does the coercer stand in any different relation to the coerced person than the criminal law stands to individuals in society?

Suppose the person who is threatened disregards the order and gets the threatened harm. Now suppose he is told, "Well, you did after all bring it upon yourself." There is clearly something strange in this. It is the person doing the threatening and not the person threatened who is responsible. But our reaction to punishment, at least in a system that resembles the one I have described, is precisely that the person violating the rules brought it upon himself. What lies behind these different reactions?

There exist situations in the law, of course, which resemble coercion situations. There are occasions when in the law a person might justifiably say "I am not being treated as a person but being used" and where he might properly react to the punishment as something "he was hardly responsible for." But it is possible to have a system in which it would be misleading to say, over a wide range of cases of punishment for noncompliance, that we are using persons. The clearest case in which it would be inappropriate to so regard punishment would be one in which there were explicit agreement in advance that punishment should follow on the voluntary doing of certain acts. Even if one does not have such conditions satisfied, and obviously such explicit agreements are not characteristic, one can see significant differences between our system of just punishment and a coercion situation.

First, unlike the case with one person coercing another "to do his will," the rules in our system apply to all, with the benefits and burdens equally distributed. About such a system it cannot be said that some are being subordinated to others or are being used by others or gotten to do things by others. To the extent that the rules are thought to be to the advantage of only some or to the extent there is a maldistribution of benefits and burdens, the difference between coercion and law disappears.

Second, it might be argued that at least any person inclined to act in a manner violative of the rules stands to all others as the person coerced stands to his coercer, and that he, at least, is a person disadvantaged as others are not. It is important here, I think, that he is part of a system in which it is commonly agreed that forbearance from the acts proscribed by the rules provides advantages for all. This system is the accepted setting; it is the norm. Thus, in any coercive situation, it is the coercer who deviates from the norm, with the responsibility of the person he is attempting to coerce defeated. In a just punishment situation, it is the person deviating from the norm, indeed he might be a coercer, who is responsible, for it is the norm to restrain oneself from acts of that kind. A voluntary agent diverging in his conduct from what is expected or what the norm is, on general causal principles, is regarded as the cause of what results from his conduct.

There is, then, some plausibility in the claim that, in a system of punishment of the kind I have sketched, a person chooses the punishment that is meted out to him. If, then, we can say in such a system that the rules provide none with advantages that others do not have, and further, that what happens to a person is conditioned by that person's choice and not that of others, then we can say that it is a system responding to one as a person.

We treat a human being as a person provided: first, we permit the person to make the choices that will determine what happens to him, and second, our responses to the person are responses respecting the person's choices. When we respond to a person's illness by treating the illness it is neither a case of treating or not treating the individual as a person. When we give a person a gift we are neither treating or not treating him as a person, unless, of course, he does not wish it, chooses not to have it, but we compel him to accept it.

3. This right to be treated as a person is a fundamental human right belonging to all human beings by virtue of their being human. It is also a natural, inalienable, and absolute right. I want now to defend these claims so reminiscent of an era of philosophical thinking about rights that many consider to have been seriously confused.

If the right is one that we possess by virtue of being human beings, we are immediately confronted with an apparent dilemma. If, to treat another as a person requires that we provide him with reasons for acting and avoid force or deception, how can we justify the force and deception we exercise with respect to children and the mentally ill? If they, too, have a right to be treated as persons are we not constantly infringing their rights? One way out of this is simply to restrict the right to those who satisfy the conditions of being a person. Infants and the insane, it might be argued, do not meet these conditions, and they would not then have the right. Another approach would be to describe the right they possess as a prima facie right to be treated as a person. This right might then be outweighed by other considerations. This approach generally seems to me, as I shall later argue, inadequate.

I prefer this tack. Children possess the right to be treated as persons but they possess this right as an individual might be said in the law of property to possess a future interest. There are advantages in talking of individuals as having a right though complete enjoyment of it is postponed. Brought to our attention, if we ascribe to them the right, is the legitimacy of their complaint if they are not provided with opportunities and conditions assuring their full enjoyment of the right when they acquire the characteristics of persons. More than this, all persons are charged with the sensitive task of not denying them the right to be a person and to be treated as a person by failing to provide the conditions for their becoming individuals who are able freely and in an informed way to choose and who are prepared themselves to assume responsibility for their choices. There is an obligation imposed upon us all, unlike that we have with respect to animals, to respond to children in such a way as to maximize the chances of their becoming persons. This may well impose upon us the obligation to treat them as persons from a very early age, that is, to respect their choices and to place upon them the responsibility for the choices to be made. There is no need to say that there is a close connection between how we respond to them and what they become. It also imposes upon us all the duty to display constantly the qualities of a person, for what they become they will largely become because of what they learn from us is acceptable behavior.

In claiming that the right is a right that human beings have by virtue of being human, there are several other features of the right that should be noted, perhaps better conveyed by labelling them "natural." First, it is a right we have apart from any voluntary agreement into which we have entered. Second, it is not a right that derives from some defined position or status. Third, it is equally apparent that one has the right regardless of the society or community of which one is a member. Finally, it is a right linked to certain features of a class of beings. Were we fundamentally different than we now are, we would not have it. But it is more than that, for the right is linked to a feature of human beings which, were that feature absent — the capacity to reason and to choose on the basis of reasons — , profound conceptual changes would be involved in the thought about human beings. It is a right, then, connected with a feature of men that sets men apart from other natural phenomena.

The right to be treated as a person is inalienable. To say of a right that it is inalienable draws attention not to limitations placed on what others may do with respect to the possessor of the right but rather to limitations placed on the dispositive capacities of the possessor of the right. Something is to be gained in keeping the issues of alienability and absoluteness separate.

There are a variety of locutions qualifying what possessors of rights may and may not do. For example, on this issue of alienability, it would be worthwhile to look at, among other things, what is involved in abandoning, abdicating, conveying, giving up, granting, relinquishing, surrendering, transferring, and waiving one's rights. And with respect to each of these concepts we should also have to be sensitive to the variety of uses of the term "rights." What it is, for example, to waive a Hohfeldian "right" in his strict sense will differ from what it is to waive a right in his "privilege" sense.

Let us look at only two concepts very briefly, those of transferring and waiving rights. The clearest case of transferring rights is that of transferring rights with respect to specific objects. I own a watch and owning it I have a complicated relationship, captured in this area rather well I think by Hohfeld's four basic legal relationships, to all persons in the world with respect to the watch. We crudely capture these complex relationships by talking of my "property rights" in or with respect to the watch. If I sell the watch, thus exercising a capacity provided by the rules of property, I have transferred rights in or with respect to the watch to someone else, the buyer, and the buyer now stands, as I formerly did, to all persons in the world in a series of complex relationships with respect to the watch.

While still the owner, I may have given to another permission to use it for several days. Had there not been the permission and had the person taken the watch, we should have spoken of interfering with or violating or, possibly, infringing my property rights. Or, to take a situation in which transferring rights is inappropriate, I may say to another "go ahead and slap me — you have my permission." In these types of situations philosophers and others have spoken of "surrendering" rights or, alternatively and, I believe, less strangely, of "waiving one's rights." And recently, of course, the whole topic of "waiving one's right to remain silent" in the context of police interrogation of suspects has been a subject of extensive litigation and discussion.

I confess to feeling that matters are not entirely perspicuous with respect to what is involved in "waiving" or "surrendering" rights. In conveying to another permission to take a watch or slap one, one makes legally permissible what otherwise would not have been. But in saying those words that constitute permission to take one's watch one is, of course, exercising precisely one of those capacities that leads us to say he has, while others have not, property rights with respect to the watch. Has one then waived his right in Hohfeld's strict sense in which the correlative is a duty to forbear on the part of others?

We may wish to distinguish here waiving the right to have others forbear to which there is a corresponding duty on their part to forbear, from placing oneself in a position where one has no legitimate right to complain. If I say the magic words "take the watch for a couple of days" or "go ahead and slap me," have I waived my right not to have my property taken or a right not to be struck or have I, rather, in saying what I have, simply stepped into a relation in which the rights no longer apply with respect to a specified other person? These observations find support in the following considerations. The right is that which gives rise, when infringed, to a legitimate claim against another person. What this suggests is that the right is that sphere interference with which entitles us to complain or gives us a right to complain. From this it seems to follow that a right to bodily security should be more precisely described as "a right that others not interfere without permission." And there is the corresponding duty not to interfere unless provided permission. Thus when we talk of waiving our rights or "giving up our rights" in such cases we are not waiving or giving up our right to property nor our right to bodily security, for we still, of course, possess the right not to have our watch taken without permission. We have rather placed ourselves in a position where we do not possess the capacity, sometimes called a right, to complain if the person takes the watch or slaps us.

There is another type of situation in which we may speak of waiving our rights. If someone without permission slaps me, there is an infringement of my right to bodily security. If I now acquiesce or go further and say "forget it" or "you are forgiven," we might say that I had waived my right to complain. But here, too, I feel uncomfortable about what is involved. For I do have the right to complain (a right without a corresponding duty) in the event I am slapped and I have that right whether I wish it or not. If I say to another after the slap, "you are forgiven" what I do is not waive the right to complain but rather make illegitimate my subsequent exercise of that right.

Now, if we turn to the right to be treated as a person, the claim that I made was that it was inalienable, and what I meant to convey by that word of respectable age is that (a) it is a right that cannot be transferred to another in the way one's right with respect to objects can be transferred and (b) that it cannot be waived in the ways in which people talk of waiving rights to property or waiving, within certain limitations, one's right to bodily security.

While the rules of the law of property are such that persons may, satisfying certain procedures, transfer rights, the right to be treated as a person logically cannot be transferred any more than one person can transfer to another his right to life or privacy. What, indeed, would it be like for another to have our right to be treated as a person? We can understand transferring a right with respect to certain objects. The new owner stands where the old owner stood. But with a right to be treated as a person what could this mean? My having the right meant that my choices were respected. Now if I transfer it to another this will mean that he will possess the right that my choices be respected? This is nonsense. It is only each person himself that can have his choices respected. It is no more possible to transfer this right than it is to transfer one's right to life.

Nor can the right be waived. It cannot be waived because any agreement to being treated as an animal or an instrument does not provide others with the moral permission to so treat us. One can volunteer to be a shield, but then it is one's choice on a particular occasion to be a shield. If without our permission, without our choosing it, someone used us as a shield, we may, I should suppose, forgive the person for treating us as an object. But we do not thereby waive our right to be treated as a person, for that is a right that has been infringed and what we have at most done is put ourselves in a position where it is inappropriate any longer to exercise the right to complain.

This is the sort of right, then, such that the moral rules defining relationships among persons preclude anyone from morally giving others legitimate permissions or rights with respect to one by doing or saying certain things. One stands, then, with respect to one's person as the nonowner of goods stands to those goods. The nonowner cannot, given the rule-defined relationships, convey to others rights and privileges that only the owner possesses. Just as there are agreements nonenforceable because void is contrary to public policy, so there are permissions our moral outlook regards as without moral force. With respect to being treated as a person, one is "disabled" from modifying relations of others to one.

The right is absolute. This claim is bound to raise eyebrows. I have an innocuous point in mind in making this claim.

In discussing alienability we focused on incapacities with respect to disposing of rights. Here what I want to bring out is a sense in which a right exists despite considerations for refusing to accord the person his rights. As with the topic of alienability there are a host of concepts that deserve a close look in this area. Among them are according, acknowledging, annulling, asserting, claiming, denying, destroying, exercising, infringing, insisting upon, interfering with, possessing, recognizing, and violating.

The claim that rights are absolute has been construed to mean that "assertions of rights cannot, for any reason under any circumstances, be denied." When there are considerations which warrant refusing to accord persons their rights, there are two prevalent views as to how this should be described: there is, first, the view that the person does not have the right, and second, the view that he has rights but of a prima facie kind and that these have been outweighed or overcome by the other considerations. "We can conceive times when such rights must give way, and, therefore, they are only prima facie and not absolute rights." (Brandt)

Perhaps there are cases in which a person claims a right to do a certain thing, say with his property, and argues that his property rights are absolute, meaning by this he has a right to do whatever he wishes with his property. Here, no doubt, it has to be explained to the person that the right he claims he has, he does not in fact possess. In such a case the person does not have and never did have, given a certain description of the right, a right that was prima facie or otherwise, to do what he claimed he had the right to do. If the assertion that a right is absolute implies that we have a right to do whatever we wish to do, it is an absurd claim and as such should not really ever have been attributed to political theorists arguing for absolute rights. But, of course, the claim that we have a prima facie right to do whatever we wish to do is equally absurd. The right is not prima facie either, for who would claim, thinking of the right to be free, that one has a prima facie right to kill others, if one wishes, unless there are moral considerations weighing against it?

There are, however, other situations in which it is accepted by all that a person possesses rights of a certain kind, and the difficulty we face is that of according the person the right he is claiming when this will promote more evil than good. The just act is to give the man his due and giving a man what it is his right to have is giving him his due. But it is a mistake to suppose that justice is the only dimension of morality. It may be justifiable not to accord to a man his rights. But it is no less a wrong to him, no less an infringement. It is seriously misleading to turn all justifiable infringements into noninfringements by saying that the right is only prima facie, as if we have, in concluding that we should not accord a man his rights, made out a case that he had none. To use the language of "prima facie rights" misleads, for it suggests that a presumption of the existence of a right has been overcome in these cases where all that can be said is that the presumption in favor of according a man his rights has been overcome. If we begin to think the right itself is prima facie, we shall, in cases in which we are justified in not according it, fail sufficiently to bring out that we have interfered where justice says we should not. Our moral framework is unnecessarily and undesirably impoverished by the theory that there are such rights.

When I claim, then, that the right to be treated as a person is absolute what I claim is that given that one is a person, one always has the right so to be treated, and that while there may possibly be occasions morally requiring not according a person this right, this fact makes it no less true that the right exists and would be infringed if the person were not accorded it.

4. Having said something about the nature of this fundamental right I want now, in conclusion, to suggest that the denial of this right entails the denial of all moral rights and duties. This requires bringing out what is surely intuitively clear—that any framework of rights and duties presupposes individuals that have the capacity to choose on the basis of reasons presented to them, and that what makes legitimate actions within such a system are the free choices of individuals. There is, in other words, a distribution of benefits and burdens in accord with a respect for the freedom of choice and freedom of action of all. I think that the best way to make this point may be to sketch some of the features of a world in which rights and duties are possessed.

First, rights exist only when there is some conception of some things valued and others not. Secondly, and implied in the first point, is the fact that there are dispositions to defend the valued commodities. Third, the valued commodities may be interfered with by others in this world. A group of animals might be said to satisfy these first three conditions. Fourth, rights exist when there are recognized rules establishing the legitimacy of some acts and ruling out others. Mistakes in the claim of rights are possible. Rights imply the concepts of interference and infringement, concepts the elucidation of which requires the concept of a rule applying to the conduct of persons. Fifth, to possess a right is to possess something that constitutes a legitimate restraint on the freedom of action of others. It is clear, for example, that if individuals were incapable of controlling their actions we would have no notion of a legitimate claim that they do so. If, for example, we were all disposed to object or disposed to complain, as the elephant seal is disposed to object when his territory is invaded, then the objection would operate in a causal way, or approximating a causal way, in getting the behavior of noninterference. In a system of rights, on the other hand, there is a point to appealing to the rules in legitimating one's complaint. Implied, then, in any conception of rights is the existence of individuals capable of choosing and capable of choosing on the basis of considerations with respect to rules. The distribution of freedom throughout such a system is determined by the free choice of individuals. Thus any denial of the right to be treated as a person would be a denial undercutting the whole system, for the system rests on the assumption that spheres of legitimate and illegitimate conduct are to be delimited with regard to the choices made by persons.

This conclusion stimulates one final reflection on the therapy world we imagined.

The denial of this fundamental right will also carry with it, ironically, the denial of the right to treatment to those who are ill. In the world as we now understand it, there are those who do wrong and who have a right to be responded to as persons who have done wrong. And there are those who have not done wrong but who are suffering from illnesses that in a variety of ways interfere with their capacity to live their lives as complete persons. These persons who are ill have a claim upon our compassion. But more than this they have, as animals do not, a right to be treated as persons. When an individual is ill he is entitled to that assistance which will make it possible for him to resume his functioning as a person. If it is an injustice to punish an innocent person, it is no less an injustice, and a far more significant one in our day, to fail to promote as best we can through adequate facilities and medical care the treatment of those who are ill. Those human beings who fill our mental institutions are entitled to more than they do in fact receive; they should be viewed as possessing the right to be treated as a person so that our responses to them may increase the likelihood that they will enjoy fully the right to be so treated. Like the child the mentally ill person has a future interest we cannot rightly deny him. Society is today sensitive to the infringement of justice in punishing the innocent; elaborate rules exist to avoid this evil. Society should be no less sensitive to the injustice of failing to bring back to the community of persons those whom it is possible to bring back.

A Paternalistic Theory
of Punishment

Herbert Morris

I

Nothing is more necessary to human life, and fortunately nothing more common, than parents' concern for their children. The infant's relatively lengthy period of helplessness requires that others nourish and protect it. And the child's existence as a vital being with an interest in the world, a capacity for eagerness and trust, and a sense of its own worth, all depend upon its receiving loving care, understanding, and attention. With time the normally developing child relinquishes its almost total dependence; it acquires the capacity to conceive of itself as an agent, to set out on its own, and to live in a world less dominated by its bodily needs and by its parents. Inevitably, this growth in competence and strength brings greater potential for self-harm, for the child's fantasies of its power and knowledge stand in marked contrast to the reality of its relative ignorance and vulnerability. In the ordinary course of events, the more powerful and knowledgeable parent often interferes with the child's choices in order to prevent harm and to bring about good and the reason for this is frequently, if the appropriate degree of parental selflessness is present, the child's own best interests, not primarily the interests of the parents or others.

Concern for the child often, of course, is manifested in allowing and encouraging experimentation just as it sometimes is in forceful intrusion. The child's developing

From *American Philosophical Quarterly*, vol. 18, no. 4, October 1981. Reprinted with permission.

individuality and sense of personal responsibility require that others encourage in it a sense of its own power and competence, support its venturing out, and exercise judgment in forbearing from intrusion, permitting it to err and to learn some painful truths from painful consequences suffered. God commanded Adam and Eve but left them free to disobey, thereby providing evidence both of his love and respect. The Devil, preferring for humans a state of permanent infantilism, would, no doubt, have acted differently as Dostoevsky's *Grand Inquisitor* nicely illustrates.[1]

The rational love of parents for their children then guides the parents' conduct so that their children may one day be fortunate enough to say with St. Paul, ". . . when I became a man, I put away childish things." A central drama of many lives is a result of imbalance in the relations between parents and children in this area—of being left too much on one's own or too little, of counting on one's parents too much, or of not being able to count upon them enough, of parental conduct that fosters too great dependence or conduct that imposes upon the child too great a personal responsibility, creating in the child not self-confidence but a sense of being alone and insecure in a threatening world.

Paternalism as a social phenomenon is prefigured in this elemental and universal situation of solicitous parental conduct that has its roots in our common humanity. But paternalism is of philosophic interest, not because of the way parents legitimately relate to their children—indeed there is oddity in describing this conduct as "paternalistic"—but rather because something like this practice is introduced into relations among adults. If our responses to adults mirror intrusive and solicitous parental responses to children we behave paternalistically.

Contemporary discussions of paternalism, understood in this way, proceed by focusing primarily on specific laws, laws that either prohibit or require certain conduct and that, arguably, have as their principal or sole reason for existence the good of those individuals to whom they are addressed. My focus in this paper is entirely different, for I consider paternalism, its meaning and its possible legitimacy, not in the context of specific laws prohibiting or requiring conduct, but rather with regard to the existence of a system of punitive responses for the violation of any law. I shall consider several issues and make a number of proposals. First, I define my particular version of a paternalistic theory of punishment. Second, I argue for, and consider a variety of objections to, this paternalistic theory. Third, I argue that the paternalistic theory I have constructed implies, in a more natural way than other common justifications for punishment, certain restrictions on the imposition of punishment.

II

Let us turn to the first topic. My aim here is to describe the paternalistic theory of punishment I later defend. I set out a variety of moral paternalism, for the good that is sought is a specific moral good.

First, then, in order to punish paternalistically we must be punishing. I assume that

---

1. What is gained and what is lost by allowing a choice to disobey is also brought out in C. S. Lewis's engaging replay of the Adam and Eve myth in his novel *Perelandra*.

the human institution of punishment presupposes, of course among other things, that certain conduct has been determined to be wrongful, that what are generally recognized as deprivations are imposed in the event of such conduct, that these deprivations are imposed upon the wrongdoer by someone in a position of authority, that wrongdoers are generally made aware that the deprivation is imposed because of the wrongdoing, and that the context makes evident that the deprivation is not a tax on a course of conduct or in some way a compensation to injured individuals but rather a response to the doing of what one was not entitled to do.

I have placed a logical constraint on the concept of punishment that is not customarily explicitly associated with it. I have claimed that in order for a person to be punished there must be an intention—one normally simply taken for granted—to convey to the wrongdoer, and where it is punishment for breach of a community's requirement, to others as well, that the deprivation is imposed because of wrongdoing. A communicative component is a defining characteristic of punishment and in part distinguishes it from mere retaliation or acting out of revenge where the goal of bringing about evil for another may achieve all that one desires. The paternalistic theory I present relies essentially on the idea of punishment as a complex communicative act—the components of which I hope will become clear as I proceed.[2]

A central theme in paternalism is to justify one's conduct out of a concern for the good of another. And so a paternalistic theory of punishment will naturally claim that a principal justification for punishment and a principal justification for restrictions upon it are that the system furthers the good of potential and actual wrongdoers. This contrasts with views—though many of the practices supported may be the same—that it is justice that requires the guilty persons be punished or that it is the utility to society that requires punishment. The theory I put forward emphasizes what retributivist and utilitarian theories largely, if not entirely, ignore, that a principal justification for punishment is the potential and actual wrongdoer's good. The theory should not, however, be confused with "reform" or "rehabilitative" theories. First, these theories may be based, not on consideration of what promotes the good of actual and potential wrongdoers, but on what promotes value for society generally. A reform theory, further, may countenance responses ruled out under the paternalistic theory proposed in these pages. And, finally, reform theories usually fail to address the issue of how instituting a practice of punishment, meaning by this both the threat of punishment and its actual infliction, may promote a specific moral good and this is a central feature of the theory I propose.[3]

I also assume that paternalistic measures characteristically involve disregard of, indeed conflict with, a person's desires. Giving a person what they want and being motivated to do so for that person's good is benevolence not paternalism. And so, if a

---

2. See generally Walter Moberly's splendid *The Ethics of Punishment* (London: Faber and Faber, 1968), particularly pp. 201 ff.
3. The reform theories discussed by H. L. A. Hart and found to be unacceptable as answers to the question what could be "the general justifying aim of punishment" differ, then, from the theory developed in these pages. Hart's change of mind in the notes to his collection of essays is occasioned by consideration of theories that still differ markedly from the one I propose. See *Punishment and Responsibility* (New York and Oxford: Oxford University Press, 1968), pp. 24–27, 240–41.

longing for punishment were characteristically the way in which people responded to the prospect of its imposition, there would, I think, be no role for a paternalistic theory regarding the practice, for it would simply be a practice that generally supplied people with what they acknowledged wanting. We may speak meaningfully of a paternalistic theory of punishment for two reasons: first, punishment by its nature characteristically involves a deprivation that individuals seek to avoid, with the implication that there is some conflict between what people want and what they get; second, the practice is such that the desires of a person at the time of the deprivation are not determinative of what they receive. Thus, while there are obviously persons guilty of wrongdoing who desire punishment, this fact will not affect either its being punishment that is meted out to such a person or the punishment being possibly based on paternalistic consideration, for what is customarily viewed as a deprivation is being imposed independently of the individual's desires.

Most importantly, the theory I am proposing requires that the practice of punishment promote a particular kind of good for potential and actual wrongdoers. The good is a moral one, and it is, arguably, one upon which all morality is grounded.

What is the character of this good? It has a number of component parts but it is essentially one's identity as a morally autonomous person attached to the good. This statement obviously needs explanation. First, it is a part of this good that one comes to appreciate the nature of the evil involved for others and for oneself in one's doing wrong. This requires empathy, a putting oneself in another's position; it also requires the imaginative capacity to take in the implications for one's future self of the evil one has done; it further requires an attachment to being a person of a certain kind. The claim is that it is good for the person, and essential to one's status as a moral person, that the evil underlying wrongdoing and the evil radiating from it be comprehended, comprehended not merely, if at all, in the sense of one's being able to articulate what one has done, but rather comprehended in the way remorse implies comprehension of evil caused. A person's blindness about such matters—this view assumes—is that person's loss. The Devil's splendid isolation is his hell.

Of course, this element of the good makes it apparent that for this theory, as with other moral justifications for punishment, that the rules defining wrongdoing, the rules whose violation occasions punishment, themselves meet certain minimal moral conditions. I assume, and do not argue for the view, that attachment to the values underlying these rules partly defines one's identity as a moral being and as a member of a moral community, that it gives one a sense of who one is and provides some meaning to one's life, and that the price paid for unconcern is some rupture in relationships, a separation from others, a feeling ill at ease with oneself, and some inevitable loss of emotional sustenance and sense of identity. I further assume that attachment to these values is a natural by-product of certain early forms of caring, understanding and respect and that the practice of punishment applies to those with such an attachment and not to those who because of some early disasters in primary relationships might value nothing or possess values we might attribute to the Devil.

Second, it is part of the good that one feel guilt over the wrongdoing, that is, that one be pained at having done wrong, that one be distressed with oneself, that one be disposed to restore what has been damaged, and that one accept the appropriateness of some deprivation, and the making of amends. Not to experience any of this would be to evidence an indifference to separation from others that could only, given the assumptions I have made, diminish one as a person.

Third, it is also part of the good that one reject the disposition to do what is wrong and commit oneself to forbearance in the future. I assume that this makes possible, indeed that it is inextricably bound up with, one's forgiving oneself, one's relinquishing one's guilt, and one's having the capacity fully to enter into life.

Finally, it is part of the good that one possess and vividly retain a conception of oneself as an individual worthy of respect, a conception of oneself as a responsible person, responsible for having done wrong and responsible, through one's own efforts at understanding and reflection, at more clearly coming to see things as they are with a deepened attachment to what is good. This conception of oneself is further nourished by freely accepting the moral conditions placed upon restoring relationships with others and oneself that one has damaged.

It is a moral good, then, that one feel contrite, that one feel the guilt that is appropriate to one's wrongdoing, that one be repentant, that one be self-forgiving and that one have reinforced one's conception of oneself as a responsible being. Ultimately, then, the moral good aimed at by the paternalism I propose is an autonomous individual freely attached to that which is good, those relationships with others that sustain and give meaning to a life.

The theory I propose claims that the potential of punishment to further the realization of this moral good is one principal justification for its existence. From the perspective of this form of paternalism there must be full respect in the design of the practice of punishment for the individual's moral and intellectual capacities. The good places logical and moral constraints on the means that it is permissible to employ to realize it. This is the principal reason that I earlier emphasized the communicative aspect of punishment, for on this theory we seek to achieve a good entirely through the mediation of the wrongdoer's efforts to understand the full significance of the wrongful conduct, the significance of the punishment being imposed, and the significance of acceptance of that punishment. Thus, unacceptable to this theory would be any response that sought the good of a wrongdoer in a manner that bypassed the human capacity for reflection, understanding, and revision of attitude that may result from such efforts. Any punitive response to a fully responsible being, then, and it might be no more than the giving of an evil-tasting pill or some form of conditioning, that directly in some causal way, with or without the agent's consent, sought to bring about a good, say, instantaneous truth or aversion to acting violently, would be incompatible with this constraint. There is, then, a good to be achieved but one cannot, logically or morally, be compelled to obtain it. Throughout there must be complete respect for the moral personality of the wrongdoer; it is a respect also, as I later argue, that must be given despite the wrongdoer's consent to be treated otherwise.

It is evident that this paternalistic goal is not to make people feel less burdened or more content. Once the good is achieved, these may be likely results; they are not, however, what is sought. It is important, too, to recognize that this good differs markedly from those particular goods associated with specific paternalistic legislation. It is not one's health; it is not even one's moral health with respect to any particular matter that is sought to be achieved; it is one's general character as a morally autonomous individual attached to the good.

III

What might be said in favor of such a theory and what might be objections to it? Two major issues will be considered. First, can a plausible case be presented that punishment is connected with the good as I have defined it? Second is there anything morally offensive or otherwise objectionable, as there often is with particular legislation, in having as one's goal in limiting freedom, the person's own good?

Let us direct attention again to the relationship between parent and child with which I commenced this essay and in which paternalistic-like elements seem clearly and appropriately present. The range of situations here is very great. Sometimes parents coercively interfere to protect the child from hurting itself, sometimes to assure its continued healthy growth, sometimes so that the child will learn to move about comfortably in a world of social conventions. But sometimes, of course, coercion enters in with respect to matters that are moral; certain modes of conduct are required if valued relationships among individuals within the family and outside the family are to come into existence and be maintained.

Slowly such values as obedience, respect, loyalty, and a sense of personal responsibility are integrated into the young person's life. This results to a considerable degree—of course not entirely and in differing degrees in different stages of development—from the child's conduct sometimes meeting with unpleasant responses. Written vividly upon children are lessons associated with some loss or some pain visited upon them by those to whom they are attached. It is important for my purposes that a difference in the significance of the painful responses be noted. The pain experienced by the child subjected to a parent's anger or disapproval only has the significance of punishment if the parent deliberately visits upon the child some pain because of the perceived wrongdoing. The parent's spontaneous anger or disapproval or blame causes the child distress. They may motivate future compliant conduct. They may arouse in the child guilt. They are not, however, by themselves requital for wrongdoing and by themselves do not relieve guilt. My view is that punishment has some special and logical relationship to wrongdoing and to the possibility of a child's acquiring the concept. Because of this relationship, punishment is connected with the good that I have described in a way that blame or disapproval by themselves are not.

First, because of punishment children come to acquire an understanding of the meaning of a limit on conduct. Logically connected with the concept of wrongdoing is the concept of a painful response that another is entitled to inflict because of the wrongful conduct.[4] Second, a punitive response conveys to children the depth of parental attachment to the values underlying the limit. Just as children know from experience that they are disposed to strike out when they or what they care for are injured, so they come to appreciate the seriousness of their parents' attachment to the limit and to the values supported by its existence by the parents' visiting some pain upon them. The degree of punishment, then, conveys to the child the importance parents attach to their child's responding to the limit and promotes in children, not just an appreciation that some-

---

4. Fingarette, "Punishment and Suffering," *Proceedings of the American Philosophical Association,* vol. 51 (1977).

thing is wrong, but how seriously wrong it is. It conveys, too, the significance of different degrees of fault in the doing of what is wrong. Further, particular punishments that are chosen often communicate to children the peculiar character of the evil caused by their disregard of the limit, the evil to others and the evil to themselves. Thus, even young children will find it particularly fitting to penalize a cheater by not permitting, for a time at least, further play, for such punishment conveys the central importance of honesty in the playing of the game and one's placing oneself outside the community of players by dishonesty. "If you will not abide by what makes this segment of our lives together possible, suffer the consequence of not being here a part of our lives."

Finally, punishment "rights the wrong." It has, in contrast to blame and disapproval, the character of closure, of matters returning to where they were before, of relationships being restored. Just as a limit being placed upon conduct serves to provide a bounded, manageable, world for the child, so the punitive response to a breach defines a limit to separation that is occasioned by wrongdoing. The debt is paid, life can go on.

The young hero in Styron's *Sophie's Choice* gives in to a desire for an exciting ride with a friend and forgets his agreeing to tend the fire before which his invalided mother sits for heat in the freezing weather. The young man is guilty and remorseful. Why, we may wonder, was he grateful to his father for placing him for a period of time in a shed without heat? The answer seems clear. It diminished the young boy's guilt, diminished it in a way that it would not have been were the father merely to have said, "You did something dreadful; I know you feel bad; don't let it happen again!" The young boy's guilt and remorse were painful; but because they were not deprivations imposed because of wrongdoing, they could not serve to reestablish what had been upset in the relations between parents and child.

What I have described is familiar. What needs emphasizing is that this parental practice of punishing is a complex communication to the child. It aids the child in learning what as a moral person it must know, that some things are not permitted, that some wrongs are more serious than others, that it is sometimes responsible for doing wrong and sometimes not, and that its degree of blameworthiness is not always the same. Further, the child's response to wrongdoing by feeling guilt, its willingness to accept some deprivation, and its commitment to acting differently in the future, all play an indispensable role in its restoring relationships it has damaged, relationships with others and with itself. The claim, then, is that this practice is, in fact, a significant contributing factor in one's development as a moral person.

Now, what more acceptably motivates a parent when it punishes its child than the desire to achieve a goal such as I have described? It would be perverse if the parent were generally to punish primarily from motives of retributive justice or optimal utility for the family. These ends are secondary to, though with retributive ends, to some extent essential to, the child's acquiring the characteristics of a moral person. This much may seem plausible but also quite beside the point. The topic is, after all, punishment in the adult world and there are significant differences between adults and children that may carry fatal implications for a paternalistic theory. I do not believe this is so, but before moving on I want to note a phenomenon that may cast doubt upon the legitimacy of the parental practice itself.

Parents sometimes, when imposing some deprivation upon their children, say, "I'm only doing this for your own good!" There is, I think, something offensive about this.

Does it affect the legitimacy of parental concern primarily for the child's moral development in inflicting punishment?

The answer I think is clearly "no," for the offensiveness of those words is not limited to situations in which punishment is imposed. Giving some unpleasant medicine or compelling the child to eat some distasteful but allegedly nourishing food, if accompanied by a statement that it is for the child's own good, is equally offensive. The words are customarily uttered in response to some sign of resistance, of some anger, and what they neglect to address is the child's unhappiness. They rather defend the parents before the child, making the child feel guilty because of its failure to be grateful for the good done it. And so imposed upon the child is the burden of getting what it does not want, the burden of checking its understandable anger because of this, and, finally, the burden of having to be grateful for getting what it does not want and, if not grateful, then guilty. It is not the motive of promoting the child's good that is suspect in these cases; it is communicating to the child what one's motive is, with its distressing consequences for the child, and with the still more serious problem, perhaps, that the parent's own guilt is unconsciously sought to be transferred to the child.

IV

One can acknowledge the place of punishment in the moral development of children and acknowledge, too, that it must to some degree be imposed to further this development and wonder what all this has to do with legal punishment of adults. For the law as a means of social control presupposes that the individuals to whom it applies are already responsible persons, responsible both in the sense of having the capacity to govern their actions through an understanding of the meaning of the norms addressed to them and responsible in the sense that they possess a knowledge of and an attachment to the values embodied in the society's laws. There is, nevertheless, a place for punishment in society analogous to its role in the family. I shall briefly sketch what this is.

Through promulgation of laws, through provision of sanctions for their violation, and through the general imposition of sanctions in the event of violation, each citizen learns what is regarded as impermissible by society, the degree of seriousness to be attached to wrongdoing of different kinds, and the particular significance—especially when the punishment is in its severity and character linked to the offense—of the evil underlying offenses. Punishment is a forceful reminder of the evil that is done to others and oneself. Were it not present, or were it imposed in circumstances markedly at odds with criteria for its imposition during the process of moral development, only confusion would result. Brandeis, in a quite different context, observed: "Our government is the potent, the omnipresent teacher. For good or for ill, it teaches the whole people by its example." My point is that law plays an indispensable role in our knowing what for society is good and evil. Failure to punish serious wrongdoing, punishment of wrongdoing in circumstances where fault is absent, would serve only to baffle our moral understanding and threaten what is so often already precarious.

Further, our punitive responses guide the moral passions as they come into play with respect to interests protected by the law. Punishment, among other things, permits purgation of guilt and ideally restoration of damaged relationships. Punishment, then, communicates what is wrong and in being imposed both rights the wrong and serves, as well, as a reminder of the evil done to others and to oneself in the doing of what is wrong.

Now in addition to making out that punishment may reasonably be thought to play its part, even with adults, in promoting the good of one's moral personality, the paternalist has to have some argument for this as a morally permissible way of proceeding. The paternalist is, I believe, on firm ground here. The guilty wrongdoer is not viewed as damned by his wrongful conduct to a life forever divorced from others. He is viewed as as responsible being, responsible for having done wrong and possessing the capacity for recognizing the wrongfulness of his conduct. Further, the evil—as Socrates long ago pointed out—that he has done himself by his wrongdoing is a moral evil greater than he has done others. His soul is in jeopardy as his victim's is not. What could possibly justify an unconcern with this evil if the person is one of us and, if we sense, rightly I believe, that there but for the grace of God go we? In considering, for example, why we might wish to have a society of laws, of laws associated with sanctions for their violation, of laws that are in fact enforced against others and ourselves, it would be rational, indeed it would be, I think, among the most persuasive of considerations for establishing such a social practice, that it would promote our own good as moral persons. Thinking of ourselves as potential, and thinking of ourselves as actual wrongdoers, and appreciating the connection of punishment with one's attachment to the good, to one's status as a moral person, and to the possibility it provides of closure and resumption of relationships, would we not select such a system, if for no other reason, than that it would promote our own good?

V

We have now to consider certain objections to the theory. First, does it fail to respect one as an autonomous being? The answer is that it does not. One's choices are throughout respected, and it is one's status as a moral person that is sought to be affirmed. But is there not something offensively demeaning in instituting punishment for such a reason? More demeaning, one might ask, than addressing the wrongdoer's sense of fear to which others appeal in their theories of punishment? More demeaning than an indifference to the moral status of the person but totally committed to retributive justice? I am not convinced that this is so either. On the theory I propose one is throughout responded to as a moral person.

But does not a paternalistic theory lead to two unacceptable extremes with respect to punishment, the first that we should always warn before punishing, and wait to see the effects of our warning, the other that we should continue punishing until we achieve the desired effects? The answers here can be brief. First, the announcement of the norm and the provision for punishment in the event of its violation is itself the warning and to allow a person to disobey and threaten that next time there will be punishment is to issue not one but two warnings. Second, the practice of punishment, given the paternalistic goals I have described, cannot permit open-ended punishments, repeated punishments or punishments that are excessively severe. For, first, the goal is not repentance at all costs, if that has meaning, but repentance freely arrived at and not merely a disposition toward conformity with the norms; secondly, the punishment provided for wrongdoing must reflect judgments of the seriousness of the wrong done; such punishment cannot focus on some end state of the person and disregard the potential for moral confusion that would arise from repeated or excessive punishment.

Another criticism might go as follows: "You have ruled out conditioning a person, even with their consent, so that they might not be disposed to do evil in the future. But surely, while perhaps an unjustifiable practice without consent, it is acceptable with it, for it provides a person what they freely choose and delivers them from an affliction that promotes evil." Two points need to be made here. First, the theory would not preclude freely chosen forms of conditioning, surgery and the like in those circumstances in which it is acknowledged that the person is not, with respect to the conduct involved, an autonomous agent. There is nothing wrong, for example, in a person choosing surgery to remove a tumor that is causally related to outbursts of violence over which the person has no control. The class of person, then, whose choice would be accorded respect is made up of those we should be disposed to excuse from criminal liability. Second, the theory would regard as morally unacceptable a response, conditioning or otherwise, that had as its goal, not just aversion to doing wrong, but obliteration of one's capacity to choose to do so. What must be aimed at is that the afflicted become autonomous not automatons. There must be freedom to disobey, for the moral price is too high that is paid in purchasing immunity from temptation and guaranteed conformity.

The most troubling objections to the theory are, I think, these: First, it cannot account for the accepted disposition to punish those who are already, as it were, awakened and repentant. And, second, even more seriously, it cannot account for the disposition to punish those who know what the values of society are but who are indifferent to or opposed to them. Someone, for example, may feel inclined to say: "Look—most serious crimes—and your theory surely most neatly fits such crimes not petty offenses—are committed by individuals who are perfectly aware of what they are doing and perfectly aware that society's values are being flouted. These individuals are not going to be instructed about evil or brought to any moral realization about themselves by punishment. Surely, you can't be serious about repentance when considering them, and they certainly do not care a jot about paying off any debt because they do not feel any guilt over what they have done. Your theory fails so to match reality as to be just one more tedious example of a philosopher spinning out fantastic yarns without any genuine relevance to reality." What can be said in response to these points?

As to the first, I would claim that the guilty and repentant wrongdoers are naturally disposed to accept the appropriateness of the punishment provided, both because this will evidence to them and to others the genuineness of their feelings and because the punishment rights the wrong, brings about closure and restores relationships that have been damaged. The experience of guilt and remorse, the avowal of repentance do not by themselves achieve this.[5] A general practice of pardoning persons who claimed that they were repentant would destroy the principal means of reestablishing one's membership in the community.

---

5. On the connections of guilt and suffering, see Morris, *On Guilt and Innocence* (Berkeley and Los Angeles: University of California Press, 1976), pp. 89–110.

Now for the second major objection. A response here requires that attention be paid to certain general features of the theory that has been put forward. The theory is, of course, not intended as a description of any actual practice of legal punishment or even as realistically workable in a society such as ours. Things are in such a state that it is not. What is proposed is a moral theory of punishment and, as such, it includes at least two conditions that may be only marginally congruent with our social world. The first is that the norms addressed to persons are generally just and that the society is to some substantial extent one in which those who are liable to punishment have roughly equal opportunities to conform to those just norms. The second condition is equally important. The theory presupposes that there is a general commitment among persons to whom the norms apply to the values underlying them. If these two conditions are not met, we do not have what I understand as a practice of punishment for which any moral justification can be forthcoming.

At this point it may be thought, "fair enough, but then what is the point of the whole exercise?" My response is this: First, the theory is not without applicability to significant segments of our society. Second, it has value, for it provides an important perspective upon actual practices; it throws into relief our society's failures to realize the conditions I have stipulated. And, finally, it assists us in sensitive and intelligent forbearance from putting our moral imprimatur upon practices which the paternalistic model would find unacceptable. Excessively lengthy prison terms and the inhumane conditions under which they are served, for example, can be effectively criticized with a clear conception of the good defined by the paternalistic theory. The theory may serve as a guide in our attempts to adjust present practices so that they more closely accord with moral dictates, to work for precisely that society in which the paternalistic conception provides not just the ring of moral truth but descriptive truth as well.

VI

I want now to shift attention to the issue of restrictions on punishment. The proposed paternalistic theory limits punishment, I believe, in a way that accords more closely with our moral intuitions than a number of alternative theories. First, it follows from the theory that any class of persons incapable of appreciating the significance of the norms addressed to them cannot justifiably be punished. Absence of a free and knowing departure from the norm makes pointless imposition of punishment. Second, it also follows that excuses must be recognized and that mitigating factors be taken into account, including as an excuse, of course, reasonable ignorance or mistake of law.

Perhaps most significantly, a paternalistic orientation implies a position that matches our moral intuitions more closely than other theories on the issue of what kinds of punishment may be inflicted. Punishments that are aimed at degrading or brutalizing a person are not conducive to moral awakening but only to bitterness and resentment. But there is also, I believe, another paternalistic route to limitations upon certain modes of punishment, a limitation that follows from the conception of the moral good.

The wrongdoer has, as we all do, a basic right to be free. How, we may wonder, are we able to justify our imposing our will upon him and limiting his freedom? One answer is that by wrongful conduct he has forfeited his right to freedom. The wrongdoer is in no position to complain if he meets with a response that is similar to what has been visited by him upon another. Such a theory of forfeiture places great weight upon an individual's choice. It holds that rights are forfeitable, waivable and relinquishable—just so long as the choice involved is informed and free. A person might forfeit his right to life by murdering; a person might relinquish his right to be free by selling himself into slavery. The paternalistic position that I have proposed holds otherwise. It implies that there is a non-waivable, non-forfeitable, non-relinquishable right—the right to one's status as a moral being, a right that is implied in one's being a possessor of any rights at all.

Such a view, when punishment is at issue, makes morally impermissible any response to a person, despite what that person has done, that would be inconsistent with this fundamental right, even though the person were unattached to it, indifferent to its moral value and eager to forfeit it. A retributivist might respond in kind to any wrong done. A social utilitarian might calculate the effects on people and society in doing so. A paternalist, attached to the good of the wrongdoer, would reject retributive justice and utility as the sole determinative criteria, and would propose a good to be realized that is independent of these values. Punishment will not be permitted that destroys in some substantial way one's character as an autonomous creature. Certain cruel punishments, then, may be ruled out, not merely because they are conducive to hardening the heart but, more importantly, because they destroy a good that can never rightly be destroyed. As I see it, this precludes, on moral grounds, punishment that may be like for like but which nevertheless violates one's humanity by either destroying one's life or destroying one's capacity for rejecting what is evil and again attaching oneself to the good.

Let me be more specific. Suppose that a sadist has cruelly destroyed another human being's capacity for thought while leaving the person alive. Is there a retributivist argument that would bar a like treatment for the sadist? I do not know of it. Certainly, the lex talionis would seem to sanction it. Is our inclination to forbear from treating the sadist in a manner that he has treated his victim derived exclusively, then, from social evils that we foresee might flow from such punishment? I do not find this persuasive. Our moral repugnance precedes such calculation and findings inconsistent with this repugnance would be rejected. Is it simply revulsion at the thought of oneself or one's agents deliberately perpetrating such acts? Is it a concern for our own good that motivates us? No doubt, this may play a role, but my conviction is that something else is involved. It is the ingredient to which the moral paternalist draws attention. The wrongdoer possesses something destroyed in another. The wrongdoer may desire to destroy it in himself as well, but that is not his moral prerogative. It is immune from moral transformations brought about by free choice.

VII

I would like, in conclusion, to make somewhat clearer what I am and am not claiming for the theory proposed in these pages and, further, to draw attention to two ironies connected with it.

I have claimed that to have as one's aim in punishing the good of the wrongdoer counts strongly in favor of the moral legitimacy of punishing. I do not claim, of course, that this is the sole justification for punishment, though I do believe that what it seeks to promote is among the most important, if not the most important, of human goods. The practice of punishment is complex and any justification proposed as an exclusive one must, in my judgment, be met with skepticism, if not scorn. There is, too, as I earlier briefly noted, a significant logical overlapping of this theory with retributivism, though at a certain point, when one considers types of punishment, they diverge. A paternalistic theory, given the good as defined, would support principles that are familiar dictates of retributivism—that only the guilty may be punished, that the guilty must be, and that the punishment inflicted reflect the degree of guilt. Failure to comply with the demands of retributivism would preclude realization of the paternalist's goal. I have also, however, suggested that retributivism needs supplementing if it is to meet our intuitions of what is morally permissible punishment. But, of course, this overlapping of justifications for punishment includes as well some form of utilitarianism, for if our goal is as I have defined it, and punishments are threatened and imposed, deterrent values are also furthered. I do not question the rich over-determination of goods promoted by the practice of punishment. I do urge that weight be given, and on the issue of restrictions on punishment, determinative weight, to paternalistic ends.

There are, finally, two ironies to which I wish to draw attention. The first is this. I have selected as the good to be realized by this paternalistic theory of punishment the very good to which philosophers often make appeal in their principled objections to paternalism with regard to specific prohibitions and requirements. Secondly, I have proposed a theory that justifies forceful intrusion into the lives of people. But it is also an atypical paternalistic theory, for it prohibits certain types of intrusion. I reach this conclusion because the good sought does not allow weight to be given to an individual's free choice when the issue is relinquishment of one's status as a moral being. The paternalistic aspect in this derives from the fact that there is a good for the person to which we are attached, though the person might not be, and which we continue to respect in disregard of the usual consequences of a person's free choice. I would guess that something like these thoughts underlies the view that we possess some goods as gifts from God and that it is not within our moral prerogative to dispose of them. It is easy to suppose, but a mistake nevertheless, that because we may be favored by the gods that we are one of them.

Punishment and Utility

Jeremy Bentham

Of the Principle of Utility

I.   Nature has placed mankind under the governance of two sovereign masters, *pain* and *pleasure*. It is for them alone to point out what we ought to do, as well as to determine what we shall do. On the one hand the standard of right and wrong, on the other the chain of causes and effects, are fastened to their throne. They govern us in all we do, in all we say, in all we think: every effort we can make to throw off our subjection, will serve but to demonstrate and confirm it. In words a man may pretend to abjure their empire: but in reality he will remain subject to it all the while. The *principle of utility*[1] recognises this subjection, and assumes it for the foundation of that system,

From Chapters I, III, VII, XIII, and XIV of *An Introduction to the Principles of Morals and Legislation* (1823 edition). Some footnotes have been omitted. Bentham, an English utilitarian and philosophical radical, was one of the most influential moral writers and social reformers of the nineteenth century.

1. *Note by the Author, July 1822.* To this denomination has of late been added, or substituted, the *greatest happiness* or *greatest felicity* principle: this for shortness, instead of saying at length *that principle* which states the greatest happiness of all those whose interest is in question, as being the right and proper, and only right and proper and universally desirable, end of human action: of human action in every situation,. and in particular in that of functionary or set of functionaries exercising the powers of Government. The word *utility* does not so clearly point to the ideas of *pleasure* and *pain* as the words *happiness* and *felicity* do: nor does it lead us to the consideration of the *number,* of the interests affected; to the *number,* as being the circumstance, which contributes, in the largest proportion, to the formation of the standard here in question; the *standard of right and*

the object of which is to rear the fabric of felicity by the hands of reason and law. Systems which attempt to question it, deal in sounds instead of sense, in caprice instead of reason, in darkness instead of light.

But enough of metaphor and declamation: it is not by such means that moral science is to be improved.

II.   The principle of utility is the foundation of the present work: it will be proper therefore at the outset to give an explicit and determinate account of what is meant by it. By the principle of utility is meant that principle which approves or disapproves of every action whatsoever, according to the tendency which it appears to have to augment or diminish the happiness of the party whose interest is in question: or, what is the same thing in other words, to promote or to oppose that happiness. I say of every action whatsoever; and therefore not only of every action of a private individual, but of every measure of government.

III.   By utility is meant that property in any object, whereby it tends to produce benefit, advantage, pleasure, good, or happiness, (all this in the present case comes to the same thing) or (what comes again to the same thing) to prevent the happening of mischief, pain, evil, or unhappiness to the party whose interest is considered: if that party be the community in general, then the happiness of the community: if a particular individual, then the happiness of that individual.

IV.   The interest of the community is one of the most general expressions that can occur in the phraseology of morals: no wonder that the meaning of it is often lost. When it has a meaning, it is this. The community is a fictitious *body,* composed of the individual persons who are considered as constituting as it were its *members.* The interest of the community then is, what?—the sum of the interests of the several members who compose it.

V.   It is in vain to talk of the interest of the community, without understanding what is the interest of the individual. A thing is said to promote the interest, or to be *for* the interest, of an individual, when it tends to add to the sum total of his pleasures: or, what comes to the same thing, to diminish the sum total of his pains.

VI.   An action then may be said to be conformable to the principle of utility, or, for shortness sake, to utility, (meaning with respect to the community at large) when the tendency it has to augment the happiness of the community is greater than any it has to diminish it.

VII.   A measure of government (which is but a particular kind of action, performed by a particular person or persons) may be said to be conformable to or dictated by the principle of utility, when in like manner the tendency which it has to augment the happiness of the community is greater than any which it has to diminish it.

VIII.   When an action, or in particular a measure of government, is supposed by a man to be conformable to the principle of utility, it may be convenient, for the purposes

---

wrong, by which alone the propriety of human conduct, in every situation, can with propriety be tried. This want of a sufficiently manifest connexion between the ideas of *happiness* and *pleasure* on the one hand, and the idea of *utility* on the other, I have every now and then found operating, and with but too much efficiency, as a bar to the acceptance, that might otherwise have been given, to this principle.

of discourse, to imagine a kind of law or dictate, called a law or dictate of utility: and to speak of the action in question, as being conformable to such a law or dictate. . . .

Of the Four Sanctions or Sources of Pain and Pleasure

I.   It has been shown that the happiness of the individuals, of whom a community is composed, that is their pleasures and their security, is the end and the sole end which the legislator ought to have in view: the sole standard, in conformity to which each individual ought, as far as depends upon the legislator, to be *made* to fashion his behaviour. But whether it be this or any thing else that is to be *done,* there is nothing by which a man can ultimately be *made* to do it, but either pain or pleasure. Having taken a general view of these two grand objects (*viz.* pleasure, and what comes to the same thing, immunity from pain) in the character of *final* causes; it will be necessary to take a view of pleasure and pain itself, in the character of *efficient* causes or means.

II.   There are four distinguishable sources from which pleasure and pain are in use to flow: considered separately, they may be termed the *physical,* the *political,* the *moral,* and the *religious:* and inasmuch as the pleasures and pains belonging to each of them are capable of giving a binding force to any law or rule of conduct, they may all of them be termed *sanctions.* . . .

IV.   If at the hands of a *particular* person or set of persons in the community, who under names correspondent to that of *judge,* are chosen for the particular purpose of dispensing it, according to the will of the sovereign or supreme ruling power in the state, it may be said to issue from the *political sanction.* . . .

Of Human Actions in General

I.   The business of government is to promote the happiness of the society, by punishing and rewarding. That part of its business which consists in punishing, is more particularly the subject of penal law. In proportion as an act tends to disturb that happiness, in proportion as the tendency of it is pernicious, will be the demand it creates for punishment. What happiness consists of we have already seen: enjoyment of pleasures, security from pains.

II.   The general tendency of an act is more or less pernicious, according to the sum total of its consequences: that is, according to the difference between the sum of such as are good, and the sum of such as are evil.

III.   It is to be observed, that here, as well as henceforward, wherever consequences are spoken of, such only are meant as are *material.* Of the consequences of any act, the multitude and variety must needs be infinite: but such of them only as are material are worth regarding. Now among the consequences of an act, be they what they may, such only, by one who views them in the capacity of a legislator, can be said to be material, as either consist of pain or pleasure, or have an influence in the production of pain or pleasure. . . .

Cases Unmeet for Punishment

1. General View of Cases Unmeet for Punishment

I. The general object which all laws have, or ought to have, in common, is to augment the total happiness of the community; and therefore, in the first place, to exclude, as far as may be, every thing that tends to subtract from that happiness: in other words, to exclude mischief.

II. But all punishment is mischief: all punishment in itself is evil. Upon the principle of utility, if it ought at all to be admitted, it ought only to be admitted in as far as it promises to exclude some greater evil.[2]

III. It is plain, therefore, that in the following cases punishment ought not to be inflicted.

1. Where it is *groundless:* where there is no mischief for it to prevent; the act not being mischievous upon the whole.
2. Where it must be *inefficacious:* where it cannot act so as to prevent the mischief.
3. Where it is *unprofitable,* or too *expensive:* where the mischief it would produce would be greater than what it prevented.
4. Where it is *needless:* where the mischief may be prevented, or cease of itself, without it: that is, at a cheaper rate.

2. Cases in Which Punishment Is Groundless

These are,

IV. 1. Where there has never been any mischief: where no mischief has been produced to any body by the act in question. Of this number are those in which the act was such as might, on some occasions, be mischievous or disagreeable, but the person whose interest it concerns gave his *consent* to the performance of it. This consent, provided it be free, and fairly obtained, is the best proof that can be produced, that, to

---

2. What follows, relative to the subject of punishment, ought regularly to be preceded by a distinct chapter on the ends of punishment. But having little to say on that particular branch of the subject, which has not been said before, it seemed better, in a work, which will at any rate be but too voluminous, to omit this title, reserving it for another, hereafter to be published entitled *The Theory of Punishment.* To the same work I must refer the analysis of the several possible modes of punishment, a particular and minute examination of the nature of each, and of its advantages and disadvantages, and various other disquisitions, which did not seem absolutely necessary to be inserted here. A very few words, however, concerning the *ends* of punishment, can scarcely be dispensed with.

The immediate principal end of punishment is to control action. This action is either that of the offender, or of others: that of the offender it controls by its influence, either on his will, in which case it is said to operate in the way of *reformation;* or on his physical power, in which case it is said to operate by *disablement:* that of others it can influence no otherwise than by its influence over their wills; in which case it is said to operate in the way of *example.* A kind of collateral end, which it has a natural tendency to answer, is that of affording a pleasure or satisfaction to the party injured, where there is one, and, in general, to parties whose ill-will, whether on a self-regarding account, or on the account of sympathy or antipathy, has been excited by the offence. This purpose, as far as it can be answered *gratis,* is a beneficial one. But no punishment ought to be allotted merely to this purpose, because (setting aside its effects in the way of control) no such pleasure is

the person who gives it, no mischief, at least no immediate mischief upon the whole, is done. For no man can be so good a judge as the man himself, what it is gives him pleasure or displeasure.

V. 2. Where the mischief was *outweighed:* although a mischief was produced by that act, yet the same act was necessary to the production of a benefit which was of greater value than the mischief. This may be the case with any thing that is done in the way of precaution against instant calamity, as also with any thing that is done in the exercise of the several sorts of powers necessary to be established in every community, to wit, domestic, judicial, military, and supreme.

VI. 3. Where there is a certainty of an adequate compensation: and that in all cases where the offence can be committed. This supposes two things: 1. That the offence is such as admits of an adequate compensation: 2. That such a compensation is sure to be forthcoming. Of these suppositions, the latter will be found to be a merely ideal one: a supposition that cannot, in the universality here given to it, be verified by fact. It cannot, therefore, in practice, be numbered amongst the grounds of absolute impunity. It may, however, be admitted as a ground for an abatement of that punishment, which other considerations, standing by themselves, would seem to dictate.

3. Cases in Which Punishment Must Be Inefficacious

These are,

VII. 1. Where the penal provision is *not established* until after the act is done. Such are the cases, 1. Of an *ex-post-facto* law; where the legislator himself appoints not a punishment till after the act is done. 2. Of a sentence beyond the law; where the judge, of his own authority, appoints a punishment which the legislator had not appointed.

VIII. 2. Where the penal provision, though established, is *not conveyed* to the notice of the person on whom it seems intended that it should operate. Such is the case where the law has omitted to employ any of the expedients which are necessary, to make sure that every person whatsoever, who is within the reach of the law, be apprized of all the cases whatsoever, in which (being in the station of life he is in) he can be subjected to the penalties of the law.

IX. 3. Where the penal provision, though it were conveyed to a man's notice, *could produce no effect* on him, with respect to the preventing him from engaging in any act of the *sort* in question. Such is the case, 1. In extreme *infancy;* where a man has not yet attained that state or disposition of mind in which the prospect of evils so distant as those which are held forth by the law, has the effect of influencing his conduct. 2. In *insanity;* where the person, if he has attained to that disposition, has since been deprived of it through the influence of some permanent though unseen cause. 3. In

---

ever produced by punishment as can be equivalent to the pain. The punishment, however, which is allotted to the other purpose, ought, as far as it can be done without expense, to be accommodated to this. Satisfaction thus administered to a party injured, in the shape of a dissocial pleasure, may be styled a vindictive satisfaction or compensation: as a compensation, administered in the shape of a self-regarding profit, or stock of pleasure, may be styled a lucrative one. See. B. I. tit. vi. [Compensation]. Example is the most important end of all, in proportion as the *number* of the persons under temptation to offend is to *one.*

intoxication; where he has been deprived of it by the transient influence of a visible cause: such as the use of wine, or opium, or other drugs, that act in this manner on the nervous system: which condition is indeed neither more nor less than a temporary insanity produced by an assignable cause.[3]

X. 4. Where the appeal provision (although, being conveyed to the party's notice, it might very well prevent his engaging in acts of the sort in question, provided he knew that it related to those acts) could not have this effect, with regard to the *individual* act he is about to engage in: to wit, because he knows not that it is of the number of those to which the penal provision relates. This may happen, 1. In the case of *unintentionality;* where he intends not to engage, and thereby knows not that he is about to engage, in the *act* in which eventually he is about to engage. 2. In the case of *unconsciousness;* where, although he may know that he is about to engage in the *act* itself, yet, from not knowing all the material *circumstances* attending it, he knows not of the *tendency* it has to produce that mischief, in contemplation of which it has been made penal in most instances. 3. In the case of *missupposal;* where, although he may know of the tendency the act has to produce that degree of mischief, he supposes it, though mistakenly, to be attended with some circumstance, or set of circumstances, which, if it had been attended with, it would either not have been productive of that mischief, or have been productive of such a greater degree of good, as has determined the legislator in such a case not to make it penal.

XI. 5. Where, though the penal clause might exercise a full and prevailing influence, were it to act alone, yet by the *predominant* influence of some opposite cause upon the will, it must necessarily be ineffectual; because the evil which he sets himself about to undergo, in the case of his *not* engaging in the act, is so great, that the evil denounced by the penal clause, in case of his engaging in it, cannot appear greater. This may happen, 1. In the case of *physical danger;* where the evil is such as appears likely to be brought about by the unassisted powers of *nature*. 2. In the case of a *threatened mischief;* where it is such as appears likely to be brought about through the intentional and conscious agency of *man*.[4]

---

3. Notwithstanding what is here said, the cases of infancy and intoxication (as we shall see hereafter) cannot be looked upon in practice as affording sufficient grounds for absolute impunity. But this exception in point of practice is no objection to the propriety of the rule in point of theory. The ground of the exception is neither more nor less than the difficulty there is of ascertaining the matter of fact: viz. whether at the requisite point of time the party was actually in the state in question; that is, whether a given case comes really under the rule. Suppose the matter of fact capable of being perfectly ascertained, without danger or mistake, the impropriety of punishment would be as indubitable in these cases as in any other.

  The reason that is commonly assigned for the establishing an exemption from punishment in favour of infants, insane persons, and persons under intoxication, is either false in fact, or confusedly expressed. The phrase is, that the will of these persons concurs not with the act; that they have no vicious will; or, that they have not the free use of their will. But suppose all this to be true? What is it to the purpose? Nothing: except in as far as it implies the reason given in the text.

4. The influences of the *moral* and *religious* sanctions, or, in other words, of the motives of *love of reputation* and *religion,* are other causes, the force of which may, upon particular occasions, come to be greater than that of any punishment which the legislator is *able,* or at least which he will *think proper,* to apply. These, therefore, it will be proper for him to have his eye upon. But the force of these influences is variable and different in different times and places: the force of the foregoing influences is constant and the same, at all times and every where. These, therefore, it can never be

XII. 6. Where (though the penal clause may exert a full and prevailing influence over the *will* of the party) yet his *physical faculties* (owing to the predominant influence of some physical cause) are not in a condition to follow the determination of the will: insomuch that the act is absolutely *involuntary*. Such is the case of physical *compulsion* or *restraint,* by whatever means brought about; where the man's hand, for instance, is pushed against some object which his will disposes him *not* to touch; or tied down from touching some object which his will disposes him to touch.

4. Cases Where Punishment Is Unprofitable

These are,

XIII. 1. Where, on the one hand, the nature of the offence, on the other hand, that of the punishment, are, *in the ordinary state of things,* such, that when compared together, the evil of the latter will turn out to be greater than that of the of the former.

XIV. Now the evil of the punishment divides itself into four branches, by which so many different sets of persons are affected. 1. The evil of *coercion* or *restraint:* or the pain which it gives a man not to be able to do the act, whatever it be, which by the apprehension of the punishment he is deterred from doing. This is felt by those by whom the law is *observed.* 2. The evil of *apprehension:* or the pain which a man, who has exposed himself to punishment, feels at the thoughts of undergoing it. This is felt by those by whom the law has been *broken,* and who feel themselves in *danger* of its being executed upon them. 3. The evil of *sufferance:* or the pain which a man feels, in virtue of the punishment itself, from the time when he begins to undergo it. This is felt by those by whom the law is broken, and upon whom it comes actually to be executed. 4. The pain of sympathy, and the other *derivative* evils resulting to the persons who are in *connection* with the several classes of original sufferers just mentioned. Now of these four lots of evil, the first will be greater or less, according to the nature of the act from which the party is restrained: the second and third according to the nature of the punishment which stands annexed to that offence.

XV. On the other hand, as to the evil of the offence, this will also, of course, be greater or less, according to the nature of each offence. The proportion between the one evil and the other will therefore be different in the case of each particular offence. The cases, therefore, where punishment is unprofitable on this ground, can by no other means be discovered, than by an examination of each particular offence; which is what will be the business of the body of the work.

XVI. 2. Where, although in the *ordinary state* of things, the evil resulting from the punishment is not greater than the benefit which is likely to result from the force with which it operates, during the same space of time, towards the excluding the evil of the offences, yet it may have been rendered so by the influence of some *occasional circumstances.* In the number of these circumstances may be, 1. The multitude of delinquents at a particular juncture; being such as would increase, beyond the ordinary

---

proper to look upon as safe grounds for establishing absolute impunity: owing (as in the above-mentioned cases of infancy and intoxication) to the impracticability of ascertaining the matter of fact.

measure, the *quantum* of the second and third lots, and thereby also of a part of the fourth lot, in the evil of the punishment. 2. The extraordinary value of the services of some one delinquent; in the case where the effect of the punishment would be to deprive the community of the benefit of those services. 3. The displeasure of the *people;* that is, of an indefinite number of the members of the *same* community, in cases where (owing to the influence of some occasional incident) they happen to conceive, that the offence or the offender ought not to be punished at all, or at least ought not to be punished in the way in question. 4. The displeasure of *foreign powers;* that is, of the governing body, or a considerable number of the members of some *foreign* community or communities, with which the community in question is connected.

5. Cases Where Punishment Is Needless

These are,

XVII. 1. Where the purpose of putting an end to the practice may be attained as effectually at a cheaper rate: by instruction, for instance, as well as by terror: by informing the understanding; as well as by exercising an immediate influence on the will. This seems to be the case with respect to all those offences which consist in the disseminating pernicious principles in matters of *duty;* of whatever kind the duty be; whether political, or moral, or religious. And this, whether such principles be disseminated *under,* or even *without,* a sincere persuasion of their being beneficial. I say, even *without:* for though in such a case it is not instruction that can prevent the writer from endeavouring to inculcate his principles, yet it may the readers from adopting them: without which, his endeavouring to inculcate them will do no harm. In such a case, the sovereign will commonly have little need to take an active part: if it be the interest of *one* individual to inculcate principles that are pernicious, it will as surely be the interest of *other* individuals to expose them. But if the sovereign must needs take a part in the controversy, the pen is the proper weapon to combat error with, not the sword.

Of the Proportion Between Punishments and Offences

I. We have seen that the general object of all laws is to prevent mischief; that is to say, when it is worth while; but that, where there are no other means of doing this than punishment, there are four cases in which it is *not* worth while.

II. When it *is* worth while, there are four subordinate designs or objects, which, in the course of his endeavours to compass, as far as may be, that one general object, a legislator, whose views are governed by the principle of utility, comes naturally to propose to himself.

III. 1. His first, most extensive, and most eligible object, is to prevent, in as far as it is possible, and worth while, all sorts of offences whatsoever:[5] in other words, so to manage, that no offence whatsoever may be committed.

---

5. By *offences* I mean, at present, acts which appear to him to have a tendency to produce mischief.

IV. 2. But if a man must needs commit an offence of some kind or other, the next object is to induce him to commit an offence *less* mischievous, *rather* than one *more* mischievous: in other words, to choose always the *least* mischievous, of two offences that will either of them suit his purpose.

V. 3. When a man has resolved upon a particular offence, the next object is to dispose him to do *no more* mischief than is *necessary* to his purpose: in other words, to do as little mischief as is consistent with the benefit he has in view.

VI. 4. The last object is, whatever the mischief be, which it is proposed to prevent, to prevent it at as *cheap* a rate as possible.

VII. Subservient to these four objects, or purposes, must be the rules or canons by which the proportion of punishments to offences is to be governed.

VIII. Rule 1. 1. The first object, it has been seen, is to prevent, in as far as it is worth while, all sorts of offences; therefore,

The value of the punishment must not be less in any case than what is sufficient to outweigh that of the profit of the offence. [6]

If it be, the offence (unless some other considerations, independent of the punishment, should intervene and operate efficaciously in the character of tutelary motives) will be sure to be committed notwithstanding: the whole lot of punishment will be thrown away: it will be altogether *inefficacious*.

IX. The above rule has been often objected to, on account of its seeming harshness: but this can only have happened for want of its being properly understood. The strength of the temptation, *caeteris paribus,* is as the profit of the offence: the quantum of the punishment must rise with the profit of the offence: *caeteris paribus,* it must therefore rise with the strength of the temptation. This there is no disputing. True it is, that the stronger the temptation, the less conclusive is the indication which the act of delinquency affords of the depravity of the offender's disposition. So far then as the absence of any aggravation, arising from extraordinary depravity of disposition, may operate, or at the utmost, so far as the presence of a ground of extenuation, resulting from the innocence or beneficence of the offender's disposition, can operate, the strength of the temptation may operate in abatement of the demand for punishment. But it can never operate so far as to indicate the propriety of making the punishment ineffectual, which it is sure to be when brought below the level of the apparent profit of the offence.

The partial benevolence which should prevail for the reduction of it below this level, would counteract as well those purposes which such a motive would actually have in

---

6. By the profit of an offence, it to be understood, not merely the pecuniary profit, but the pleasure or advantage, of whatever kind it be, which a man reaps, or expects to reap, from the gratification of the desire which prompted him to engage in the offence. It is the profit (that is, the expectation of the profit) of the offence that constitutes the *impelling* motive, or, where there are several, the sum of the impelling motives, by which a man is prompted to engage in the offence. It is the punishment, that is, the expectation of the punishment, that constitutes the *restraining* motive, which, either by itself, or in conjunction with others, is to act upon him in a *contrary* direction, so as to induce him to abstain from engaging in the offence. Accidental circumstances apart, the strength of the temptation is as the force of the seducing, that is, of the impelling motive or motives. To say then, as authors of great merit and great name have said, that the punishment ought not to increase with the strength of the temptation, is as much as to say in mechanics, that the moving force or *momentum* of the *power* need not increase in proportion to the momentum of the *burthen*.

view, as those more extensive purposes which benevolence ought to have in view: it would be cruelty not only to the public, but to the very persons in whose behalf it pleads: in its effects, I mean, however opposite in its intention. Cruelty to the public, that is cruelty to the innocent, by suffering them, for want of an adequate protection, to lie exposed to the mischief of the offence: cruelty even to the offender himself, by punishing him to no purpose, and without the chance of compassing that beneficial end, by which alone the introduction of the evil of punishment is to be justified.

X. Rule 2. But whether a given offence shall be prevented in a given degree by a given quantity of punishment, is never any thing better than a chance; for the purchasing of which, whatever punishment is employed, is so much expended in advance. However, for the sake of giving it the better chance of outweighing the profit of the offence,

The greater the mischief of the offence, the greater is the expense, which it may be worth while to be at, in the way of punishment.

XI. Rule 3. The next object is, to induce a man to choose always the least mischievous of two offences; therefore

Where two offences come in competition, the punishment for the greater offence must be sufficient to induce a man to prefer the less.

XII. Rule 4. When a man has resolved upon a particular offence, the next object is, to induce him to do no more mischief than what is necessary for his purpose: therefore

The punishment should be adjusted in such a manner to each particular offence, that for every part of the mischief there may be a motive to restrain the offender from giving birth to it.

XIII. Rule 5. The last object is, whatever mischief is guarded against, to guard against it at as cheap a rate as possible: therefore

The punishment ought in no case to be more than what is necessary to bring it into conformity with the rules here given.

XIV.   Rule 6. It is further to be observed, that owing to the different manners and degrees in which persons under different circumstances are affected by the same exciting cause, a punishment which is the same in name will not always either really produce, or even so much as appear to others to produce, in two different persons the same degree of pain: therefore

That the quantity actually inflicted on each individual offender may correspond to the quantity intended for similar offenders in general, the several circumstances influencing sensibility ought always to be taken into account.

XV. Of the above rules of proportion, the four first, we may perceive, serve to mark out the limits on the side of diminution; the limits *below* which a punishment ought not to be *diminished:* the fifth, the limits on the side of increase; the limits *above* which it ought not to be *increased.* The five first are calculated to serve as guides to the legislator: the sixth is calculated, in some measure, indeed, for the same purpose; but principally for guiding the judge in his endeavours to conform, on both sides, to the intentions of the legislator.

XVI. Let us look back a little. The first rule, in order to render it more conveniently applicable to practice, may need perhaps to be a little more particularly unfolded. It is to be observed, then, that for the sake of accuracy, it was necessary, instead of the word *quantity* to make use of the less perspicuous term *value.* For the word *quantity* will not properly include the circumstances either of certainty or proximity: circumstances which, in estimating the value of a lot of pain or pleasure, must always be taken into the account. Now, on the one hand, a lot of punishment is a lot of pain; on the other hand, the profit of an offence is a lot of pleasure, or what is equivalent to it. But the profit of the offence *is* commonly more *certain* than the punishment, or, what comes to the same thing, *appears* so at least to the offender. It is at any rate commonly more *immediate.* It follows, therefore, that, in order to maintain its superiority over the profit of the offence, the punishment must have its value made up in some other way, in proportion to that whereby it falls short in the two points of *certainty* and *proximity.* Now there is no other way in which it can receive any addition to its *value,* but by receiving an addition in point of *magnitude.* Wherever then the value of the punishment falls short, either in point of *certainty,* or of *proximity,* of that of the profit of the offence, it must receive a proportionable addition in point of *magnitude.*[7]

XVII. Yet farther. To make sure of giving the value of the punishment the superiority over that of the offence, it may be necessary, in some cases, to take into the account the profit not only of the *individual* offence to which the punishment is to be annexed, but also of such *other* offences of the *same sort* as the offender is likely to have already committed without detection. This random mode of calculation, severe as it is, it will be impossible to avoid having recourse to, in certain cases: in such, to wit, in which the profit is pecuniary, the chance of detection very small, and the obnoxious act of such a nature as indicates a habit: for example, in the case of frauds agains the coin. If it be *not* recurred to, the practice of committing the offence will be sure to be, upon the balance of the account, a gainful practice. That being the case, the legislator will be absolutely sure of *not* being able to suppress it, and the whole punishment that is bestowed upon it will be thrown away. In a word (to keep to the same expressions we set out with) that whole quantity of punishment will be *inefficacious.*

XVIII. Rule 7. These things being considered, the three following rules may be laid down by way of supplement and explanation to Rule 1.

To enable the value of the punishment to outweigh that of the profit of the offence, it must be increased, in point of magnitude, in proportion as it falls short in point of certainty.

XIX. Rule 8. *Punishment must be further increased in point of magnitude, in proportion as it falls short in point of proximity.*

XX. Rule 9. *Where the act is conclusively indicative of a habit, such an increase must be given to the punishment as may enable it to outweigh the profit not only of the individual offence, but of such other like offences as are likely to have been committed with impunity by the same offender.*

XXI. There may be a few other circumstances or considerations which may influence, in some small degree, the demand for punishment: but as the propriety of these is either not so demonstrable, or not so constant, or the application of them not so determinate, as that of the foregoing, it may be doubted whether they be worth putting on a level with the others.

XXII. Rule 10. *When a punishment, which in point of quality is particularly well calculated to answer its intention, cannot exist in less than a certain quantity, it may sometimes be of use, for the sake of employing it, to stretch a little beyond that quantity which, on other accounts, would be strictly necessary.*

XXIII. Rule 11. *In particular, this may sometimes be the case, where the punishment*

---

7. It is for this reason, for example, that simple compensation is never looked upon as sufficient punishment for theft or robbery.

proposed is of such a nature as to be particularly well calculated to answer the purpose of a moral lesson.[8]

XXIV. Rule 12. The tendency of the above considerations is to dictate an augmentation in the punishment: the following rule operates in the way of diminution. There are certain cases (it has been seen) in which, by the influence of accidental circumstances, punishment may be rendered unprofitable in the whole: in the same cases it may chance to be rendered unprofitable as to a part only. Accordingly,

In adjusting the quantum of punishment, the circumstances, by which all punishment may be rendered unprofitable, ought to be attended to.

XXV. Rule 13. It is to be observed, that the more various and minute any set of provisions are, the greater the chance is that any given article in them will not be borne in mind: without which, no benefit can ensure from it. Distinctions, which are more complex than what the conceptions of those whose conduct it is designed to influence can take in, will even be worse than useless. The whole system will present a confused appearance: and thus the effect, not only of the proportions established by the articles in question, but of whatever is connected with them, will be destroyed. To draw a precise line of direction in such case seems impossible. However, by way of memento, it may be of some use to subjoin the following rule.

Among provisions designed to perfect the proportion between punishments and offences, if any occur, which, by their own particular good effects, would not make up for the harm they would do by adding to the intricacy of the Code, they should be omitted.

XXVI. It may be remembered, that the political sanction, being that to which the sort of punishment belongs, which in this chapter is all along in view, is but one of four sanctions, which may all of them contribute their share towards producing the same effects. It may be expected, therefore, that in adjusting the quantity of political punishment, allowance should be made for the assistance it may meet with from those other controlling powers. True it is, that from each of these several sources a very powerful assistance may sometimes be derived. But the case is, that (setting aside the moral sanction, in the case where the force of it is expressly adopted into and modified by the political) the force of those other powers is never determinate enough to be depended upon. It can never be reduced, like political punishment, into exact lots, nor meted out in number, quantity, and value. The legislator is therefore obliged to provide the full complement of punishment, as if he were sure of not receiving any assistance whatever from any of those quarters. If he does, so much the better: but lest he should not, it is necessary he should, at all events, make that provision which depends upon himself.

XXVII. It may be of use, in this place, to recapitulate the several circumstances, which, in establishing the proportion betwixt punishments and offences, are to be attended to. These seem to be as follows:

I. *On the part of the offence:*
    1. The profit of the offence;

---

8. A punishment may be said to be calculated to answer the purpose of a moral lesson, when, by reason of the ignominy it stamps upon the offence, it is calculated to inspire the public with sentiments of aversion towards those pernicious habits and dispositions with which the offence appears to be connected; and thereby to inculcate the opposite beneficial habits and dispositions.

2. The mischief of the offence;
3. The profit and mischief of other greater or lesser offences, of different sorts, which the offender may have to choose out of;
4. The profit and mischief of other offences, of the same sort, which the same offender may probably have been guilty of already.

II. *On the part of the punishment:*
5. The magnitude of the punishment: composed of its intensity and duration;
6. The deficiency of the punishment in point of certainty;
7. The deficiency of the punishment in point of proximity:
8. The quality of the punishment;
9. The accidental advantage in point of quality of a punishment, not strictly needed in point of quantity;
10. The use of a punishment of a particular quality, in the character of a moral lesson.

III. *On the part of the offender:*
11. The responsibility of the class of persons in a way to offend;
12. The sensibility of each particular offender;
13. The particular merits or useful qualities of any particular offender, in case of a punishment which might deprive the community of the benefit of them;
14. The multitude of offenders on any particular occasion.

IV. *On the part of the public,* at any particular conjuncture:
15. The inclinations of the people, for or against any quantity or mode of punishment;
16. The inclinations of foreign powers.

V. *On the part of the law:* that is, of the public for a continuance:
17. The necessity of making small sacrifices, in point of proportionality, for the sake of simplicity.

XXVIII. There are some, perhaps, who, at first sight, may look upon the nicety employed in the adjustment of such rules, as so much labour lost: for gross ignorance, they will say, never troubles itself about laws, and passion does not calculate. But the evil of ignorance admits of cure: and as to the proposition that passion does not calculate, this, like most of these very general and oracular propositions, is not true. When matters of such importance as pain and pleasure are at stake, and these in the highest degree (the only matters, in short, that can be of importance) who is there that does not calculate? Men calculate, some with less exactness, indeed, some with more: but all men calculate. I would not say, that even a madman does not calculate.[9] Passion calculates, more or less, in every man: in different men, according to the warmth or coolness of their dispositions: according to the firmness or irritability of their minds: according to the nature of the motives by which they are acted upon. Happily, of all passions, that is the most given to calculation, from the excess of which, by reason of its strength, constancy, and universality, society has most to apprehend: I mean that which corresponds to the motive of pecuniary interest: so that these niceties, if such they are to be called, have the best chance of being efficacious, where efficacy is of the most importance.

---

9. There are few madmen but what are observed to be afraid of the strait waistcoat.

Punishment as a Practice

John Rawls

T he subject of punishment, in the sense of attaching legal penalties to the violation of legal rules, has always been a troubling moral question. The trouble
about it has not been that people disagree as to whether or not punishment is
justifiable. Most people have held that, freed from certain abuses, it is an acceptable
institution. Only a few have rejected punishment entirely, which is rather surprising
when one considers all that can be said against it. The difficulty is with the justification
of punishment: various arguments for it have been given by moral philosophers, but so
far none of them has won any sort of general acceptance; no justification is without those
who detest it. I hope to show that the use of the aforementioned distinction[1] enables
one to state the utilitarian view in a way which allows for the sound points of its critics.

Excerpted from John Rawls, "Two Concepts of Rules," *The Philosophical Review* 64 (1955), pp.
3–32. Reprinted with permission of *The Philosophical Review* and the author. The footnotes have
been renumbered and some have been omitted. John Rawls is a Professor of Philosophy at Harvard University and is the author of *A Theory of Justice,* Harvard, 1971.

1. [Rawls begins his paper by claiming that he wants to show "the importance of the distinction
between justifying a practice and justifying a particular action falling under it. . . . The word
'practice' is used throughout as a sort of technical term meaning any form of activity specified by a
system of rules which defines offices, roles, moves, penalties, defenses, and so on, and which gives
the activity its structure. As examples one may think of games and rituals, trials and parliaments."
The importance of the distinction, Rawls argues, lies in "the way it strengthens the utilitarian
view regardless of whether or not that view is completely defensible." Ed.]

For our purposes we may say that there are two justifications of punishment. What we may call the retributive view is that punishment is justified on the grounds that wrongdoing merits punishment. It is morally fitting that a person who does wrong should suffer in proportion to his wrongdoing. That a criminal should be punished follows from his guilt, and the severity of the appropriate punishment depends on the depravity of his act. The state of affairs where a wrongdoer suffers punishment is morally better than the state of affairs where he does not; and it is better irrespective of any of the consequences of punishing him.

What we may call the utilitarian holds that on the principle that bygones are bygones and that only future consequences are material to present decisions, punishment is justifiable only by reference to the probable consequences of maintaining it as one of the devices of the social order. Wrongs committed in the past are, as such, not relevant considerations for deciding what to do. If punishment can be shown to promote effectively the interest of society it is justifiable; otherwise it is not.

I have stated these two competing views very roughly to make one feel the conflict between them: one feels the force of *both* arguments and one wonders how they can be reconciled. From my introductory remarks it is obvious that the resolution which I am going to propose is that in this case one must distinguish between justifying a practice as a system of rules to be applied and enforced, and justifying a particular action which falls under these rules; utilitarian arguments are appropriate with regard to questions about practices, while retributive arguments fit the application of particular rules to particular cases.

We might try to get clear about this distinction by imagining how a father might answer the question of his son. Suppose the son asks, "Why was *J* put in jail yesterday?" The father answers, "Because he robbed the bank at *B*. He was duly tried and found guilty. That's why he was put in jail yesterday." But suppose the son had asked a different question, namely, "Why do people put other people in jail?" Then the father might answer, "To protect good people from bad people" or "To stop people from doing things that would make it uneasy for all of us; for otherwise we wouldn't be able to go to bed at night and sleep in peace." There are two very different questions here. One question emphasizes the proper name: it asks why *J* was punished rather than someone else, or it asks what he was punished for. The other question asks why we have the institution of punishment: why do people punish one another rather than, say, always forgiving one another?

Thus the father says in effect that a particular man is punished, rather than some other man, because he is guilty, and he is guilty because he broke the law (past tense). In his case the law looks back, the judge looks back, the jury looks back, and a penalty is visited upon him for something he did. That a man is to be punished, and what his punishment is to be, is settled by its being shown that he broke the law and that the law assigns that penalty for the violation of it.

On the other hand we have the institution of punishment itself, and recommend and accept various changes in it, because it is thought by the (ideal) legislator and by those to whom the law applies that, as a part of a system of law impartially applied from case to case arising under it, it will have the consequence, in the long run, of furthering the interests of society.

One can say, then, that the judge and the legislator stand in different positions and look in different directions: one to the past, the other to the future. The justification of what the judge does, *qua* judge, sounds like the retributive view; the justification of what the (ideal) legislator does, *qua* legislator, sounds like the utilitarian view. Thus both views have a point (this is as it should be since intelligent and sensitive persons have been on both sides of the argument); and one's initial confusion disappears once one sees that these views apply to persons holding different offices with different duties, and situated differently with respect to the system of rules that make up the criminal law.

One might say, however, that the utilitarian view is more fundamental since it applies to a more fundamental office, for the judge carries out the legislator's will so far as he can determine it. Once the legislator decides to have laws and to assign penalties for their violation (as things are there must be both the law and the penalty) an institution is set up which involves a retributive conception of particular cases. It is part of the concept of the criminal law as a system of rules that the application and enforcement of these rules in particular cases should be justifiable by arguments of a retributive character. The decision whether or not to use law rather than some other mechanism of social control, and the decision as to what laws to have and what penalties to assign, may be settled by utilitarian arguments; but if one decides to have laws then one has decided on something whose working in particular cases is retributive in form.

The answer, then, to the confusion engendered by the two views of punishment is quite simple: one distinguishes two offices, that of the judge and that of the legislator, and one distinguishes their different stations with respect to the system of rules which make up the law; and then one notes that the different sorts of considerations which would usually be offered as reasons for what is done under the cover of these offices can be paired off with the competing justifications of punishment. One reconciles the two views by the time-honored device of making them apply to different situations.

But can it really be this simple? Well, this answer allows for the apparent intent of each side. Does a person who advocates the retributive view necessarily advocate, as an *institution*, legal machinery whose essential purpose is to set up and preserve a correspondence between moral turpitude and suffering? Surely not. What retributionists have rightly insisted upon is that no man can be punished unless he is guilty, that is, unless he has broken the law. Their fundamental criticism of the utilitarian account is that, as they interpret it, it sanctions an innocent person's being punished (if one may call it that) for the benefit of society.

On the other hand, utilitarians agree that punishment is to be inflicted only for the violation of law. They regard this much as understood from the concept of punishment itself. The point of the utilitarian account concerns the institution as a system of rules: utilitarianism seeks to limit its use by declaring it justifiable only if it can be shown to foster effectively the good of society. Historically it is a protest against the indiscriminate and ineffective use of the criminal law. It seeks to dissuade us from assigning to penal institutions the improper, if not sacrilegious, task of matching suffering with moral turpitude. Like others, utilitarians want penal institutions designed so that, as far as humanly possible, only those who break the law run afoul of it. They hold that no official should have discretionary power to inflict penalties whenever he thinks it for the benefit of society; for on utilitarian grounds an institution granting such power could not be justified.

The suggested way of reconciling the retributive and the utilitarian justifications of punishment seems to account for what both sides have wanted to say. There are, however, two further questions which arise, and I shall devote the remainder of this section to them.

First, will not a difference of opinion as to the proper criterion of just law make the proposed reconciliation unacceptable to retributionists? Will they not question whether, if the utilitarian principle is used as the criterion, it follows that those who have broken the law are guilty in a way which satisfies their demand that those punished deserve to be punished? To answer this difficulty, suppose that the rules of the criminal law are justified on utilitarian grounds (it is only for laws that meet his criterion that the utilitarian can be held responsible). Then it follows that the actions which the criminal law specifies as offenses are such that, if they were tolerated, terror and alarm would spread in society. Consequently, retributionists can only deny that those who are punished deserve to be punished if they deny that such actions are wrong. This they will not want to do.

The second question is whether utilitarianism doesn't justify too much. One pictures it as an engine of justification which, if consistently adopted, could be used to justify cruel and arbitrary institutions. Retributionists may be supposed to concede that utilitarians *intend* to reform the law and to make it more humane; that utilitarians do not *wish* to justify any such thing as punishment of the innocent; and that utilitarians may appeal to the fact that punishment presupposes guilt in the sense that by punishment one understands an institution attaching penalties to the infraction of legal rules, and therefore that it is logically absurd to suppose that utilitarians in justifying *punishment* might also have justified punishment (if we may call it that) of the innocent. The real question, however, is whether the utilitarian, in justifying punishment, hasn't used arguments which commit him to accepting the infliction of suffering on innocent persons if it is for the good of society (whether or not one calls this punishment). More generally, isn't the utilitarian committed in principle to accepting many practices which he, as a morally sensitive person, wouldn't want to accept? Retributionists are inclined to hold that there is no way to stop the utilitarian principle from justifying too much except by adding to it a principle which distributes certain rights to individuals. Then the amended criterion is not the greatest benefit of society *simpliciter,* but the greatest benefit of society subject to the constraint that no one's rights may be violated. Now while I think that the classical utilitarians proposed a criterion of this more complicated sort, I do not want to argue that point here. [2] What I want to show is that there is *another* way of preventing the utilitarian principle from justifying too much, or at least of making it much less likely to do so: namely, by stating utilitarianism in a way which accounts for the distinction between the justification of an institution and the justification of a particular action falling under it.

I begin by defining the institution of punishment as follows: a person is said to suffer punishment whenever he is legally deprived of some of the normal rights of a citizen on the ground that he has violated a rule of law, the violation having been established by trial according to the due process of law, provided that the deprivation is carried out by the recognized legal authorities of the state, that the rule of law clearly specifies both the offense and the attached penalty, that the courts construe statutes strictly, and that the statute was on the books prior to the time of the offense. This definition specifies

---

2. By the classical utilitarians I understand Hobbes, Hume, Bentham, J. S. Mill, and Sidgwick.

what I shall understand by punishment. The question is whether utilitarian arguments may be found to justify institutions widely different from this and such as one would find cruel and arbitrary.

This question is best answered, I think, by taking up a particular accusation. Consider the following from Carritt:

> The utilitarian must hold that we are justified in inflicting pain always and only to prevent worse pain or bring about greater happiness. This, then, is all we need to consider in so-called punishment, which must be purely preventive. But if some kind of very cruel crime becomes common, and none of the criminals can be caught, it might be highly expedient, as an example, to hang an innocent man, if a charge against him could be so framed that he were universally thought guilty; indeed this would only fail to be an ideal instance of utilitarian "punishment" because the victim himself would not have been so likely as a real felon to commit such a crime in the future; in all other respects it would be perfectly deterrent and therefore felicific.[3]

Carritt is trying to show that there are occasions when a utilitarian argument would justify taking an action which would be generally condemned; and thus that utilitarianism justifies too much. But the failure of Carritt's argument lies in the fact that he makes no distinction between the justification of the general system of rules which constitutes penal institutions and the justification of particular applications of these rules to particular cases by the various officials whose job it is to administer them. This becomes perfectly clear when one asks who the "we" are of whom Carritt speaks. Who is this who has a sort of absolute authority on particular occasions to decide that an innocent man shall be "punished" if everyone can be convinced that he is guilty? Is this person the legislator, or the judge, or the body of private citizens, or what? It is utterly crucial to know who is to decide such matters, and by what authority, for all of this must be written into the rules of the institution. Until one knows these things one doesn't know what the institution is whose justification is being challenged; and as the utilitarian principle applies to the institution one doesn't know whether it is justifiable on utilitarian grounds or not.

Once this is understood it is clear what the countermove to Carritt's argument is. One must describe more carefully what the *institution* is which his example suggests, and then ask oneself whether or not it is likely that having this institution would be for the benefit of society in the long run. One must not content oneself with the vague thought that, when it's a question of *this* case, it would be a good thing if *somebody* did something even if an innocent person were to suffer.

Try to imagine, then, an institution (which we may call "telishment") which is such that the officials set up by it have authority to arrange a trial for the condemnation of an innocent man whenever they are of the opinion that doing so would be in the best interests of society. The discretion of officials is limited, however, by the rule that they may not condemn an innocent man to undergo such an ordeal unless there is, at the

---

3. *Ethical and Political Thinking* (Oxford, 1947), p. 65.

time, a wave of offenses similar to that with which they charge him and telish him for. We may imagine that the officials having the discretionary authority are the judges of the higher courts in consultation with the chief of police, the minister of justice, and a committee of the legislature.

Once one realizes that one is involved in setting up an *institution,* one sees that the hazards are very great. For example, what check is there on the officials? How is one to tell whether or not their actions are authorized? How is one to limit the risks involved in allowing such systematic deception? How is one to avoid giving anything short of complete discretion to the authorities to telish anyone they like? In addition to these considerations, it is obvious that people will come to have a very different attitude towards their penal system when telishment is adjoined to it. They will be uncertain as to whether a convicted man has been punished or telished. They will wonder whether or not they should feel sorry for him. They will wonder whether the same fate won't at any time fall on them. If one pictures how such an institution would actually work, and the enormous risks involved in it, it seems clear that it would serve no useful purpose. A utilitarian justification for this institution is most unlikely.

It happens in general that as one drops off the defining features of punishment one ends up with an institution whose utilitarian justification is highly doubtful. One reason for this is that punishment works like a kind of price system: by altering the prices one has to pay for the performance of actions it supplies a motive for avoiding some actions and doing others. The defining features are essential if punishment is to work in this way; so that an institution which lacks these features, e.g., an institution which is set up to "punish" the innocent, is likely to have about as much point as a price system (if one may call it that) where the prices of things change at random from day to day and one learns the price of something after one has agreed to buy it. [4]

If one is careful to apply the utilitarian principle to the institution which is to authorize particular actions, then there is *less* danger of its justifying too much. Carritt's example gains plausibility by its indefiniteness and by its concentration on the particular case. His argument will only hold if it can be shown that there are utilitarian arguments which justify an institution whose publicly ascertainable offices and powers are such as to permit officials to exercise that kind of discretion in particular cases. But the requirement of having to build the arbitrary features of the particular decision into the institutional practice makes the justification much less likely to go through.

---

4. The analogy with the price system suggests an answer to the question of how utilitarian considerations insure that punishment is proportional to the offense. It is interesting to note that Sir David Ross, after making the distinction between justifying a penal law and justifying a particular application of it, and after stating that utilitarian considerations have a large place in determining the former, still holds back from accepting the utilitarian justification of punishment on the grounds that justice requires that punishment be proportional to the offense, and that utilitarianism is unable to account for this. Cf. *The Right and the Good,* pp. 61–62. I do not claim that utilitarianism can account for this requirement as Sir David might wish, but it happens, nevertheless, that if utilitarian considerations are followed penalties will be proportional to offenses in this sense: the order of offenses according to seriousness can be paired off with the order of penalties according to severity. Also the absolute level of penalties will be as low as possible. This follows from the assumption that people are rational (i.e., that they are able to take into account the "prices" the state puts on actions), the utilitarian rule that a penal system should provide a motive for preferring the less serious offense, and the principle that punishment as such is an evil. All this was carefully worked out by Bentham in *The Principles of Morals and Legislation,* chs. xiii–xv.

Marxism and Retribution

Jeffrie G. Murphy

Punishment in general has been defended as a means either of ame-
liorating or of intimidating. Now what right have you to punish me for
the amelioration or intimidation of others? And besides there is history — there is such a thing as statistics — which prove with the most
complete evidence that since Cain the world has been neither intimidated nor ameliorated by punishment. Quite the contrary. From the
point of view of abstract right, there is only one theory of punishment
which recognizes human dignity in the abstract, and that is the theory
of Kant, especially in the more rigid formula given to it by Hegel. Hegel
says: "Punishment is the *right* of the criminal. It is an act of his own
will. The violation of right has been proclaimed by the criminal as his
own right. His crime is the negation of right. Punishment is the negation of this negation, and consequently an affirmation of right, solicited
and forced upon the criminal by himself."

There is no doubt something specious in this formula, inasmuch as
Hegel, instead of looking upon the criminal as the mere object, the slave
of justice, elevates him to the position of a free and self-determined being.
Looking, however, more closely into the matter, we discover that Ger-

Reprinted from *Philosophy and Public Affairs*, Vol. 2, No. 3 (Spring 1973), 217–243. Copyright ©
1973 by Princeton University Press. Reprinted by permission of the publisher.

man idealism here, as in most other instances, has but given a transcendental sanction to the rules of existing society. Is it not a delusion to substitute for the individual with his real motives, with multifarious social
circumstances pressing upon him, the abstraction of "free will" — one
among the many qualities of man for man himself? . . . Is there not a
necessity for deeply reflecting upon an alteration of the system that breeds
these crimes, instead of glorifying the hangman who executes a lot of
criminals to make room only for the supply of new ones?

Karl Marx, "Capital Punishment,"
New York Daily Tribune, *18 February 1853*[1]

Philosophers have written at great length about the moral problems involved in
punishing the innocent—particularly as these problems raise obstacles to an
acceptance of the moral theory of Utilitarianism. Punishment of an innocent
man in order to bring about good social consequences is, at the very least, not always
clearly wrong on utilitarian principles. This being so, utilitarian principles are then to
be condemned by any morality that may be called Kantian in character. For punishing
an innocent man, in Kantian language, involves using that man as a mere means or
instrument to some social good and is thus not to treat him as an end in himself, in
accord with his dignity or worth as a person.

The Kantian position on the issue of punishing the innocent, and the many ways in
which the utilitarian might try to accommodate that position, constitute extremely
well-worn ground in contemporary moral and legal philosophy.[2] I do not propose to
wear the ground further by adding additional comments on the issue here. What I do
want to point out, however, is something which seems to me quite obvious but which
philosophical commentators on punishment have almost universally failed to see—
namely, that problems of the very same kind and seriousness arise for the utilitarian
theory with respect to the punishment of the guilty. For a utilitarian theory of punishment (Bentham's is a paradigm) must involve justifying punishment in terms of its
social results—e.g., deterrence, incapacitation, and rehabilitation. And thus even a
guilty man is, on this theory, being punished because of the instrumental value the
action of punishment will have in the future. He is being used as a means to some

---

1. In a sense, my paper may be viewed as an elaborate commentary on this one passage, excerpted
from a discussion generally concerned with the efficacy of capital punishment in eliminating crime.
For in this passage, Marx (to the surprise of many I should think) expresses a certain admiration for
the classical retributive theory of punishment. Also (again surprisingly) he expresses this admiration
in a kind of language he normally avoids—i.e., the moral language of rights and justice. He then, of
course, goes on to reject the applicability of that theory. But the question that initially perplexed me is
the following: what is the explanation of Marx's ambivalence concerning the retributive theory; why is
he both attracted and repelled by it? (This ambivalence is not shared, for example, by utilitarians—
who feel nothing but repulsion when the retributive theory is even mentioned.) Now except for some
very brief passages in *The Holy Family,* Marx himself has nothing more to say on the topic of punishment beyond what is contained in this brief *Daily Tribune* article. Thus my essay is in no sense an
exercise in textual scholarship (there are not enough texts) but is rather an attempt to construct an
assessment of punishment, Marxist at least in spirit, that might account for the ambivalence found in
the quoted passage. My main outside help comes, not from Marx himself, but from the writings of
the Marxist criminologist Willem Bonger.
2. Many of the leading articles on this topic have been reprinted in *The Philosophy of Punishment,* ed.
H. B. Acton (London, 1969). Those papers not included are cited in Acton's excellent bibliography.

future good—e.g., the deterrence of others. Thus those of a Kantian persuasion, who see the importance of worrying about the treatment of persons as mere means, must, it would seem, object just as strenuously to the punishment of the guilty on utilitarian grounds as to the punishment of the innocent. Indeed the former worry, in some respects, seems more serious. For a utilitarian can perhaps refine his theory in such a way that it does not commit him to the punishment of the innocent. However, if he is to approve of punishment at all, he must approve of punishing the guilty in at least some cases. This makes the worry about punishing the guilty formidable indeed, and it is odd that this has gone generally unnoticed.[3] It has generally been assumed that if the utilitarian theory can just avoid entailing the permissibility of punishing the innocent, then all objections of a Kantian character to the theory will have been met. This seems to me simply not to be the case.

What the utilitarian theory really cannot capture, I would suggest, is the notion of persons having rights. And it is just this notion that is central to any Kantian outlook on morality. Any Kantian can certainly agree that punishing persons (guilty or innocent) may have either good or bad or indifferent consequences and that insofar as the consequences (whether in a particular case or for an institution) are good, this is something in favor of punishment. But the Kantian will maintain that this consequential outlook, important as it may be, leaves out of consideration entirely that which is most morally crucial—namely, the question of rights. Even if punishment of a person would have good consequences, what gives us (i.e., society) the moral right to inflict it? If we have such a right, what is its origin or derivation? What social circumstances must be present for it to be applicable? What does this right to punish tell us about the status of the person to be punished—e.g., how are we to analyze his rights, the sense in which he must deserve to be punished, his obligations in the matter? It is this family of questions which any Kantian must regard as morally central and which the utilitarian cannot easily accommodate into his theory. And it is surely this aspect of Kant's and Hegel's retributivism, this seeing of rights as basic, which appeals to Marx in the quoted passage. As Marx himself puts it: "What right have you to punish me for the amelioration or intimidation of others?" And he further praises Hegel for seeing that punishment, if justified, must involve respecting the rights of the person to be punished.[4] Thus Marx, like Kant, seems prepared to draw the important distinction between (a) what it would be good to do on grounds of utility and (b) what we have a right to do. Since we do not always have the right to do what it would be good to do, this distinction is of the greatest moral importance; and missing the distinction is the Achilles' heel of all forms of Utilitarianism. For consider the following example: A Jehovah's

---

3. One writer who has noticed this is Richard Wasserstrom. See his "Why Punish the Guilty?" *Princeton University Magazine* 20 (1964), pp. 14–19.
4. Marx normally avoids the language of rights and justice because he regards such language to be corrupted by bourgeois ideology. However, if we think very broadly of what an appeal to rights involves—namely, a protest against unjustified coercion—there is no reason why Marx may not legitimately avail himself on occasion of this way of speaking. For there is surely at least some moral overlap between Marx's protests against exploitation and the evils of a division of labor, for example, and the claims that people have a right not to be used solely for the benefit of others and a right to self-determination.

Witness needs a blood transfusion in order to live; but, because of his [some might say absurd] religious belief that such transfusions are against God's commands, he instructs his doctor not to give him one. Here is a case where it would seem to be good or for the best to give the transfusion and yet, at the very least, it is highly doubtful that the doctor has a right to give it. This kind of distinction is elementary, and any theory which misses it is morally degenerate.[5]

To move specifically to the topic of punishment: How exactly does retributivism (of a Kantian or Hegelian variety) respect the rights of persons? Is Marx really correct on this? I believe that he is. I believe that retributivism can be formulated in such a way that it is the only morally defensible theory of punishment. I also believe that arguments, which may be regarded as Marxist at least in spirit, can be formulated which show that social conditions as they obtain in most societies make this form of retributivism largely inapplicable within those societies. As Marx says, in those societies retributivism functions merely to provide a "transcendental sanction" for the status quo. If this is so, then the only morally defensible theory of punishment is largely inapplicable in modern societies. The consequence: modern societies largely lack the moral right to punish.[6] The upshot is that a Kantian moral theory (which in general seems to me correct) and a Marxist analysis of society (which, if properly qualified, also seems to me correct) produces a radical and not merely reformist attack not merely on the scope and manner of punishment in our society but on the institution of punishment itself. Institutions of punishment constitute what Bernard Harrison has called structural injustices[7] and are, in the absence of a major social change, to be resisted by all who take human rights to be morally serious—i.e., regard them as genuine action guides and not merely as rhetorical devices which allow people to morally sanctify institutions which in fact can only be defended on grounds of social expediency.

Stating all of this is one thing and proving it, of course, is another. Whether I can ever do this is doubtful. That I cannot do it in one brief article is certain. I cannot, for example, here defend in detail my belief that a generally Kantian outlook on moral matters is correct.[8] Thus I shall content myself for the present with attempting to render at least plausible two major claims involved in the view that I have outlined thus far: (1) that a retributive theory, in spite of the bad press that it has received, is a

---

5. I do not mean to suggest that under no conceivable circumstances would the doctor be justified in giving the transfusion even though, in one clear sense, he had no right to do it. If, for example, the Jehovah's Witness was a key man whose survival was necessary to prevent the outbreak of a destructive war, we might well regard the transfusion as on the whole justified. However, even in such a case, a morally sensitive man would have to regretfully realize that he was sacrificing an important principle. Such a realization would be impossible (because inconsistent) for a utilitarian, for his theory admits only one principle—namely, do that which on the whole maximizes utility. An occupational disease of utilitarians is a blindness to the possibility of genuine moral dilemmas—i.e., a blindness to the possibility that important moral principles can conflict in ways that are not obviously resolvable by a rational decision procedure.

6. I qualify my thesis by the word "largely" to show at this point my realization, explored in more detail later, that no single theory can account for all criminal behavior.

7. Bernard Harrison, "Violence and the Rule of Law," in *Violence*, ed. Jerome A. Shaffer (New York, 1971), pp. 139–176.

8. I have made a start toward such a defense in my "The Killing of the Innocent," in *The Monist* 57, no. 4 (October 1973).

morally credible theory of punishment—that it can be, H. L. A. Hart to the contrary,[9] a reasonable general justifying aim of punishment; and (2) that a Marxist analysis of a society can undercut the practical applicability of that theory.

The Right of the State to Punish

It is strong evidence of the influence of a utilitarian outlook in moral and legal matters that discussions of punishment no longer involve a consideration of the right of anyone to inflict it. Yet in the eighteenth and nineteenth centuries, this tended to be regarded as the central aspect of the problem meriting philosophical consideration. Kant, Hegel, Bosanquet, Green—all tended to entitle their chapters on punishment along the lines explicitly used by Green: "The Right of the State to Punish."[10] This is not just a matter of terminology but reflects, I think, something of deeper philosophical substance. These theorists, unlike the utilitarian, did not view man as primarily a maximizer of personal satisfactions—a maximizer of individual utilities. They were inclined, in various ways, to adopt a different model of man—man as a free or spontaneous creator, man as autonomous. (Marx, it may be noted, is much more in line with this tradition than with the utilitarian outlook.)[11] This being so, these theorists were inclined to view punishment (a certain kind of coercion by the state) as not merely a causal contributor to pain and suffering, but rather as presenting at least a prima facie challenge to the values of autonomy and personal dignity and self-realization—the very values which, in their view, the state existed to nurture. The problem as they saw it, therefore, was that of reconciling punishment as state coercion with the value of individual autonomy. (This is an instance of the more general problem which Robert Paul Wolff has called the central problem of political philosophy—namely, how is individual moral autonomy to be reconciled with legitimate political authority?)[12] This kind of problem, which I am inclined to agree is quite basic, cannot even be formulated intelligibly from a utilitarian perspective. Thus the utilitarian cannot even see the relevance of Marx's charge: Even if punishment has wonderful social consequences, what gives anyone the right to inflict it . . .?

Now one fairly typical way in which others acquire rights over us is by our own consent. If a neighbor locks up my liquor cabinet to protect me against my tendencies to drink too heavily, I might well regard this as a presumptuous interference with my own freedom, no matter how good the result intended or accomplished. He had no right to do it and indeed violated my rights in doing it. If, on the other hand, I had asked him to do this or had given my free consent to his suggestion that he do it, the same sort of objection on my part would be quite out of order. I had given him the right to do it, and he had the

---

9. H. L. A. Hart, "Prolegomenon to the Principles of Punishment," from *Punishment and Responsibility* (Oxford, 1968), pp. 1–27.

10. Thomas Hill Green, *Lectures on the Principles of Political Obligation* (1885), (Ann Arbor, 1967), pp. 180–205.

11. For an elaboration of this point, see Steven Lukes, "Alienation and Anomie," in *Philosophy, Politics and Society* (Third Series), ed. Peter Laslett and W. G Runciman (Oxford, 1967), pp. 134–156.

12. Robert Paul Wolff, *In Defense of Anarchism* (New York, 1970).

right to do it. In doing it, he violated no rights of mine—even if, at the time of his doing it, I did not desire or want the action to be performed. Here then we seem to have a case where my autonomy may be regarded as intact even though a desire of mine is thwarted. For there is a sense in which the thwarting of the desire can be imputed to me (my choice or decision) and not to the arbitrary intervention of another.

How does this apply to our problem? The answer, I think, is obvious. What is needed, in order to reconcile my undesired suffering of punishment at the hands of the state with my autonomy (and thus with the state's right to punish me), is a political theory which makes the state's decision to punish me in some sense my own decision. If I have willed my own punishment (consented to it, agreed to it) then— even if at the time I happen not to desire it—it can be said that my autonomy and dignity remain intact. Theories of the General Will and Social Contract theories are two such theories which attempt this reconciliation of autonomy with legitimate state authority (including the right or authority of the state to punish). Since Kant's theory happens to incorporate elements of both, it will be useful to take it for our sample.

Moral Rights and the
Retributive Theory of Punishment

To justify government or the state is necessarily to justify at least some coercion.[13] This poses a problem for someone, like Kant, who maintains that human freedom is the ultimate or most sacred moral value. Kant's own attempt to justify the state, expressed in his doctrine of the *moral title (Befugnis)*,[14] involves an argument that coercion is justified only in so far as it is used to prevent invasions against freedom. Freedom itself is the only value which can be used to limit freedom, for the appeal to any other value (e.g., utility) would undermine the ultimate status of the value of freedom. Thus Kant attempts to establish the claim that some forms of coercion (as opposed to violence) are morally permissible because, contrary to appearance, they are really consistent with rational freedom. The argument, in broad outline, goes in the following way. Coercion may keep people from doing what they desire or want to do on a particular occasion and is thus prima facie wrong. However, such coercion can be shown to be morally justified (and thus not absolutely wrong) if it can be established that the coercion is such that it could have been rationally willed even by the person whose desire is interfered with:

---

13. In this section, I have adapted some of my previously published material: *Kant: The Philosophy of Right* (London, 1970), pp. 109–112 and 140–144; "Three Mistakes About Retributivism," *Analysis* (April 1971): 166–169; and "Kant's Theory of Criminal Punishment," in *Proceedings of the Third International Kant Congress*, ed. Lewis White Beck (Dordrecht, 1972), pp. 434–441. I am perfectly aware that Kant's views on the issues to be considered here are often obscure and inconsistent—e.g., the analysis of "willing one's own punishment" which I shall later quote from Kant occurs in a passage the primary purpose of which is to argue that the idea of "willing one's own punishment" makes no sense! My present objective, however, is not to attempt accurate Kant scholarship. My goal is rather to build upon some remarks of Kant's which I find philosophically suggestive.

14. Immanuel Kant, *The Metaphysical Elements of Justice* (1797), trans. John Ladd (Indianapolis, 1965), pp. 35ff.

Accordingly, when it is said that a creditor has a right to demand from his debtor the payment of a debt, this does not mean that he can *persuade* the debtor that his own reason itself obligates him to this performance; on the contrary, to say that he has such a right means only that the use of coercion to make anyone do this is entirely compatible with everyone's freedom, *including the freedom of the debtor,* in accordance with universal laws.[15]

Like Rousseau, Kant thinks that it is only in a context governed by social practice (particularly civil government and its Rule of Law) that this can make sense. Laws may require of a person some action that he does not desire to perform. This is not a violent invasion of his freedom, however, if it can be shown that in some antecedent position of choice (what John Rawls calls "the original position"),[16] he would have been rational to adopt a Rule of Law (and thus run the risk of having some of his desires thwarted) rather than some other alternative arrangement like the classical State of Nature. This is, indeed, the only sense that Kant is able to make of classical Social Contract theories. Such theories are to be viewed, not as historical fantasies, but as ideal models of rational decision. For what these theories actually claim is that the only coercive institutions that are morally justified are those which a group of rational beings could agree to adopt in a position of having to pick social institutions to govern their relations:

The contract, which is called *contractus originarius,* or *pactum sociale* . . . need not be assumed to be a fact, indeed it is not [even possible as such. To suppose that would be like insisting] that before anyone would be bound to respect such a civic constitution, it be proved first of all from history that a people, whose rights and obligations we have entered into as their descendants, had *once upon a time* executed such an act and had left a reliable document or instrument, either orally or in writing, concerning this contract. Instead, this contract is a *mere idea* of reason which has undoubted practical reality; namely, to oblige every legislator to give us laws in such a manner that the laws *could* have originated from the united will of the entire people and to regard every subject in so far as he is a citizen as though he had consented to such [an expression of the general] will. This is the testing stone of the rightness of every publicly-known law, for if a law were such that it was impossible for an entire people to give consent to it (as for example a law that a certain class of subjects, by inheritance, should have the privilege of the *status of lords*), then such a law is unjust. On the other hand, if there is a mere *possibility* that a people might consent to a (certain) law, then it is a duty to consider that the law is just even though at the moment the people might be in such a position or have a point of view that would result in their refusing to give their consent to it if asked.[17]

---

15. *Ibid.,* p. 37.

16. John Rawls, "Justice as Fairness," *The Philosophical Review* 67 (1958): 164–194; and *A Theory of Justice* (Cambridge, Mass., 1971), especially pp. 17–22.

17. Immanuel Kant, "Concerning the Common Saying: This May be True in Theory but Does Not Apply in Practice (1793)," in *The Philosophy of Kant,* ed. and trans. Carl J. Friedrich (New York, 1949), pp. 421–422.

The problem of organizing a state, however hard it may seem, can be solved even for a race of devils, if only they are intelligent. The problem is: "Given a multiple of rational beings requiring universal laws for their preservation, but each of whom is secretly inclined to exempt himself from them, to establish a constitution in such a way that, although their private intentions conflict, they check each other, with the result that their public conduct is the same as if they had no such intentions."[18]

Though Kant's doctrine is superficially similar to Mill's later self-protection principle, the substance is really quite different. For though Kant in some general sense argues that coercion is justified only to prevent harm to others, he understands by "harm" only certain invasions of freedom and not simply disutility. Also, his defense of the principle is not grounded, as is Mill's, on its utility. Rather it is to be regarded as a principle of justice, by which Kant means a principle that rational beings could adopt in a situation of mutual choice:

> The concept [of justice] applies only to the relationship of a will to another person's will, not to his wishes or desires (or even just his needs) which are the concern of acts of benevolence and charity. . . . In applying the concept of justice we take into consideration only the form of the relationship between the wills insofar as they are regarded as free, and whether the action of one of them can be conjoined with the freedom of the other in accordance with universal law. Justice is therefore the aggregate of those conditions under which the will of one person can be conjoined with the will of another in accordance with a universal law of freedom.[19]

How does this bear specifically on punishment? Kant, as everyone knows, defends a strong form of a retributive theory of punishment. He holds that guilt merits, and is a sufficient condition for, the infliction of punishment. And this claim has been universally condemned particularly by utilitarians—as primitive, unenlightened and barbaric.

But why is it so condemned? Typically, the charge is that infliction of punishment on such grounds is nothing but pointless vengeance. But what is meant by the claim that the infliction is "pointless"? If "pointless" is tacitly being analyzed as "disutilitarian," then the whole question is simply being begged. You cannot refute a retributive theory merely by noting that it is a retributive theory and not a utilitarian theory. This is to confuse redescription with refutation and involves an argument whose circularity is not even complicated enough to be interesting.

Why, then, might someone claim that guilt merits punishment? Such a claim might be made for either of two very different reasons. (1) Someone (e.g., a Moral Sense theorist) might maintain that the claim is a primitive and unanalyzable proposition that is morally ultimate—that we can just intuit the "fittingness" of guilt and punishment. (2) It might be maintained that the retributivist claim is demanded by a general theory of political obligation which is more plausible than any alternative the-

---

18. Immanuel Kant, *Perpetual Peace* (1795), trans. Lewis White Beck in the Kant anthology *On History* (Indianapolis 1963), p. 112.

19. Immanuel Kant, *The Metaphysical Elements of Justice*, p. 34.

ory. Such a theory will typically provide a technical analysis of such concepts as crime and punishment and will thus not regard the retributivist claim as an indisputable primitive. It will be argued for as a kind of theorem within the system.

Kant's theory is of the second sort. He does not opt for retributivism as a bit of intuitive moral knowledge. Rather he offers a theory of punishment that is based on his general view that political obligation is to be analyzed, quasi-contractually, in terms of reciprocity. If the law is to remain just, it is important to guarantee that those who disobey it will not gain an unfair advantage over those who do obey voluntarily. It is important that no man profit from his own criminal wrongdoing, and a certain kind of "profit" (i.e., not bearing the burden of self-restraint) is intrinsic to criminal wrongdoing. Criminal punishment, then, has as its object the restoration of a proper balance between benefit and obedience. The criminal himself has no complaint, because he has rationally consented to or willed his own punishment. That is, those very rules which he has broken work, when they are obeyed by others, to his own advantage as a citizen. He would have chosen such rules for himself and others in the original position of choice. And, since he derives and voluntarily accepts benefits from their operation, he owes his own obedience as a debt to his fellow-citizens for their sacrifices in maintaining them. If he chooses not to sacrifice by exercising self-restraint and obedience, this is tantamount to his choosing to sacrifice in another way—namely, by paying the prescribed penalty:

> A transgression of the public law that makes him who commits it unfit to be a citizen is called . . . a crime. . . .

> What kind [and] what degree of punishment does public legal justice adopt as its principle and standard? None other than the principle of equality (illustrated by the pointer of the scales of justice), that is, the principle of not treating one side more favorably than the other. Accordingly, any undeserved evil that you inflict on someone else among the people is one you do to yourself. If you vilify him, you vilify yourself; if you steal from him, you steal from yourself; if you kill him, you kill yourself. . . .

> To say, "I will to be punished if I murder someone" can mean nothing more than, "I submit myself along with everyone else to those laws which, if there are any criminals among the people, will naturally include penal laws."[20]

This analysis of punishment regards it as a debt owed to the law-abiding members of one's community; and, once paid, it allows reentry into the community of good citizens on equal status.

Now some of the foregoing no doubt sounds implausible or even obscurantist. Since criminals typically desire not to be punished, what can it really mean to say that they have, as rational men, really willed their own punishment? Or that, as Hegel says, they have a right to it? Perhaps a comparison of the traditional retributivist views with those

---

20. *Ibid.*, pp. 99, 101, and 105, in the order quoted.

of a contemporary Kantian—John Rawls—will help to make the points clearer.[21] Rawls (like Kant) does not regard the idea of the social contract as an historical fact. It is rather a model of rational decision. Respecting a man's autonomy, at least on one view, is not respecting what he now happens, however uncritically, to desire; rather it is to respect what he desires (or would desire) as a rational man. (On Rawls's view, for example, rational men are said to be unmoved by feelings of envy; and thus it is not regarded as unjust to a person or a violation of his rights, if he is placed in a situation where he will envy another's advantage or position. A rational man would object, and thus would never consent to, a practice where another might derive a benefit from a position at his expense. He would not, however, envy the position *simpliciter,* would not regard the position as itself a benefit.) Now on Kant's (and also, I think, on Rawls's) view, a man is genuinely free or autonomous only in so far as he is rational. Thus it is man's rational will that is to be respected.

Now this idea of treating people, not as they in fact say that they want to be treated, but rather in terms of how you think they would, if rational, will to be treated, has obviously dangerous (indeed Fascistic) implications. Surely we want to avoid cramming indignities down the throats of people with the offhand observation that, no matter how much they scream, they are really rationally willing every bit of it. It would be particularly ironic for such arbitrary repression to come under the mask of respecting autonomy. And yet, most of us would agree, the general principle (though subject to abuse) also has important applications—for example, preventing the suicide of a person who, in a state of psychotic depression, wants to kill himself. What we need, then, to make the general view work, is a check on its arbitrary application; and a start toward providing such a check would be in the formulation of a public, objective theory of rationality and rational willing. It is just this, according to both Kant and Rawls, which the social contract theory can provide. On this theory, a man may be said to rationally will X if, and only if, X is called for by a rule that the man would necessarily have adopted in the original position of choice—i.e., in a position of coming together with others to pick rules for the regulation of their mutual affairs. This avoids arbitrariness because, according to Kant and Rawls at any rate, the question of whether such a rule would be picked in such a position is objectively determinable given certain (in their view) noncontroversial assumptions about human nature and rational calculation. Thus I can be said to will my own punishment if, in an antecedent position of choice, I and my fellows would have chosen institutions of punishment as the most rational means of dealing with those who might break the other generally beneficial social rules that had been adopted.

Let us take an analogous example: I may not, in our actual society, desire to treat a

---

21. In addition to the works on justice by Rawls previously cited, the reader should consult the following for Rawls's application of his general theory to the problem of political obligation: John Rawls, "Legal Obligation and the Duty of Fair Play," in *Law and Philosophy,* ed. Sidney Hook (New York, 1964), pp. 3–18. This has been reprinted in my anthology *Civil Disobedience and Violence* (Belmont, Calif., 1971), pp. 39–52. For a direct application of a similar theory to the problem of punishment, see Herbert Morris, "Persons and Punishment," *The Monist* 52, no. 4 (October 1968): 475–501.

certain person fairly—e.g., I may not desire to honor a contract I have made with him because so doing would adversely affect my own self-interest. However, if I am forced to honor the contract by the state, I cannot charge (1) that the state has no right to do this, or (2) that my rights or dignity are being violated by my being coerced into doing it. Indeed, it can be said that I rationally will it since, in the original position, I would have chosen rules of justice (rather than rules of utility) and the principle, "contracts are to be honored," follows from the rules of justice.

Coercion and autonomy are thus reconciled, at least apparently. To use Marx's language, we may say (as Marx did in the quoted passage) that one virtue of the retributive theory, at least as expounded by Kant and Hegel on lines of the General Will and Social Contract theory, is that it manifests at least a formal or abstract respect for rights, dignity, and autonomy. For it at least recognizes the importance of attempting to construe state coercion in such a way that it is a product of each man's rational will. Utilitarian deterrence theory does not even satisfy this formal demand.

The question of primary interest to Marx, of course, is whether this formal respect also involves a material respect; i.e., does the theory have application in concrete fact in the actual social world in which we live? Marx is confident that it does not, and it is to this sort of consideration that I shall now pass.

Alienation and Punishment

What can the philosopher learn from Marx? This question is a part of a more general question: What can philosophy learn from social science? Philosophers, it may be thought, are concerned to offer a priori theories, theories about how certain concepts are to be analyzed and their application justified. And what can the mundane facts that are the object of behavioral science have to do with exalted theories of this sort?

The answer, I think, is that philosophical theories, though not themselves empirical, often have such a character that their intelligibility depends upon certain empirical presuppositions. For example, our moral language presupposes, as Hart has argued,[22] that we are vulnerable creatures—creatures who can harm and be harmed by each other. Also, as I have argued elsewhere,[23] our moral language presupposes that we all share certain psychological characteristics—e.g., sympathy, a sense of justice, and the capacity to feel guilt, shame, regret, and remorse. If these facts were radically different (if, as Hart imagines for example, we all developed crustaceanlike exoskeletons and thus could not harm each other), the old moral language, and the moral theories which employ it, would lack application to the world in which we live. To use a crude example, moral prohibitions against killing presuppose that it is in fact possible for us to kill each other.

Now one of Marx's most important contributions to social philosophy, in my judgment, is simply his insight that philosophical theories are in peril if they are constructed

---

22. H. L. A. Hart, *The Concept of Law* (Oxford, 1961), pp. 189–195.
23. Jeffrie G. Murphy, "Moral Death: A Kantian Essay on Psychopathy," *Ethics* 82, no. 4 (July 1972): 284–298.

in disregard of the nature of the empirical world to which they are supposed to apply.[24] A theory may be formally correct (i.e., coherent, or true for some possible world) but materially incorrect (i.e., inapplicable to the actual world in which we live). This insight, then, establishes the relevance of empirical research to philosophical theory and is a part, I think, of what Marx meant by "the union of theory and practice." Specifically relevant to the argument I want to develop are the following two related points:

1. The theories of moral, social, political, and legal philosophy presuppose certain empirical propositions about man and society. If these propositions are false, then the theory (even if coherent or formally correct) is materially defective and practically inapplicable. (For example, if persons tempted to engage in criminal conduct do not in fact tend to calculate carefully the consequences of their actions, this renders much of deterrence theory suspect.)

2. Philosophical theories may put forth as a necessary truth that which is in fact merely an historically conditioned contingency. (For example, Hobbes argued that all men are necessarily selfish and competitive. It is possible, as many Marxists have argued, that Hobbes was really doing nothing more than elevating to the status of a necessary truth the contingent fact that the people around him in the capitalistic society in which he lived were in fact selfish and competitive.)[25]

In outline, then, I want to argue the following: that when Marx challenges the material adequacy of the retributive theory of punishment, he is suggesting (a) that it presupposes a certain view of man and society that is false and (b) that key concepts involved in the support of the theory (e.g., the concept of "rationality" in Social Contract theory) are given analyses which, though they purport to be necessary truths, are in fact mere reflections of certain historical circumstances.

In trying to develop this case, I shall draw primarily upon Willem Bonger's *Criminality and Economic Conditions* (1916), one of the few sustained Marxist analyses of crime and punishment.[26] Though I shall not have time here to qualify my support of Bonger in certain necessary ways, let me make clear that I am perfectly aware that his analysis is not the whole story. (No monolithic theory of anything so diverse as criminal behavior could be the whole story.) However, I am convinced that he has discovered part of the

---

24. Banal as this point may seem, it could be persuasively argued that all Enlightenment political theory (e.g., that of Hobbes, Locke and Kant) is built upon ignoring it. For example, once we have substantial empirical evidence concerning how democracies really work in fact, how sympathetic can we really be to classical theories for the justification of democracy? For more on this, see C. B. Macpherson, "The Maximization of Democracy," in *Philosophy, Politics and Society* (Third Series), ed. Peter Laslett and W. G. Runciman (Oxford, 1967), pp. 83–103. This article is also relevant to the point raised in note 11 above.

25. This point is well developed in C. B. Macpherson, *The Political Theory of Possessive Individualism* (Oxford, 1962). In a sense, this point affects even the formal correctness of a theory. For it demonstrates an empirical source of corruption in the analyses of the very concepts in the theory.

26. The writings of Willem Adriaan Bonger (1876–1940), a Dutch criminologist, have fallen into totally unjustified neglect in recent years. Anticipating contemporary sociological theories of crime, he was insisting that criminal behavior is in the province of normal psychology (though abnormal society) at a time when most other writers were viewing criminality as a symptom of psychopathology. His major works are: *Criminality and Economic Conditions* (Boston, 1916); *An Introduction to Criminology* (London, 1936); and *Race and Crime* (New York, 1943).

story. And my point is simply that insofar as Bonger's Marxist analysis is correct, then to that same degree is the retributive theory of punishment inapplicable in modern societies. (Let me emphasize again exactly how this objection to retributivism differs from those traditionally offered. Traditionally, retributivism has been rejected because it conflicts with the moral theory of its opponent, usually a utilitarian. This is not the kind of objection I want to develop. Indeed, with Marx, I have argued that the retributive theory of punishment grows out of the moral theory—Kantianism—which seems to me generally correct. The objection I want to pursue concerns the empirical falsity of the factual presuppositions of the theory. If the empirical presuppositions of the theory are false, this does indeed render its application immoral. But the immorality consists, not in a conflict with some other moral theory, but immorality in terms of a moral theory that is at least close in spirit to the very moral theory which generates retributivism itself—i.e., a theory of justice.)[27]

To return to Bonger. Put bluntly, his theory is as follows. Criminality has two primary sources: (1) need and deprivation on the part of disadvantaged members of society, and (2) motives of greed and selfishness that are generated and reinforced in competitive capitalistic societies. Thus criminality is economically based—either directly in the case of crimes from need, or indirectly in the case of crimes growing out of motives or psychological states that are encouraged and developed in capitalistic society. In Marx's own language, such an economic system alienates men from themselves and from each other. It alienates men from themselves by creating motives and needs that are not "truly human." It alienates men from their fellows by encouraging a kind of competitiveness that forms an obstacle to the development of genuine communities to replace mere social aggregates.[28] And in Bonger's thought, the concept of community is central. He argues that moral relations and moral restraint are possible only in genuine communities characterized by bonds of sympathetic identification and mutual aid resting upon a perception of common humanity. All this he includes under the general rubric of reciprocity.[29] In the absence of reciprocity in this rich sense, moral relations among men will break down and criminality will increase.[30] Within bourgeois society,

---

27. I say "at least in spirit" to avoid begging the controversial question of whether Marx can be said to embrace a theory of justice. Though (as I suggested in note 4) much of Marx's own evaluative rhetoric seems to overlap more traditional appeals to rights and justice (and a total lack of sympathy with anything like Utilitarianism), it must be admitted that he also frequently ridicules at least the terms "rights" and "justice" because of their apparent entrenchment in bourgeois ethics. For an interesting discussion of this issue, see Allen W. Wood, "The Marxian Critique of Justice," *Philosophy & Public Affairs* 1, no. 3 (Spring 1972): 244–282.

28. The importance of community is also, I think, recognized in Gabriel de Tarde's notion of "social similarity" as a condition of criminal responsibility. See his *Penal Philosophy* (Boston, 1912). I have drawn on de Tarde's general account in my "Moral Death: A Kantian Essay on Psychopathy."

29. By "reciprocity" Bonger intends something which includes, but is much richer than, a notion of "fair trading or bargaining" that might initially be read into the term. He also has in mind such things as sympathetic identification with others and tendencies to provide mutual aid. Thus, for Bonger, reciprocity and egoism have a strong tendency to conflict. I mention this lest Bonger's notion of reciprocity be too quickly identified with the more restricted notion found in, for example, Kant and Rawls.

30. It is interesting how greatly Bonger's analysis differs from classical deterrence theory—e.g., that of Bentham. Bentham, who views men as machines driven by desires to attain pleasure and avoid pain, tends to regard terror as the primary restraint against crime. Bonger believes that, at

then, crimes are to be regarded as normal, and not psychopathological, acts. That is, they grow out of need, greed, indifference to others, and sometimes even a sense of indignation—all, alas, perfectly typical human motives.

To appreciate the force of Bonger's analysis, it is necessary to read his books and grasp the richness and detail of the evidence he provides for his claims. Here I can but quote a few passages at random to give the reader a tantalizing sample in the hope that he will be encouraged to read further into Bonger's own text:

> The abnormal element in crime is a social, not a biological, element. With the exception of a few special cases, crime lies within the boundaries of normal psychology and physiology. . . .

> We clearly see that [the egoistic tendencies of the present economic system and of its consequences] are very strong. Because of these tendencies the social instinct of man is not greatly developed; they have weakened the moral force in man which combats the inclination towards egoistic acts, and hence toward the crimes which are one form of these acts . . . . Compassion for the misfortunes of others inevitably becomes blunted, and a great part of morality consequently disappears. . . .

> As a consequence of the present environment, man has become very egoistic and hence more *capable of crime,* than if the environment had developed the germs of altruism. . . .

> There can be no doubt that one of the factors of criminality among the bourgeoisie is bad [moral] education. . . . The children—speaking of course in a general way—are brought up with the idea that they must succeed, no matter how; the aim of life is presented to them as getting money and shining in the world. . . .

> Poverty (taken in the sense of absolute want) kills the social sentiments in man, destroys in fact all relations between men. He who is abandoned by all can no longer have any feeling for those who have left him to his fate. . . .

> [Upon perception that the system tends to legalize the egoistic actions of the bourgeoisie and to penalize those of the proletariat], the oppressed resort to means which they would otherwise scorn. As we have seen above, the basis of the social feeling is reciprocity. As soon as this is trodden under foot by the ruling class the social sentiments of the oppressed become weak towards them.[31]

---

least in a healthy society, moral motives would function as a major restraint against crime. When an environment that destroys moral motivation is created, even terror (as statistics tend to confirm) will not eradicate crime.

31. *Introduction to Criminology,* pp. 75–76, and *Criminality and Economic Conditions,* pp. 532, 402, 483–484, 436, and 407, in the order quoted. Bonger explicitly attacks Hobbes: "The adherents of [Hobbes's theory] have studied principally men who live under capitalism, or under civilization; their correct conclusion has been that egoism is the predominant characteristic of these men, and they have adopted the simplest explanation of the phenomenon and say that this trait is inborn." If Hobbists can site Freud for modern support, Bonger can cite Darwin. For, as Darwin had argued in the *Descent of Man,* men would not have survived as a species if they had not initially had considerably greater social sentiments than Hobbes allows them.

The essence of this theory has been summed up by Austin J. Turk. "Criminal behavior," he says, "is almost entirely attributable to the combination of egoism and an environment in which opportunities are not equitably distributed."[32]

No doubt this claim will strike many as extreme and intemperate—a sample of the old-fashioned Marxist rhetoric that sophisticated intellectuals have outgrown. Those who are inclined to react in this way might consider just one sobering fact: of the 1.3 million criminal offenders handled each day by some agency of the United States correctional system, the vast majority (80 percent on some estimates) are members of the lowest 15-percent income level—that percent which is below the "poverty level" as defined by the Social Security Administration.[33] Unless one wants to embrace the belief that all these people are poor because they are bad, it might be well to reconsider Bonger's suggestion that many of them are "bad" because they are poor.[34] At any rate, let us suppose for purposes of discussion that Bonger's picture of the relation between crime and economic conditions is generally accurate. At what points will this challenge the credentials of the contractarian retributive theory as outlined above? I should like to organize my answer to this question around three basic topics:

1. *Rational choice.* The model of rational choice found in Social Contract theory is egoistic—rational institutions are those that would be agreed to by calculating egoists ("devils" in Kant's more colorful terminology). The obvious question that would be raised by any Marxist is: Why give egoism this special status such that it is built, a priori, into the analysis of the concept of rationality? Is this not simply to regard as necessary that which may be only contingently found in the society around us? Starting from such an analysis, a certain result is inevitable—namely, a transcendental sanction for the status quo. Start with a bourgeois model of rationality and you will, of course, wind up defending a bourgeois theory of consent, a bourgeois theory of justice, and a bourgeois theory of punishment.

---

32. Austin J. Turk, in the Introduction to his abridged edition of Bonger's *Criminality and Economic Conditions* (Bloomington, 1969), p. 14.

33. Statistical data on characteristics of offenders in America are drawn primarily from surveys by the Bureau of Census and the National Council on Crime and Delinquency. While there is of course wide disagreement on how such data are to be interpreted, there is no serious disagreement concerning at least the general accuracy of statistics like the one I have cited. Even government publications openly acknowledge a high correlation between crime and socioeconomic disadvantages: "From arrest records, probation reports, and prison statistics a 'portrait' of the offender emerges that progressively highlights the disadvantaged character of his life. The offender at the end of the road in prison is likely to be a member of the lowest social and economic groups in the country, poorly educated and perhaps unemployed. . . . Material failure, then, in a culture firmly oriented toward material success, is the most common denominator of offenders" (*The Challenge of Crime in a Free Society, A Report by the President's Commission on Law Enforcement and Administration of Justice,* U.S. Government Printing Office, Washington, D.C., 1967, pp. 44 and 160). The Marxist implications of this admission have not gone unnoticed by prisoners. See Samuel Jorden, "Prison Reform: In Whose Interest?" *Criminal Law Bulletin* 7, no. 9 (November 1971): 779–787.

34. There are, of course, other factors which enter into an explanation of this statistic. One of them is the fact that economically disadvantaged guilty persons are more likely to wind up arrested or in prison (and thus be reflected in this statistic) than are economically advantaged guilty persons. Thus economic conditions enter into the explanation, not just of criminal behavior, but of society's response to criminal behavior. For a general discussion on the many ways in which crime and poverty are related, see Patricia M. Wald, "Poverty and Criminal Justice," *Task Force Report: The Courts,* U.S. Government Printing Office, Washington, D.C., 1967, pp. 139–151.

Though I cannot explore the point in detail here, it seems to me that this Marxist claim may cause some serious problems for Rawls's well-known theory of justice, a theory which I have already used to unpack some of the evaluative support for the retributive theory of punishment. One cannot help suspecting that there is a certain sterility in Rawls's entire project of providing a rational proof for the preferability of a certain conception of justice over all possible alternative evaluative principles, for the description which he gives of the rational contractors in the original position is such as to guarantee that they will come up with his two principles. This would be acceptable if the analysis of rationality presupposed were intuitively obvious or argued for on independent grounds. But it is not. Why, to take just one example, is a desire for wealth a rational trait whereas envy is not? One cannot help feeling that the desired result dictates the premises.[35]

2. *Justice, benefits, and community.* The retributive theory claims to be grounded on justice; but is it just to punish people who act out of those very motives that society encourages and reinforces? If Bonger is correct, much criminality is motivated by greed, selfishness, and indifference to one's fellows; but does not the whole society encourage motives of greed and selfishness ("making it," "getting ahead"), and does not the competitive nature of the society alienate men from each other and thereby encourage indifference—even, perhaps, what psychiatrists call psychopathy? The moral problem here is similar to one that arises with respect to some war crimes. When you have trained a man to believe that the enemy is not a genuine human person (but only a gook, or a chink), it does not seem quite fair to punish the man if, in a war situation, he kills indiscriminately. For the psychological trait you have conditioned him to have, like greed, is not one that invites fine moral and legal distinctions. There is something perverse in applying principles that presuppose a sense of community in a society which is structured to destroy genuine community.[36]

---

35. The idea that the principles of justice could be proved as a kind of theorem (Rawls's claim in "Justice as Fairness") seems to be absent, if I understand the work correctly, in Rawls's recent *A Theory of Justice.* In this book, Rawls seems to be content with something less than a decision procedure. He is no longer trying to pull his theory of justice up by its own bootstraps, but now seems concerned simply to *exhibit* a certain elaborate conception of justice in the belief that it will do a good job of systematizing and ordering most of our considered and reflective intuitions about moral matters. To this, of course, the Marxist will want to say something like the following: "The considered and reflective intuitions current in our society are a product of bourgeois culture, and thus any theory based upon them begs the question against us and in favor of the status quo." I am not sure that this charge cannot be answered, but I am sure that it deserves an answer. Someday Rawls may be remembered, to paraphrase Georg Lukács's description of Thomas Mann, as the last and greatest philosopher of bourgeois liberalism. The virtue of this description is that it perceives the limitations of his outlook in a way consistent with acknowledging his indisputable genius. (None of my remarks here, I should point out, are to be interpreted as denying that our civilization derived major moral benefits from the tradition of bourgeois liberalism. Just because the freedoms and procedures we associate with bourgeois liberalism—speech, press, assembly, due process of law, etc.—are not the only important freedoms and procedures, we are not to conclude with some witless radicals that these freedoms are not terribly important and that the victories of bourgeois revolutions are not worth preserving. My point is much more modest and noncontroversial—namely, that even bourgeois liberalism requires a critique. It is not self-justifying and, in certain very important respects, is not justified at all.)

36. Kant has some doubts about punishing bastard infanticide and dueling on similar grounds. Given the stigma that Kant's society attached to illegitimacy and the halo that the same society

Related to this is the whole allocation of benefits in contemporary society. The retributive theory really presupposes what might be called a "gentlemen's club" picture of the relation between man and society—i.e., men are viewed as being part of a community of shared values and rules. The rules benefit all concerned and, as a kind of debt for the benefits derived, each man owes obedience to the rules. In the absence of such obedience, he deserves punishment in the sense that he owes payment for the benefits. For, as rational man, he can see that the rules benefit everyone (himself included) and that he would have selected them in the original position of choice.

Now this may not be too far off for certain kinds of criminals—e.g., business executives guilty of tax fraud. (Though even here we might regard their motives of greed to be a function of societal reinforcement.) But to think that it applies to the typical criminal, from the poorer classes, is to live in a world of social and political fantasy. Criminals typically are not members of a shared community of values with their jailers; they suffer from what Marx calls alienation. And they certainly would be hard-pressed to name the benefits for which they are supposed to owe obedience. If justice, as both Kant and Rawls suggest, is based on reciprocity, it is hard to see what these persons are supposed to reciprocate for. Bonger addresses this point in a passage quoted earlier (p. 236): "The oppressed resort to means which they would otherwise scorn. . . . The basis of social feelings is reciprocity. As soon as this is trodden under foot by the ruling class, the social sentiments of the oppressed become weak towards them."

3. *Voluntary acceptance.* Central to the Social Contract idea is the claim that we owe allegiance to the law because the benefits we have derived have been voluntarily accepted. This is one place where our autonomy is supposed to come in. That is, having benefited from the Rule of Law when it was possible to leave, I have in a sense consented to it and to its consequences—even my own punishment if I violate the rules. To see how silly the factual presuppositions of this account are, we can do no better than quote a famous passage from David Hume's essay "Of the Original Contract":

> Can we seriously say that a poor peasant or artisan has a free choice to leave his country — when he knows no foreign language or manners, and lives from day to day by the small wages which he acquires? We may as well assert that a man, by remaining in a vessel, freely consents to the dominion of the master, though he was carried on board while asleep, and must leap into the ocean and perish the moment he leaves her.

A banal empirical observation, one may say. But it is through ignoring such banalities that philosophers generate theories which allow them to spread iniquity in the ignorant belief that they are spreading righteousness.

It does, then, seem as if there may be some truth in Marx's claim that the retributive theory, though formally correct, is materially inadequate. At root, the retributive theory fails to acknowledge that criminality is, to a large extent, a phenomenon of economic class. To acknowledge this is to challenge the empirical presupposition of the retributive theory—the presupposition that all men, including criminals, are volun-

---

placed around military honor, it did not seem totally fair to punish those whose criminality in part grew out of such approved motives. See *Metaphysical Elements of Justice,* pp. 106–107.

tary participants in a reciprocal system of benefits and that the justice of this arrangement can be derived from some eternal and ahistorical concept of rationality.

The upshot of all this seems rather upsetting, as indeed it is. How can it be the case
that everything we are ordinarily inclined to say about punishment (in terms of utility
and retribution) can be quite beside the point? To anyone with ordinary language sympathies (one who is inclined to maintain that what is correct to say is a function of what
we do say), this will seem madness. Marx will agree that there is madness, all right, but
in his view the madness will lie in what we do say—what we say only because of our
massive (and often self-deceiving and self-serving) factual ignorance or indifference to
the circumstances of the social world in which we live. Just as our whole way of talking
about mental phenomena hardened before we knew any neurophysiology—and this
leads us astray, so Marx would argue that our whole way of talking about moral and
political phenomena hardened before we knew any of the relevant empirical facts about
man and society—and this, too, leads us astray. We all suffer from what might be
called the *embourgeoisment* of language, and thus part of any revolution will be a linguis-
tic or conceptual revolution. We have grown accustomed to modifying our language or
conceptual structures under the impact of empirical discoveries in physics. There is no
reason why discoveries in sociology, economics, or psychology could not and should not
have the same effect on entrenched patterns of thought and speech. It is important to
remember, as Russell remarked, that our language sometimes enshrines the metaphysics of the Stone Age.

Consider one example: a man has been convicted of armed robbery. On investigation, we learn that he is an impoverished black whose whole life has been one of frus-
trating alienation from the prevailing socio-economic structure—no job, no transpor-
tation if he could get a job, substandard education for his children, terrible housing
and inadequate health care for his whole family, condescending-tardy-inadequate welfare payments, harassment by the police but no real protection by them against the
dangers in his community, and near total exclusion from the political process. Learning
all this, would we still want to talk—as many do—of his suffering punishment under
the rubric of "paying a debt to society"? Surely not. Debt for what? I do not, of course,
pretend that all criminals can be so described. But I do think that this is a closer picture
of the typical criminal than the picture that is presupposed in the retributive theory—
i.e., the picture of an evil person who, of his own free will, intentionally acts against
those just rules of society which he knows, as a rational man, benefit everyone including
himself.

But what practical help does all this offer, one may ask. How should we design our
punitive practices in the society in which we now live? This is the question we want to
ask, and it does not seem to help simply to say that our society is built on deception and
inequity. How can Marx help us with our real practical problem? The answer, I think, is
that he cannot and obviously does not desire to do so. For Marx would say that we have
not focused (as all piecemeal reform fails to focus) on what is truly the real problem.
And this is changing the basic social relations. Marx is the last person from whom we
can expect advice on how to make our intellectual and moral peace with bourgeois
society. And this is surely his attraction and his value.

What does Bonger offer? He suggests, near the end of his book, that in a properly designed society all criminality would be a problem "for the physician rather than the judge." But this surely will not do. The therapeutic state, where prisons are called hospitals and jailers are called psychiatrists, simply raises again all the old problems about the justification of coercion and its reconciliation with autonomy that we faced in worrying about punishment. The only difference is that our coercive practices are now surrounded with a benevolent rhetoric which makes it even harder to raise the important issues. Thus the move to therapy, in my judgment, is only an illusory solution— alienation remains and the problem of reconciling coercion with autonomy remains unsolved. Indeed, if the alternative is having our personalities involuntarily restructured by some state psychiatrist, we might well want to claim the "right to be punished" that Hegel spoke of.[37]

Perhaps, then, we may really be forced seriously to consider a radical proposal. If we think that institutions of punishment are necessary and desirable, and if we are morally sensitive enough to want to be sure that we have the moral right to punish before we inflict it, then we had better first make sure that we have restructured society in such a way that criminals genuinely do correspond to the only model that will render punishment permissible—i.e., make sure that they are autonomous and that they do benefit in the requisite sense. Of course, if we did this then—if Marx and Bonger are right— crime itself and the need to punish would radically decrease if not disappear entirely.

---

37. This point is pursued in Herbert Morris, "Persons and Punishment." Bonger did not appreciate that "mental illness," like criminality, may also be a phenomenon of social class. On this, see August B. Hollingshead and Frederick C. Redlich, *Social Class and Mental Illness* (New York, 1958).

PART II

THE DEATH PENALTY

L et us suppose that we regard the practice of punishment as justified and that we believe that we have adopted justified standards and procedures for judging criminal responsibility. This still leaves open the question of what type of punishment is proper (either by statute or judicial discretion) for particular classes of offenses and particular classes of offenders. This question forces us to think about both the *kinds* of punishments we shall employ and—with respect to the kinds of punishment—the *amounts* of those punishments we shall impose. (There is, of course, only one "amount" of certain punishments—for example, death.) Our general theoretical reasons (utilitarian deterrence or Kantian retributive) for adopting the practice of punishment will, of course, largely determine the kind and amount of punishment. However, other factors will also be involved. In the United States legal system, for example, certain punishments identified in the Eighth Amendment as "cruel and unusual" are ruled out in principle, even if they would deter and even if they are, in some sense, what the criminal deserves.

In recent years, worries about kind and amount of punishment have been brought into focus in various Supreme Court cases dealing with the death penalty and the question of whether it is cruel and unusual and thus constitutionally impermissible. In the 1972 case of *Furman v. Georgia* (408 U.S. 238), the court identified three main ways in which a punishment could count as cruel and unusual: it could be (1) a kind of punishment (for example, torture) that is intrinsically or per se cruel; (2) a punishment out of all reasonable proportion to the seriousness of the individual's offense; or (3) a punishment that tends to be administered in an arbitrary and capricious manner. Though there was strong dissent from some justices, a majority of the Court held that death is not per se cruel (death is not like torture) and is not disproportionate to some murders. (In *Coker v. Georgia*, 433 U.S. 584 [1977], the Court held that capital punishment is disproportionate to rape.) The Court did hold, however, that capital punishment has historically been inflicted in an arbitrary and capricious manner; that is, it tended to be administered mainly on racial and economic grounds rather than on grounds of genuine criminal desert. (For example, a black criminal who had performed a certain heinous action was much more likely to be sentenced to death than a white criminal who had performed an act of similar gravity.) This was held to be cruel and unusual punishment. Basically, the court reasoned in this way: The more serious the harm that the state proposes to inflict on individuals (the more seriously at risk the state proposes to put individuals), the more rigorous and careful must be the procedures surrounding the administration of that harm. Since death is the most serious harm the state can inflict, it must surround that punishment with greater due process than it uses with any other punishment. Until the states do this, capital punishment will be cruel and unusual and thus constitutionally impermissible.

The 1972 Court ruling held out to the states the following challenge: Either abandon the death penalty or design procedures (a kind of super due process) that will guarantee that the punishment of death will not be administered in an arbitrary and capricious manner. Most of the subsequent death penalty cases involved the constitutional test of various state statutes that attempted to retain the punishment of death without violating the principles laid down in *Furman v. Georgia*.

The first reading in this section, a substantial excerpt from *Gregg v. Georgia* (428 U.S. 153 [1976]), finds the court evaluating the death sentence of an individual sentenced under a capital punishment statute designed by Georgia to pass the *Furman v. Georgia* test: a statute attempting to provide enough due process protections to guarantee that the punishment is not administered in an arbitrary and capricious manner. The majority of the justices held that the Georgia statute did pass the test, and thus the death penalty is upheld in this case as not being cruel and unusual. Two of the justices strongly dissent, and their opinions are also printed here. The majority and dissenting opinions are interesting not merely for the position taken on this particular Georgia statute, of course, but also for the insight they give us into the general philosophies of punishment stated by the various justices.

Following the legal case are two theoretical discussions of the death penalty. David A. Conway's "Capital Punishment and Deterrence" explores the justification of punishment from a generally utilitarian point of view, one that sees deterrence of crime to be the dominant rationale of punishment. Margaret Jane Radin's "Cruel Punishment and Respect for Persons" explores the death penalty from both a legal and philosophical perspective. Radin's own perspective on punishment is basically that of a Kantian retributivist, a perspective that, she argues, illuminates the constitutional concept of cruel and unusual punishment.

Gregg v. Georgia,
United States Supreme Court (1976)

Mr. Justice Stewart,
with Justices Powell and Stevens Concurring

We address initially the basic contention that the punishment of death for the crime of murder is, under all circumstances, "cruel and unusual" in violation of the Eighth and Fourteenth Amendments of the Constitution. In Part IV of this opinion, we will consider the sentence of death imposed under the Georgia statutes at issue in this case.

The Court on a number of occasions has both assumed and asserted the constitutionality of capital punishment. In several cases that assumption provided a necessary foundation for the decision, as the Court was asked to decide whether a particular method of carrying out a capital sentence would be allowed to stand under the Eighth Amendment.[12] But until *Furman v. Georgia,* 408 U.S. 238, 92 S.Ct. 2726, 33 L.Ed.2d 346 (1972), the Court never confronted squarely the fundamental claim that the punish-

428 U.S. 153 (1976). This decision is abridged and begins in Part III. Footnotes are numbered as in original.

12. *Louisiana ex rel. Francis v. Resweber,* 329 U.S. 459, 464, 67 S.Ct. 374, 376, 91 L.Ed. 422 (1947); *In re Kemmler,* 136 U.S. 436, 447, 10 S.Ct. 930, 933, 34 L.Ed. 519 (1890); *Wilkerson v. Utah,* 99 U.S. 130, 134–135, 25 L.Ed. 345 (1879). See also *McGautha v. California,* 402 U.S. 183, 91 S.Ct. 1454, 28 L.Ed.2d 711 (1971); *Witherspoon v. Illinois,* 391 U.S. 510, 88 S.Ct. 1770, 20 L.Ed. 2d 776 (1968); *Trop v. Dulles,* 356 U.S. 86, 100, 78 S.Ct. 590, 597, 2 L.Ed. 2d 630 (1958) (plurality opinion).

ment of death always, regardless of the enormity of the offense or the procedure followed in imposing the sentence, is cruel and unusual punishment in violation of the Constitution. Although this issue was presented and addressed in *Furman,* it was not resolved by the Court. Four Justices would have held that capital punishment is not unconstitutional *per se*;[13] two Justices would have reached the opposite conclusion;[14] and three Justices, while agreeing that the statutes then before the Court were invalid as applied, left open the question whether such punishment may ever be imposed.[15] We now hold that the punishment of death does not invariably violate the Constitution.

A

[1] The history of the prohibition of "cruel and unusual" punishment already has been reviewed by this Court at length.[16] The phrase first appeared in the English Bill of Rights of 1689, which was drafted by Parliament at the accession of William and Mary. See Granucci, "Nor Cruel and Unusual Punishments Inflicted:" The Original Meaning, 57 Cal. L. Rev. 839, 852–853 (1969). The English version appears to have been directed against punishments unauthorized by statute and beyond the jurisdiction of the sentencing court, as well as those disproportionate to the offense involved. *Id.,* at 860. The American draftsmen, who adopted the English phrasing in drafting the Eighth Amendment, were primarily concerned, however, with proscribing "tortures" and other "barbarous" methods of punishment. *Id.,* at 842.[17]

In the earliest cases raising Eighth Amendment claims, the Court focused on particular methods of execution to determine whether they were too cruel to pass constitutional muster. The constitutionality of the sentence of death itself was not at issue, and the criterion used to evaluate the mode of execution was its similarity to "torture" and other "barbarous" methods. See *Wilkerson v. Utah,* 99 U.S., at 136 ("[I]t is safe to affirm

---

13. 408 U.S., at 375, 92 S.Ct., at 2796 (Burger, C. J., dissenting), 405, 92 S.Ct. 2812 (Blackmun, J., dissenting), 414, 92 S.Ct. 2816 (Powell, J., dissenting), 465, 92 S.Ct. 2842 (Rehnquist, J., dissenting).

14. *Id.,* at 257, 92 S.Ct., at 2736 (Brennan, J., concurring), 314, 92 S.Ct. 2765 (Marshall, J., concurring).

15. *Id.,* at 240, 92 S.Ct., at 2727 (Douglas, J., concurring), 306, 92 S.Ct. 2760 (Stewart, J., concurring), 310, 92 S.Ct. 2763 (White, J., concurring).

   Since five Justices wrote separately in support of the judgments in *Furman,* the holding of the Court may be viewed as that position taken by those Members who concurred in the judgments on the narrowest grounds—Mr. Justice Stewart and Mr. Justice White. See n. 35, *infra.*

16. *Id.,* at 316–328, 92 S.Ct., at 2765–2772 (Marshall, J., concurring).

17. This conclusion derives primarily from statements made during the debates in the various state conventions called to ratify the Federal Constitution. For example, Virginia delegate Patrick Henry objected vehemently to the lack of a provision banning "cruel and unusual punishments": "What has distinguished our ancestors?—That they would not admit of tortures, or cruel and barbarous punishment. But Congress may introduce the practice of the civil law, in preference to that of the common law. They may introduce the practice of France, Spain, and Germany—of torturing, to extort a confession of the crime." 3 J. Elliot, The Debates in the Several State Conventions On the Adoption of the Federal Constitution 447–448 (1861). A similar objection was made in the Massachusetts convention: "They are nowhere restrained from inventing the most cruel and unheard-of punishments and annexing them to crimes; and there is no constitutional check on them, but that *racks* and *gibbets* may be amongst the most mild instruments of their discipline." 2 *id.,* at 111 (1876).

that punishments of torture, . . . and all others in the same line of unnecessary cruelty, are forbidden by that amendment. . . ."); *In re Kemmler,* 136 U.S., at 447, 10 S.Ct., at 933 ("Punishments are cruel when they involve torture or a lingering death. . . ."). See also *Louisiana ex rel. Francis v. Resweber,* 329 U.S. 459, 464, 67 S.Ct. 374, 376, 91 L.Ed. 422 (1947) (A second attempt at electrocution found not to violate the Eighth Amendment, since the failure of the initial execution attempt was "an unforeseeable accident" and " [t]here [was] no purpose to inflict unnecessary pain nor any unnecessary pain involved in the proposed execution.").

[2] But the Court has not confined the prohibition embodied in the Eighth Amendment to "barbarous" methods that were generally outlawed in the 18th century. Instead, the Amendment has been interpreted in a flexible and dynamic manner. The Court early recognized that "a principle to be vital, must be capable of wider application than the mischief which gave it birth." *Weems v. United States,* 217 U.S. 349, 373, 30 S.Ct. 544, 551, 54 L.Ed. 793 (1910). Thus the clause forbidding "cruel and unusual" punishments "is not fastened to the obsolete but may acquire meaning as public opinion becomes enlightened by a humane justice." *Id.,* at 378, 30 S.Ct., at 553. See also *Furman v. Georgia,* 408 U.S., at 429–430, 92 S.Ct., at 2823–2824 (Powell, J., dissenting); *Trop v. Dulles,* 356 U.S., at 100–101, 78 S.Ct., at 597–598 (plurality opinion).

In *Weems* the Court addressed the constitutionality of the Philippine punishment of *cadena temporal* for the crime of falsifying an official document. That punishment included imprisonment for at least 12 years and one day, in chains, at hard and painful labor; the loss of many basic civil rights; and subjection to lifetime surveillance. Although the Court acknowledged the possibility that "the cruelty of pain" may be present in the challenged punishment, 217 U.S., at 366, 30 S.Ct., at 549, it did not rely on that factor, for it rejected the proposition that the Eighth Amendment reaches only punishments that are "inhuman and barbarous, torture and the like." *Id.,* at 368, 30 S.Ct., at 549. Rather, the Court focused on the lack of proportion between the crime and the offense:

> Such penalties for such offenses amaze those who have formed their conception of the relation of a state to even its offending citizens from the practice of the American commonwealths, and believe that it is a precept of justice that punishment for crime should be graduated and proportioned to offense. [*Id.,* at 366–367, 30 S.Ct., at 549.[18]]

Later, in *Trop v. Dulles,* 356 U.S. 86, 78 S.Ct. 590, 2 L.Ed.2d 630 (1958), the Court reviewed the constitutionality of the punishment of denationalization imposed upon a soldier who escaped from an Army stockade and became a deserter for one day. Although the concept of proportionality was not the basis of the holding, the plurality

---

18. The Court remarked on the fact that the law under review "has come to us from a government of a different form and genius from ours," but it also noted that the punishments it inflicted "would have those bad attributes even if they were found in a Federal enactment and not taken from an alien source." 217 U.S., at 377, 30 S.Ct., at 553.

observed in dicta that "[f]ines, imprisonment and even execution may be imposed depending upon the enormity of the crime." *Id.,* at 100, 78 S.Ct., at 598.

The substantive limits imposed by the Eighth Amendment on what can be made criminal and punished were discussed in *Robinson v. California,* 370 U.S. 660, 82 S.Ct. 1417, 8 L.Ed.2d (1962). The Court found unconstitutional a state statute that made the status of being addicted to a narcotic drug a criminal offense. It held in effect, that it is "cruel and unusual" to impose any punishment at all for the mere status of addiction. The cruelty in the abstract of the actual sentence imposed was irrelevant: "Even one day in prison would be cruel and unusual punishment for the 'crime' of having a common cold." *Id.,* at 667, 82 S.Ct. at 1421. Most recently, in *Furman v. Georgia,* 408 U.S. 238, 92 S.Ct. 2726, 33 L.Ed.2d 346 (1972), three Justices in separate concurring opinions found the Eighth Amendment applicable to procedures employed to select convicted defendants for the sentence of death.

[3, 4] It is clear from the foregoing precedents that the Eighth Amendment has not been regarded as a static concept. As Chief Justice Warren said, in an oft-quoted phrase, "[t]he Amendment must draw its meaning from the evolving standards of decency that mark the progress of a maturing society." *Trop v. Dulles, supra,* 356 U.S. at 101, 78 S.Ct., at 598. See also *Jackson v. Bishop,* 404 F.2d 571, 579 (CA 8 1968). Cf. *Robinson v. California, supra,* 370 U.S., at 666, 82 S.Ct., at 1420. Thus, an assessment of contemporary values concerning the infliction of a challenged sanction is relevant to the application of the Eighth Amendment. As we develop below more fully, see pp. 2926–2927, *infra,* this assessment does not call for a subjective judgment. It requires, rather, that we look to objective indicia that reflect the public attitude toward a given sanction.

[5] But our cases also make clear that public perceptions of standards of decency with respect to criminal sanctions are not conclusive. A penalty also must accord with "the dignity of man," which is the "basic concept underlying the Eighth Amendment." *Trop v. Dulles, supra,* 356 U.S., at 100, 78 S.Ct., at 597 (plurality opinion). This means, at least, that the punishment not be "excessive." When a form of punishment in the abstract (in this case, whether capital punishment may ever be imposed as a sanction for murder) rather than in the particular (the propriety of death as a penalty to be applied to a specific defendant for a specific crime) is under consideration, the inquiry into "excessiveness" has two aspects. First, the punishment must not involve the unnecessary and wanton infliction of pain. *Furman v. Georgia, supra,* 408 U.S., at 392–393, 92 S.Ct., at 2805–2806 (Burger, C.J., dissenting). See *Wilkerson v. Utah,* 99 U.S., at 136; *Weems v. United States,* 217 U.S., at 381, 30 S.Ct., at 554. Second, the punishment must not be grossly out of proportion to the severity of the crime. *Trop v. Dulles, supra,* 356 U.S., at 100, 78 S.Ct., at 597 (plurality opinion) (dictum); *Weems v. United States, supra,* 217 U.S., at 367, 30 S.Ct., at 549.

B

[6–8] Of course, the requirements of the Eighth Amendment must be applied with an awareness of the limited role to be played by the courts. This does not mean that judges have no role to play, for the Eighth Amendment is a restraint upon the exercise of legislative power.

> Judicial review by definition, often involves a conflict between judicial and legislative judgment as to what the Constitution means or requires. In this respect, Eighth Amendment cases come to us in no different posture. It seems conceded by all that the Amendment imposes some obligations on the judiciary to judge the constitutionality of punishment and that there are punishments that the Amendment would bar whether legislatively approved or not. [*Furman v. Georgia, supra,* 408 U.S., at 313–314, 92 S.Ct., at 2764 (White, J., concurring).]

See also *id.,* at 433, 92 S.Ct., at 2825 (Powell, J., dissenting).[19] But, while we have an obligation to insure that constitutional bounds are not overreached, we may not act as judges as we might as legislators.

> Courts are not representative bodies. They are not designed to be a good reflex of a democratic society. Their judgment is best informed, and therefore most dependable, within narrow limits. Their essential quality is detachment, founded on independence. History teaches that the independence of the judiciary is jeopardized when courts become embroiled in the passions of the day and assume primary responsibility in choosing between competing political, economic and social pressures. [*Dennis v. United States,* 341 U.S. 494, 525, 71 S.Ct. 857, 875, 95 L.Ed. 1137 (1951) (Frankfurter, J., concurring in affirmance).[20]]

[9–11] Therefore, in assessing a punishment selected by a democratically elected legislature against the constitutional measure, we presume its validity. We may not require the legislature to select the least severe penalty possible so long as the penalty selected is not cruelly inhumane or disproportionate to the crime involved. And a heavy burden rests on those who would attack the judgment of the representatives of the people.

---

19. Although legislative measures adopted by the people's chosen representatives provide one important means of ascertaining contemporary values, it is evident that legislative judgments alone cannot be determinative of Eighth Amendment standards since that Amendment was intended to safeguard individuals from the abuse of legislative power. See *Weems v. United States, supra,* 217 U.S., at 371–373, 30 S.Ct., at 550–551; *Furman v. Georgia, supra,* 408 U.S., at 258–269, 92 S.Ct., at 2736–2742 (Brennan, J., concurring). *Robinson v. California,* 370 U.S. 660, 82 S.Ct. 1417, 8 L.Ed.2d 758 (1962), illustrates the proposition that penal laws enacted by state legislatures may violate the Eighth Amendment because "in the light of contemporary human knowledge" they "would doubtless be universally thought to be an infliction of cruel and unusual punishment." *Id.,* at 666, 82 S.Ct., at 1420. At the time of *Robinson* nine States in addition to California had criminal laws that punished addiction similar to the law declared unconstitutional in *Robinson.* See Brief for Appellant in *Robinson v. California,* No. 61–554, at 15.

20. See also *Furman v. Georgia, supra,* at 411, 92 S.Ct., at 2815 (Blackmun, J., dissenting): "We should not allow our personal preferences as to the wisdom of legislative and congressional action, or our distaste for such action, to guide our judicial decision in cases such as these. The temptations to cross that policy line are very great."

[12] This is true in part because the constitutional test is intertwined with an assessment of contemporary standards and the legislative judgment weighs heavily in ascertaining such standards. "[I]n a democratic society legislatures, not courts, are constituted to respond to the will and consequently the moral values of the people." *Furman v. Georgia*, 408 U.S., at 383, 92 S.Ct., at 2800 (Burger, C. J., dissenting). The deference we owe to the decisions of the state legislatures under our federal system, *id.*, at 465–470, 92 S.Ct., at 2842–2844 (Rehnquist, J., dissenting), is enhanced where the specification of punishments is concerned, for "these are peculiarly questions of legislative policy." *Gore v. United States*, 357 U.S. 386, 393, 78 S.Ct. 1280, 1285, 2 L.Ed.2d 1405 (1958). Cf. *Robinson v. California*, 370 U.S., at 664–665, 82 S.Ct., at 1419–1420; *Trop v. Dulles*, 356 U.S., at 103, 78 S.Ct., at 599 (plurality opinion); *In re Kemmler*, 136 U.S., at 447, 10 S.Ct., at 933. Caution is necessary lest this Court become, "under the aegis of the Cruel and Unusual Punishment Clause, the ultimate arbiter of the standards of criminal responsibility . . . throughout the country." *Powell v. Texas*, 392 U.S. 514, 533, 88 S.Ct. 2145, 2154, 20 L.Ed.2d 1254 (1968). A decision that a given punishment is impermissible under the Eighth Amendment cannot be reversed short of a constitutional amendment. The ability of the people to express their preference through the normal democratic processes, as well as through ballot referenda, is shut off. Revisions cannot be made in the light of further experience. See *Furman v. Georgia*, *supra*, 408 U.S., at 461–462, 92 S.Ct., at 2839–2840 (Powell, J., dissenting).

C

In the discussion to this point we have sought to identify the principles and considerations that guide a court in addressing an Eighth Amendment claim. We now consider specifically whether the sentence of death for the crime of murder is a *per se* violation of the Eighth and Fourteenth Amendments to the Constitution. We note first that history and precedent strongly support a negative answer to this question.

[13] The imposition of the death penalty for the crime of murder has a long history of acceptance both in the United States and in England. The common-law rule imposed a mandatory death sentence on all convicted murderers. *McGautha v. California*, 402 U.S., at 197–198, 91 S.Ct., at 1462–1463. And the penalty continued to be used into the 20th century by most American States, although the breadth of the common-law rule was diminished, initially by narrowing the class of murders to be punished by death and subsequently by widespread adoption of laws expressly granting juries the discretion to recommend mercy. *Id.*, at 199–200, 91 S.Ct., at 1463–1464. See *Woodson v. North Carolina*, — U.S. —, 96 S.Ct. 2978, 48 L.Ed.2d —.

It is apparent from the text of the Constitution itself that the existence of capital punishment was accepted by the Framers. At the time the Eighth Amendment was ratified, capital punishment was a common sanction in every State. Indeed, the First Congress of the United States enacted legislation providing death as the penalty for specified crimes. 1 Stat. 112 (1790). The Fifth Amendment, adopted at the same time as the Eighth, contemplated the continued existence of the capital sanction by imposing certain limits on the prosecution of capital cases:

No person shall be held to answer for a capital, or otherwise infamous crime, unless on a presentment or indictment of a Grand Jury . . . ; nor shall any person be subject for the same offense to be twice put in jeopardy of life or limb; . . . nor be deprived of life, liberty or property, without due process of law.

And the Fourteenth Amendment, adopted over three-quarters of a century later, similarly contemplates the existence of the capital sanction in providing that no State shall deprive any person of "life, liberty, or property" without due process of law.

For nearly two centuries, this Court, repeatedly and often expressly, has recognized that capital punishment is not invalid *per se.* In *Wilkerson v. Utah,* 99 U.S., at 134–135, where the Court found no constitutional violation in inflicting death by public shooting, it said:

Cruel and unusual punishments are forbidden by the Constitution, but the authorities referred to are quite sufficient to show that the punishment of shooting as a mode of executing the death penalty for the crime of murder in the first degree is not included in that category, within the meaning of the eighth amendment.

Rejecting the contention that death by electrocution was "cruel and unusual," the Court in *In re Kemmler,* 136 U.S., at 447, 10 S.Ct., at 933 reiterated:

[T]he punishment of death is not cruel, within the meaning of that word as used in the Constitution. It implies there something inhuman and barbarous, something more than the mere extinguishment of life.

Again, in *Louisiana ex rel. Francis v. Resweber,* 329 U.S., at 464, 67 S.Ct., at 376, the Court remarked: "The cruelty against which the Constitution protects a convicted man is cruelty inherent in the method of punishment, not the necessary suffering involved in any method employed to extinguish life humanely." And in *Trop v. Dulles,* 356 U.S., at 99, 78 S.Ct., at 597, Chief Justice Warren, for four Justices, wrote:

Whatever the arguments may be against capital punishment, both on moral grounds and in terms of accomplishing the purposes of punishment . . . the death penalty has been employed throughout our history, and, in a day when it is still widely accepted, it cannot be said to violate the constitutional concept of cruelty.

Four years ago, the petitioners in *Furman* and its companion cases predicated their argument primarily upon the asserted proposition that standards of decency had evolved to the point where capital punishment no longer could be tolerated. The petitioners in those cases said, in effect, that the evolutionary process had come to an end, and that standards of decency required that the Eighth Amendment be construed finally as prohibiting capital punishment for any crime regardless of its depravity and impact on society. This view was accepted by two Justices.[21] Three other Justices were unwilling to

---

21. See concurring opinions of Mr. Justice Brennan and Mr. Justice Marshall, 408 U.S., at 257 and 314, 92 S.Ct. at 2736 and 2765.

go so far; focusing on the procedures by which convicted defendants were selected for the death penalty rather than on the actual punishment inflicted, they joined in the conclusion that the statutes before the Court were constitutionally invalid.[22]

[14] The petitioners in the capital cases before the Court today renew the "standards of decency" argument, but developments during the four years since *Furman* have undercut substantially the assumptions upon which their argument rested. Despite the continuing debate, dating back to the 19th century, over the morality and utility of capital punishment, it is now evident that a large proportion of American society continues to regard it as an appropriate and necessary criminal sanction.

The most marked indication of society's endorsement of the death penalty for murder is the legislative response to *Furman*. The legislatures of at least 35 States[23] have enacted new statutes that provide for the death penalty for at least some crimes that result in the death of another person. And the Congress of the United States, in 1974, enacted a statute providing the death penalty for aircraft piracy that results in death.[24] These recently adopted statutes have attempted to address the concerns expressed by the Court in *Furman* primarily (i) by specifying the factors to be weighed and the procedures to be followed in deciding when to impose a capital sentence, or (ii) by making the death penalty mandatory for specified crimes. But all of the post-*Furman* statutes make clear that capital punishment itself has not been rejected by the elected representatives of the people.

In the only statewide referendum occurring since *Furman* and brought to our attention, the people of California adopted a constitutional amendment that authorized capital punishment, in effect negating a prior ruling by the Supreme Court of California in *People v. Anderson,* 6 Cal.3d 628, 100 Cal.Rptr. 152, 493 P.2d 880, cert. denied,

---

22. See concurring opinions of Mr. Justice Douglas, Mr. Justice Stewart, and Mr. Justice White, 408 US., at 240, 306, and 310, 92 S.Ct., at 2727, 2760 and 2763.
23. Ala.H.B. 212, §§ 2 –4, 6 –7 (1975); Ariz.Rev.Stat.Ann. §§ 13–452 to 13–454 (Supp. 1973); Ark.Stat.Ann. § 41–4706 (Cum.Supp. 1975); Cal.Penal Code §§ 190.1, 209, 219 (West Supp. 1974); Col.S.B.No. 46, § 4 (1974 Sess.); Gen.Stat.Conn. §§53a–25, 53a–35(b), 53a–46a, 53a–54b (1975); 11 Del.Code Ann. § 4209 (Cum.Supp. 1975); Fla.Stat.Ann. §§ 782.04, 921.141 (Cum.Supp. 1975–1976); Ga.Code Ann. §§ 26–3102, 27–2528, 27–2534.1, 27–2537 (Supp. 1975); Idaho Code § 18–4004 (Cum.Supp. 1975); Ill.Rev.Stat c. 38. §§ 9–1, 1005–5–3, 1005–8–1A (1973); Burns' Ind.Stat.Ann. § 35–13–4–1 (1975); 16 Ky.Rev.Stat. § 507.020 (1975); La.Rev.Stat.Ann. § 14:30 (Supp. 1974); Md.Code Ann., Art. 27, § 413 (Cum.Supp. 1975); Miss.Code Ann. §§ 97–3–19, 97–3–21, 97–25–55, 99–17–20 (Cum. Supp. 1975); Vernon's Mo.Stat.Ann. §§ 559.009, 559.005 (Supp. 1976); Mont.Rev.Codes Ann. § 94–5–105 (Spec.Crim.Code Supp. 1973), as amended, c. 262, 43d Legislative Assembly (Mar. 21, 1974); Neb.Rev.Stat. §§ 28–401, 29–2521 to 29–2523 (Cum.Supp. 1974); Nev.Rev. Stat. § 200.030 (1973); N.H.Rev.Stat.Ann. § 630.1 (1974); N.M.Stat.Ann. § 40A–29–2 (Supp. 1973); N.Y.Penal Law § 60.06 (added by S. 21028 (Cal.No. 1548) (Ass.B 11474–A), N.Y.Laws 1974); N.C.Gen.Stat. § 14–17 (Cum.Supp. 1974); Ohio Rev. Code Ann. §§ 2929.02–2929.04 (Page Spec.Supp. 1973); 21 Okla.Stat.Ann. §§ 701.1–701.3 (Supp. 1973); Pa.Act.No. 46, 158th General Assembly (Mar. 26, 1974); R.I.Gen.Laws Ann. § 11–23–2 (Supp. 1975); S.C.Code § 16–52 (Cum.Supp. 1975); Tenn.Code Ann. §§ 39–2402, 39–2406 (1975); Vernon's Tex.Pen.Code Ann. § 19–03(a)(1974); Utah Code Ann. §§ 76–3–206–207, 76–5–202 (Supp. 1975); Va.Code §§ 18.2–10, 18.2–31 (1975); Wash.Rev.Code §§ 9A.32.045, 9A.32.046 (Supp. 1975); Wyo.Stat.Ann. § 6–54 (Cum.Supp. 1975).
24. Antihijacking Act of 1974, 49 U.S.C. §§ 1472(i), (n) (Supp. IV).

406 U.S. 958, 92 S.Ct. 2060, 32 L.Ed.2d 344 (1972), that the death penalty violated the California Constitution.[25]

[15] The jury also is a significant and reliable objective index of contemporary values because it is so directly involved. See *Furman v. Georgia,* 408 U.S., at 439–440, 92 S.Ct., at 2828–2829 (Powell, J., dissenting). See generally Powell, Jury Trial of Crimes, 23 Wash. & Lee L.Rev. 1 (1966). The Court has said that "one of the most important functions any jury can perform in making . . . a selection [between life imprisonment and death for a defendant convicted in a capital case] is to maintain a link between contemporary community values and the penal system." *Witherspoon v. Illinois,* 391 U.S. 510, 519 n. 15, 88 S.Ct. 1770, 1775, 20 L.Ed.2d 776 (1968). It may be true that evolving standards have influenced juries in recent decades to be more discriminating in imposing the sentence of death.[26] But the relative infrequency of jury verdicts imposing the death sentence does not indicate rejection of capital punishment *per se.* Rather, the reluctance of juries in many cases to impose the sentence may well reflect the humane feeling that this most irrevocable of sanctions should be reserved for a small number of extreme cases. See *Furman v. Georgia, supra,* 408 U.S., at 388, 92 S.Ct., at 2803 (Burger, C.J., dissenting). Indeed, the actions of juries in many States since *Furman* is fully compatible with the legislative judgments, reflected in the new statutes, as to the continued utility and necessity of capital punishment in appropriate cases. At the close of 1974 at least 254 persons had been sentenced to death since *Furman,*[27] and by the end of March 1976, more than 460 persons were subject to death sentences.

[16] As we have seen, however, the Eighth Amendment demands more than that a challenged punishment be acceptable to contemporary society. The Court also must ask whether it comports with the basic concept of human dignity at the core of the Amendment. *Trop v. Dulles,* 356 U.S., at 100, 78 S.Ct., at 597 (plurality opinion). Although we cannot "invalidate a category of penalties because we deem less severe penalties adequate to serve the ends of penology," *Furman v. Georgia, supra,* 408 U.S., at

---

25. In 1968, the people of Massachusetts were asked "Shall the commonwealth . . . retain the death penalty for crime?" A substantial majority of the ballots cast answered "Yes." Of 2,348,005 ballots cast, 1,159,348 voted "Yes," 730,649 voted "No," and 458,008 were blank. See *Commonwealth v. O'Neal,* 339 N.E.2d 676, 708 and n. 1 (Mass. 1975) (Reardon, J., dissenting). A December 1972 Gallup poll indicated that 57% of the people favored the death penalty, while a June 1973 Harris survey showed support of 59%. Vidmar & Ellsworth, Public Opinion and the Death Penalty, 26 Stan.L.Rev. 1245, 1249 n. 22 (1974). In a December 1970 referendum the voters of Illinois also rejected the abolition of capital punishment by 1,218,791 votes to 676,302 votes. Report of the Governor's Study Commn. on Capital Punishment, p. 43 (Pa. 1973).

26. The number of prisoners who received death sentences in the years from 1961 to 1972 varied from a high of 140 in 1961 to a low of 75 in 1972, with wide fluctuations in the intervening years: 103 in 1962; 93 in 1963; 106 in 1964; 86 in 1965; 118 in 1966; 85 in 1967; 102 in 1968; 97 in 1969; 127 in 1970; and 104 in 1971. Department of Justice, Capital Punishment 1971–1972, National Prisoner Statistics Bulletin, p. 20 (December 1974). It has been estimated that before *Furman* less than 20% of those convicted of murder were sentenced to death in those States that authorized capital punishment. See *Woodson v. North Carolina, post,* —— U.S. p. —— n. 31, 96 S. Ct. p. 2987.

27. Law Enforcement Assistance Administration, Capital Punishment 1974, p. 1 and Table 7, p. 26 (1975).

451, 92 S.Ct., at 2834 (Powell, J., dissenting), the sanction imposed cannot be so totally without penological justification that it results in the gratuitous infliction of suffering. Cf. *Wilkerson v. Utah,* 99 U.S., at 135–136; *In re Kemmler,* 136 U.S., at 447, 10 S.Ct., at 933.

[17] The death penalty is said to serve two principal social purposes: retribution and deterrence of capital crimes by prospective offenders.[28]

[18] In part, capital punishment is an expression of society's moral outrage at particularly offensive conduct.[29] This function may be unappealing to many, but it is essential in an ordered society that asks its citizens to rely on legal processes rather than self-help to vindicate their wrongs.

> The instinct for retribution is part of the nature of man, and channeling that instinct in the administration of criminal justice serves an important purpose in promoting the stability of a society governed by law. When people begin to believe that organized society is unwilling or unable to impose upon criminal offenders the punishment they "deserve," then there are sown the seeds of anarchy — of self-help, vigilante justice, and lynch law. [*Furman v. Georgia, supra,* 408 U.S., at 308, 92 S.Ct., at 2761 (Stewart, J., concurring).]

"Retribution is no longer the dominant objective of the criminal law," *Williams v. New York,* 337 U.S. 241, 248, 69 S.Ct. 1079, 1084, 93 L.Ed. 1337 (1949), but neither is it a forbidden objective nor one inconsistent with our respect for the dignity of men. *Furman v. Georgia, supra,* 408 U.S., at 394–395, 92 S.Ct., at 2806–2807 (Burger, C.J., dissenting), 452–454, 92 S.Ct. 2835–2836 (Powell, J., dissenting); *Powell v. Texas,* 392 U.S., at 531, 535–536, 88 S.Ct., at 2153, 2155–2156. Indeed, the decision that capital punishment may be the appropriate sanction in extreme cases is an expression of the community's belief that certain crimes are themselves so grievous an affront to humanity that the only adequate response may be the penalty of death.[30]

---

28. Another purpose that has been discussed is the incapacitation of dangerous criminals and the consequent prevention of crimes that they may otherwise commit in the future. See *People v. Anderson,* 6 Cal.3d 628, 651, 100 Cal.Rptr. 152, 493 P.2d 880, 896, cert.denied, 406 U.S. 958, 92 S.Ct. 2060, 32 L.Ed.2d 344 (1972); *Commonwealth v. O'Neal,* 339 N.E.2d 676, 685–686 (Mass. 1975).

29. See Packer, The Limits of the Criminal Sanction 43–44 (1968).

30. Lord Justice Denning, Master of the Rolls of the Court of Appeal in England, spoke to this effect before the British Royal Commission on Capital Punishment:

> Punishment is the way in which society expresses its denunciation of wrong doing: and, in order to maintain respect for law, it is essential that the punishment inflicted for grave crimes should adequately reflect the revulsion felt by the great majority of citizens for them. It is a mistake to consider the objects of punishment as being deterrent or reformative or preventive and nothing else. . . . The truth is that some crimes are so outrageous that society insists on adequate punishment, because the wrong-doer deserves it, irrespective of whether it is a deterrent or not. [Royal Commission on Capital Punishment, Minutes of Evidence, Dec. 1, 1949, p. 207 (1950).]

A contemporary writer has noted more recently that opposition to capital punishment "has much more appeal when the discussion is merely academic than when the community is confronted with a crime, or a series of crimes, so gross, so heinous, so cold-blooded that anything

Statistical attempts to evaluate the worth of the death penalty as a deterrent to crimes by potential offenders have occasioned a great deal of debate.[31] The results simply have been inconclusive. As one opponent of capital punishment has said:

[A]fter all possible inquiry, including the probing of all possible methods of inquiry, we do not know, and for systematic and easily visible reasons cannot know, what the truth about this "deterrent" effect may be. . . .

The inescapable flaw is . . . that social conditions in any state are not constant through time, and that social conditions are not the same in any two states. If an effect were observed (and the observed effects one way or another, are not large) then one could not at all tell whether any of this effect is attributable to the presence or absence of capital punishment. A "scientific"—that is to say, a soundly based—conclusion is simply impossible, and no methodological path out of this tangle suggests itself. [C. Black, Capital Punishment: The Inevitability of Caprice and Mistake 25–26 (1974).]

Although some of the studies suggest that the death penalty may not function as a significantly greater deterrent than lesser penalties,[32] there is no convincing empirical evidence either supporting or refuting this view. We may nevertheless assume safely that there are murderers, such as those who act in passion, for whom the threat of death has little or no deterrent effect. But for many others, the death penalty undoubtedly is a significant deterrent. There are carefully contemplated murders, such as murder for hire, where the possible penalty of death may well enter into the cold calculus that precedes the decision to act.[33] And there are some categories of murder, such as murder by a life prisoner, where other sanctions may not be adequate.[34]

---

short of death seems an inadequate response." Raspberry, Death sentence, The Washington Post, March 12, 1976, at A27, col. 5–6.

31. See, *e.g.*, Peck, The Deterrent Effect of Capital Punishment: Ehrlich and His Critics, 85 Yale L.J. 359 (1976); Baldus & Cole, A Comparison of the Work of Thorsten Sellin and Isaac Ehrlich on the Deterrent Effect of Capital Punishment, 85 Yale L.J. 170 (1975); Bowers & Pierce, The Illusion of Deterrence in Isaac Ehrlich's Research on Capital Punishment, 85 Yale L.J. 187 (1975); Ehrlich, The Deterrent Effect of Capital Punishment: A Question of Life and Death, 65 Am. Econ. Rev. 397 (1975); Hook, The Death Sentence, in The Death Penalty in America 146 (H. Bedau ed. 1967); Sellin, The Death Penalty (1959).

32. See, *e.g.*, The Death Penalty in America 258–332 (H. Bedau ed. 1967); Report of the Royal Commission on Capital Punishment 1949–1953, Cmd. 8932.

33. Other types of calculated murders, apparently occurring with increasing frequency, include the use of bombs or other means of indiscriminate killings, the extortion murder of hostages or kidnap victims, and the execution-style killing of witnesses to a crime.

34. We have been shown no statistics breaking down the total number of murders into the categories described above. The overall trend in the number of murders committed in the nation, however, has been upward for some time. In 1964, reported murders totaled an estimated 9,250. During the ensuing decade, the number reported increased 123%, until it totalled approximately 20,600 in 1974. In 1972, the year *Furman* was announced, the total estimated was 18,550. Despite a fractional decrease in 1975 as compared with 1974, the number of murders increased in the three years immediately following *Furman* to approximately 20,400, an increase of almost 10%. See Federal Bureau of Investigation Crime in the United States, Uniform Crime Reports, for 1964, 1972, and 1974; 1975 Preliminary Annual Release, Uniform Crime Reports.

The value of capital punishment as a deterrent of crime is a complex factual issue the resolution of which properly rests with the legislatures, which can evaluate the results of statistical studies in terms of their own local conditions and with a flexibility of approach that is not available to the courts. *Furman v. Georgia,* 408 U.S., at 403–405, 92 S.Ct., at 2810–2812 (Burger, C. J., dissenting). Indeed, many of the post-*Furman* statutes reflect just such a responsible effort to define those crimes and those criminals for which capital punishment is most probably an effective deterrent.

[19] In sum, we cannot say that the judgment of the Georgia legislature that capital punishment may be necessary in some cases is clearly wrong. Considerations of federalism, as well as respect for the ability of a legislature to evaluate, in terms of its particular state the moral consensus concerning the death penalty and its social utility as a sanction, require us to conclude, in the absence of more convincing evidence, that the infliction of death as a punishment for murder is not without justification and thus is not unconstitutionally severe.

[20,21] Finally, we must consider whether the punishment of death is disproportionate in relation to the crime for which it is imposed. There is no question that death as a punishment is unique in its severity and irrevocability. *Furman v. Georgia, supra,* at 286–291, 92 S.Ct. at 2750–2753 (Brennan, J., concurring), 306, 92 S.Ct. 2760 (Stewart, J., concurring). When a defendant's life is at stake, the Court has been particularly sensitive to insure that every safeguard is observed. *Powell v. State of Alabama,* 287 U.S. 45, 71, 53 S.Ct. 55, 65, 77 L.Ed. 158 (1932); *Reid v. Covert,* 354 U.S. 1, 77, 77 S.Ct. 1222, 1262, 1 L.Ed.2d 1148 (1957) (Harlan J., concurring in the result). But we are concerned here only with the imposition of capital punishment for the crime of murder, and when a life has been taken deliberately by the offender,[35] we cannot say that the punishment is invariably disproportionate to the crime. It is an extreme sanction, suitable to the most extreme of crimes.

[22] We hold that the death penalty is not a form of punishment that may never be imposed, regardless of the circumstances of the offense, regardless of the character of the offender, and regardless of the procedure followed in reaching the decision to impose it.

IV

We now consider whether Georgia may impose the death penalty on the petitioner in this case.

A

While *Furman* did not hold that the infliction of the death penalty *per se* violates the Constitution's ban on cruel and unusual punishments, it did recognize that the penalty

---

35. We do not address here the question whether the taking of the criminal's life is a proportionate sanction where no victim has been deprived of life—for example, when capital punishment is imposed for rape, kidnapping, or armed robbery that does not result in the death of any human being.

of death is different in kind from any other punishment imposed under our system of criminal justice. Because of the uniqueness of the death penalty, *Furman* held that it could not be imposed under sentencing procedures that created a substantial risk that it would be inflicted in an arbitrary and capricious manner. Mr. Justice White concluded that "the death penalty is exacted with great infrequency even for the most atrocious crimes and . . . there is no meaningful basis for distinguishing the few cases in which it is imposed from the many cases in which it is not." 408 U.S., at 313, 92 S.Ct., at 2764. Indeed, the death sentences examined by the Court in *Furman* were "cruel and unusual in the same way that being struck by lightning is cruel and unusual. For, of all the people convicted of [capital crimes], many just as reprehensible as these, the petitioners [in *Furman* were] among a capriciously selected random handful upon which the sentence of death has in fact been imposed. . . . [T]he Eighth and Fourteenth Amendments cannot tolerate the infliction of a sentence of death under legal systems that permit this unique penalty to be so wantonly and so freakishly imposed." *Id,* at 309–310, 92 S.Ct., at 2762 (Stewart, J., concurring).[36]

[23] *Furman* mandates that where discretion is afforded a sentencing body on a matter so grave as the determination of whether a human life should be taken or spared, that discretion must be suitably directed and limited so as to minimize the risk of wholly arbitrary and capricious action.

It is certainly not a novel proposition that discretion in the area of sentencing be exercised in an informed manner. We have long recognized that "[f]or the determination of sentences, justice generally requires . . . that there be taken into account the circumstances of the offense together with the character and propensities of the offender." *Pennsylvania v. Ashe,* 302 U.S. 51, 55, 58 S.Ct. 59, 61, 82 L.Ed. 43 (1937). See also *Williams v. Oklahoma,* 358 U.S. 576, 585, 79 S.Ct. 421, 426, 3 L.Ed.2d. 516 (1959); *Williams v. New York,* 337 U.S. 241, 247, 69 S.Ct. 1079, 1083, 93 L.Ed. 1337 (1949).[37] Otherwise, "the system cannot function in a consistent and rational manner." ABA Standards Relating to Sentencing Alternatives and Procedures § 4.1(a), Commentary, p. 201. See also President's Comm'n on Law Enforcement & Administration of Justice, The Challenge of Crime in a Free Society 144 (1967); Model Penal Code § 7.07, Comment 1, pp. 52–53 (Tent. Draft No. 2, 1954).[38]

---

36. This view was expressed by other Members of the Court who concurred in the judgments. See 408 U.S., at 255–257, 92 S.Ct. at 2734–2736 (Douglas, J., concurring); 291–295, 92 S.Ct. 2753–2755 (Brennan, J., concurring). The dissenters viewed this concern as the basis for the *Furman* decision: "The decisive grievance of the opinions . . . is that the present system of discretionary sentencing in capital cases has failed to produce even handed justice; . . . that the selection process has followed no rational pattern." *Id.,* at 398–399, 92 S.Ct., at 2808 (Burger, C. J., dissenting).

37. The Federal Rules of Criminal Procedure require as a matter of course that a presentence report containing information about a defendant's background be prepared for use by the sentencing judge. Fed. Rule Crim. Proc. 32(c). The importance of obtaining accurate sentencing information is underscored by the Rule's direction to the sentencing court to "afford the defendant or his counsel an opportunity to comment [on the report] and, at the discretion of the court, to introduce testimony or other information relating to any alleged factual inaccuracy contained in the presentence report." Fed. Rule Crim. Proc. 32(c)(3)(A).

38. Indeed, we hold elsewhere today that in capital cases it is constitutionally required that the sentencing authority have information sufficient to enable it to consider the character and individual circumstances of a defendant prior to imposition of a death sentence. See *Woodson v. North Carolina, post,* ——— U.S., pp. ———, 96 S.Ct. pp. 2991–2992.

The cited studies assumed that the trial judge would be the sentencing authority. If an experienced trial judge, who daily faces the difficult task of imposing sentences, has a vital need for accurate information about a defendant and the crime he committed in order to be able to impose a rational sentence in the typical criminal case, then accurate sentencing information is an indispensable prerequisite to a reasoned determination of whether a defendant shall live or die by a jury of people who may never before have made a sentencing decision.

[24] Jury sentencing has been considered desirable in capital cases in order "to maintain a link between contemporary community values and the penal system—a link without which the determination of punishment could hardly reflect "the evolving standards of decency that mark the progress of a maturing society."[39] But it creates special problems. Much of the information that is relevant to the sentencing decision may have no relevance to the question of guilt, or may even be extremely prejudicial to a fair determination of that question.[40] This problem, however, is scarcely insurmountable. Those who have studied the question suggest that a bifurcated procedure—one in which the question of sentence is not considered until the determination of guilt has been made—is the best answer. The drafters of the Model Penal Code concluded that if a unitary proceeding is used

> the determination of punishment must be based on less than all the evidence that has a bearing on that issue, such for example as a previous criminal record of the accused, or evidence must be admitted on the ground that it is relevant to sentence, though it would be excluded as irrelevant or prejudicial with respect to guilt or innocence alone. Trial lawyers understandably have little confidence in a solution that admits the evidence and trusts to an instruction to the jury that it should be considered only in determining the penalty and disregarded in assessing guilt.
>
> ... The obvious solution ... is to bifurcate the proceeding, abiding strictly by the rules of evidence until and unless there is a conviction, but once guilt has been determined opening the record to further information that is relevant to sentence. This is the analogue of the procedure in the ordinary case when capital punishment is not in issue; the court conducts a separate inquiry before imposing sentence. [Model Penal Code § 201.6, Comment 5, pp. 74–75 (Tent. Draft No. 9, 1959).]

See also *Spencer v. Texas*, 385 U.S. 554, 567–569, 87 S.Ct. 648, 655–657, 17 L.Ed.2d 606; Report of the Royal Commission on Capital Punishment, 1949–1953, Cmd. 8932, ¶¶555, 574; Knowlton, Problems of Jury Discretion in Capital Cases, 101

---

39. *Witherspoon v. Illinois*, 391 U.S. 510, 519 n. 15, 88 S.Ct. 1770, 1775, 20 L.Ed.2d 776 (1968), quoting *Trop v. Dulles*, 356 U.S. 86, 101, 78 S.Ct. 590, 598, 2 L.Ed.2d 630 (1958). See also Report of the Royal Commission on Capital Punishment, 1949–1953, Cmd. 8932, ¶571.
40. In other situations this Court has concluded that a jury cannot be expected to consider certain evidence before it on one issue, but not another. See, *e.g.*, *Bruton v. United States*, 391 U.S. 123, 88 S.Ct. 1620, 20 L.Ed.2d 476 (1968); *Jackson v. Denno*, 378 U.S. 368, 84 S.Ct. 1774, 12 L.Ed.2d 908 (1964).

U. Pa. L. Rev. 1099, 1135–1136 (1953). When a human life is at stake and when the jury must have information prejudicial to the question of guilt but relevant to the question of penalty in order to impose a rational sentence, a bifurcated system is more likely to ensure elimination of the constitutional deficiencies identified in *Furman*.[41]

[25] But the provision of relevant information under fair procedural rules is not alone sufficient to guarantee that the information will be properly used in the imposition of punishment, especially if sentencing is performed by a jury. Since the members of a jury will have had little, if any, previous experience in sentencing, they are unlikely to be skilled in dealing with the information they are given. See ABA Standards Relating to Sentencing Alternatives & Procedures, § 1.1(b), Commentary, pp. 46–47; President's Comm'n on Law Enforcement & Administration of Justice: The Challenge of Crime in a Free Society, Task Force Report: The Courts 26 (1967). To the extent that this problem is inherent in jury sentencing, it may not be totally correctible. It seems clear, however, that the problem will be alleviated if the jury is given guidance regarding the factors about the crime and the defendant that the State, representing organized society, deems particularly relevant to the sentencing decision.

The idea that a jury should be given guidance in its decisionmaking is also hardly a novel proposition. Juries are invariably given careful instructions on the law and how to apply it before they are authorized to decide the merits of a lawsuit. It would be virtually unthinkable to follow any other course in a legal system that has traditionally operated by following prior precedents and fixed rules of law.[42] See *Gasoline Products Co. v. Champlin Refining Co.*, 283 U.S. 494, 498, 51 S.Ct. 513, 514, 75 L.Ed. 1188, Fed. Rule Civ. Proc. 51. When erroneous instructions are given, retrial is often required. It is quite simply a hallmark of our legal system that juries be carefully and adequately guided in their deliberations.

[26] While some have suggested that standards to guide a capital jury's sentencing deliberations are impossible to formulate,[43] the fact is that such standards have been developed. When the drafters of the Model Penal Code faced this problem, they concluded "that it is within the realm of possibility to point to the main circumstances of aggravation and of mitigation that should be weighed *and weighed against each other,*

---

41. In *United States v. Jackson*, 390 U.S. 570, 88 S.Ct. 1209, 20 L.Ed.2d 138 (1968), the Court considered a statute that provided that if a defendant pleaded guilty, the maximum penalty would be life imprisonment, but if a defendant chose to go to trial, the maximum penalty upon conviction was death. In holding that the statute was constitutionally invalid, the Court noted:

The inevitable effect of any such provision is, of course, to discourage assertion of the Fifth Amendment right not to plead guilty and to deter exercise of the Sixth Amendment right to demand a jury trial. If the provision had no other purpose or effect than to chill the assertion of constitutional rights by penalizing those who choose to exercise them, then it would be patently unconstitutional. [*Id.,* at 581, 88 S.Ct., at 1216.]

42. But see Md.Const., art. XV, § 5: "In the trial of all criminal cases, the jury shall be the Judges of the Law, as well as of fact. . . ." See also Md. Code Ann., art. 27, § 593 (1971). Maryland judges, however, typically give advisory instructions on the law to the jury. See Md. Rule 756; *Wilson v. State,* 239 Md. 245, 210 A.2d 824 (1965).

43. See *McGautha v. California,* 402 U.S. 183, 204–207, 91 S.Ct. 1454, 1465–1467, 28 L.Ed.2d 711 (1971); Report of the Royal Commission on Capital Punishment, 1949–1953, Cmd. 8932, ¶595.

when they are presented in a concrete case." Model Penal Code § 201.6, Comment 3, p. 71 (Tent. Draft No. 9, 1959) (emphasis original).[44] While such standards are by necessity somewhat general, they do provide guidance to the sentencing authority and thereby reduce the likelihood that it will impose a sentence that fairly can be called capricious or arbitrary.[45] Where the sentencing authority is required to specify the factors it relied upon in reaching its decision, the further safeguard of meaningful appellate review is available to ensure that death sentences are not imposed capriciously or in a freakish manner.

[27] In summary, the concerns expressed in *Furman* that the penalty of death not be imposed in an arbitrary or capricious manner can be met by a carefully drafted statute that ensures that the sentencing authority is given adequate information and guidance. As a general proposition these concerns are best met by a system that provides for a bifurcated proceeding at which the sentencing authority is apprised of the information relevant to the imposition of sentence and provided with standards to guide its use of the information.

---

44. The Model Penal Code proposes the following standards:

(3) Aggravating Circumstances.

(a) The murder was committed by a convict under sentence of imprisonment.

(b) The defendant was previously convicted of another murder or of a felony involving the use or threat of violence to the person.

(c) At the time the murder was committed the defendant also committed another murder.

(d) The defendant knowingly created a great risk of death to many persons.

(e) The murder was committed while the defendant was engaged or was an accomplice in the commission of, or an attempt to commit, or flight after committing or attempting to commit robbery, rape or deviate sexual intercourse by force or threat of force, arson, burglary or kidnapping.

(f) The murder was committed for the purpose of avoiding or preventing a lawful arrest or effecting an escape from lawful custody.

(g) The murder was committed for pecuniary gain.

(h) The murder was especially heinous, atrocious or cruel, manifesting exceptional depravity.

(4) Mitigating Circumstances.

(a) The defendant has no significant history of prior criminal activity.

(b) The murder was committed while the defendant was under the influence of extreme mental or emotional disturbance.

(c) The victim was a participant in the defendant's homicidal conduct or consented to the homicidal act.

(d) The murder was committed under circumstances which the defendant believed to provide a moral justification or extenuation for his conduct.

(e) The defendant was an accomplice in a murder committed by another person and his participation in the homicidal act was relatively minor.

(f) The defendant acted under duress or under the domination of another person.

(g) At the time of the murder, the capacity of the defendant to appreciate the criminality [wrongfulness] of his conduct or to conform his conduct to the requirements of law was impaired as a result of mental disease or defect or intoxication.

(h) The youth of the defendant at the time of the crime

Model Penal Code § 210.6 (Proposed Official Draft, 1962).

45. As Mr. Justice Brennan noted in *McGautha v. California*, 402 U.S. 183, 285–286, 91 S.Ct. 1454, 1507, 28 L.Ed.2d 711 (1971) (dissenting opinion):

[E]ven if a State's notion of wise capital sentencing policy is such that a policy cannot be implemented through a formula capable of mechanical application . . . there is no reason that it should not give some guidance to those called upon to render decision.

We do not intend to suggest that only the above-described procedures would be permissible under *Furman* or that any sentencing system constructed along these general lines would inevitably satisfy the concerns of *Furman*,[46] for each distinct system must be examined on an individual basis. Rather, we have embarked upon this general exposition to make clear that it is possible to construct capital-sentencing systems capable of meeting *Furman's* constitutional concerns.[47]

B

We now turn to consideration of the constitutionality of Georgia's capital-sentencing procedures. In the wake of *Furman*, Georgia amended its capital punishment statute, but chose not to narrow the scope of its murder provisions. See Part II, *supra*. Thus, now as before *Furman*, in Georgia "[a] person commits murder when he unlawfully and with malice aforethought, either express or implied, causes the death of another human being." Ga. Code Ann., § 26–1101(a) (1972). All persons convicted of murder "shall be punished by death or by imprisonment for life." § 26–1101(c) (1972).

Georgia did act, however, to narrow the class of murderers subject to capital punishment by specifying 10 statutory aggravating circumstances, one of which must be found by the jury to exist beyond a reasonable doubt before a death sentence can ever be imposed.[48] In addition, the jury is authorized to consider any other appropriate aggravating or mitigating circumstances. § 27–2534. 1(b) (Supp. 1975). The jury is not required to find any mitigating circumstance in order to make a recommendation of mercy that is binding on the trial court, see § 27–2302 (Supp. 1975), but it must find a *statutory* aggravating circumstance before recommending a sentence of death.

These procedures require the jury to consider the circumstances of the crime and the criminal before it recommends sentence. No longer can a Georgia jury do as *Furman's* jury did: reach a finding of the defendant's guilt and then, without guidance or direc-

---

46. A system could have standards so vague that they would fail adequately to channel the sentencing decision patterns of juries with the result that a pattern of arbitrary and capricious sentencing like that found unconstitutional in *Furman* could occur.

47. In *McGautha v. California*, 402 U.S. 183, 91 S.Ct. 1454, 28 L.Ed.2d 711 (1971), this Court held that the Due Process Clause of the Fourteenth Amendment did not require that a jury be provided with standards to guide its decision whether to recommend a sentence of life imprisonment or death or that the capital-sentencing proceeding be separated from the guilt determination process. *McGautha* was not an Eighth Amendment decision, and to the extent it purported to deal with Eighth Amendment concerns, it must be read in light of the opinions in *Furman v. Georgia*. There the Court ruled that death sentences imposed under statutes that left juries with untrammeled discretion to impose or withhold the death penalty violated the Eighth and Fourteenth Amendments. While *Furman* did not overrule *McGautha*, it is clearly in substantial tension with a broad reading of *McGautha's* holding. In view of *Furman*, *McGautha* can be viewed rationally as a precedent only for the proposition that standardless jury sentencing procedures were not employed in the cases there before the Court so as to violate the Due Process Clause. We note that *McGautha's* assumption that it is not possible to devise standards to guide and regularize jury sentencing in capital cases has been undermined by subsequent experience. In view of that experience and the considerations set forth in the text, we adhere to *Furman's* determination that where the ultimate punishment of death is at issue a system of standardless jury discretion violates the Eighth and Fourteenth Amendments.

48. The text of the statute enumerating the various aggravating circumstances is set out at n. 9, *supra*.

tion, decide whether he should live or die. Instead, the jury's attention is directed to the specific circumstances of the crime: Was it committed in the course of another capital felony? Was it committed for money? Was it committed upon a peace officer or judicial officer? Was it committed in a particularly heinous way or in a manner that endangered the lives of many persons? In addition, the jury's attention is focused on the characteristics of the person who committed the crime: Does he have a record of prior convictions for capital offenses? Are there any special facts about this defendant that mitigate against imposing capital punishment (*e.g.*, his youth, the extent of his cooperation with the police, his emotional state at the time of the crime).[49] As a result, while some jury discretion still exists, "the discretion to be exercised is controlled by clear and objective standards so as to produce non-discrimininatory application." *Coley v. State,* 231 Ga. 829, 834, 204 S.E.2d 612, 615.

As an important additional safeguard against arbitrariness and caprice, the Georgia statutory scheme provides for automatic appeal of all death sentences to the State's supreme court. That court is required by statute to review each sentence of death and determine whether it was imposed under the influence of passion or prejudice, whether the evidence supports the jury's finding of a statutory aggravating circumstance, and whether the sentence is disproportionate compared to those sentences imposed in similar cases. § 27–2537(c) (Supp. 1975).

[28] In short, Georgia's new sentencing procedures require as a prerequisite to the imposition of the death penalty, specific jury findings as to the circumstances of the crime or the character of the defendant. Moreover to guard further against a situation comparable to that presented in *Furman,* the Supreme Court of Georgia compares each death sentence with the sentences imposed on similarly situated defendants to ensure that the sentence of death in a particular case is not disproportionate. On their face these procedures seem to satisfy the concerns of *Furman.* No longer should there be "no meaningful basis for distinguishing the few cases in which [the death penalty] is imposed from the many cases in which it is not." 408 U.S., at 313, 92 S.Ct., at 2764 (White, J., concurring).

The petitioner contends, however, that the changes in the Georgia sentencing procedures are only cosmetic, that the arbitrariness and capriciousness condemned by *Furman* continue to exist in Georgia—both in traditional practices that still remain and in the new sentencing procedures adopted in response to *Furman.*

First, the petitioner focuses on the opportunities for discretionary action that are inherent in the processing of any murder case under Georgia law. He notes that the state prosecutor has unfettered authority to select those persons whom he wishes to prosecute for a capital offense and to plea bargain with them. Further, at the trial the jury may choose to convict a defendant of a lesser included offense rather than find him guilty of a crime punishable by death, even if the evidence would support a capital verdict. And finally, a defendant who is convicted and sentenced to die may have his sentence commuted by the Governor of the State and the Georgia Board of Pardons and Paroles.

---

49. See *Moore v. State,* 233 Ga. 861, 865, 213 S.E.2d 829, 832 (1975).

[29 –32] The existence of these discretionary stages is not determinative of the issues before us. At each of these stages an actor in the criminal justice system makes a decision which may remove a defendant from consideration as a candidate for the death penalty. *Furman,* in contrast, dealt with the decision to impose the death sentence on a specific individual who had been convicted of a capital offense. Nothing in any of our cases suggests that the decision to afford an individual defendant mercy violates the Constitution. *Furman* held only that, in order to minimize the risk that the death penalty would be imposed on a capriciously selected group of offenders, the decision to impose it had to be guided by standards so that the sentencing authority would focus on the particularized circumstances of the crime and the defendant.[50]

The petitioner further contends that the capital-sentencing procedures adopted by Georgia in response to *Furman* do not eliminate the dangers of arbitrariness and caprice in jury sentencing that were held in *Furman* to be violative of the Eighth and Fourteenth Amendments. He claims that the statute is so broad and vague as to leave juries free to act as arbitrarily and capriciously as they wish in deciding whether to impose the death penalty. While there is no claim that the jury in this case relied upon a vague or overbroad provision to establish the existence of a statutory aggravating circumstance, the petitioner looks to the sentencing system as a whole (as the Court did in *Furman* and we do today) and argues that it fails to reduce sufficiently the risk of arbitrary infliction of death sentences. Specifically, Gregg urges that the statutory aggravating circumstances are too broad and too vague, that the sentencing procedure allows for arbitrary grants of mercy, and that the scope of the evidence and argument that can be considered at the presentence hearing is too wide.

[33] The petitioner attacks the seventh statutory aggravating circumstance, which authorizes imposition of the death penalty if the murder was "outrageously or wantonly vile, horrible or inhuman in that it involved torture, depravity of mind, or an aggravated battery to the victim," contending that it is so broad that capital punishment could be imposed in any murder case.[51] It is, of course, arguable that any murder

---

50. The petitioner's argument is nothing more than a veiled contention that *Furman* indirectly outlawed capital punishment by placing totally unrealistic conditions on its use. In order to repair the alleged defects pointed to by the petitioner, it would be necessary to require that prosecuting authorities charge a capital offense whenever arguably there had been a capital murder and that they refuse to plea bargain with the defendant. If a jury refused to convict even though the evidence supported the charge, its verdict would have to be reversed and a verdict of guilty entered or a new trial ordered, since the discretionary act of jury nullification would not be permitted. Finally, acts of executive clemency would have to prohibited. Such a system, of course, would be totally alien to our notions of criminal justice.

Moreover, it would be unconstitutional. Such a system in many respects would have the vices of the mandatory death penalty statutes we hold unconstitutional today in *Woodson v. North Carolina, post,* —— U.S., p. ——, 96 S.Ct. p. 2978, and *Roberts v. Louisiana, post,* ——U.S., p. ——, 96 S.Ct. p. 3001. The suggestion that a jury's verdict of acquittal could be overturned and a defendant retried would run afoul of the Sixth Amendment jury trial guarantee and the Double Jeopardy Clause of the Fifth Amendment. In the federal system it also would be unconstitutional to prohibit a President from deciding, as an act of executive clemency, to reprieve one sentenced to death. U.S. Const. Art. II. § 2.

51. In light of the limited grant of certiorari, see p. 2920, *supra,* we review the "vagueness" and "overbreadth" of the statutory aggravating circumstances only to consider whether their impreci-

involves depravity of mind or an aggravated battery. But this language need not be construed in this way, and there is no reason to assume that the Supreme Court of Georgia will adopt such an open-ended construction.[52] In only one case has it upheld a jury's decision to sentence a defendant to death when the only statutory aggravating circumstance found was that of § 7, see *McCorquodale v. State*, 233 Ga. 369, 211 S. E. 2d 577 (1974), and that homicide was a horrifying torture-murder.[53]

[34] The petitioner also argues that two of the statutory aggravating circumstances are vague and therefore susceptible to widely differing interpretations, thus creating a substantial risk that the death penalty will be arbitrarily inflicted by Georgia juries.[54] In light of the decisions of the Supreme Court of Georgia we must disagree. First, the petitioner attacks that part of §1 that authorizes a jury to consider whether a defendant has a "substantial history of serious assaultive criminal convictions." The Supreme Court of Georgia, however, has demonstrated a concern that the new sentencing procedures provide guidance to juries. It held this provision to be impermissibly vague in *Arnold v. State*, 236 Ga. 534, 540, 224 S.E.2d 386, 391 (1976), because it did not provide the jury with "sufficiently 'clear and objective standards.'" Second, the petitioner points to §3 which speaks of creating a "great risk of death to more than one person." While such a phrase might be susceptible to an overly broad interpretation, the Supreme Court of Georgia has not so construed it. The only case in which the court upheld a conviction in reliance on this aggravating circumstance involved a man who stood up in a church and fired a gun indiscriminately into the audience. See *Chenault v. State*, 234 Ga. 216, 215 S.E.2d 223 (1975). On the other hand, the court expressly reversed a finding of great risk when the victim was simply kidnapped in a parking lot. See *Jarrell v. State*, 234 Ga. 410, 424, 216 S.E.2d 258, 269 (1975).[55]

[35] The petitioner next argues that the requirements of *Furman* are not met here because the jury has the power to decline to impose the death penalty even if it finds

---

sion renders this capital-sentencing system invalid under the Eighth and Fourteenth Amendments because it is incapable of imposing capital punishment other than by arbitrariness or caprice.

52. In the course of interpreting Florida's new capital-sentencing statute, the Supreme Court of Florida has ruled that the phrase "especially heinous, atrocious or cruel" means a "conscienceless or pitiless crime which is unnecessarily torturous to the victim." *State v. Dixon*, 283 So.2d 1, 9 (1973). See *Proffitt v. Florida*,——U.S.——, p.——, 96 S. Ct. 2960, pp. 2968–2969, 48 L. Ed. 2d——.

53. Two other reported cases indicate that juries have found aggravating circumstances based on §7. In both cases a separate statutory aggravating circumstance was also found, and the Supreme Court of Georgia did not explicitly rely on the finding of the §7 circumstance when it upheld the death sentence. See *Jarrell v. State*, 234 Ga. 410, 216 S.E.2d 258 (1975) (state supreme court upheld finding that defendant committed two other capital felonies—kidnapping and armed robbery—in the course of the murder (§2); jury also found that the murder was committed for money (§4) and that a great risk of death to bystanders was created (§3)); *Floyd v. State*, 233 Ga. 280, 210 S.E.2d 810 (1974) (found to have committed a capital felony—armed robbery—in the course of the murder (§2)).

54. The petitioner also attacks §7 as vague. As we have noted in answering his overbreadth argument concerning §7, however, the state court has not given a broad reading to the scope of this provision, and there is no reason to think that juries will not be able to understand it. See n. 51, *supra: Proffitt v. Florida, post*, ——U.S., p.——, 96 S. Ct. p. 2960.

55. The petitioner also objects to the last part of §3 which requires that the great risk be created "by means of a weapon or device which would normally be hazardous to the lives of more than one person." While the state court has not focused on this section, it seems reasonable to assume that if a great risk in fact is created, it will be likely that a weapon or device normally hazardous to more than one person will have created it.

that one or more statutory aggravating circumstances is present in the case. This contention misinterprets *Furman*. See p. 2937, *supra*. Moreover, it ignores the role of the Supreme Court of Georgia which reviews each death sentence to determine whether it is proportional to other sentences imposed for similar crimes. Since the proportionality requirement on review is intended to prevent caprice in the decision to inflict the penalty, the isolated decision of a jury to afford mercy does not render unconstitutional death sentences imposed on defendants who were sentenced under a system that does not create a substantial risk of arbitrariness or caprice.

[36] The petitioner objects, finally, to the wide scope of evidence and argument allowed at presentence hearings. We think that the Georgia court wisely has chosen not to impose unnecessary restrictions on the evidence that can be offered at such a hearing and to approve open and far-ranging argument. See, *e.g., Brown v. State*, 235 Ga. 644, 220 S.E.2d 922 (1975). So long as the evidence introduced and the arguments made at the presentence hearing do not prejudice a defendant, it is preferable not to impose restrictions. We think it desirable for the jury to have as much information before it as possible when it makes the sentencing decision. See pp. 2932–2933, *supra*.

[37,38] Finally, the Georgia statute has an additional provision designed to assure that the death penalty will not be imposed on a capriciously selected group of convicted defendants. The new sentencing procedures require that the state supreme court review every death sentence to determine whether it was imposed under the influence of passion, prejudice, or any other arbitrary factor, whether the evidence supports the findings of a statutory aggravating circumstance, and "[w]hether the sentence of death is excessive or disproportionate to the penalty imposed in similar cases, considering both the crime and the defendant." §27–2537(c)(3) (Supp. 1975).[56] In performing its sentence review function, the Georgia court has held that "if the death penalty is only rarely imposed for an act or it is substantially out of line with sentences imposed for other acts it will be set aside as excessive." *Coley v. State*, 231 Ga. 829, 834, 204 S.E.2d 612, 616 (1974). The court on another occasion stated that "we view it to be our duty under the similarity standard to assure that no death sentence is affirmed unless in similar cases throughout the state death penalty has been imposed generally. . . . " *Moore v. State*, 233 Ga. 861, 864, 213 S.E.2d 829, 832 (1975). See also *Jarrell v. State*,

---

56. The court is required to specify in its opinion the similar cases which it took into consideration. §27–2537(e) (Supp. 1975). Special provision is made for staff to enable the court to compile data relevant to its consideration of the sentence's validity. §§ 27–2537(f)–(h) (Supp. 1975). See generally pp. 2922–2923, *supra*.

The petitioner claims that this procedure has resulted in an inadequate basis for measuring the proportionality of sentences. First, he notes that nonappealed capital convictions where a life sentence is imposed and cases involving homicides where a capital conviction is not obtained are not included in the group of cases which the Supreme Court of Georgia uses for comparative purposes. The Georgia court has the authority to consider such cases, see *Ross v. State*, 233 Ga. 361, 365–366, 211 S.E.2d 356, 359, (1974), and it does consider appealed murder cases where a life sentence has been imposed. We do not think that the petitioner's argument establishes that the Georgia courts review process is ineffective. The petitioner further complains about the Georgia court's current practice of using some pre-*Furman* cases in its comparative examination. This practice was necessary at the inception of the new procedure in the absence of any post-*Furman* capital cases available for comparison. It is not unconstitutional.

234 Ga. 410, 425, 216 S.E. 2d 258, 270 (1975) (standard is whether "juries generally throughout the state have imposed the death penalty"); *Smith v. State,* 236 Ga. 12, 24, 222 S.E. 2d 308 (1976) (found "a clear pattern" of jury behavior).

It is apparent that the Supreme Court of Georgia has taken its review responsibilities seriously. In *Coley,* it held that "[t]he prior cases indicate that the past practice among juries faced with similar factual situations and like aggravating circumstances has been to impose only the sentence of life imprisonment for the offense of rape, rather than death." 231 Ga., at 835, 204 S.E. 2d at, 617. It thereupon reduced Coley's sentence from death to life imprisonment. Similarly, although armed robbery is a capital offense under Georgia law, §26–1902 (1972), the Georgia court concluded that the death sentences imposed in this case for that crime were "unusual in that they are rarely imposed for [armed robbery]. Thus, under the test provided by statute, they must be considered to be excessive or disproportionate to the penalties imposed in similar cases." *Gregg v. State,* 233 Ga. 117, 127, 210 S.E. 2d 659, 667 (1974). The court therefore vacated Gregg's death sentences for armed robbery and has followed a similar course in every other armed robbery death penalty case to come before it. See *Floyd v. State,* 233 Ga. 280, 285, 210 S.E. 2d 810, 814 (1974); *Jarrell v. State,* 234 Ga. 410, 424–425, 216 S.E. 2d 258, 270 (1975). See *Dorsey v. State,* 236 Ga. 591, 225 S.E. 2d 418 (1976).

The provision for appellate review in the Georgia capital-sentencing system serves as a check against the random or arbitrary imposition of the death penalty. In particular, the proportionality review substantially eliminates the possibility that a person will be sentenced to die by the action of an aberrant jury. If a time comes when juries generally do not impose the death sentence in a certain kind of murder case, the appellate review procedures assure that no defendant convicted under such circumstances will suffer a sentence of death.

V

The basic concern of *Furman* centered on those defendants who were being condemned to death capriciously and arbitrarily. Under the procedures before the Court in that case, sentencing authorities were not directed to give attention to the nature or circumstances of the crime committed or to the character or record of the defendant. Left unguided, juries imposed the death sentence in a way that could only be called freakish. The new Georgia sentencing procedures, by contrast, focus the jury's attention on the particularized nature of the crime and the particularized characteristics of the individual defendant. While the jury is permitted to consider any aggravating or mitigating circumstances, it must find and identify at least one statutory aggravating factor before it may impose a penalty of death. In this way the jury's discretion is channeled. No longer can a jury wantonly and freakishly impose the death sentence; it is always circumscribed by the legislative guidelines. In addition, the review function of the Supreme Court of Georgia affords additional assurance that the concerns that prompted our decision in *Furman* are not present to any significant degree in the Georgia procedure applied here.

For the reasons expressed in this opinion, we hold that the statutory system under which Gregg was sentenced to death does not violate the Constitution. Accordingly, the judgment of the Georgia Supreme Court is affirmed.

It is so ordered.

Mr. Justice BRENNAN, dissenting.

The Cruel and Unusual Punishments Clause "must draw its meaning from the evolving standards of decency that mark the progress of a maturing society."[1] The opinions of Mr. Justice STEWART, Mr. Justice POWELL, and Mr. Justice STEVENS today hold that "evolving standards of decency" require focus not on the essence of the death penalty itself but primarily upon the procedures employed by the State to single out persons to suffer the penalty of death. Those opinions hold further that, so viewed, the Clause invalidates the mandatory infliction of the death penalty but not its infliction under sentencing procedures that Mr. Justice STEWART, Mr. Justice POWELL, and Mr. Justice STEVENS conclude adequately safeguard against the risk that the death penalty was imposed in an arbitrary and capricious manner.

In *Furman v. Georgia*, 408 U.S. 238, 257, 92 S.Ct. 2726, 2735, 33 L.Ed.2d 346 (1972), I read "evolving standards of decency" as requiring focus upon the essence of the death penalty itself and not primarily or solely upon the procedures under which the determination to inflict the penalty upon a particular person was made. I there said:

> From the beginning of our Nation, the punishment of death has stirred acute public controversy. Although pragmatic arguments for and against the punishment have been frequently advanced, this longstanding and heated controversy cannot be explained solely as the result of differences over the practical wisdom of a particular government policy. At bottom, the battle has been waged on moral grounds. The country has debated whether a society for which the dignity of the individual is the supreme value can, without a fundamental inconsistency, follow the practice of deliberately putting some of its members to death. In the United States, as in other nations of the western world, "the struggle about this punishment has been one between ancient and deeply rooted beliefs in retribution, atonement or vengeance on the one hand, and, on the other, beliefs in the personal value and dignity of the common man that were born of the democratic movement of the eighteenth century, as well as beliefs in the scientific approach to an understanding of the motive forces of human conduct, which are the result of the growth of the sciences of behavior during the nineteenth and twentieth centuries." It is this essentially moral conflict that forms the backdrop for the past changes in and the present operation of our system of imposing death as a punishment for crime. [*Id.*, at 296, 92 S.Ct., at 2755.[2]]

That continues to be my view. For the Clause forbidding cruel and unusual punishments under our constitutional system of government embodies in unique degree

---

1. *Trop v. Dulles*, 356 U.S. 86, 101, 78 S.Ct. 590, 598, 2 L.Ed.2d 630 (1958) (opinion of Warren, C.J.).

2. Quoting T. Sellin, The Death Penalty, A Report for the Model Penal Code Project of the American Law Institute 15 (1959).

moral principles restraining the punishments that our civilized society may impose on those persons who transgress its laws. Thus, I too say: "For myself, I do not hesitate to assert the proposition that the only way the law has progressed from the days of the rack, the screw and the wheel is the development of moral concepts, or, as stated by the Supreme Court . . . the application of 'evolving standards of decency. . . .'"[3]

This Court inescapably has the duty, as the ultimate arbiter of the meaning of our Constitution, to say whether, when individuals condemned to death stand before our Bar, "moral concepts" require us to hold that the law has progressed to the point where we should declare that the punishment of death, like punishments on the rack, the screw and the wheel, is no longer morally tolerable in our civilized society.[4] My opinion in *Furman v. Georgia* concluded that our civilization and the law had progressed to this point and that therefore the punishment of death, for whatever crime and under all circumstances, is "cruel and unusual" in violation of the Eighth and Fourteenth Amendments of the Constitution. I shall not again canvass the reasons that led to that conclusion. I emphasize only that foremost among the "moral concepts" recognized in our cases and inherent in the Clause is the primary moral principle that the State, even as it punishes, must treat its citizens in a manner consistent with their intrinsic worth as human beings—a punishment must not be so severe as to be degrading to human dignity. A judicial determination whether the punishment of death comports with human dignity is therefore not only permitted but compelled by the Clause. 408 U.S., at 270, 92 S.Ct., at 2742.

I do not understand that the Court disagrees that "[i]n comparison to all other punishments today . . . the deliberate extinguishment of human life by the State is uniquely degrading to human dignity." *Id.,* at 291, 92 S.Ct., at 2752. For three of my Brethren hold today that mandatory infliction of the death penalty constitutes the penalty cruel and unusual punishment. I perceive no principled basis for this limitation. Death for whatever crime and under all circumstances "is truly an awesome punishment. The calculated killing of a human being by the State involves, by its very nature, a denial of the executed person's humanity. . . . An executed person has indeed 'lost the right to have rights.'" *Id.,* at 290, 92 S.Ct. at 2752. Death is not only an unusually severe punishment, unusual in its pain, in its finality, and in its enormity, but it serves no penal purpose more effectively than a less severe punishment; therefore the principle inherent in the Clause that prohibits pointless infliction of excessive punishment when less severe punishment can adequately achieve the same purposes invalidates the punishment. *Id.,* at 279, 92 S.Ct., at 2747.

The fatal constitutional infirmity in the punishment of death is that it treats "members of the human race as nonhumans, as objects to be toyed with and discarded. [It is] thus inconsistent with the fundamental premise of the Clause that even the vilest criminal remains a human being possessed of common human dignity." *Id.,* at 273, 92 S. Ct., at 2743. As such it is a penalty that "subjects that individual to a fate forbidden by

---

3. *Novak v. Beto,* 453 F.2d 661, 672 (CA5 1971) (Tuttle, J., concurring in part and dissenting in part).
4. Tao, Beyond *Furman v. Georgia:* The Need for a Morally Based Decision on Capital Punishment, 51 Notre Dame Lawyer 722, 736 (1976).

the principle of civilized treatment guaranteed by the [Clause]."[5] I therefore would hold, on that ground alone, that death is today a cruel and unusual punishment prohibited by the Clause. "Justice of this kind is obviously no less shocking than the crime itself, and the new 'official' murder, far from offering redress for the offense committed against society, adds instead a second defilement to the first."[6]

I concur in the judgments in No. 75–5491, *Woodson v. North Carolina,* and No. 75–5844, *Roberts v. Louisiana,* that set aside the death sentences imposed under the North Carolina and Louisiana death sentence statues as violative of the Eighth and Fourteenth Amendments.

I dissent, however, from the judgments in No. 74–6257, *Gregg v. Georgia,* No. 75–5706, *Proffitt v. Florida,* and No. 75–5394, *Jurek v. Texas,* insofar as each upholds the death sentences challenged in those cases. I would set aside the death sentences imposed in those cases as violative of the Eighth and Fourteenth Amendments.

Mr. Justice MARSHALL, dissenting.

In *Furman v. Georgia,* 408 U.S. 238, 314, 92 S.Ct. 2726, 2764, 33 L.Ed.2d 346 (1972), I set forth at some length my views on the basic issue presented to the Court in these cases. The death penalty, I concluded, is a cruel and unusual punishment prohibited by the Eighth and Fourteenth Amendments. That continues to be my view.

I have no intention of retracing the "long and tedious journey," *id.,* at 370, 92 S.Ct., at 2793, that led to my conclusion in *Furman.* My sole purposes here are to consider the suggestion that my conclusion in *Furman* has been undercut by developments since then, and briefly to evaluate the basis for my Brethren's holding that the extinction of life is a permissible form of punishment under the Cruel and Unusual Punishments Clause.

In *Furman* I concluded that the death penalty is constitutionally invalid for two reasons. First, the death penalty is excessive. *Id.,* at 331–332; 342–359, 92 S.Ct., at 2773; 2778–2787. And second, the American people, fully informed as to the purposes of the death penalty and its liabilities would in my view reject it as morally unacceptable. *Id.,* at 360–369, 92 S.Ct., at 2788–2792.

Since the decision in *Furman,* the legislatures of 35 States have enacted new statutes authorizing the imposition of the death sentence for certain crimes, and Congress has enacted a law providing the death penalty for air piracy resulting in death. 49 U.S.C. (Supp. IV) §§ 1472, 1473. I would be less than candid if I did not acknowledge that these developments have a significant bearing on a realistic assessment of the moral acceptability of the death penalty to the American people. But if the constitutionality of the death penalty turns, as I have urged, on the opinion of an *informed* citizenry, then even the enactment of new death statutes cannot be viewed as conclusive. In *Furman,* I observed that the American people are largely unaware of the information critical to a judgment on the morality of the death penalty, and concluded that if they were better informed they would consider it shocking, unjust, and unacceptable. 408 U.S., at 360–369, 92 S.Ct., at 2788–2792. A recent study, conducted after the enactment of

5. *Trop v. Dulles, supra,* 356 U.S. at 99, 78 S.Ct. at 597 (opinion of Warren, C.J.).
6. A. Camus, Reflections on the Guillotine 5–6 (Fredjof-Karla Pub. 1960).

the post-*Furman* statutes, has confirmed that the American people know little about the death penalty, and that the opinions of an informed public would differ significantly from those of a public unaware of the consequences and effects of the death penalty.[1]

Even assuming, however, that the post-*Furman* enactment of statutes authorizing the death penalty renders the prediction of the views of an informed citizenry an uncertain basis for a constitutional decision, the enactment of those statutes has no bearing whatsoever on the conclusion that the death penalty is unconstitutional because it is excessive. An excessive penalty is invalid under the Cruel and Unusual Punishments Clause "even though popular sentiment may favor" it. *Id.,* at 331, 92 S.Ct., at 2773; *ante,* at 2925–2930 (Opinion of STEWART, POWELL, and STEVENS, JJ.); *Roberts v. Louisiana*——U.S.——,——,96 S.Ct. 3016, 48 L.Ed.2d——(White, J., dissenting). The inquiry here, then, is simply whether the death penalty is necessary to accomplish the legitimate legislative purposes in punishment, or whether a less severe penalty—life imprisonment—would do as well. *Furman, supra,* at 342, 92 S.Ct., at 2778 (Marshall, J., concurring).

The two purposes that sustain the death penalty as nonexcessive in the Court's view are general deterrence and retribution. In *Furman,* I canvassed the relevant data on the deterrent effect of capital punishment. 408 U.S., at 347–354, 92 S.Ct., at 2781–2785.[2] The state of knowledge at that point, after literally centuries of debate, was summarized as follows by a United Nations Committee:

> It is generally agreed between the retentionists and abolitionists, whatever their opinions about the validity of comparative studies of deterrence, that the data which now exist show no correlation between the existence of capital punishment and lower rates of capital crime. (Footnote omitted.)[3]

The available evidence, I concluded in *Furman,* was convincing that "capital punishment is not necessary as a deterrent to crime in our society." *Id.,* at 353, 92 S.Ct., at 2784.

The Solicitor General in his *amicus* brief in these cases relies heavily on a study by Isaac Ehrlich,[4] reported a year after *Furman,* to support the contention that the death penalty does deter murder. Since the Ehrlich study was not available at the time of *Furman* and since it is the first scientific study to suggest that the death penalty may have a deterrent effect, I will briefly consider its import.

---

1. Sarat and Vidmar, Public Opinion, The Death Penalty, and the Eighth Amendment: Testing the Marshall Hypothesis, 1976 Wisc. L. Rev. 171.
2. See *e.g.,* T. Sellin, The Death Penalty, A Report for the Model Penal Code Project of the American Law Institute (ALI) (1959).
3. United Nations, Department of Economic and Social Affairs, Capital Punishment, Pt. II, ¶ 159, at 123.
4. I. Ehrlich, The Deterrent Effect of Capital Punishment: A Question of Life and Death (Working Paper No. 18, National Bureau of Economic Research, November 1973); Ehrlich, The Deterrent Effect of Capital Punishment: A Question of Life and Death, 65 Am.Econ.Rev. 397 (1975) [hereinafter cited as Ehrlich 1975].

The Ehrlich study focused on the relationship in the Nation as a whole between the homicide rate and "execution risk" — the fraction of persons convicted of murder who were actually executed. Comparing the differences in homicide rate and execution risk for the years 1933 to 1969, Ehrlich found that increases in execution risk were associated *with increases in the homicide* rate.[5] But when he employed the statistical technique of multiple regression analysis to control for the influence of other variables posited to have an impact on the homicide rate,[6] Ehrlich found a negative correlation between changes in the homicide rate and changes in execution risk. His tentative conclusion was that for the period from 1933 to 1967 each additional execution in the United States might have saved eight lives.[7]

The methods and conclusions of the Ehrlich study have been severely criticized on a number of grounds.[8] It has been suggested, for example, that the study is defective because it compares execution and homicide rates on a nationwide, rather than a State-by-State, basis. The aggregation of data from all States—including those that have abolished the death penalty—obscures the relationship between murder and execution rates. Under Ehrlich's methodology, a decrease in the execution risk in one State combined with an increase in the murder rate in another State would, all other things being equal, suggest a deterrent effect that quite obviously would not exist. Indeed, a deterrent effect would be suggested if, once again all other things being equal, one State abolished the death penalty and experienced no change in the murder rate, while another State experienced an increase in the murder rate.[9]

The most compelling criticism of the Ehrlich study is that its conclusions are extremely sensitive to the choice of the time period included in the regression analysis. Analysis of Ehrlich's data reveals that all empirical support for the deterrent effect of capital punishment disappears when the five most recent years are removed from his time series—that is to say, whether a decrease in the execution risk corresponds to an increase or a decrease in the murder rate depends on the ending point of the sample period.[10] This finding has cast severe doubts on the reliability of Ehrlich's tentative

---

5. Ehrlich 1975, *supra*, n. 4, 409.

6. The variables other than execution risk included probability of arrest, probability of conviction given arrest, national aggregate measures of the percentage of the population between age 14 and 24, the unemployment rate, the labor force participation rate, and estimated per capita income.

7. Ehrlich 1975, *supra*, n. 4, at 398, 414.

8. See Passell & Taylor, The Deterrent Effect of Capital Punishment: Another View (March 1975) (unpublished Columbia University Discussion Paper 74–7509); Passell, The Deterrent Effect of the Death Penalty: A Statistical Test, 28 Stan. L. Rev. 61 (1975); Baldus & Cole, A Comparison of the Work of Thorsten Sellin and Isaac Ehrlich on the Deterrent Effect of Capital Punishment, 85 Yale L. J. 170 (1975); Bowers & Pierce, The Illusion of Deterrence in Isaac Ehrlich's Research on Capital Punishment, 85 Yale L. J. 187 (1975); Peck, The Deterrent Effect of Capital Punishment: Ehrlich and His Critics, 85 Yale L. J. 359 (1976). See also Ehrlich, Deterrence: Evidence and Inference, 85 Yale L. J. 209 (1975); Ehrlich, Rejoinder, 85 Yale L. J. 368 (1976). In addition to the items discussed in text, criticism has been directed at the quality of Ehrlich's data, his choice of explanatory variables, his failure to account for the interdependence of those variables, and his assumptions as to the mathematical form of the relationship between the homicide rate and the explanatory variables.

9. See Baldus & Cole, *supra*, n. 8, at 175–177.

10. Bowers & Pierce, *supra*, n. 8, at 197–198. See also Passell & Taylor, *supra*, n. 8 (Appendix E to Brief for Petitioner in *Jurek v. Texas*, No. 75–5394, at 2–66—2–68).

conclusions.[11] Indeed, a recent regression study, based on Ehrlich's theoretical model but using cross-section state data for the years 1950 and 1960 found no support for the conclusion that executions act as a deterrent.[12]

The Ehrlich study, in short, is of little, if any, assistance in assessing the deterrent impact of the death penalty. Accord, *Commonwealth v. O'Neal,* 339 N.E.2d 676, 684 (Mass. 1975). The evidence I reviewed in *Furman*[13] remains convincing, in my view that "capital punishment is not necessary as a deterrent to crime in our society." 408 U.S., at 353, 92 S.Ct., at 2784. The justification for the death penalty must be found elsewhere.

The other principal purpose said to be served by the death penalty is retribution.[14] The notion that retribution can serve as a moral justification for the sanction of death finds credence in the opinion of my Brothers STEWART, POWELL, and STEVENS, and that of my Brother White in *Roberts v. Louisiana, post.* See also *Furman v. Georgia,* 408 U.S. 238, 394–395, 92 S.Ct., 2726, 2806, 33 L.Ed.2d 346 (1972)(Burger, C. J., dissenting). It is this notion that I find to be the most disturbing aspect of today's unfortunate decision.

The concept of retribution is a multifaceted one, and any discussion of its role in the criminal law must be undertaken with caution. On one level, it can be said that the notion of retribution or reprobation is the basis of our insistence that only those who have broken the law be punished, and in this sense the notion is quite obviously central to a just system of criminal sanctions. But our recognition that retribution plays a crucial role in determining who may be punished by no means requires approval of retribution as a general justification for punishment.[15] It is the question whether retribution can provide a moral justification for punishment—in particular, capital punishment—that we must consider.

My Brothers STEWART, POWELL, and STEVENS offer the following explanation of the retributive justification for capital punishment:

> The instinct for retribution is part of the nature of man, and chan-
> neling that instinct in the administration of criminal justice serves an
> important purpose in promoting the stability of a society governed by
> law. When people begin to believe that organized society is unwilling or
> unable to impose upon criminal offenders the punishment they "de-

---

11. See Bowers & Pierce, *supra,* n. 8, at 197–198; Baldus & Cole, *supra,* n. 8, at 181, 183–185; Peck, *supra,* n. 8, at 366–367.

12. Passell, *supra,* n. 8.

13. See also Bailey, Murder and Capital Punishment: Some Further Evidence, 45 Am.J. Orthopsychiatry 669 (1975); Bowers, Executions in America 121–162 (1974).

14. In *Furman,* I considered several additional purposes arguably served by the death penalty. 408 U.S., at 342, 355–358, 92 S. Ct., at 2778, 2785–2787. The only additional purpose mentioned in the opinions in these cases is specific deterrence—preventing the murderer from committing another crime. Surely life imprisonment and, if necessary, solitary confinement would fully accomplish this purpose. Accord, *Commonwealth v. O'Neal,* 339 N.E.2d 676, 685 (Mass. 1975); *People v. Anderson,* 6 Cal.3d 628, 651, 100 Cal.Rptr. 152, 168, 493, P2d 880 (1972), cert. denied *sub nom. California v. Anderson,* 406 U.S. 958, 92 S.Ct. 2060, 32 L.Ed.2d 344 (1972).

15. See, *e.g.,* H. L. A. Hart, Punishment and Responsibility 8–10, 71–83 (1968); H. Packer, The Limits of the Criminal Sanction 38–39, 66 (1968).

serve," then there are sown the seeds of anarchy — of self-help, vigilante justice, and lynch law. [*Ante,* at 2930, quoting from *Furman v. Georgia,* 408 U.S., at 308, 92 S.Ct., at 2761 (Stewart, J., concurring).]

This statement is wholly inadequate to justify the death penalty. As my Brother BREN-NAN stated in *Furman,* "[t]here is no evidence whatever that utilization of imprisonment rather than death encourages private blood feuds and other disorders." 408 U.S., at 303, 92 S.Ct., at 2758.[16] It simply defies belief to suggest that the death penalty is necessary to prevent the American people from taking the law into their own hands.

In a related vein, it may be suggested that the expression of moral outrage through the imposition of the death penalty serves to reinforce basic moral values—that it marks some crimes as particularly offensive and therefore to be avoided. The argument is akin to a deterrence argument, but differs in that it contemplates the individual's shrinking from anti-social conduct not because he fears punishment, but because he has been told in the strongest possible way that the conduct is wrong. This contention, like the previous one, provides no support for the death penalty. It is inconceivable that any individual concerned about conforming his conduct to what society says is "right" would fail to realize that murder is "wrong" if the penalty were simply life imprisonment.

The foregoing contentions—that society's expression of moral outrage through the imposition of the death penalty pre-empts the citizenry from taking the law into its own hands and reinforces moral values—are not retributive in the purest sense. They are essentially utilitarian in that they portray the death penalty as valuable because of its beneficial results. These justifications for the death penalty are inadequate because the penalty is, quite clearly I think, not necessary to the accomplishment of those results.

There remains for consideration, however, what might be termed the purely retributive justification for the death penalty—that the death penalty is appropriate, not because of its beneficial effect on society, but because the taking of the murderer's life is itself morally good.[17] Some of the language of the plurality's opinion appears positively to embrace this notion of retribution for its own sake as a justification for capital punishment.[18] My Brothers STEWART, POWELL, and STEVENS state:

[T]he decision that capital punishment may be the appropriate sanction in extreme cases is an expression of the community's belief that

---

16. See *Commonwealth v. O'Neal,* 339 N.E.2d 676, 687 (Mass. 1975); Bowers, *supra,* n. 13, at 335; Sellin *supra,* n. 2, at 79.

17. See H. L. A. Hart, *supra,* n. 15, at 72, 74–75, 234–235; H. Packer, *supra,* n. 15, at 37–39.

18. Mr. Justice White's view of retribution as a justification for the death penalty is not altogether clear. "The widespread reenactment of the death penalty," he states at one point, "answers any claims that life imprisonment is adequate punishment to satisfy the need for reprobation or retribution." *Roberts v. Louisiana,*——U.S.——,——, 96 S.Ct. 3001, 3016,——L.Ed.2d——(White, J., dissenting). But Mr. Justice White later states: "It will not do to denigrate these legislative judgments as some form of vestigial savagery or as purely retributive in motivation; for they are solemn judgments, reasonably based, that imposition of the death penalty will save the lives of innocent persons." *Id.,* at——, 96 S. Ct. at 3017.

certain crimes are themselves so grievous an affront to humanity that the only adequate response may be the penalty of death. [*Ante,* at 2930 (footnote omitted).]

The plurality then quotes with approval from Lord Justice Denning's remarks before the British Royal Commission on Capital Punishment:

The truth is that some crimes are so outrageous that society insists on adequate punishment, because the wrongdoer deserves it, irrespective of whether it is a deterrent or not. [*Ante,* at 2930 n. 30.]

Of course it may be that these statements are intended as no more than observations as to the popular demands that it is thought must be responded to in order to prevent anarchy. But the implication of the statements appears to me to be quite different— namely, that society's judgment that the murderer "deserves" death must be respected not simply because the preservation of order requires it, but because it is appropriate that society make the judgment and carry it out. It is this latter notion, in particular, that I consider to be fundamentally at odds with the Eighth Amendment. See *Furman v. Georgia,* 408 U.S., at 343–345, 92 S.Ct., at 2779–2780 (Marshall, J., concurring). The mere fact that the community demands the murderer's life in return for the evil he has done cannot sustain the death penalty, for as the plurality reminds us, "the Eighth Amendment demands more than that a challenged punishment be acceptable to contemporary society." *Ante,* at 2929. To be sustained under the Eighth Amendment, the death penalty must "[comport] with the basic concept of human dignity at the core of the Amendment," *ante,* at 2929 (opinion of STEWART, POWELL and STEVENS, JJ.); the objective in imposing it must be "[consistent] with our respect for the dignity of other men." *Id.,* at 2930. *See Trop v. Dulles,* 356 U.S. 86, 100, 78 S.Ct., 590, 598, 2 L. Ed.2d 630 (1958). Under these standards, the taking of life "because the wrongdoer deserves it" surely must fall, for such a punishment has as its very basis the total denial of the wrongdoer's dignity and worth.[19]

The death penalty, unnecessary to promote the goal of deterrence or to further any legitimate notion of retribution, is an excessive penalty forbidden by the Eighth and Fourteenth Amendments. I respectfully dissent from the Court's judgment upholding the sentences of death imposed upon the petitioners in these cases.

---

19. See *Commonwealth v. O'Neal,* 339 N.E.2d 676, 687 (Mass. 1975); *People v. Anderson,* 6 Cal. 3d 628, 651, 100 Cal.Rptr. 152, 168, 493 P.2d 880 (1972), cert. denied *sub nom. California v. Anderson,* 406 U.S. 958, 92 S.Ct. 2060, 32 L.Ed.2d 344 (1972).

Capital Punishment and Deterrence: Some Considerations in Dialogue Form

David A. Conway

P: I am happy to learn that our state legislature is trying to restore C.P.[1] Many of the legislators think they can pass a bill prescribing C.P. that the Supreme Court would not find unconstitutional.

O: Yes, that is true in many legislatures.[2] But it is hardly something I am happy about. Not only do I think C.P. is wrong, but I see a great danger in the present situation. The prime question in the minds of too many legislators seems to be, How do we draft laws that the court would not object to? The more basic question, Is C.P. ethically justifiable? may be lost sight of altogether.

P: Perhaps, but if necessary, I think C.P. can be justified easily enough.

O: Are you some sort of retributivist?

P: Not at all. I hold that deterrence is the aim of punishment and that it is the central issue in the minds of legislators. They, as I am, are worried about the sheer lack of personal safety in our society.

Reprinted with permission from *Philosophy and Public Affairs,* vol. 3, no. 4 (Summer 1974). Copyright © 1974 by Princeton University Press. David A. Conway is an Associate Professor of Philosophy at the University of Missouri—St. Louis.

1. I shall use "C.P." for "capital punishment" throughout this paper.
2. In addition, President Nixon in March of 1973 called for restoration of C.P., saying that he is convinced that it deters the commission of some types of crimes.

O: I didn't know that you had any strong feelings on this subject.

P: I didn't until recently. Then I read an interview in a newspaper. Ernest van den Haag, in response to questions from Philip Nobile, gives some arguments for C.P. that I find very convincing.[3] And I would bet that legislators do too.

I. The Preference Argument

O: How can you think that C.P. is an effective deterrent? What about all of the statistical studies that have failed to show that this is true?[4]

P: I admit that such studies are inconclusive. But I am not relying on them to show the deterrent value of C.P. A simpler fact will do the job. Consider this exchange in the van den Haag interview:

> *Nobile:* Is it true that capital punishment is a better deterrent than irrevocable life imprisonment?
>
> *van den Haag:* Yes, and that I can prove. I noticed a story in the paper the other day about a French heroin smuggler who pleaded guilty in a New York court because, as his lawyer admitted, he preferred irrevocable life imprisonment here to the guillotine in France.
>
> In fact, all prisoners prefer life. For even if the sentence is irrevocable, as long as there's life, psychologically, there's hope.

O: That argument is pretty popular among policemen and some editorial writers. In fact, Hugo Bedau in *The Death Penalty in America* includes a passage from Police Chief Allen which gives this argument. Bedau also mentions it in one of his essays in that volume, but he does not argue against it, although he does argue against some pro-C.P. views of Sidney Hook and Jacques Barzun.[5]

P: What does that mean? That serious philosophers do not bother to argue against policemen and editorial writers? or that this particular argument is too stupid to bother with?

O: I'm not sure what it means. But I do think this argument is worth taking seriously. For it is intuitively plausible, and it rests on an empirical premise which seems to me to be almost indisputably true. That is, almost all of us would, at least consciously, given the present choice between being subjected to life imprisonment and to C.P., choose the former. Still, the argument is not convincing.

P: Why not?

O: There are a couple of reasons. First, you are saying that if, given that I must choose between some punishment x and another punishment y, I would strongly prefer y,

---

3. *St. Louis Globe-Democrat*, 6–7 January 1973. The arguments that van den Haag puts forth in this interview are currently quite popular among "intellectual conservatives" (e.g. writers for the *National Review* and conservative newspapers). The importance of his views is much greater than would be indicated just by the fact that one person happened to express them in a newspaper interview.

4. See, for instance, Hugo Bedau, *The Death Penalty in America* (Garden City: Doubleday, 1967) especially chapters 6 and 7.

5. Ibid., pp. 135–136, 220.

then it follows that knowing that x will be inflicted on me if I perform some action will more effectively deter me from performing that action than will knowing that y will be inflicted. But consider that, given the choice, I would strongly prefer one thousand years in hell to eternity there. Nonetheless, if one thousand years in hell were the penalty for some action, it would be quite sufficient to deter me from performing that action. The additional years would do nothing to discourage me further.

Similarly, the prospect of the death penalty, while worse, may not have any greater deterrent effect than does that of life imprisonment. In fact, I would imagine that either prospect would normally deter the rational man, while the man irrational enough not to be deterred by life imprisonment wouldn't be deterred by anything. [6] So, the deterrent value of the two may be indistinguishable in practice even though one penalty may be definitely preferable to the other, if one is forced to choose between them.

P: I see. Still there could be potential killers who are deterred by one and not by the other.

O: Of course there *could be*. But have you forgotten what this discussion is about? You were supposed to have a proof that there are such people.

P: OK. What is your other argument?

O: Well, before, I argued that C.P. may not be an additional deterrent even if we assume that the criminal expects to be caught. But surely most do not expect to be caught or they hold no expectations at all, i.e. they are acting in "blind passion." In these cases, the punishment is irrelevant. If, however, we assume at least minimal rationality on the part of the criminal, he knows that there is some chance that he will be caught. Let us say that he believes that there is a one in ten chance that he will be, and also that the actuality of punishment x is sufficient to deter him from performing some actions from which punishment y would not deter him. It does not follow from this that a one in ten chance of x would deter him from performing any actions that a one in ten chance of y would not. To put it abstractly, we can assign to the death penalty 100 "disutility units" and to life imprisonment 50 "disutility units" to represent a significant difference between their undesirability. If the chance of either punishment actually being inflicted, however, is only one in ten, the difference becomes much less significant (i.e. $1/10 \cdot 100$ vs. $1/10 \cdot 50$, or 10 vs. 5 disutility units). We do not, of course, actually think in such precise terms of probability and utility units, but we do often approximate such reasoning. For instance, if it is important that I get to my destination quickly, I may be willing to (actually) be fined for speeding while I am not willing to (actually) smash up my car and possibly myself. The difference between the two "penalties," if actually inflicted, is very great, great enough that one deters and the other does not. If, however, I know that there is only a slight chance of either occurring, the deterrent effect of the threats may be virtually indistinguishable, and I may speed on my way.

There are, then, at least two reasons for not equating "what we fear the most" with "what will most effectively deter us." Both of these are overlooked by those of you who give the "preference argument."

---

6. For a similar supposition, see Bedau, p. 272. There, however, the point is not made specifically in relation to the "Preference Argument."

II. The Rational Person –
Deterrent Argument

O: What else did you find in the van den Haag interview?

P: Well, there is this.

> *Nobile:* Most capital crimes are crimes of passion in which family members or friends kill each other. You can't stop this sort of thing with the threat of execution.
>
> *van den Haag:* It's perfectly true that the irrational person won't be deterred by any penalty. But to the extent that murder is an act of passion, the death penalty has already deterred all rational persons.

O: And you agree with that?

P: I suppose not. It does seem to be a pretty clear case of *post hoc, ergo propter hoc* reasoning. [7] Still, there is a smaller point to be made here. Van den Haag says that C.P. has deterred rational persons. We do not know that it has. But, we also don't know that it hasn't. You opponents of C.P. are always saying something like, "Virtually all capital crimes are committed by persons in an irrational frame of mind. Therefore, C.P. (or any other punishment) cannot be regarded as a deterrent." So, you say, rational persons just do not (often) murder; I say, maybe they do not because of the threat of C.P. And so you cannot simply cite the fact that they do not as an argument against C.P.

O: I have to grant you that point. What you say has been often enough said before, and, yet, without attempting to answer the point, my fellow opponents of C.P. too often just go on saying "rational people seldom murder." We must seriously try to show that rational people seldom murder even in the absence of C.P., rather than just continuing to recite "rational people seldom murder."

III. The Best-bet Argument

O: Do you have any more arguments to trot out?

P: There is another in the van den Haag interview, and I have been saving the best for last.

O: Let's hear it.

P: All right.

> *Nobile:* You're pretty cavalier about executions, aren't you?
>
> *van den Haag:* If we have capital punishment, our risk is that it is unnecessary and no additional deterrence is achieved. But if we do not have it, our risk is that it might have deterred future murderers and spared future victims. Then it's a matter of which risk you prefer and I prefer to protect the victims.
>
> *Nobile:* But you're gambling with the lives of condemned men who might otherwise live.
>
> *van den Haag:* You're right. But we're both gambling. I'm gambling by executing and you're gambling by not executing.

---

7. For a more complete critique of the same argument, see Bedau, pp. 268–269.

We can see the force of this more clearly if we specify all of the possible outcomes ("C.P. works" means "C.P. is a uniquely effective deterrent.")

	C.P. Works	C.P. Does Not Work
We bet C.P. works	(a) We win: some murderers die, but innocents, who would otherwise die, are spared.	(b) We lose: Some murderers die for no purpose. The lives of others are unaffected.
We bet C.P. does not work	(c) We lose: Murderers live, but some innocents needlessly die.	(d) We win: Murderers live and the lives of others are unaffected.

To make it more clear, suppose that we assign utility values in this way:

Each murderer saved (not executed)	$+5$
Each murderer executed	-5
Each innocent person saved (not murdered)	$+10$
Each innocent person murdered	-10

And assume also that, if C.P. works, each execution saves five innocents (a conservative estimate, surely). Potential gains and losses can be represented as:

$$
\begin{array}{ll}
\text{(a)} & -5 \\
& \underline{+50} \\
& +45
\end{array}
\qquad
\begin{array}{ll}
\text{(b)} & -5
\end{array}
$$

$$
\begin{array}{ll}
\text{(c)} & +5 \\
& \underline{-50} \\
& -45
\end{array}
\qquad
\begin{array}{ll}
\text{(d)} & +5
\end{array}
$$

Now we can clearly see that not only do we have less to lose by betting on C.P., but we also have more to gain. It would be quite irrational not to bet on it.

O: Pascal lives.

P: What's that?

O: Nothing. But look, you have to admit that there is an unsavory air about the argument. Nobile is right; the very notion of gambling with human lives seems morally repugnant.

P: Maybe. But the fact is, as van den Haag says, we are also gambling if we do not execute, so you would do so as much as I.

O: If so, then what your argument does is make very apparent the sort of point retributivists have always made. In Kantian terms, this sort of gambling with human lives is a particularly crude form of treating human beings as means rather than ends.

P: You are willing to take a retributivist position in order to avoid the force of the argument?

O: No. I will leave vengeance to the Lord, if he wants it. Anyway, I am not convinced there are not other reasons for rejecting your argument. I cannot get over the feeling that, in some sense, you are gambling with lives in a way that I am not.

P: Maybe that is a feeling that requires therapy to get over. Let me say it once more: If either of us loses our wager, human lives are needlessly lost. Granted, if you win yours, no life is lost at all, while if I win mine, the criminal loses his; but since he loses it and others gain theirs, that cannot be what is disturbing you. There is nothing disturbing about the prospect of saving many innocents.

O: Wait now. I think that I am beginning to see what is going on here. Look at your utility summary again. You rightly say that (a) which represents the situation *if* we bet on C. P. *and win* is the best possible outcome, while (c), the situation which results *if* we bet against it *and lose,* is the worst. Now if this were a case of pure uncertainty, if we had no idea at all whether C. P. deters, these outcomes might be the only thing to consider. But surely this is not such a case: We do have statistical studies; we do have some rudimentary knowledge of criminal psychology; at least, we have some common sense idea of how people behave and why. All of this may be very inconclusive, but still we cannot say we have total uncertainty.

P: No. I never imagined we did have that.

O: So when we are weighing the alternative outcomes, we cannot *just* consider which is most or least desirable; we must consider the probability of that outcome occurring, even though our probability estimates must be very subjective.

P: Of course. I had that in mind all along.

O: It seems to me that that might be at least obscured in van den Haag's statements and in your earlier ones. You sounded as if it were just a matter of both of us gambling and recommending that we decide which to take on the basis of the possible outcomes alone, without taking into account the probabilities of those outcomes occurring. Anyway, can we now, for the sake of argument if nothing else, find a probability we can agree on?

P: I really think that it is at least as likely that it deters as that it does not.

O: I can see no reason at all for such an evaluation.

P: All right. I was going to add that I will not insist on it. Grant me that there is at least a one in five chance that C.P. deters. That is asking little enough. And it is all I need for my argument. In fact, that such a low assessment of the probabilities is all that is needed is, essentially, the point of the argument.

O: Let's see how that works.

P: It's very simple. Even if there is only a .2 probability that C. P. works, the calculations come out this way: if we bet for C. P.,

(a) $.2 \cdot +45 = +9$. That is, there is a one in five chance of gaining 45 utility units. Similarly, there is a .8 chance that I would take a life needlessly.

(b) $.8 \cdot -5 = -4$

And, if we bet against C. P., then

(c) $.2 \cdot -45 = -9$
(d) $.8 \cdot +5 = +4$

So, even if it is improbable that C. P. deters, we should bet that it does.

O: But that calculation is all wrong.

P: Wrong? All I did was multiply possible outcomes by the probability of obtaining those outcomes. What can be wrong with that?

O: In (a), there is not a .2 chance of gaining 45 utility units. There is certainty of there being -5 utility units, a certainty of the criminal losing his life, and a .2 chance of a compensating $+50$ units, of C. P. being a deterrent. And in (b), there isn't a .8 chance of taking a life needlessly; there is a certainty of taking a life. That it is needless simply means there is no compensating gain. So the outcome for (a) is not $+9$, it is $+5$. Let me put the whole thing properly.

(a) $-5 + .2 \cdot +50 = +5$
(b) -5
(c) $+5 + .2 \cdot -50 = -5$
(d) $+5$

This looks very different than it did before.[8] And once the betting situation is put in this way, the correct way, the source of the "worry" that the argument causes becomes clear, and we can seriously evaluate the argument.

P: I see how what you have said changes the advisability of the various wagers, but you seem to mean more than that.

O: I think I do. The argument was put badly from the start. It was put in a way which is reflected in your erroneous utility calculation. Van den Haag says, "It's a matter of which risk you prefer and I prefer to protect the victims." This immediately makes us think of the situation in a misleading way, for it seems to imply that while I would risk the lives of potential victims, he would risk the lives of convicted criminals. Or, minimally, it implies that there are risks of a like kind on both sides. But he isn't *risking* the lives of criminals; he is taking their lives and risking that some further good will come of this.

Put the same thing a slightly different way. It has been said in our discussion that on either bet, the result could be the needless loss of life. This makes the bets look more parallel than they are. If we bet your way, lives *have been lost,* and the risk is that this is needless. If we bet my way, it is *possible* that *lives may be lost,* needlessly. The difference between *lives lost,* perhaps needlessly, and *perhaps lives lost,* strikes me as a very significant one.

Now it should be clear that there is a sense in which you are gambling and I am not. It is exactly the sense in which I would be gambling if I used my last ten dollars to buy a lottery ticket but would not be if I used the money for groceries. Opting for a certain good, rather than risking it on a chance of a greater future good, is exactly what we mean when we say we refuse to gamble. Not gambling is taking the sure thing.

On the plausible moral principle, gambling with human lives is wrong, I can, then, reject the "Best-bet Argument."

P: But if you understand "gambling" as not taking the sure thing, that moral principle is much too strong. Unless you have infallible knowledge that C.P. deters, on that principle it could never be justified, even under conditions in which you would want to adopt it. For even if it were ninety *percent* certain that it deters, you would still be gambling. And there are other circumstances in which we must gamble with lives in this way. Suppose you were almost, but not quite, certain a madman was about to set off all the bombs in the Western hemisphere. On that principle, you would not be justified in shooting him, even if it were the only possible way to stop him.

O: Yes, I suppose that I must grant you that. But perhaps my suppositions that

---

8. The precise number of utility units assigned to the alternatives is, of course, not significant. What is significant is the difference that results from the two ways of calculating. (I do not think that the rather simple uses I make of utility calculations in this paper assume any particular interpretation of utility theory; whether they are taken as a measure of "satisfaction" on the basis of which we prefer some thing or they simply reflect the fact that we prefer some things, the calculations would be the same and, I take it, at least roughly parallel our rational decision making.)

gambling is taking the risk and that gambling with human lives is wrong, taken together, at least partially account for my intuitive revulsion with van den Haag's argument.

P: That may be. But so far, your intuitions have come to nothing in producing a genuine objection to the argument. I might add that I cannot even agree with your intuition that not gambling is taking the sure thing. Don't we sometimes disapprove of the person who refuses to take out life insurance or automobile liability insurance on the grounds that he is unwisely gambling that he will not die prematurely or be responsible for a highway accident? And he is taking the sure thing, keeping the premium money in his pocket. So, in common sense terms, failure to take a wise bet is sometimes "gambling."

O: You are right again. And I thank you.

P: For what?

O: For saying just what I needed to hear in order to get straight on this whole business. As I indicated before, once we properly set out the betting situation, it does not appear that your proponents *have* such a good bet. But in addition, I have (along with Nobile) been plagued by the feeling that there is something *in principle* wrong with the argument, that you would gamble with human lives while I would not. Now I understand that these two objections are actually only one objection.

P: How so?

O: Your insurance examples make the point. They show that what we intuitively think of as "gambling" is simply taking the more risky course of action, i.e. making a bad bet. So, my intuitive worry resulted simply from my conviction that your bet on C.P. is "gambling," i.e. that it is the riskier course of action; or, and this comes to the same thing, it is a *bad* bet.

P: So you admit that there is nothing in principle wrong with my argument. That it all depends on whether the bet on C.P. is a good bet.

O: I think I must. But that does not change my views about C.P. Once the bet is clarified, it should be clear that you are asking us to risk too much, to actually take a human life on far too small a chance of saving others. It is just a rotten bet.

P: But it is not. As I have said, the life of each murderer is clearly worth much less than the life of an innocent, and, besides, each criminal life lost may save many innocents.

O: This business about how much lives are "worth" seems pretty suspicious to me. According to some, human life qua human life is sacred and so all lives have the same value. According to others, the continued life of an innocent child is of much less importance than that of a criminal, since it is the criminal, qua criminal, who needs a chance to cleanse his soul. Or we could consider the potential social usefulness of the individual. If we do this, it is by no means obvious that the average murderer has less potential than the average person (consider Chessman or Leopold).

P: How can you talk like that? Have you ever seen the battered, maimed body of an innocent child, raped and brutally murdered? Compare the value of that life against that of the beast who performed the deed, and then can you doubt that the child is worth 10,000 times the criminal?

O: That seems to me to be based on a desire for revenge against "the beast," rather than on any evaluation of the "value of different lives." I admit to sharing such feelings, in some moods, at least, but it is not at all clear how they are relevant. Anyway, let's drop this. I am willing to rely on my feelings and grant, for argument purposes, that the life of a murderer is worth somewhat less than that of an innocent.

The basic problem with your wager is simply that we have no reason to think C.P does work, and in the absence of such reason, the probability that it does is virtually zero. In general, your proponents seem confused about evidence. First, you say C.P. deters. Then you are confronted with evidence such as: State A and State B have virtually identical capital crime rates but State A hasn't had C.P. for one hundred years. You reply, for instance, that this could be because State A has more Quakers, who are peace-loving folk and so help to keep the crime rate down. And, you say, with C.P. and all those Quakers, State A, perhaps, could have had an even lower crime rate.[9] Since we do not know about all such variables, the evidence is "inconclusive."[10] Here, "inconclusive" can only mean that while the evidence does not indicate that C.P. deters, it also does not demonstrate that it does not.

The next thing we see is your proponents saying that we just do not know whether C.P. deters or not, since the evidence is "inconclusive." But for this to follow, "inconclusive" must mean something like "tends to point both ways." The only studies available, on your own account, fail to supply any evidence at all that it *does* deter. From this, we cannot get "inconclusive" in the latter sense; we can't say that "we just don't know" whether it deters; we can only conclude, "we have no reason to think it does." Its status as a deterrent is no different from, e.g. prolonged tickling of murderers' feet. It could deter, but why think it does?

P: That's an absurd comparison that only a professional philosopher could think of. Common sense tells us that C.P. is a likely deterrent and foot-tickling is not.

O: I don't see how we can rely very heavily on the common sense of a law-abiding man to tell us how murderers think and why they act. Common sense also tells us that pornography should inflame the passions and therefore increase sex crimes, but Denmark's recent experience indicates quite the opposite.

P: So you demand that we have definite, unequivocal evidence and very high probability that C.P. deters before it could be said to be justifiable.

O: No, I never said that. That is what most of my fellow opponents of C.P. seem to demand. In fact, even though this would probably horrify most opponents, I think the "Best-bet Argument" shows that that demand is too strong. Given the possible gains and losses, if there is even a strong possibility that it works, I do not think it would be irrational to give it another try. But we should do so in full cognizance of the betting situation. We would be taking lives on the chance that there will be more than compensating saving of lives. And, I also think that it is damned difficult to show that there is even a strong possibility that C.P. deters.

P: Not really. Consider the fact that, given a choice between life imprisonment and C.P., prisoners always prefer . . .

O: Good night.

---

9. Neglecting the fact that, with C.P., the crime rate also could have been higher (cf. Sidney Hook, "The Death Sentence," in Bedau, pp. 147 –148).

10. For such a use of "inconclusive," see J. Edgar Hoover, in Bedau, p. 134.

Cruel Punishment and Respect for Persons: Super Due Process for Death

Margaret Jane Radin

T he Supreme Court now holds that in death penalty cases the eighth amendment, which speaks only of "cruel and unusual punishments," requires sentencing procedures amounting to a kind of super due process. In *Lockett v. Ohio*,[1] Chief Justice Burger reasoned that the "degree of respect due the uniqueness of the individual" renders execution a cruel punishment if sentence is imposed under a statute limiting the scope of evidence that the defendant may offer in mitigation of her crime. In its focus on procedural safeguards, *Lockett* is the child of *Gregg v. Georgia* and

---

Reprinted with permission from *Southern California Law Review*, vol. 53, no. 4, May 1980. Copyright 1980 by the University of Southern California. Margaret Jane Radin is a Professor of Law at the University of Southern California.

[Author's note] I am grateful to many colleagues and friends whose support and criticism contributed to this paper, especially Drucilla L. Cornell, Herbert Morris and Michael H. Shapiro. I also wish to acknowledge the able research assistance of Michael O'Halloran, a third-year student at the U.S.C. Law Center.

1. 438 U.S. 586, 605 (1978). *Lockett* was decided together with a companion case, Bell v. Ohio, 438 U.S. 637 (1978). The super due process theory was relied on by a four judge plurality. In effect, super due process is the holding of the Court, since Justices Brennan and Marshall, who oppose the death penalty per se, always vote with the plurality who espouse the super due process theory when that theory results in reversal of a death sentence. For a more extensive discussion of *Lockett*, see text accompanying notes 31–34 and note 64 *infra*.

its four companions.[2] Those five 1976 cases validated the death penalty if imposed under procedural statutes that guide the sentencer's discretion by directing the sentencer to weigh aggravating and mitigating factors. Three members of the Court in *Gregg* (Justices Stewart, Powell, and Stevens) rendered this the reigning approach to analysis of the cruelty (vel non) of execution for murder,[3] and in *Lockett,* Justice Burger joined in following their approach. Thus, four members of the Court have embraced the proposition that a process, and not just the event it authorizes, can be considered cruel in the constitutional sense.[4] Since 1971, no majority approach to review of executions for murder has existed.[5] The Court has wrestled for almost a decade with the death penalty, but has not yet worked out an analysis that can be applied satisfactorily and consistently either to permit or to prevent execution.

This Article will draw out some implications of the super due process approach to judicial review of execution for murder, and the underlying notion that a process may be considered cruel. In particular it will explore the concept of respect for persons in its relationship both to the procedural due process strain in eighth amendment analysis and to retributivism as a justification of—and limitation on—punishment. The "respect due the uniqueness of the individual" that Justice Burger articulated as forming the basis of the analysis in *Lockett* is, in fact, the moral substance behind retributivism as well as behind all due process guarantees. This Article will ultimately argue that in the context of our system of government this moral substance dictates that execution is always, and not merely sometimes, a cruel punishment.

---

2. Roberts v. Louisiana, 428 U.S. 325 (1976); Woodson v. North Carolina, 428 U.S. 280 (1976); Jurek v. Texas, 428 U.S. 262 (1976); Proffitt v. Florida, 428 U.S. 242 (1976); Gregg v. Georgia, 428 U.S. 153 (1976).

3. *See* Jurek v. Texas, 428 U.S. 262, 276 (Stevens, J., plurality opinion); Proffitt v. Florida, 428 U.S. 242, 259 (Powell, J., plurality opinion); Gregg v. Georgia, 428 U.S. 153, 197 (Stewart, J., plurality opinion).

4. In Godfrey v. Georgia, 100 S.Ct. 1759 (1980), Justice Blackmun joined a Stewart opinion relying on the eighth amendment super due process approach to invalidate a death sentence imposed under a standard too vague to avoid arbitrariness. That opinion was joined also by Justices Powell and Stevens, who, with Justice Stewart, gave the approach its first definite articulation in *Gregg* and its companions. Justice Blackmun has not authored an opinion adopting this rationale.

5. In McGautha v. California, 402 U.S. 183 (1971), a due process attack on the death penalty was rejected in an opinion written by Justice Harlan and joined by four others (Chief Justice Burger and Justices Stewart, White and Blackmun). The five-judge consensus was short-lived. The Court splintered in 1972 in Furman v. Georgia, 408 U.S. 238 (1972), reversing a death sentence for murder under the eighth amendment with nine separate opinions resting on three separate rationales. Two justices thought the death penalty was intrinsically cruel, three justices thought the process of inflicting it was cruel, and four justices would have deferred to state legislatures on both questions. In Gregg v. Georgia, 428 U.S. 153 (1976), and its four companion cases, the same three types of rationale appeared but none commanded a majority. In Coker v. Georgia, 433 U.S. 584 (1977) (reversing a death sentence for rape under the eighth amendment), a new rationale based on proportionality appeared, which was espoused by Justice White and three others, Justices Stewart, Blackmun and Stevens.

In Lockett v. Ohio, 438 U.S. 586, another minority rationale appeared, under which execution for murder is cruel where the defendant has no intent to kill. Justice White related this theory to disproportionality, while Justice Blackmun also seemed to espouse it but related it more vaguely to mens rea. *See* note 64 *infra.* For extended discussion of the various rationales in the eighth amendment case law prior to *Lockett,* see Radin, *The Jurisprudence of Death: Evolving Standards for the Cruel and Unusual Punishments Clause,* 126 U. PA. L. REV. 989 (1978).

The most plausible interpretation of the Supreme Court's eighth amendment juris-prudence is that there is a dual limitation on punishment.[6] A punishment is cruel in the constitutional sense if it cannot be justified by both utilitarian and retributivist arguments.[7] To be justified in the utilitarian mode, a punishment must generate a net

---

6. This dual limitation is the most plausible view of how the Supreme Court interpreted the eighth amendment limitation on punishment in the landmark case of Coker v. Georgia, 433 U.S. 584 (1977). In *Coker,* the plurality held that a punishment is excessive, and hence cruel, if it "(1) makes no measurable contribution to acceptable goals of punishment and hence is nothing more than the purposeless and needless imposition of pain and suffering; *or* (2) is grossly out of propor-tion to the severity of the crime." *Id.* at 592 (emphasis added). The first prong of this test is best viewed as implicitly utilitarian, excluding punishments that do not result in a net social gain. The second prong is best viewed as implicitly retributivist, excluding punishments that violate the dignity of the individual by being more than the individual deserves for the crime. The Court in *Coker* found that execution for the rape of an adult woman violated the second prong; execution is disproportionate to the crime of rape. Thus, the Court would find the punishment excessive, even assuming arguendo that execution of persons convicted of rape could make a "measurable contri-bution" to social welfare.

Justice White, in his *Coker* plurality opinion, considered both prongs of his stated dual limita-tion as aspects of "excessiveness." There can be a retributivist aspect of excessiveness (more punish-ment than a person deserves) as well as a utilitarian one (more punishment than necessary to achieve a given social goal). Nevertheless, excessiveness as a limitation on punishment comports best with the utilitarian mode of justification with its connotation of inquiry into goals and means to achieve them most efficiently. On the other hand, the concept of proportionality seems to ally most readily with the ideas of desert and human dignity. Desert and human dignity are both characteristic formulations of a retributivist (that is to say, deontological and individualist) nature. So far, the Court has preferred to subsume both types of limitation under the umbrella concept of human dignity. "A penalty . . . must accord with the 'dignity of man,' which is the basic concept underlying the Eighth Amendment. This means, at least, that the punishment not be 'excessive.'" Gregg v. Georgia, 428 U.S. at 173 (Stewart, J., plurality opinion). Justice Stewart went on to delineate two "aspects" of excessiveness, one implicitly utilitarian and one implicitly retributivist. Justice White, in *Coker,* merely amplified the formulation.

To add to the confusion, the Court has sometimes seemed to view "evolving standards of de-cency" as a third inquiry, separate from "excessiveness" and "the dignity of man." *See, e.g.,* Gregg v. Georgia, 428 U.S. at 173 (plurality opinion); Trop v. Dulles, 356 U.S. 86, 101 (1958) (plurality opinion). Yet "evolving standards of decency" is merely the method of making the moral judgment called for by the inquiry about human dignity. With the possible exception of Justice Rehnquist, all members of the current Court accept the view that the moral content of the cruelty limitation on punishment is variable over time (*i.e.,* subject to "evolving standards"). *See* Radin, *supra* note 5, at 1030–33; *cf.* Munzer & Nickel, *Does the Constitution Mean What it Always Meant?* 77 COLUM. L. REV. 1029 (1977) (present content of the Constitution is determined by authoritative interpreta-tion that results from the interaction, over time, of framers, judges, legislatures and executive officials).

7. The two justifications of punishment most often proffered are utilitarianism and retributiv-ism—roughly speaking, deterrence and deserts. (As Hugo Bedau has pointed out, it may be possible to formulate the retributivist conception without reference to desert. Bedau, *Retribution and the Theory of Punishment,* 75 J. PHILOSOPHY 601, 607–11 (1978). *See* text accompanying notes 51–66 *infra* (retributivism explored in more detail). Other proffered justifications of punish-ment, such as isolation and rehabilitation, can probably be assimilated to utilitarianism.

The argument for the dual limitation theory of the eighth amendment rests on two important premises: (1) for the purposes of the Constitution, cruel punishment is *unjustified* punishment, and (2) a punishment is unjustified and hence cruel unless it can be justified in both modes. *See* Radin, *supra* note 5, at 1046 (as to the former); *id.* at 1056 (as to the latter). A mixed approach to justification of punishment harmonizes the two modes by holding that the general practice of punishment is justified by net social gain while application to specific individuals is justified by deserts or appropriateness to a crime committed. *See e.g.,* H.L.A. HART, PUNISHMENT AND RE-SPONSIBILITY 1–27 (1968); Rawls, *Two Concepts of Rules,* 64 PHILOSOPHICAL REV. 3 (1955). Because the two modes of justification reflect two contradictory but complementary modes of self-social gain;[8] to be justified in the retributivist mode, a punishment must be deserved by a person for an offense.[9]

A majority of the Supreme Court has been willing to assume that execution might engender a net social gain, or that the states may decide it might.[10] To pursue the implications of the retributivist limitation formulated in terms of human dignity or respect for persons, I will accept arguendo both the Court's assumption and its propriety.[11] I will ignore the utilitarian prong of the dual limitation, with its concomitant

---

perception, in my view the attempt to unite them with such a metatheory is unsatisfactory. Professor Soper has recently expressed a similar view:

> The relevance of moral philosophy to the development of norms for governing a society of ordinary people lies in a few broad generalizations: Utilitarianism, for example, emphasizes that we are part of a social whole; Kantianism reminds us, on the other hand, that we are not mere appendages of the social body. And the task of judges, to maintain the balance between these poles while the philosophers are still out, requires practical reasoning that does not yield easily to unified field theories.

Soper, *On the Relevance of Philosophy to Law: Reflections on Ackerman's* Private Property and the Constitution, 79 COLUM. L. REV. 44, 64 (1979).

8. To be justified, punishment X must produce a net gain in social welfare over use of the next preferred alternative, and a gain great enough to outweigh any social losses attributable to the use of punishment X. Thus, the utilitarian justification generates an implied limitation. For example, for execution to be justifiable in the utilitarian mode, it must produce a net social gain over life imprisonment that is great enough to outweigh any social losses attributable to the existence of the death penalty in our system.

9. The retributivist justification also generates an implied limitation: if punishment Y is not deserved by a person for an offense, it is unjustified. For example, if a person cannot deserve to die for a crime, then the death penalty is not justified in the retributivist mode. The nature of the retributivist limitation will be explored in more detail. *See* text accompanying notes 71–87 *infra*.

10. *See* Radin, *supra* note 5, at 1055 n. 254; *see, e.g.,* Bailey, *Murder and the Death Penalty*, 65 J. CRIM. L. & CRIMINOLOGY 416 (1974); Bailey, *Imprisonment v. the Death Penalty as a Deterrent to Murder*, 1 LAW & HUMAN BEHAVIOR 239 (1977); Bailey, *The Deterrent Effect of the Death Penalty for Murder in California*, 52 S. CAL. L. REV. 743 (1979).

Statistical attempts to show any deterrent effect of the death penalty are likely to remain inconclusive because of the number of variables that cannot be controlled. Of course, even solid proof of some incremental deterrence attributable to execution over life imprisonment would not constitute a complete utilitarian justification of execution, because increases in violence or other social losses attributable to the existence of execution would not have been taken into account.

With regard to execution as permissible punishment for murder, the Court has placed the burden of proof of nonjustification on the defendants seeking to stay alive rather than the burden of proof of justification on the government seeking to kill. Settled moral principles of our system regarding who should bear the risk of error or uncertainty make it clear that the Court is wrong to do so when the interests at stake are life on the one hand, and questionable incremental deterrence—or a questionable retributive "fit"—on the other. The Court should have reviewed execution with strictest scrutiny, and with no presumptions in favor of the legislature. *See* Radin, *supra* note 5, at 1027–30.

11. So far, the Court has concluded that execution of all murderers would be cruel to some of them. *See, e.g.,* Roberts v. Louisiana, 428 U.S. 325 (1976); Woodson v. North Carolina, 428 U.S. 280 (1976). But some murderers may be executed without violating human dignity or the respect due the individual. *See, e.g.,* Jurek v. Texas, 428 U.S. 262 (1976); Proffitt v. Florida, 428 U.S. 242 (1976); Gregg v. Georgia, 428 U.S. 153 (1976). The prevailing plurality has tended to rely on its perception of what the majority public opinion is on the moral issue of whether execution violates human dignity. If this perception is based upon what the legislature in fact enacted, the result is not merely deference but complete abdication of any check on legislative power. *See* Radin, *supra* note 5, at 1034–39; *see also* Ely, *Foreward: On Discovering Fundamental Values*, 92 HARV. L. REV. 5, 51–52 (1978). Justice White, writing for the plurality in *Coker*, recognized this problem when he noted that "the Constitution contemplates that in the end our own judgment will be brought to bear on the question of the acceptability of the death penalty under the Eighth Amendment."

empirical questions. Under the retributivist prong, the questions are moral and not empirical, unless moral standards are properly determined by empirical inquiry.

This Article will suggest that the human dignity or personhood standard has both a "substantive" and "procedural" aspect; that the same respect for persons that gives form to the retributivist substantive limitation on punishment also engenders a super due process procedural limitation. To show the plausibility and power of this suggestion, this Article will: (1) review the super due process rationale in terms of a risk of error theory;[12] (2) detour to review the concept of retributivism;[13] (3) explicate the function of a dignity standard a retributivist system, in terms of a theory of respect for persons;[14] and, (4) show that this theory of limitation precludes execution as punishment.[15]

Coker v. Georgia, 433 U.S. 584, 597 (1977). Nevertheless, there is persistent tendency to think that when "the people" say they want the death penalty, that automatically renders it constitutional (*i.e.,* noncruel).

There are two fundamental mistakes in this rationale. First, the content of noncruel punishment, or of any moral concept, cannot be captured by taking a vote on it. Second, even if it could, it is very likely that many of the voters desire the death penalty precisely because they desire to be cruel. Taking the second problem first, such a desire is a constitutionally impermissible purpose. The fact that people sometimes desire to be cruel is one reason there is a constitutional safeguard in the first place. Thus, to evaluate any such vote, it seems that the question of what percentage of the populace votes for the death penalty because they think it *is* cruel could and should be empirically investigated.

To return to the first problem, assuming arguendo that all voters who would vote for the death penalty would do so because they thought it not cruel, can a majority vote suffice to prove it is not cruel, or in fact to *define* it as not cruel? It could serve to *define* it as not cruel only on a radically subjective view of morality that assumes (1) that the statement, "It is right," is exactly equivalent to, "I want it," and (2) that what is "right" for a society is what a majority "wants" at any given moment. Still, can a popular vote in favor of the death penalty (again, assuming all supporters think it not cruel) be taken as mere evidence that it in fact is not cruel? There seems to be nothing inherently wrong with this idea, although it will not be very *good* evidence unless there is some reason to believe all voters have reached a reflective equilibrium on the subject. At any rate, it cannot be conclusive evidence because to treat it as such would be either to slip back into the radically subjective definitional approach or at least to assume that people do not make moral mistakes. People do, however, make moral mistakes, and the fact that they do is another reason to have a constitutional safeguard. Judges must decide when moral mistakes are being made by the voters; they cannot properly abdicate this decision by pointing to what the voters have done. *See* Moore, *The Semantics of Judging* (54 S. CAL. L. REV. (1981)). Whether judges should use their "own values" in making this decision is a separate question. *Cf.* note 109, *infra* (sources from which judges make such moral judgments).

The situation is rendered more complicated when voters, by initiative, amend their state constitution to declare that the death penalty is not cruel. The Constitution of the State of California, for example, now states: "The death penalty provided for under [statutes previously in effect] shall not be deemed to be, or to constitute, the infliction of cruel or unusual punishments within the meaning of Article I, Section 6 [proscribing 'cruel or unusual punishments']." CAL. CONST. art. 1, §27. This outflanks any argument that execution violates the state analogue to the federal cruel and unusual punishments clause, but does not decide whether the voters may so amend their state constitution consistently with the eighth amendment, unless the meaning of cruelty in the federal provision is subject to majority vote on a state-by-state basis. *See* People v. Frierson, 25 Cal. 3d 142, 599 P. 2d 587, 158 Cal. Rptr. 281 (1979).

12. *See* text accompanying notes 16–69 *infra.*

13. *See* text accompanying notes 70–95 *infra.*

14. *See* text accompanying notes 96–119 *infra.*

15. *See* text accompanying notes. 120–127 *infra.*

I. Super Due Process and
Respect for Persons

A. *The Dilemma of Discretion*

In 1971, Dennis McGautha argued to the Supreme Court that unfettered jury discretion in imposing death for murder resulted in arbitrary or capricious sentencing and, hence, violated the fourteenth amendment right to due process of law. He lost.[16] Justice Harlan, for himself, Chief Justice Burger, and Justices Stewart, White and Blackmun, wrote: "In light of history, experience, and the present limitations of human knowledge, we find it quite impossible to say that committing to the untrammeled discretion of the jury the power to pronounce life or death in capital cases is offensive to anything in the Constitution."[17] In the following year, William Henry Furman argued that unfettered jury discretion in imposing death for murder resulted in arbitrary or capricious sentencing and, hence, violated the eighth amendment right not to be subjected to cruel and unusual punishment. He won—and thus a due process strain was imported into the eighth amendment.[18]

This due process strain in eighth amendment analysis was elaborated in *Gregg v. Georgia* and its four companion cases in 1976.[19] Validating an approach suggested by the Model Penal Code,[20] the three judge plurality, composed of Justices Stewart, Powell and Stevens, held that execution for murder is not cruel only if there is guided discretion vested in the sentencer. The sentencer must weigh "aggravating factors" against "mitigating factors" pertaining to the crime and the defendant.

After these five cases, both poles on the jury discretion continuum resulted in unconstitutional sentences. "Unfettered" discretion was unconstitutional,[21] while no discretion—mandatory sentence of death legislatively prescribed for certain crimes—was also unconstitutional.[22] The prevailing plurality said that the constitutional vice of the no-discretion pole was its lack of focus on the "circumstances of the [particular] offense

---

16. McGautha v. California, 402 U.S. 183 (1971).
17. *Id.* at 207.
18. Furman v. Georgia, 408 U.S. 238 (1972). The dissenters in *Furman* argued vigorously that this was merely an attempt to get around *McGautha*. See 408 U.S. at 399–403 (Burger, C.J., dissenting). The new procedural strain of eighth amendment reasoning was espoused—with considerable differences in reasoning and emphasis—in only three of the nine separate opinions (those of Justices Douglas, Stewart and White). The alliance of these three Justices with the two who found execution substantively cruel (Justices Brennan and Marshall) resulted in reversal. In *Lockett,* the procedural strain gained one more adherent in Chief Justice Burger. In fact, although the procedural rationale still did not command a majority of the Court, only one Justice found that it would have been constitutional to execute Sandra Lockett. 438 U.S. at 636 (Rehnquist, J., concurring in part and dissenting in part).
19. *See* note 2 *supra.*
20. MODEL PENAL CODE §210.6 (1962).
21. Furman v. Georgia, 408 U.S. 238 (1972) (opinions of Justices Douglas, Stewart and White).
22. Roberts v. Louisiana, 428 U.S. 325 (1976); Woodson v. North Carolina, 428 U.S. 280 (1976).

together with the character and propensities of the offender."[23] This focus was required to treat defendants as "uniquely individual human beings."[24]

By these decisions, the Court put itself between the "rock and the hard place"; here arises the dilemma of discretion. In *Furman v. Georgia*,[25] the Court had realized that discretion leads to arbitrariness, which fails to treat people equally, and hence fails to treat them with respect. Now the Court has also realized that lack of discretion leads to inflexibility, which fails to treat people as unique individuals, and hence fails to treat them with respect. The Court, in *Gregg* and its companion cases, did not address in any systematic way what principles would govern drawing the line, or delineate the allowable space on the continuum between the amount of sentencing discretion *required* in order to save execution from being unconstitutionally cruel and the amount of sentencing discretion which itself *renders* execution unconstitutionally cruel. The Court instead assumed that the compromise reached in a statute that gives the jury lists of aggravating and mitigating factors to guide its moral judgment on proportionality and individual desert is acceptable.

But is it acceptable? Requiring *some* discretion reflects a loathness to risk moral error against an individual by applying a class rule—*e.g.,* all killers must die—that may punish her disproportionately to her own particular deserts. Moral loathness increases as the severity of the risk increases, so that the requirement of individualization must be strongest if the risk of undeserved death is the worst type of risk. On the other hand, a limitation on discretion reflects moral loathness to risk moral error against an individual by arbitrarily punishing her more severely than others whose deserts are the same as hers. Here too, moral loathness increases as the severity of the risk increases, so that the requirement of consistency must be strongest if death is worst. *The achievable or imaginable level of individualization varies inversely with the achievable or imaginable level of consistency.* Thus it is quite possible that a process accurate enough with respect to individual deserts may require so much discretion as to be unacceptably arbitrary; and that a process that can avoid being unacceptably arbitrary can never be accurate enough with respect to individual deserts. If this is so, then the Court's 1976 compromise cannot stand, and the dilemma of discretion cannot be resolved. This dilemma stems from the strength of two core moral principles of the super due process approach, both of which are related to respect for persons. One dictates that individuals must be evaluated in all their uniqueness. The other dictates that like cases must be treated alike. The first is the Kantian notion of desert,[26] necessary in order to respect persons; the second is the notion that equal treatment is required in order to respect persons.

Since the super due process rationale surfaced in *Furman,* the idea that we commit moral error against an individual if we arbitrarily punish her more severely than others whose deserts are the same as hers has been a central moral premise, consistently espoused by the Court's prevailing plurality.[27] To characterize this type of unequal treatment as moral error requires the assumption that there exists a right to equal treatment

---

23. Woodson v. North Carolina, 408 U.S. 280, 304 (1976) (citation omitted).
24. *Id.*
25. 408 U.S. 238 (1972).
26. *See* note 70 and accompanying text *infra.*
27. *See* Godfrey v. Georgia, 100 S. Ct. 1759 (1980); note 4 *supra.*

such that like cases must be treated alike. It means that someone who a Kantian ideal observer would decree "deserves" to die nevertheless is treated unfairly if we spare someone else who is equally deserving. Although the Supreme Court does not describe it as such, this can be characterized as a "comparative" or "equal protection" notion of proportionality.[28] This commitment to an "equal protection" conception of fairness in punishment probably rests primarily on the recognition of a right to equal treatment as a core notion of human dignity that can negate any condemnation from the viewpoint of an ideal observer unless all those deserving are equally punished. It may rest also on a recognition that in a real life system the imposer of punishment can never be an ideal observer about people's deserts, so that apparent equal treatment may be all we can readily rely on to satisfy our aspirations of fairness. The Court's commitment to the equality premise in the super due process rationale also reflects concern that the system not countenance use of factors other than desert (*e.g.,* race) to single people out for more severe punishment.[29]

Thus, the dilemma of discretion reflects the strength of both equal treatment and individual desert as moral aspects of the respect for persons that must delineate the bounds of acceptable punishment. We must be sure we treat like cases alike; we must be sure we consider each case as that of a unique individual. We cannot simultaneously maximize the extent to which we satisfy both of these moral requirements.[30]

---

28. *See* text accompanying notes 83–85 *infra.*

29. *See, e.g.,* Furman v. Georgia, 408 U.S. 238, 242 (1972) (Douglas, J., concurring).

30. The dilemma of discretion is inherent in all fields of adjudication, but only occasionally will it be unresolvable. In order to judge, we must first classify, and in order to classify, we risk error in determining the appropriate level of generality. The use of comprehensive rules (*e.g.,* mandatory execution for murder) as applied to individuals contains a risk of error because those rules are both underinclusive and overinclusive with regard to the substantive objective sought (execution only of individuals who deserve it). Case-by-case adjudication also risks error because it leads to inconsistent and arbitrary results. Ordinarily the dilemma does not prevent us from judging; we simply evaluate which risk is worse in the particular context and choose the other. *Cf.* Kennedy, *Form and Substance in Private Law Adjudication,* 89 HARV. L. REV. 1685, 1688–89 (1976) ("If we adopt the rule, it is because of a judgment that this kind of arbitrariness is less serious than the arbitrariness and uncertainty that would result from empowering the official to apply the standard . . . directly to the facts of each case").

It is only when the risk associated with either choice cannot be countenanced that the dilemma cannot be resolved. The horns of the dilemma are nicely illustrated in McGautha v. California, 402 U.S. 183 (1971), by the opinions of Justices Harlan, *id.* at 183 (majority opinion), and, Brennan, *id.* at 248 (dissenting). Justice Harlan preferred to apply a standard, *i.e.,* to allow unfettered jury discretion, because no "attempt to catalog the appropriate factors in this elusive area" could be complete and precise enough. *Id.* at 208. *See also* note 56 *infra.* Justice Brennan, dissenting, thought that a rule approach, *i.e.,* lists of aggravating and mitigating factors, could supply such precision and that without such precision execution must be disallowed:

> [The Court assumes] that the legislatures of Ohio and California are incompetent to express with clarity the basis upon which they have determined that some persons guilty of some crimes should be killed, while others should live. . . . [E]ven if I shared the Court's view that the rule of law and the power of the States to kill are in irreconcilable conflict, I would have no hesitation in concluding that the rule of law must prevail.

Id. at 249–50 (Brennan, J., dissenting). In other other words, if the type of arbitrariness or risk of error inherent in standards is perceived as too serious to permit the government act in question, and if the type of arbitrariness or risk of error inherent in rules is also perceived as too serious to permit the act, then that form of government action must be precluded under the rule of law. As Justice Marshall recently put this argument:

The Court, on its next occasion to invoke eighth amendment super due process, did not explicitly face the dilemma of discretion. Yet its decision on that occasion, in *Lockett v. Ohio*,[31] seems to render its 1976 compromise shaky. In *Lockett,* the *Gregg* plurality, now augmented by Chief Justice Burger, found Ohio's guided discretion death sentencing statute to be too far on the continuum toward the "lack of discretion" pole. A death sentence rendered under that statute was unconstitutionally cruel because the statute limited the "mitigating factors" that the sentencer could consider. Sandra Lockett, a twenty-one year old woman, was an accomplice to the robbery of a pawnbroker, which was apparently planned by her older brother. During the robbery, an unplanned killing occurred while Lockett was outside the shop behind the wheel of the getaway car. Under Ohio's death sentencing statute, Lockett's youth, her lack of intent to kill, her status as a mere accomplice and her absence from the scene when the shooting occurred could not count as "mitigating factors" that could be weighed in favor of sparing her life.[32] Chief Justice Burger held not only that withholding these factors from consideration resulted in cruel punishment, but also that *any* curtailment of the range of admissible mitigating evidence would result in cruel punishment. He wrote:

> [W]e conclude that the Eighth and Fourteenth Amendments require that the sentencer . . . not be precluded from considering *as a mitigating factor,* any aspect of a defendant's character or record and any of the circumstances of the offense that the defendant proffers as a basis for a sentence less than death.[33]

To understand the significance of this decision for the dilemma of discretion, recall that the level of individualization and the level of consistency must vary inversely. By requiring more individualization in capital murder cases after *Lockett* the Court has necessarily increased the area of possible arbitrariness beyond the limits established under the 1976 compromise. Is the level of arbitrariness now too high to produce the degree of equal treatment required by respect for persons? Although the Court has not

---

I remain hopeful that even if the Court is unwilling to accept the view that the death penalty is so barbaric that it is in all circumstances cruel and unusual punishment . . . it may eventually conclude that the effort to eliminate arbitrariness in the infliction of that ultimate sanction is so plainly doomed to failure that it—and the death penalty—must be abandoned altogether.

Godfrey v. Georgia, 100 S. Ct. 1759, 1772 (1980) (Marshall, J., concurring).

31. 438 U.S. 586 (1978).

32. The Ohio death penalty statute provided:

[T]he death penalty . . . is precluded when, considering the nature and circumstances of the offense and the history, character, and condition of the offender, one or more of the following is established by a prepondence [*sic*] of the evidence:

(1) The victim of the offense induced or facilitated it.

(2) It is unlikely that the offense would have been committed, but for the fact that the offender was under duress, coercion, or strong provocation.

(3) The offense was primarily the product of the offender's psychosis or mental deficiency, though such condition is insufficient to establish the defense of insanity.

OHIO REV. CODE ANN. §2929.04(B) (Page 1975).

33. 438 U.S. at 604 (emphasis in original). Burger excluded from this holding "the rarest kind of capital case," reserving the question of whether mandatory death sentences might be justified by the need for deterrence in cases of murder by convicts already sentenced to life imprisonment. *Id.* at n. 11.

yet faced the issue directly, a majority of the justices think not, since two executions have been allowed to proceed since the *Lockett* decision.[34]

With regard to mitigating factors, the plurality has now, in effect, declared that the "unfettered" discretion found permissible in *McGautha v. California*,[35] but impermissible in *Furman,* is now not merely permissible but constitutionally required. The situation with regard to aggravating factors seems to have fluctuated. The Court has not yet declared that there are any constitutional limitations on what may be considered as aggravating factors.[36] Although the aggravating factors must be specified, so that discretion will be "guided," the states may draft statutes allowing on their face for almost total discretion by simply including as aggravating circumstances those factors that

---

34. *See* Lenhard v. Wolff, 443 U.S. 1306 (1979) (execution of Jesse Bishop); note 125 *infra* (execution of John Spenkelink).

35. 402 U.S. 183 (1971).

36. Some possible sources of constitutional limitations on the appropriateness of aggravating factors are equal protection, vagueness or overbreadth, and the cruel and unusual punishments clause. A state could not, of course, designate race as an aggravating factor, *see, e.g.,* McGautha v. California, 402 U.S. 183, 207 n. 17 (1971); and probably it could not rely on factors that de facto are predictable of nonwhite defendants without regard to their degree of culpability. So far the Supreme Court has refused to take the problem of vagueness or overbreadth on the face of the statute too seriously. For example, in Jurek v. Texas, 428 U.S. 262 (1976), the Court approved a statute that included, as an aggravating factor, "the probability that the defendant would commit criminal acts of violence that would constitute a continuing threat to society." *Id.* at 269. *See generally* Black, *Due Process for Death: Jurek v. Texas and Companion Cases,* 26 CATH. U.L. REV. 1 (1976). In Proffitt v. Florida, 428 U.S. 242 (1976), the Court rejected petitioner's contention that the language, "especially heinous, atrocious, or cruel" is vague and overbroad and looked to the Florida courts for an adequate narrowing interpretation. *Id.* at 255. Later developments suggested that the Court's reliance on state courts was misplaced, to an extent that "appalled" Justice Marshall. *See* Gardner v. Florida, 430 U.S. 349, 365–70 (1977) (Marshall, J., dissenting). In Gregg v. Georgia, 428 U.S. 153 (1976), the plurality relied on the Georgia court to provide an adequate narrowing interpretation of "outrageously or wantonly vile, horrible or inhuman in that [the offense] involved torture, depravity of mind or an aggravated battery to the victim." In Godfrey v. Georgia, 100 S. Ct. 1759 (1980), the Court found its earlier reliance upon the state misplaced as it reversed a death sentence because, in its moral judgment, "[t]he petitioner's crimes cannot be said to have reflected a consciousness materially more "depraved" than that of any person guilty of murder." *Id.* at 1767. Thus, while not disallowing broad or vague statutory language, the Court seems committed to review each case on its facts in light of the problem of arbitrary or inconsistent decisions by state courts under broadly or ambiguously worded aggravating factors.

There is also a potential class of eighth amendment issues, not yet considered by the Court, involving whether aggravating factors must bear some relation to culpability. If so, aggravating factors that are motivated wholly by utilitarian considerations may be unjustified. *E.g.,* "[t]he murder of a judicial officer, former judicial officer, district attorney or solicitor or former district attorney or solicitor during or because of the exercise of his official duty," GA. CODE ANN. §27–2534.1 (5) (1978); "[t]he offense of murder was committed by a person in, or who has escaped from, the lawful custody of a peace officer or place of lawful confinement," GA. CODE ANN. §27–2534.1(9) (1978). If punishment must be "for" an offense, deterrence, and recidivist factors also may be unjustified. *E.g.,* "[t]he defendant was previously convicted of murder in the first or second degree. For the purpose of this paragraph an offense committed in another jurisdiction which if committed in California would be punishable as first or second degree murder shall be deemed murder in the first or second degree." CAL. PENAL CODE §190.2(a)(2) (West Supp. 1980). Finally, in an appropriate felony murder case, the Supreme Court may eventually address the eighth amendment proportionality issue raised by Justice White in *Lockett,* 438 U.S. at 621 (White, J., concurring in part, concurring in the judgment, and dissenting in part). *See* note 5 *supra.* For example, it appears that under California's new death penalty statute it would be permissible to execute someone who is found to be an intentional accomplice to a murder during which oral copulation occurs. CAL. PENAL CODE §190.2(a)(1)(iv) (West Supp. 1980).

tend to make a homicide first-degree murder.[37] Yet in *Godfrey v. Georgia*,[38] the Court held that a sentence supported by a broadly worded aggravating circumstance will be unconstitutionally cruel if the statute is not applied by the state court in such a way as to execute consistently only those murderers whose crimes are bad enough to be clearly distinguishable from ordinary first degree murder.[39] Thus, in its effort to achieve a satisfactory level of consistency in death cases, the Court has paradoxically committed itself to a case-by-case review. This too undermines its 1976 compromise.

It may seem that the jurisprudence of death has come almost full circle—from the discretion of *McGautha* to the guided discretion of *Lockett* and back to the discretion of *Godfrey*. A cynic might suspect that all the intervening words merely reflect the necessity of dealing with the confusion caused by *Furman* without facing the political disruption that forthrightly overruling *Furman* would cause.[40] Yet there are two other more important and less cynical observations to be made.

First, the Court's struggle with the death penalty has resulted in some intellectual progress. By the time it decided *Coker v. Georgia*,[41] the Court was on the right track regarding how to evaluate legislatively prescribed punishments for cruelty in light of the political and philosophical justifications advanced for them.[42] The thesis of this Article is that in deciding *Lockett,* a plurality put itself on the right track regarding why an analysis of cruelty appropriately involves an analysis of legislatively prescribed sentencing procedures.

Second, the Court's struggle may reflect something profound about the death penalty issue owing to the dilemma of discretion. The Court has determined that flexibility and consistency (nonarbitrariness) are both required for fairness (equal respect for persons), and that the level of each requirement rises as the gravity of the punishment increases. Thus, if death as punishment requires both maximum flexibility and nonarbitrariness, and these requirements cannot both be met (because flexibility and nonarbitrariness must vary inversely), then death cannot be a permissible punishment. The dilemma may become clear in practice by attempting to implement first one requirement and then the other, followed by attempting to harmonize them, and finally by concluding that there is no level at which they can be satisfactorily harmonized. Although the Court has not yet reached the end of this road, in the case law from *McGautha* to *Lockett* and *Godfrey* it has completed the greater part of the journey.

---

37. For example, some statutes include as an aggravating circumstance the fact that the killing was "especially heinous, atrocious, or cruel." *See, e.g.,* FLA. STAT. ANN. §921.141(5)(h) (West Supp. 1980); N.C. GEN. STAT. §15A –2000(c)(9) (Supp. 1979). Arguably, this standard is not much stricter than that required for a first degree murder conviction. *But see* Godfrey v. Georgia, 100 S. Ct. 1759, 1767 (1980) (sentence of death under such a statute will be unconstitutional, if in the Court's perception the murderer's culpability is not clearly distinguishable from that of other murderers not sentenced to death).

38. 100 S. Ct. 1759 (1980).

39. *Id.* at 1759.

40. *See e.g.,* Lockett v. Ohio, 438 U.S. 586, 628–36 (1978) (Rehnquist, J., dissenting). *See also id.* at 623 (White, J., concurring in part, concurring in the judgment and dissenting in part): "I greatly fear that the effect of the Court's decision today will be to constitutionally compel a restoration of the state of affairs at the time *Furman* was decided . . . when the death penalty was generally reserved for those very few for whom society has least consideration."

41. 433 U.S. 584 (1977). *See* note 6 *supra.*

42. *See* Radin, *supra* note 5, at 1052–56.

B. Risk of Error and Respect for Persons

1. Allocation of Risk of Error as a General Moral Rule of Adjudication　Because it attaches substantive significance to risk of error, the super due process analysis is part of the broader normative evaluation of risk of error that pervades our system of criminal adjudication and our system of adjudication generally. It is similar in form to a set of developed moral / legal rules regarding allocation of risk of error. The moral question to which these risk allocation rules address themselves is, in a given case or with respect to a given issue, at the given level of uncertainty, whether the Court should risk error in favor of one side or the other?[43] Risk of error principles accord moral significance to the appreciation that judicial decisions are always made under uncertainty, in a nonideal world.[44] Our system contains moral risk of error principles relating to three separate categories of errors: factual, legal and moral.

First, there are possible factual errors; *e.g.,* did the defendant pull the trigger or was it someone else? Rules regarding the requisite burden of persuasion respond to this type of error risk. On moral grounds, *A* cannot be convicted even if it is more likely that she and not *B* pulled the trigger. Proof beyond a reasonable doubt is required.

Second, there are possible legal errors; *e.g.,* should a court apply the exclusionary rule to this evidence? The doctrine of harmless error is an example of a response to this type of error risk. There is yet another sort of legal error that arises when the law

---

43. For example, given the allocation of burdens of persuasion as to fact *X* in an ordinary civil action against defendant *B*, if the evidence shows a 50-50 chance that *X* is true, the rule directs the trier to risk error in favor of *B*. The burden of proof beyond a reasonable doubt in criminal cases reflects the moral principle that it is preferable to risk error in favor of the individual even when guilt is more likely than not. For further discussion and examples, see generally Grey, *Procedural Fairness and Substantive Rights,* in DUE PROCESS 182 (1977); Radin, *supra* note 5, at 1017–30.

In contexts other than eighth amendment review, the Supreme Court at times speaks of due process as involving the relationship of the level of risk of error to the gravity of the substantive interests involved. For example, the Court stated in Greenholz v. Inmates of Neb. Penal & Correctional Complex, 442 U.S. 1 (1979):

> The function of legal process, as that concept is embodied in the Constitution, and in the realm of factfinding, is to minimize the risk of erroneous decisions. Because of the broad spectrum of concerns to which the term must apply, flexibility is necessary to gear the process to the particular need; the quantum and quality of the process due in a particular situation depend upon the need to serve the purpose of minimizing the risk of error. [*Id.* at 13.]

44. The philosophical significance of the fact that all social actions take place in a nonideal world, what might be called a philosophical problem of "second best," is rarely dealt with specifically, though it is implicit in works such as Murphy, *Marxism and Retribution,* 2 PHILOSOPHY & PUB. AFF. 217 (1973). This problem relates not only to the ability of any social institution to make the "right" decisions with certainty, but also to the larger problem of whether such decisions could be "right," even if made with certainty, given an imperfect social order. One commentator has stated the problem as follows:

> It *could* be the case that certain defects in a society such as inequitable distribution of wealth and opportunities would dictate also a change in the way in which offenders should be treated. . . . [I]t is not clear that *as a general rule* whatever kind of institutions characterize an ideally just society are also the kinds of institutions which should be brought about in a less-than-just society. It is particularly in the discussion of punishment that this issue is of pressing importance, since those who are punished have often been victims of injustice.

J. CEDERBLOM & BLIZER, JUSTICE AND PUNISHMENT 19 (1977) (emphasis in original). *See also* G. CALABRESI & P. BOBBITT, TRAGIC CHOICES 72–79, 211–12 n. 42 (1978).

changes or constitutional requirements are reevaluated. Failure to provide counsel for an indigent defendant or permitting jurors to be "death-qualified" are errors of this sort. Gideon and Witherspoon were convicted at trials found to be unfair because of such legal error.[45] These errors are also properly considered moral errors insofar as the content of due process is determined by moral analysis.

In the context of punishment, similar morally based legal error can occur when wrong standards of proportionality or culpability are applied to a whole class of crimes or offenders. In *Coker v. Georgia,* the Court recognized that it was wrong to punish rapists by death.[46] In *Lockett,* Justice White argued, in principle, that a murderer who does not intend to kill cannot ever be guilty enough to deserve execution.[47] In *Robinson v. California,*[48] the Court recognized it was wrong to make being a addict a crime.[49]

Finally, there is a category of case-specific moral errors. In the context of punishment, this type of moral error occurs when too much blame is ascribed to, and too much punishment is inflicted upon, a particular defendant. It is this third type of risk of error to which the *Lockett* plurality rule responds.

Behind the general risk of error theory there lies a problem of metaethics. The notion that our system contains a class of risk of error rules, of which the *Lockett* rule is an example, lacks coherence unless we can assume that moral truth exists in some sense adequate enough to make sense of the notion of moral error.[50] The required assumption need not be moral truth in the sense of eternal objectivity in ethics, but can instead encompass the idea of time- and culture-bound morality, as long as changes in central values are slow and slight. While I cannot claim that the Court has a coherent or consistent metaethical position, it seems clear that the Court does not adopt a radically subjectivist view, at least with respect to errors drawing their significance from the moral content of due process. Indigents tried and convicted prior to *Gideon* were retried with counsel; people convicted of murder and sentenced to death by "death-qualified" juries prior to *Witherspoon v. Illinois,*[51] were resentenced.[52] Even though the Court's reliance on "evolving standards of decency"[53] leads one to believe it holds that what is a cruel punishment *can* change over time, if the men convicted of rape and executed prior to *Coker* could be brought back to life, no doubt they would be brought back.[54] At least

---

45. Witherspoon v. Illinois, 391 U.S. 510 (1968) (exclusion for cause of jurors generally opposed to capital punishment violates sixth and fourteenth amendments); Gideon v. Wainright, 372 U.S. 335 (1963) (failure to provide counsel for indigent defendant in state criminal trial violates sixth and fourteenth amendments).

46. 433 U.S. 584, 592 (1977).

47. 438 U.S. at 624–25 (1978) (White, J., concurring in part, concurring in the judgment and dissenting in part).

48. 370 U.S. 660 (1962).

49. *Id.* at 667.

50. There can be no error if what is morally correct is only what the Court says from time to time; there is only arbitrariness and inconsistency.

51. 391 U.S. 510 (1968).

52. Though the Court in *Witherspoon* declared its decision to be "fully retroactive," it overturned only the sentences and not the convictions of other death row inmates whose juries had been selected like Witherspoon's. 391 U.S. at 518.

53. *See* Trop v. Dulles, 356 U.S. 86, 101 (1958); note 6 *supra.*

54. "On June 29, 1977, we finally won a decision from the Supreme Court of the United States that the death penalty is excessively harsh and therefore unconstitutional for the crime of rape.

it would appear to speakers of the ordinary language of the legal system that recently executed rapists had been executed in error, not that what was right suddenly became wrong by fiat on the day *Coker* was decided.[55] Any legal rule relying on risk of moral error presupposes that there exists some consistent moral standard having an external source.

2. Respect for Persons as a Limitation on Allocation of Risk of Moral Error in Death Cases

The *Lockett* rule, and the super due process strain of eighth amendment analysis, fit within the general form of risk of error analysis. The substantive judgment to be made is a moral judgment: Does this person deserve death as punishment? The requirement that aggravating and mitigating factors be weighed is a requirement aimed at greater accuracy in making that moral judgment.[56] The analysis assumes that it is

---

Fine, but it comes too late for the 455 men executed for rape in this country since 1930—405 of them black." [Amsterdam, *Capital Punishment.* 1977 STAN. MAGAZINE 42, 44.]

55. In the context at least of constitutional fair trial rights, it is hard to infer any consistent metaethical position from the ordinary language of the legal system. Some changes in the law are retroactively applied; some rights exist only from the date of the decision recognizing them. Beginning with Linkletter v. Walker, 381 U.S. 618 (1965), the Supreme Court has frequently espoused the idea that only those decisions rectifying serious risk of *factual* error in the trial process should be given retroactive effect. *Id.* at 639 (exclusionary rule not applicable retroactively to state convictions prior to Mapp v. Ohio, 367 U.S. 643 (1960)). Nevertheless, this rationale does not wholly account for all of the cases in which retroactivity has been applied. *See, e.g.,* Robinson v. Neil, 409 U.S. 505 (1973) (retroactive effect to holding that double jeopardy clause bars state and municipal prosecutions for the same act); Jackson v. Denno, 378 U.S. 368 (1964) (prosecution must prove voluntariness of admission by a preponderance of the evidence); Gideon v. Wainright, 372 U.S. 335 (1963) (involving the right to counsel); Griffin v. Illinois, 351 U.S. 12 (1956) (state must furnish transcript on appeal to indigents). Justice White's gloss in Lego v. Twomey, 404 U.S. 477 (1972), stated that the holding in *Jackson* had "nothing whatever to do" with considerations of factual reliability. 404 U.S. at 486. The retroactivity doctrine has yet to be given a satisfactory systematic analysis. *See* Mishkin, *The Supreme Court, 1964 Term, Forward: The High Court, The Great Writ and the Due Process of Time and Law,* 79 HARV. L. REV. 56, 58, (1965); Schwartz, *Retroactivity, Reliability, and Due Process: A Reply to Professor Mishkin,* 33 U. CHI. L. REV. 719, 720 (1966). If the Court in fact adhered to a position that doubt about the integrity of the fact finding process is the only instance where retroactivity is called for, the Court might be an ethical skeptic: it might be saying it has always held the same position on the integrity of the fact finding process, while other constitutional values have changed from time to time. But the Court could hold the same position and still embrace objective ethics (at least in the weak sense, *see* note 109 *infra*), if it holds that other constitutional values have not changed, but simply are not important enough to apply retroactively once the Court realizes its prior holdings were wrong.

In reality the situation is more confused and complicated. The Court is not willing to rely openly either on ethical skepticism or on an implicit hierarchy of constitutional values. With respect to cruel punishment, the problem has not yet squarely confronted the Court. The only criminal punishments found to be cruel by the Burger Court have been certain instances of the death penalty, and previously executed defendants cannot be resurrected and resentenced. Those still alive, so far, on death row at the time of invalidation of the statute under which they were sentenced have been spared execution. Regardless of what rationale the Court chooses to rely on, it seems clear that if it finds the life imprisonment for crime X is cruel, all those previously convicted of crime X and sentenced to life imprisonment should have their sentences reduced.

56. The notion that accuracy in moral judgment can be improved by listing factors to be taken into consideration, or limiting the list to only certain factors, is rather strange. In making a moral judgment, one might make a conscious effort to exclude morally irrelevant factors, such as prejudice. But it seems one would not proceed by listing "factors" and then totalling them up in some

theoretically possible for a person to deserve death as punishment, and that death is not morally ruled out in all cases. The analysis focuses on the moral requirements necessary to render noncruel the *process* of *deciding* that *this* person deserves death. Thus, a judge who is reasoning in this mode does not determine that execution "is" cruel. She either decides that it is not, or thinks that the state legislature has the right to decide whether it is or is not.[57] But she holds there must be a case-by-case analysis. Even though a state may decide to punish murder by death, any given statute providing death for murder may be unconstitutional if the death sentence may be imposed by a trier of fact who has not been given adequate individuating directives. Chief Justice Burger, in *Lockett,* made clear that this holding rests on a notion of human dignity or respect for persons, the quantum of "respect due the uniqueness of the individual."[58] The holding thus rests on moral reasoning that parallels the inquiry involved in justifying punishment of an individual in the retributivist mode.[59] The difference is that rather than invoking respect for persons to assess the moral appropriateness of a particular instance of punishment, in this case respect for persons is invoked to assess the moral appropriateness of *risking an error against the defendant in making the first assessment.*

Let us refer to the judgment whether someone can deserve death as punishment as the *first-order moral judgment.* (The first-order moral judgment can be quite general: Can anyone deserve execution? Less general: Can anyone deserve execution for rape? Or specific: Does this particular person deserve to die for this particular murder?) Let us refer to the judgment on the moral appropriateness of risking an error against the defendant on the first-order question as the *second-order moral judgment.* It is then clear that the *Lockett* holding embodies a second-order moral judgment based upon respect for persons. Chief Justice Burger was explicit in stating that too great a risk of error in the required moral weighing process was a violation of the defendant's dignity (the respect due to her as a person) and therefore unjustified.[60] In support of constitutionalizing a requirement that the sentencer must consider all the mitigating evidence proffered, Chief Justice Burger said:

> Given that the imposition of death by public authority is so profoundly different from all other penalties, we cannot avoid the conclusion that an individualized decision is essential in capital cases. The

---

mechanical moral analogue to cost-benefit analysis. Justice Harlan seemed to recognize that such an attempt to mechanize moral judgment posed an "intractable" problem. He wrote that: "To identify before the fact those characteristics of criminal homicides and their perpetrators which call for the death penalty, and to express these characteristics in language which can be fairly understood and applied by the sentencing authority, appear to be tasks which are beyond present human ability. . . ." McGautha v. California, 402 U.S. 183, 204 (1971). "For a court to attempt to catalog the appropriate factors in this elusive area could inhibit rather than expand the scope of consideration, for no list of circumstances would ever be really complete. . . ." *Id.* at 208.

57. The deference position has been the typical stance of those judges who would uphold the death penalty. *See* Radin, *supra* note 5, at 1002–08. In spite of the rhetoric of standards of review, a judge who bows to the state legislature's judgment must be implicitly holding that execution "is not" cruel in any sense that would trigger constitutional preclusion.

58. 438 U.S. at 605 (Burger, C. J., separate opinion).

59. *See* text accompanying notes 71–87 *infra* (review of retributivist justification).

60. 438 U.S. at 605 (1978) (Burger, C. J., separate opinion).

need for treating each defendant in a capital case with that degree of respect due the uniqueness of the individual is far more important than in noncapital cases. . . . The nonavailability of corrective or modifying mechanisms with respect to an executed capital sentence underscores the need for individualized consideration as a constitutional requirement in imposing the death sentence.

There is no perfect procedure for deciding in which cases governmental authority should be used to impose death. But a statute that prevents the sentencer in all capital cases from giving independent mitigating weight to aspects of the defendant's character and record and to circumstances of the offense proffered in mitigation creates the risk that the death penalty will be imposed in spite of factors which may call for a less severe penalty. Where the choice is between life and death, that risk is unacceptable and incompatible with the commands of the Eighth and Fourteenth Amendments.[61]

This passage discusses the factors that the trier of fact must consider in determining whether a defendant deserves death. This decision is a moral judgment of proportionality and desert: to be just, punishment must not be greater than is warranted by the crime; it must "fit the crime." The Supreme Court has declared that not all murderers deserve death and that death would constitute cruel and unusual punishment of those murderers not deserving it.[62] The Court could have used proportionality[63] to decide the first-order question posed by the *Lockett* case. That is, it could have decided that, just as no one deserves to die for the rape of an adult woman, no one deserves to die who had no intent to kill, did not pull the trigger, and is a murderer only by virtue of the felony-murder rule. Justice White, in fact, would have decided *Lockett* on this basis, and Justices Marshall and Blackmun expressed sympathy with the same view.[64] In-

---

61. *Id.*

62. This is evidenced by the rejection by the Court of mandatory death sentence statutes. *See* Roberts v. Louisiana, 428 U.S. 325 (1976); Woodson v. North Carolina, 428 U.S. 280 (1976).

63. Proportionality is the second prong of the test articulated in Coker v. Georgia, 433 U.S. 584 (1977). *See* note 6 *supra.*

64. Justice White wrote in *Lockett:* "[T]he infliction of death upon those who had no intent to bring about the death of the victim is not only grossly out of proportion to the severity of the crime but also fails to significantly contribute to acceptable, or indeed to any perceptible goals of punishment." 438 U.S. at 626 (White, J., concurring in part, concurring in the judgment and dissenting in part). Justice Marshall agreed that "the imposition of the death penalty for this crime totally violated the principle of proportionality embodied in the Eighth Amendment's prohibition." *Id.* at 619–20 (Marshall, J., concurring in the judgment). Justice Blackmun would be unwilling to hold that execution of any defendant who lacked intent to kill is disproportionate, because he thinks that "such a rule, even if workable, is an incomplete method of assessing culpability for Eighth Amendment purposes, which necessarily is a more subtle mixture of action, inaction, and degrees of *mens rea.*" *Id.* at 615 n. 2 (Blackmun, J., concurring in part and concurring in the judgment). He stated he would prefer to "follow a proceduralist tack" and require the statute to give the sentencer discretion to consider the degree of the defendant's involvement in the crime and "the character of the defendant's *mens rea.*" *Id.* at 615–16. However, he appeared to endorse the idea that the constitutional proportionality standard is violated by a statute that requires (or permits?) "capital punishment of a mere aider and abettor in an armed felony resulting in a fatality even where *no* participant specifically intended the fatal use of a weapon." *Id.* at 616. Justice Brennan took no part in the *Lockett* decision, but given his per se opposition to the death

stead, the plurality chose to rely on the second-order judgment regarding the moral appropriateness of the procedures, perhaps wishing to "hold the line" on the scope of permissibility of the death penalty even while believing that no reasonable moral weigher could have found Lockett culpable enough to deserve execution for her crime. Thus, rather than hold that execution of any particular class of murderers constitutes cruel and unusual punishment, Chief Justice Burger held that it constitutes cruel punishment of *all* murderers (except perhaps convicts already under sentence of death) to risk moral error in favor of the government seeking to impose death by using procedures that fail to bring to bear on the trier's decision all "factors which may call for a less severe penalty."

The reason that running this risk of error constitutes cruel punishment is that it fails to accord the individual the "degree of respect due [her] uniqueness." Does it in fact do so? To impose punishment under these risk conditions is cruel only in death cases and not in every case where a defendant faces some form of punishment. Chief Justice Burger said the "need" to treat individuals with due respect[65] is "far more important" in death cases for two reasons. First, death is "profoundly different" from other forms of punishment; and second, it is irrevocable. In Chief Justice Burger's euphemism, there are no "modifying mechanisms" to resurrect an erroneously executed defendant. The connections between these two reasons and "respect" are obscure, but seem to be as follows.

First is the idea that death is different. It is "enormous,"[66] mysterious, of overwhelming gravity, and incommensurate with imprisonment, even for life.[67] To inflict it on someone unjustly would be the highest indignity at the hands of the government, even if it could be undone. (The fact it cannot be undone is part of what makes it "enormous," however.) Hence, willingly and knowingly to risk this injustice is also to subject the individual to an indignity.

Second is the idea of irrevocability. If any punishment is inflicted wrongly, the fact that its effects can be undone or mitigated does not make the original infliction less unjust. Nor does irrevocability by itself make it more unjust. However, insofar as subjecting an individual to the risk of unjustified punishment constitutes disrespect, to subject an individual to the risk that an irrevocable punishment will be unjustly imposed may be more disrespectful than to subject her to the risk that a "revocable" punishment will be

---

penalty, one may suppose he would agree with Justice Marshall. Thus, the status of execution under the felony-murder rule is now shaky. If an appropriate case could persuade either Justice Stewart or Justice Stevens (who, with Justice White and Justice Blackmun, endorsed the proportionality analysis in Coker v. Georgia, 433 U.S. 584 (1977)) one would expect the Court to hold that execution of a "non-triggerperson" is grossly disproportionate, and hence precluded by the eighth amendment.

65. Although Chief Justice Burger stated that the need to treat individuals with appropriate respect is far more important in death cases, he probably instead meant that the need is equally important in all cases but far harder to satisfy in death cases because of the greater gravity of the harm threatened the individual.

66. *See, e.g.,* Furman v. Georgia, 408 U.S. 238, 286–88 (1972) (Brennan, J., concurring).

67. It is difficult to capture what is involved in the notion that death is different. For an interesting recent attempt, see J. MURPHY, *Cruel and Unusual Punishments,* in RETRIBUTION, JUSTICE AND THERAPY 223–49 (1979).

unjustly imposed.[68] This may be true because the former shows lack of concern for the individual's future in addition to that degree of lack of concern for present justice toward her corresponding to the degree of risk of injustice being tolerated. Or it may be true simply because the former shows arrogance toward the individual, an arrogation of power characterized by behaving as if one's decisions were infallible when one knows they are fallible. In a liberal democracy, the government may not play God. The arrogance stems not merely from the fact that we know our factual decisions as well as our moral judgments are subject to some risk of error. Although some can imagine what it is like to be imprisoned, none can imagine what it is like to be executed, so as to know that someone deserves it the same way we know other things.

Moral considerations involving risk of injustice are relevant in all cases of punishment and not just when the government proposes to execute someone. But the degree of injustice risked, and the degree of disrespect to the individual engendered by it, will vary according to the importance of the interest threatened. Chief Justice Burger's argument may be interpreted as saying that since life is the individual's most important interest, where life is at stake these considerations are peremptory.[69] To tolerate a certain level of risk under these circumstances is cruel. Thus, we arrive at *Lockett:* At least it constitutes cruelty to sentence an individual to death under procedures allowing that particular level of risk of moral error engendered by legislative delineation of some subset of permissible factors to be considered (exclusive of all others) as militating against the death sentence.

II. Retributivism and Respect for Persons

The preceding discussion assumed that the notion of "respect for persons" is allied with or equivalent to the notion of "the dignity of man." It also assumed that these notions are characteristics of retributivist modes of justification of punishment and that they form limitations on what punishments can be justified in the retributivist mode. These matters now require examination.

The view of retributivism thus adopted may be described as Kantian.[70] In this view, a distinguishing feature of the retributivist mode of justification is the idea of proportionality—the punishment must fit the crime and must not be more or other than the person deserves. Another distinguishing feature is that the reason persons must get what they

---

68. The notion that a punishment could be "revocable" is problematic. *See* Radin, *supra* note 5, at 1022 n.132; *cf.* J MURPHY, *supra* note 67, at 240–41 ("if we already know the harm of death is greater than the harm of loss of liberty, we do not need the concept of irrevocability at all").

69. The increased standards traditionally applied in death cases reflect the perception, though incompletely articulated, that the level of certainty regarding factual and moral issues required to justify a threatened infliction increases as the gravity of the individual interests invaded increases. *See, e.g.,* Furman v. Georgia, 408 U.S. 238, 290 (1972) (Brennan, J., concurring). It can be argued that a consistent application of this perception would result in a "spectrum" theory of review regarding justification of punishment. *See* Radin, *supra* note 5, at 1016–30.

70. *See generally* I. KANT, *The Metaphysical Elements of Justice,* pt. I of THE METAPHYSICS OF MORALS (Berlin 1902–1938) (Königsberg 1797).

deserve as punishment is that we are required to give them their deserts in order to respect their status as persons or as autonomous moral entities. Because of these features, the limitation on punishment generated by retributivism seems to have two aspects: (1) any punishment that is not proportional to the crime is unjustified; and, (2) any punishment that fails to respect the personhood of the offender is unjustified. The proportionality limitation follows from the idea that more punishment than one deserves is not justified as deserts; the personhood limitation follows from the idea that if just deserts is required out of respect for one's status as a person, one cannot deserve that which fails to respect one's status as a person. This view of retributivism generates a "rights thesis": everyone has a right to be punished proportionately and with respect for her personhood, and these rights are not defined by majority opinion.[71]

A. Old and New Retributivism: Some Touchstones

To clarify the retributivist limitation and its relationship to the second-order moral judgment involved in a super due process case like *Lockett*, it will be helpful first to review some forms of retributivism varying in some aspects from the view just outlined, and to distinguish retributivism from revenge and revenge-utilitarianism. There has lately been a renaissance in retributivism, as faith in the supposedly more humanitarian ideals of utilitarianism has come to seem misplaced. Yet there is a strange split among the new retributivists. Some modern writers think there should be *less* punishment in the world than might be justified if utilitarian arguments were accepted, and urge retributivism as a means of *curtailing* punishment and the class of punishable people.[72] Others think there should be *more* punishment in the world than now exists, and urge retributivism as a means of *augmenting* punishment and the class of those punishable.[73] Retributivism is espoused by both liberals and conservatives; it is seen as both a new way to limit inhumane practices and to exorcise permissiveness and coddling of criminals. This phenomenon stems from both the existence of several different and conflicting historical threads associated with retributivism, and from some confusion surrounding the treatment of

---

71. *See* R. DWORKIN, TAKING RIGHTS SERIOUSLY 81–84, 190–200, 269 (1978). For Dworkin, "a claim of political right is a claim to a trump over the general welfare [the "background collective justification" which in our society and legal system is "normally decisive"] for the account of a particular individual." *Id.* at 364. Such rights rest on a right to equal concern and respect for each individual, which Dworkin takes to be "fundamental and axiomatic." *Id.* at xiv–xv.

72. *See, e.g.,* J. MURPHY, *supra* note 67: A. VON HIRSCH, REPORT OF THE COMMITTEE FOR THE STUDY OF INCARCERATION ON DOING JUSTICE (1976) [hereinafter cited as DOING JUSTICE]; Morris, *Persons and Punishment,* 52 MONIST 475 (1968). Two members of the committee that wrote *Doing Justice* reveal the reason for their retreat to retributivism:

> Under the rehabilitative model, we have been able to abuse our charges, the prisoners, without disabusing our consciences. . . . And so we as a group, trained in humanistic traditions, have ironically embraced the seemingly harsh principle of just deserts. . . . In so stating our position, we have become free to set reasonable limits to the extent of punishment. When we honestly face the fact that our purpose is retributive, we may, with a re-found compassion and a renewed humanity, limit the degree of retribution we will exact. [Goodell & Rothman, *Introduction* to DOING JUSTICE at xxxviii–xxxix.]

73. *E.g.,* W. BERNS, FOR CAPITAL PUNISHMENT: CRIME AND THE MORALITY OF THE DEATH PENALTY (1979); G. NEWMAN, THE PUNISHMENT RESPONSE (1978); E. VAN DEN HAAG, PUNISHING CRIMINALS (1975).

what is here called revenge-utilitarianism—defense of punishment as creating a net social gain over the private revenge that would occur without it.

1. Transcendent Order   There are several historical threads in retributivism that may ultimately be incompatible. First, there is the idea that punishment of those who break the law is required to vindicate or restore some transcendent order.[74] From this view, punishment of criminals is a good in itself, aside from its instrumental effect on the community; this is what Kant's famous pronouncement about the last murderer suggests.[75] It seems that this view requires punishment in order to keep the human community free from taint. And apparently this condition of the community is in turn required to be pursued, either to stay in the gods' good favor or to stay in harmony with objective natural law.[76] Those who invoke vindication of the moral order today may probably be assumed to be relying on objective natural law, although they tend to avoid making their reliance explicit, because they will be faced with embarrassing questions about where this natural law comes from.[77]

2. Collective Vengeance   Second, in retributivism there seems to be a thread of community vengeance. That is, under this interpretation vengeance is necessary for the community, or the community is entitled to it.[78] This might mean that punishment of criminals is acceptable simply because criminals "hurt" the community (considered in a personified, anthropomorphic sense) and the community then "hurts" them back. The modern writers who speak of collective vengeance probably intend to invoke not this mystical notion, but rather the idea that collective action is necessary to forestall

---

74. *See* W. BERNS, *supra* note 73, at 172 (death penalty must be retained "to remind us of the majesty of the moral order"); E. VAN DEN HAAG, *supra* note 73, at 11 ("[r]etribution is to restore an objective order rather than to satisfy a subjective craving for revenge").

75. "Even if a civil society were to dissolve itself by common agreement of all its members (for example, if the people inhabiting an island decided to separate and disperse themselves around the world), the last murderer remaining in prison must first be executed, so that everyone will duly receive what his actions are worth and so that the blood guilt thereof will not be fixed on the people because they failed to insist on carrying out the punishment." [I. KANT, *supra* note 70, at 333.]

76. For a discussion of the historical notion of tainting and the distinction between blaming and tainting, see G. FLETCHER, RETHINKING CRIMINAL LAW 343–49 (1978):

> In the Biblical view, the person who slays another was thought to acquire control over the blood—the life force—of the victim. The only way that this life force could be returned to God, the origin of all life, was the execute the slayer himself. In this conception of crime and punishment, capital execution for homicide served to expiate the desecration of the natural order. The desecration, it is worth stressing, inhered in causing death, regardless whether the actor was fairly to blame for the killing; the expiation for the desecration worked by terminating the violation of the sacred order—namely, the slayer's control over the victim's blood. [*Id.* at 236 (footnotes omitted).]

77. Van den Haag's treatment of the question is perhaps typical of the way such theorists shunt it aside: "This objective order [which retribution is to 'restore'] was often thought to have a divine or 'natural' source. But whatever its origin, a transpersonal social order objectively does exist. If it is to continue, it must be vindicated through the punishment of offenders." E. VAN DEN HAAG, *supra* note 73, at 11–12.

78. *See generally* W. BERNS, *supra* note 73, at 174–75.

more costly private vengeance. As will be shown, however, collectivized private vengeance is not properly considered a retributivist justification for punishment.[79]

3. Debt   Third, retributivists often invoke the idea that criminals owe a debt to the community. Assuming that the criminal had free choice to break the social compact, punishment evens the score by counterbalancing the unfair gains the criminal secured as against others who restrained themselves.[80] A variant of this idea, stemming from confusion with restitution, is that some extent of the criminal's personal interests are forfeited to the community as payment for the personal interests of which she deprived her victim.[81]

4. Desert   Fourth, retributivism almost always involves the general idea that criminals *deserve* punishment. There are at least two notions associated with desert, which may be called positive and negative. Punishment can expiate a person's guilt and restore the person to equal status in the community; a person has a "right" to be punished and thus purged of wrongdoing. (It is important not to confuse this notion with the "right" to live under a punishment *system*.)[82] This is the "positive" aspect of desert. The "negative" aspect of desert is simply that pain ought to be the consequence of bad acts; in a just state of affairs a wrong evokes reciprocal suffering in the person responsible for bringing about the wrong.

5. Proportionality   The characteristic retributivist notion of proportionality figures in all these threads.[83] The retributivist criterion in any given case is satisfied not by just any punishment, but only by the "right" punishment in the "right" amount. There is a comparative (or equal treatment) aspect of proportionality—like crimes ought to be met with like punishment.[84] There is also an absolute aspect which remains elusively

---

79. *See* text accompanying notes 88–95 *infra*.

80. This argument is stated most clearly by Herbert Morris. *See* Morris, *supra* note 72, at 476–79. It depends on the notion that the criminal had free choice in committing her crime. It also seems to depend on the notion that the social order is justly constituted. *See* Murphy, *supra* note 44; *cf.* Bedau, *supra* note 7, at 616–17 (social justice, rather than retribution, is the rationale for punishment in a system based on free will). It is also subject to the criticism that its notion of law-abiders restraining themselves because of reliance on others doing likewise makes much more sense for traffic offenses and shoplifting than for murder and rape. *See, e.g.,* G. FLETCHER, *supra* note 76, at 417.

81. As Bedau points out it is hard to see why, if this is the case, that the criminal should "pay" the community rather than the victim. *See* Bedau, *Concessions to Retribution in Punishment,* in JUSTICE AND PUNISHMENT 68 (J. Cederblom & W. Blizek eds. 1977). In other words it is hard to see, from this view, what justifies punishment over and above tort liability.

82. Both of these ideas are set forth in Morris, *supra* note 72, at 475–77. *See also* H. MORRIS, *Guilt and Suffering,* in ON GUILT AND INNOCENCE 89 (1976).

83. A utilitarian interpretation of proportionality is not impossible, but seems out of touch with the ordinary understanding of the term and apparently leads to philosophical problems very quickly. *See* Radin, *supra* note 5, at 1053, 1057.

84. *See* Radin, *supra* note 5, at 1057–60; Wheeler, *Toward a Theory of Limited Punishment II: The Eighth Amendment After Furman v. Georgia,* 25 STAN. L. REV. 62 (1972); Wheeler, *Toward a Theory of Limited Punishment: An Examination of the Eighth Amendment,* 24 STAN. L. REV. 838 (1972). In the context of a system in which the imposer of punishment cannot be an ideal observer of the criminal's deserts in the absolute sense, the comparative aspect of proportionality takes on more significance. *See* text accompanying notes 25–30 *supra*.

murky: the punishment should "fit" the crime.[85] The comparative notion and the absolute notion may be inconsistent with each other in a world where an ideal observer could discern each person's deserts. If death "fits" the crimes of 100 persons but we only execute fifty of them, it seems we would be unfair to those fifty on the comparative view of proportionality but not on the absolute view.

6. *Personhood*   The notion of respect for persons also figures in some, but not all, of the modes of thought called retributivism. Respect for persons does not seem to be a major factor if the main perspective pertains to some mystical notion of community prophylaxis like collective vengeance. But the notion assumes primary importance in the Kantian individualist perspectives expressed in the ideas of desert and debt to the community. People ought to be treated as autonomous moral beings—as ends, not means. Such treatment constitutes the respect due persons. A person who chooses to wrong others deserves punishment; not to punish her would amount to failure to respect her status as an autonomous moral agent.[86]

7. *"Protective" vs. "Assaultive" Retributivists*   It is now possible to see how retributivism can succor both those who want more punishment and those who want less. New retributivists wishing to argue for less punishment in the world—let us call them "protective" retributivists—are likely to stress the *comparative* aspect of proportionality (*e.g.,* it is unfair to execute X and let Y live when there is no principled distinction between the two cases).[87] Protective retributivists also stress the "positive" aspect of desert, and the Kantian notion of respect for persons associated with desert and debt to the community.

On the other hand, new retributivists wishing to argue for more punishment in the world—let us call them "assaultive" retributivists—are likely to stress the *absolute* aspect of proportionality (*e.g.,* a killer ought to be killed; a rapist ought to be raped(?)) and will argue that the equality issue could be solved by executing more people. Assaultive retributivists will also stress the ill-defined ideas of vindication of the moral order and collective vengeance. Perhaps because those who profess these ideas do not want to be pressed to clarify them, assaultive retributivists also often rely covertly on a form of utilitarianism, or on a social contract theory that assumes what they are trying to prove. It is to these arguments that this Article now turns.

---

85. *See* Radin, *supra* note 5, at 1060–62. This is the "object all sublime" ridiculed in the person of Gilbert & Sullivan's Mikado, who decrees that billiard sharks should be punished by being made to play with a twisted cue and elliptical billiard balls. Apparently not much philosophical progress has been made on the issue of how punishment can "fit" crime since Immanuel Kant suggested that rape and pederasty be punished by castration. *See* Bedau, *supra* note 80, at 63–65; Gibbs, *The Death Penalty, Retribution and Penal Policy,* 69 J. CRIM. L. & CRIMINOLOGY 291, 295–98 (1978).

86. *See* Fingarette, *Punishment and Suffering,* 50 AM. PHILOSOPHY PROC. & ADDRESSES 499, 509–10 (1977); Morris, *supra* note 72, at 476.

87. Although they did not call themselves retributivists, this equality issue was at the heart of the reasoning of Justices Douglas, Stewart and White, in Furman v. Georgia, 408 U.S. 238 (1972), and it has remained a primary rationale of the super due process approach. *See* Godfrey v. Georgia, 100 S. Ct. 1759 (1980).

B. Revenge and Revenge-Utilitarianism

Revenge occurs when one person, with the idea of retaliation, injures someone she believes is responsible for an injury either to herself or to someone she cares about. Revenge is a private act between one person or group and another. Revenge may be unjustified, as when one of the McCoys shoots one of the Hatfields for an imagined slight. Retribution, on the other hand, is a public act. It is the formal act of a community against one of its members, and is carried out in the manner and for the reasons that are justified under the political constitution of the community. Unlike revenge, it would be incorrect to speak of unjustified retribution. If governmental infliction of pain on someone is not justified, then it is lawless and not properly retribution.

It can be argued that the purpose of retribution is to obviate personal revenge. This argument may take one of two forms, resting on either notions of social contract or upon notions of deterrence. The contract argument states that in civilized society, people agree not to take personal revenge only because the government has been constituted as agent to do it for the people. The contract argument need not be utilitarian—the sovereign could be constituted agent to give people their just deserts—but many who adopt the contract argument do rely on the idea of net social gain.[88] The deterrence argument posits that governmental revenge is necessary to deter those who commit private acts of violence in the name of revenge. The implicit idea in both formulations is that the social costs of systematic governmental revenge will be less than the social costs of random private revenge. In its latter form, the argument is clearly utilitarian, and this Article refers to it as revenge-utilitarianism. The basic proposition of revenge-utilitarianism seems to be that the government may impose whatever punishments are necessary to deter private revenge.[89] Thus, Ernest van den Haag writes:

> James Fitzjames Stephen was right about human motivation when he suggested that revenge plays a major role in retribution. . . . Abolition [of legal retribution] would be no more likely to reduce "the passion of revenge," which finds sanctioned satisfaction in retribution, than the abolition of marriage would be to reduce the "sexual appetite," which finds sanctioned satisfaction in marriage. Marriage and retribution both serve to control impulses that might otherwise be gratified in socially more destructive ways. When legal retribution is not imposed for what is felt to be wrong, or when retribution is felt to be less than deserved — when it is felt to be insufficient, not inclusive, certain, or severe enough — public control falters, and "the passion of revenge" tends to be gratified privately.[90]

---

88. *See, e.g.,* J. BUCHANAN, THE LIMITS OF LIBERTY (1975).

89. Those who rely on a contract argument based on welfare maximization or directly consequentialist reasoning about social costs, should not be thought of as retributivists, since the distinctive feature of retributivism is its deontological and individualist character. Contract theory proponents aiming to maximize welfare should show why people in the original position would constitute the government as agent for revenge rather than simply abandoning revenge. Those who rely on cost-benefit analysis without reference to a contract should be held to show empirically that revenge-utilitarianism results in a net social gain in order to justify it (or at least give reasons why the burden of proof should be on the other side). This probably cannot be done; at any rate, assaultive "retributivists" have not seen the need to attempt to do so.

90. E. VAN DEN HAAG, *supra* note 73, at 12–13.

The implicit premise cannot withstand even minimal scrutiny. Assume A desires to injure X, for purposes of revenge. If the government is justified in injuring X enough to deter A from herself injuring X, then one must first assume at least that A has a "right" to injure X, that is, that revenge is self-justifying in all cases. In a case where A has no right to injure X, her desire to do so cannot confer upon the government a right to do so. Instead we would expect a utilitarian theory to require that the government deter A by threatening to punish *her* instead of X. If social disorder from private revenge is to be discouraged, then "taking the law into one's own hands" would be a crime, not an entitlement that the government must respect, and not something endemic to social life that must be dealt with as a "given." If it were, why not all other forms of social wrong as well? Why not deter theft by taking money from others and distributing it to would-be thieves?

In the quoted passage van den Haag might be read as asserting that if even one person "feels" that punishment is too little, the government is justified in inflicting more punishment to deter her from vengeance. Let us, however, read him charitably and assume he means to reply to the above argument with the typical revenge-utilitarian assertion that private vengeance only flourishes where *people in general* perceive the government as punishing too little. For the government to punish more would save large social costs in private vengeance for a smaller increased social cost in pain suffered by convicted persons. This attempted rejoinder refers back to what justifies punishment in general. Assume the government proposes to punish X too little to suit A, B, C, et cetera. If punishment is justified by some general sense of what the populace thinks is right, and if the populace generally perceives the government as punishing X too little, then the government is justified in meting out more punishment by that fact alone. The government need not resort to revenge-utilitarianism; it would not need to justify itself by the need to deter A, B, C, etc., from private vengeance. Of course, someone who says punishment is justified by the need to restore an objective order cannot consistently rely on this popular preference argument.

There are intractable problems in trying to determine what is meant by "what the populace thinks is right,"[91] assuming that popular preference could constitute justification. But if punishment must be justified other than by popular preference, either wholly or in part, then revenge-utilitarianism cannot convert unjustified desires to see people suffer into justified punishment. If punishment must be justified other than by popular preference the justification probably contains a nonutilitarian component,[92] so that justification cannot be accomplished by preference summing. Even if the justification of punishment could be wholly utilitarian—our "assaultive retributivist" now revealing herself as a complete Benthamite—it is hard to see how revenge-utilitarianism could result in more of a net social gain than the "right" amount of ordinary deterrence applied to would be revengers in the same way as all other would be lawbreakers.

Further, consider the claim implicit in the contract argument that under the social compact people constitute the government their agent for revenge as a condition for

91. Some possible interpretations would be (1) what is enacted by majority vote (*e.g.*, in initiative or referendum measures); (2) what is enacted by a duly constituted representative legislature as proxy for the people as a whole; (3) what is ascertained as the majority view from time to time by public opinion polls; (4) what is ascertained by polls as a measure of "informed" public opinion; (5) what is counted as societal or institutional consensus.

92. This is especially likely in the context of a constitutional limitation on punishment. Even

restraining themselves from taking private vengeance. This formulation is similar in form to the "debt" theory of retributivism discussed earlier.[93] Even if this is an adequate general theory of the source of governmental power to punish, it cannot by itself support the idea that the government is justified in inflicting the exact amount of injury a group of individual citizens would wish to see upon their targeted fellows, nor that groups of citizens are free to cease restraining themselves from private revenge unless the government inflicts the exact amount of injury they would wish to see. To support such claims, the contract would have to be based on shifting popular preferences; in which case the argument again reduces to revenge-utilitarianism.

Under a contract theory, one way that one might have a right to collectivized private revenge is if she is justified in retaliating against another and may justly "transfer" that right to the government, constituting the government her agent for retaliation. The proposition that a personal right to justified retaliation can naturally be transferred or delegated to the government is very dubious.[94] In any case, assaultive retributivists usually do not stipulate that the revenge to be carried out by the government must first be justified as between private parties. They rather seem to rely on the unstated proposition that revenge is self-justified.

If the purpose of the social contract is to achieve net gains over the state of nature for each contracting party and in the aggregate, as in the individualist "minimal-state" contract theory, people would probably be assumed to have bound themselves to accept less revenge in return for being free themselves from the threat of others' vengeance against them.[95] It is counterintuitive to assume that net gains would be achieved by requiring the government to duplicate the state of nature with regard to people's "natural" desires for vengeance. Since this kind of contract theory is supposed to justify social control by the need to reduce the amount of self-defense and violence against others present in the state of nature, it would be incoherent for the contractarian to claim that vengeance (one form of violence against others) whenever desired and in whatever amounts desired must be taken as a natural right which the contract does not curtail.

---

though a long-term, rule-utilitarian of the constitutional command might be possible, at least in the short-term punishment would not be justified merely by summing the individual preferences of everyone in society at any given time.

93. *See* text accompanying notes 80–81 *supra*.

94. In the context of existing government, justified retaliation would have to mean retaliation that is not ruled out by either tort or criminal law, such as self-defense. But it seems the personal right to self-defense (at least) arises out of the exigencies of the moment. If *A* threatens to assault *B*, then if *B* is able to say to herself, "I won't assault *A* back because I can instead escape and later get the government to do it," *B* would not be in a position where a right to self-defense would arise in the first place. In the context of existing government there are few rights to retaliation and they may, by definition, be only those that would be lost by such a transfer. But perhaps the argument really pertains to what rights would be transferred by agreement in the state of nature or the original position. Because in the state of nature no "rights" have yet been agreed upon, there are no personal rights to retaliation, there are only certain levels of desires to attack others and defend oneself, unless there are a priori "natural rights." Therefore unless one relies on natural rights it would not make sense to say that people in the original position transfer their rights to the government, but rather that they agree on some level of government protection by relinquishing some degree of their freedom to pursue their own desires.

95. For example, this idea is worked out in detail in J. BUCHANAN, *supra* note 88, at 142–46.

III. Retributivism and Personhood:
A Rights Thesis

As we have seen, assaultive retributivists tend to rely on disguised (and confused) utilitarianism, or on vague invocations of the objective moral order and *lex talionis* (the law of retribution). These notions, at least in their present state of development, have been adequately discredited.[96] On the other hand, protective retributivists rely on the Kantian notion of individual dignity allied with the desert theory, which is a viable theory. If punishment is justified because a person deserves it by virtue of the categorical imperative that she be treated with respect for her status as a person, then it follows that a punishment that itself violates that categorical imperative cannot justifiably be applied to a person. If only persons "deserve," by virtue of their personhood, then that which constitutes denial of personhood cannot be "deserved." When used in this way, the idea of respect for persons imports a "rights thesis"[97] into the justification of punishment. In the punishment context, that rights thesis has its basis in the Kantian form of retributivism.

The Supreme Court has in fact (though not in word) espoused such a retributivist rights thesis in the eighth amendment. Thus it has implicitly espoused the protective— but not the assaultive—face of retributivism. It has made clear that punishment is both "substantively" and "procedurally" limited by "respect for the uniqueness of the individual" and "the dignity of man."[98] Preliminarily, the broad notions of human dignity and respect for persons must be clarified, at least in a rudimentary and impressionistic fashion. Then a discussion will follow about whether or not it is appropriate to conflate the two concepts in the punishment context.

A. Respect for Persons

The notion of respect for persons arises in several legal contexts. It is generally at the heart of due process,[99] and also enters into contemporary thinking about privacy,[100]

---

96. In addition to the foregoing argument, see text accompanying notes 88–95 *supra* on revenge-utilitarianism. On "objective order" and *lex talionis,* see Bedau, *supra* note 81; Gibbs, *supra* note 85; Hughes, *License to Kill,* 26 N.Y. REV. BOOKS 22 (1979) (reviewing W. BERNS, *supra* note 73); Murphy, *supra* note 44.

97. *See* note 64 and accompanying text *supra.*

98. *See, e.g.,* Lockett v. Ohio, 438 U.S. 586, 605 (1978) (Burger, C. J., separate opinion); Woodson v. North Carolina, 428 U.S. 280, 304 (1976) (process of inflicting death penalty mandatorily for certain crimes "treats all persons convicted of a designated offense not as uniquely individual human beings, but as members of a faceless, undifferentiated mass"; hence, "we believe that in capital cases the fundamental respect for humanity underlying the Eighth Amendment . . . requires consideration of the character and record of the individual offender and the circumstances of the particular offense as a constitutionally indispensable part of the process of inflicting the penalty of death."); Gregg v. Georgia, 428 U.S. 153, 173 (1976) ("A penalty . . . must accord with 'the dignity of man,' which is the 'basic concept underlying the Eighth Amendment'"); Trop v. Dulles, 356 U.S. 86, 100 (1958) ("The basic concept underlying the Eighth Amendment is nothing less than the dignity of man").

99. *See, e.g.,* Michelman, *Formal and Associational Aims in Procedural Due Process,* in DUE PROCESS 126 (J. Pennock & J. Chapman eds. 1977).

100. *See, e.g.,* Benn, *Privacy, Freedom, and Respect for Persons,* in PRIVACY 1 (J. Pennock & J. Chapman eds. 1971).

property,[101] equal protection,[102] and the first amendment.[103] But is the concept useful? It is not useful if in fact society's notion of what a person is, and therefore the parameters of respecting such an entity, constitutes nothing more than a convenient label for an aggregate of other values, however they have been formulated. I do not think this is the case, for the word "person" expresses an understanding that each individual who first appears only as an object is, in fact, a subject, possessing a rich and mysterious inner life of her own. For "respect for persons" to perform an independent role as a limit on government action in any of these fields, however, it may be necessary to define what a "person" is. This problem has recently generated some interesting philosophical conundrums, which are beyond the scope of this Article.[104] In the present context, respect for persons will be briefly considered as a unitary notion. It can at least be said that to respect someone's personhood means to behave toward her in a way that manifests an understanding that every individual possesses an inner life which is no less important than anyone else's.[105] This seems to necessitate, at least, an understanding that every person can experience joy and pain in response to other people as well as to the physical environment; that every person has a sense of individuality and continuity over time; that the individual is capable of making choices; and that she constitutes herself by them.

In addition, the term respect for persons seems to indicate that one's understanding of these things must be manifested in a way that shows their significance. But it is hard to specify what manifestations are necessary in order to show respect for a person. If respect for persons is constitutionalized in some areas, society does not thereby intend to constitutionalize love, compassion, and empathy. Respect for persons may be merely a minimal quantum of these virtues, involving less affirmative actions of concern.[106]

B. Human Dignity

Is respect for persons the same thing as respect for human dignity? In the punishment context, the requirement that even a criminal not be "treated like an object" is traditionally related to the notion of dignity. It appears that respect for human dignity is either coextensive with respect for personhood or is a sub-concept included within it. When the term "dignity" is invoked, attention is focused not so much on the nature of a person as

---

101. *See, e.g.,* Reich, *The New Property,* 73 YALE L. J. 733 (1964).

102. *See, e.g.,* Michelman, *Foreward: On Protecting the Poor Through the Fourteenth Amendment,* 83 HARV. L. REV. 7 (1969).

103. *See, e.g.,* Baker, *Scope of the First Amendment Freedom of Speech,* 25 U.C.L.A. L. REV. 964 (1978).

104. *See, e.g.,* THE IDENTITIES OF PERSONS (A. Rorty ed. 1976) (with extensive bibliography); B. WILLIAMS, PROBLEMS OF THE SELF (1973); Dennett, *Intentional Systems,* 1971 J. PHILOSOPHY 87; Tooley, *Abortion and Infanticide,* 2 PHILOSOPHY & PUB. AFF. 37 (1972). *See also* P. Strawson, *Freedom and Resentment,* in FREEDOM AND RESENTMENT 1–25 (1974) (particularly suggestive with regard to the concept of treatment as a person); Morris, *supra* note 72 (every individual has a right to punishment derived from a fundamental human right to be treated as a person).

105. *See* P. STRAWSON, *supra* note 104.

106. Of course, no bright line can be drawn between affirmative and negative obligations of government, just as no bright line can be drawn between acts and omissions. Moreover, some have argued that equal concern and respect for all persons in society requires government to act affirmatively in satisfying people's "merit wants." *See, e.g.,* Michelman, *supra* note 102.

capable of and deserving of autonomous choices about her relationships to others and her environment, as on the basic understanding of intersubjectivity that distinguishes human beings from animals, trees, and stones. Thus, to say that the eighth amendment requires treatment manifesting the understanding that "even the vilest criminal remains a human being possessed of common human dignity" was equivalent in Justice Brennan's mind with saying that people must not be treated as "nonhumans, as objects to be toyed with and discarded."[107] While it may ultimately be inaccurate to think of respect for the dignity of a person as the same thing as respect for a person in general, the concepts are intertwined enough so that it is helpful to associate both of them with the retributivist rights thesis. In particular, when discussing "substantive" (first-order) limitations on punishment the Court has relied on "the dignity of man," and when discussing the "procedural" (second-order) limitations has relied on "respect due the uniqueness of the individual."[108] It is the thesis of this Article that these formulations belong to the same retributivist model or thought methodology.

C. The Retributivist Rights Thesis in Substance and Procedure

Respect for persons or human dignity is a factor in evaluating the "substantive" validity of a punishment—whether or not a person deserves it—per se or in terms of its proportionality in response to a crime. Whether or not a punishment violates human dignity is a moral judgment. In making this moral judgment under the cruel and unusual punishments clause, I have argued that judges should rely not on their own values nor on opinion polls or majority vote, but rather on a coherent moral consensus of our society.[109] In evaluating punishment some considerations relevant to dignity or

---

107. Furman v. Georgia, 408 U.S. 238, 273 (1972) (Brennan, J., concurring).

108. *See* note 6 *supra*. In his opinion for the plurality in Woodson v. North Carolina, 428 U.S. 280, 304 (1976), Justice Stewart made clear that he regards these notions as equivalent to each other and to "fundamental respect for humanity underlying the Eighth Amendment." *Id.*

109. *See* Radin, *supra* note 5, at 1030–42. The notion of deep or coherent consensus is problematic. I have embraced it because it seems less problematic than its alternatives, at least at our present stage of philosophical insight. If judges must make moral judgments, and under the cruel and unusual punishments clause they must, it seems there are four types of sources for the needed moral principles:

(1) objective ethics or moral truth of the matter—based on natural law, revelation, etc.;
(2) the judge's own personal values;
(3) "deep," institutional or "coherent" consensus;
(4) majority preference or social consensus—based on opinion polls, legislative acts, etc.

As Professor Ely, *supra* note 11, trenchantly observed, (3) has a tendency to degenerate to (4), making nonsense of the idea of constitutional limitation as a countermajoritarian check on majority rule. Some urge reliance on (1) ("objective" values) instead. *See, e.g.,* Murphy, *supra* note 67. But (1) has a tendency to degenerate to (2) just as readily as (3) does to (4). A mandate to judges to rely on the objective moral truth of the matter could result in what would be popularly perceived as travesties of justice. It is no more satisfactory to regard the Constitution as a mandate to substitute judges' personal values for majority rule than it is to regard it as a mere reinforcement of majority rule.

From this dilemma Professor Ely apparently concludes that judges are to implement *no* "substantive" values, but only "process" values. Ely, *supra* note 11, at 55; *cf.* Ely, *Toward a Representation-*

personhood are as follows: Infliction of unnecessary pain fails to manifest concerned understanding of another individual's capacity to feel pain. Humiliation and degradation seem to transgress the individual's capacity and commitment to make choices and to constitute herself by them as does manifest disregard for the individual's future life or quality of life. The greater the pain or infringement of autonomy inflicted on someone, the more likely it is that respect for persons may thereby be violated. There is a moral gray area regarding some punishments and their appropriateness in some cases.

This gray area is indeterminate, if one is wholly subjectivist in ethics; or else decisions falling within it are subject to substantial risk of error, if one embraces some form of ethical objectivity.[110] Most of us now think locking someone up in a cell does not disrespect a person; most of us think that physical torture does; many of us are unsure about execution. But in the gray area decision cannot be deferred. If no coherent consensus exists or can be discerned to resolve the moral issue of whether a specific punishment violates human dignity, and hence cannot be deserved by a person, judges should fall back to a second-order moral judgment on who should bear the risk of error in this

---

Reinforcing Mode of Judicial Review, 37 MD. L. REV. 451 (1978) (the judicial function is to preserve the substance of democracy by preserving the democratic process). But, at least in the context of review of punishment, no such escape to neutralism is possible. Professor Ely points out that the Supreme Court's "consensus" interpretation of the cruel and unusual punishments clause, involving reliance on legislative enactments as indicators of current moral standards, opened the door to a rush to re-enact the death penalty. Ely, *supra* note 11, at 46. It is true that this is the wrong use of consensus and is a danger to which consensus theory is inherently subject. Yet in a footnote Professor Ely states: "I do not by any of this mean to suggest that the death penalty is constitutional, only that its unconstitutionality must be established by some other line of argument." *Id.* at 46 n.179, (citing C. BLACK, CAPITAL PUNISHMENT: THE INEVITABILITY OF CAPRICE AND MISTAKE [1974]).

If the death penalty is unconstitutional because the process of inflicting it (like the process of doing anything) is subject to error and inconsistency, we are making the judgment that even all possible procedural due process, as pure and neutral as we can make it, in this case falls short of what is "due." This judgment is a moral judgment, and the principles upon which it is made must "come from" somewhere. I argue that those principles come from deep or institutional consensus in our system about the relationship of the decisionmaking process to the gravity of the threatened invasion of personal interests in light of the respect due to persons. The alternative would be to say they come from objective or natural law principles. Thus, Professor Ely can evade the first-order moral question but not the second. The dilemma cannot be resolved with a retreat to "neutrality."

I am hoping the dilemma can be resolved, or at least better illuminated and parsed, with some philosophical progress on what might be meant by objective morality. Hilary Putnam and others have developed a new theory of reference which relates the objective meaning of "natural kind" words to social consensus. *See, e.g.,* NAMING, NECESSITY AND NATURAL KINDS (S. Schwartz ed. 1977).

It may be that a parallel theory of objective ethics can be developed. David Wiggins' suggestion that "person" be regarded as a natural kind word seems to lead in this direction. Wiggins, *Locke, Butler and the Stream of Consciousness: And Men As a Natural Kind,* in THE IDENTITIES OF PERSONS (A. Rorty ed., 1976). If objectivity in ethics can be interpreted in this sociological light, then there apparently will be no bright-line distinction between objective ethics and what I understand as a deep or coherent moral consensus. At that point, it will be less troublesome to appeal to objective ethics in implementing the Constitution. At present I suggest that coherent consensus be considered a "weak" form of objectivity, to distinguish it clearly from radical skepticism or subjectivity of the sort that would make opinion polls decisive on moral issues.

110. As suggested above, coherent consensus should be considered for this purpose a form of ethical objectivity, since in theory, it provides a criterion for moral terms separate from preference summing (though unfortunately difficult to specify clearly) and thus makes sense of the notion of risk of error. *See* note 109 *supra.*

disputed moral weighing.[111] It seems likely that even in the absence of "substantive" (first-order) moral consensus, there might exist a moral consensus for the fallback judgment allocating risk of error. This judgment relates to factors such as the magnitude and the irrevocability of the morally dubious threatened invasion of individual interests.[112] The moral insight is that a person is not respected if subjected to the *risk* that her personhood will be degraded or negated. This is because it manifests the same sort—though not the same degree—of disregard for her inner life to do something to her with indifference or ignorance about its morality as to do something knowing it is wrong.

As elaborated above, this second-order fall-back judgment is the same type of moral judgment that is at issue in a "procedural" case like *Lockett v. Ohio*.[113] In *Lockett,* the plurality made the moral judgment that respect for persons required allocating less risk of error toward the defendant than the Ohio legislature seemed to deem appropriate. The super due process theory of adjudication requires a second-order substantive judgment similar to the first-order substantive judgment called for in a case like *Coker v. Georgia*,[114] where the determination was made that execution for rape is always disproportionate, and therefore excessive.[115] The *Lockett* limitation—punishment is cruel if

---

111. *See* Radin, *supra* note 5, at 1029–30, 1062–64; *cf.* R. DWORKIN, *supra* note 71, at 199:

> It makes sense to say that a man has a fundamental right against the Government, in the strong sense, like free speech, if that right is necessary to protect his dignity, or his standing as equally entitled to concern and respect, or some other personal value of like consequence. It does not make sense otherwise.
>
> So if rights make sense at all, then the invasion of a relatively important right must be a very serious matter. It means treating a man as less than a man, or as less worthy of concern than other men. The institution of rights rests on the conviction that this is a grave injustice, and that it is worth paying the incremental cost in social policy or efficiency that is necessary to prevent it. But then it must be wrong to say that inflating rights is as serious as invading them. If the Government errs on the side of the individual, then it simply pays a little more in social efficiency than it has to pay; it pays a little more, that is, of the same coin that it has already decided must be spent. But if it errs against the individual it inflicts an insult upon him that, on its own reckoning, it is worth a great deal of that coin to avoid.

112. Although of course it cannot be conclusive evidence for the proposition in the text, it is interesting to note that many writers think the proper allocation of burden of proof or risk of error regarding death as punishment is simply self-evident. *See, e.g.,* Amsterdam, *supra* note 54, at 44 ("[t]he deliberate judicial extinction of human life is intrinsically so final and so terrible an act as to cast the burden of proof for its justification upon those who want us to do it," a fortiori "when the act is executed through a fallible system which assures that we kill some people wrongly"); Hughes, *License to Kill,* 26 N.Y. REV. BOOKS 22, 24 (1979) (reviewing W. BERNS, *supra* note 73) ("Since we are talking about killing people we may properly place the burden of proof on the advocates of the death penalty to furnish some convincing justification"); Knorr, *Deterrence and the Death Penalty: A Temporal Cross-Sectional Approach,* 70 J. CRIM. L & CRIMINOLOGY 235, 253 (1979) ("Given the context of permanent and irreversible punishment, the answer is clear" that retentionists have the burden of proof "both morally and politically" to show that execution is a deterrent); Satre, *The Irrationality of Capital Punishment,* 6 SW. J. PHILOSOPHY 75 (1975) (arguing that risk of factual and moral error makes execution "rationally indefensible" in light of its irreversibility). *But cf.* E. VAN DEN HAAG, *supra* note 73, at 214, 219 (There is a "known" [through "intuition"] general relationship between severity and deterrence which puts the burden of proof on abolitionists. The risk of factual and moral error does not justify abolition; execution, like automobile traffic and surgery, is justified "because benefits (including justice) are felt to outweigh the statistical certainty of unintentionally killing innocents.").

113. 438 U.S. 586 (1978).

114. 433 U.S. 584 (1977).

115. *See* note 6 *supra.*

the sentence is rendered under procedures or standards allocating too much risk of moral error toward defendant—can thus be analyzed as an aspect of the retributivist rights thesis.

Classifying the super due process limitation as an aspect of the retributivist rights thesis resting on the need to keep punishment within the bounds of respect for persons does not, of course, draw those boundaries for us. How can the second-order, super due process limitation be applied? That is, how much risk of error against defendant is "too much"? *Lockett* tells us only that we fail to respect the defendant as a person if we allow her to bear the risk engendered by making some of her proffered mitigating evidence inadmissible in sentencing. It does not tell us that we do respect her as a person if we allow her to bear the risk of error remaining after her proffered mitigating evidence is admitted.

There is plenty of risk of error remaining. There is risk of legal and moral error in the use of vague or questionable aggravating circumstances such as the "probability that the defendant would commit criminal acts of violence that would constitute a continuing threat to society"[116] or the fact that the killing was "especially heinous, atrocious or cruel."[117] There is risk of moral error in not requiring a finding that aggravating circumstances outweigh mitigating circumstances.[118] There is risk of error in requiring that aggravating circumstances outweigh mitigating circumstances by a preponderance of the evidence.[119] There is less, but still some, risk of error in requiring that finding to be made beyond a reasonable doubt. There is risk of moral error in the sentencing discretion, which the Court has discovered must be kept down to some unspecified level in order to respect persons at the same time it must be kept up to some unspecified level for the same reason. There is risk of factual error regarding guilt or innocence, even when the standard for finding a person guilty is proof beyond a reasonable doubt.

IV. Respect for Persons and Execution for Homicide

The current plurality position may be that human dignity will not be violated if as much of the risk of error as "possible" is eliminated from the sentencing system. The Court has not yet done this, and it seems sure to be faced with a continuing series of cases attempting to clarify its rules.[120] But even if the Court alleviates the problems of

---

116. TEX. CRIM. PRO. CODE ANN. § 37.071(b)(2) (Vernon Supp. 1980). *See* text accompanying notes 35–39 *supra*.
117. FLA. STAT. ANN. §921.141(5)(h) (West Supp. 1980).
118. *E.g.,* CAL. PENAL CODE § 190.3 (West 1978).
119. *E.g.,* FLA. STAT. ANN. §921.141(3)(b) (West Supp. 1980).
120. Some of the unanswered questions are stated by Justice Mosk in People v. Frierson, 25 Cal. 3d 142, 193 n.8, 599 P.2d 587, 618 n.8, 158 Cal. Rptr. 281, 287 n.8 (1979) (Mosk, J., concurring):

> For example, must the jury unanimously agree on which aggravating factors are established by the evidence? Must they so find beyond a reasonable doubt? In order to permit "meaningful appellate review," must they make similar findings as to mitigating factors? Before imposing a

appropriateness, vagueness, and standards of proof in the evaluation of aggravating circumstances,[121] it will still be confronted with the dilemma of discretion—or the *Furman-Lockett* paradox. Pre-*Furman* unconstitutional discretion risks error through arbitrariness and inconsistency, and thereby fails to respect persons. Post-*Lockett* constitutional discretion is required because respect for persons necessitates a completely individualized moral judgment of desert in each case. But discretion is discretion. If the Court makes hard and fast formal rules, it will be haunted by the spirit of *Lockett*, for it knows the rules will be overinclusive as to some defendants. On the other hand, if the Court countenances conscious discretion in the system it will be haunted by the spirit of *Furman*, for it knows some defendants will be treated more harshly than the moral basis of punishment warrants, at least if that moral basis is partly grounded in a right to have like cases treated alike.

Perhaps Chief Justice Burger would want to argue that ultimately "respect" must be balanced against the "necessity" of the death penalty. But even assuming it would be appropriate to conclude that the government may accord citizens less than due respect in cases of "necessity," no one has shown that execution is necessary either for utilitarian social gain or for retributivist justice. In light of the reasoning in *Lockett*, it would be hard for the Court to disagree that due respect requires at least that necessity not be "established" by presumptions.

The Supreme Court in the Seventies saw its cases as posing both general and specific questions: (1) May anyone ever be justifiably killed by the state?; and, (2) May anyone justifiably be killed by the state using particular sentencing procedures? The Court in affirmatively answering the first question, decided to risk moral error in favor of the government. The Court in negatively answering the second question in certain cases has declared that human dignity, or the respect the government must accord its citizens as individuals, precludes risking certain moral errors in favor of the government.

I believe the ultimate import of the *Lockett* rationale is that these specific "no's" must eventually engulf the general "yes." But there is no logical proof that the quantum of risk of error inherent in the nature of the system, by virtue of the dilemma of discretion, respects or disrespects a person when that system is used to inflict death upon her. This is the ultimate second-order moral judgment the Court must make.

This Article will conclude by reviewing the state of affairs regarding both the first- and second-order retributivist rights theses as they relate to execution for homicide.

1. There is profound moral disagreement about whether any perpetrator of a homicide can ever deserve to die for the crime.

2. In case a perpetrator of a homicide can deserve to die for it:

---

sentence of death, must they unanimously agree that the aggravating factors outweigh the mitigating factors? Must that finding also be beyond a reasonable doubt? By how much must the aggravating factors "outweigh" the mitigating factors: is it enough that the former outweigh the latter by a "slight" or "mere" preponderance, or is a heavier burden required (e.g., "substantially" outweigh) in view of the nature of the penalty? At least as many questions remain unanswered concerning the process of "proportionality review."

121. *See* text accompanying note 36 *supra*.

A. there is a moral disagreement about which categories of perpetrators deserve to die,[122] and

B. there is a moral disagreement about whether their deaths should be brought about by the state.[123]

3. If a perpetrator of a homicide can deserve to die for it, if the categories of perpetrators deserving to die can be satisfactorily delineated, and if their death may be brought about by the state, we must still pass moral judgment on whether the occurrence of factual, legal, and moral errors made when the legal system tries to identify these people in the real world, as well as our knowledge that such errors are inevitable, render invalid any supposed answer to the first-order questions in the ideal world.

It seems difficult to go very far with reasoned argument about whether execution as punishment fails to treat a person with respect, such that a first-order retributivist justification cannot be made out.[124] In the context of implementing punishment

---

122. There is confusion about the criteria of culpability, such as whether an insanity defense should exist and what its scope should be. *See, e.g,* H. FINGARETTE & A. HASSE, MENTAL DISABILITIES AND CRIMINAL RESPONSIBILITY (1979); Morse, *Crazy Behavior, Morals, and Science: An Analysis of Mental Health Law,* 51 S. CAL. L. REV. 527 (1978). On the issue of how homicide offenses should be graded, see G. FLETCHER, *supra* note 76, at 351–55. For what might constitute "aggravating circumstances" that render someone deserving of death, see text accompanying note 36 *supra;* whether deserving death depends upon "mens rea" or intent to kill, see note 64 *supra* (discussing opinions of Justice White and Justice Blackmun in Lockett v. Ohio, 438 U.S. 586 (1978)).

123. *See* A. CAMUS, *Reflections on the Guillotine,* in RESISTANCE, REBELLION AND DEATH 175 (1960). In this extraordinary piece, Albert Camus rested his case on a very similar argument to the one presented here, though he stated it with fewer syllogisms and with an eloquence I can admire but not imitate.

124. Most abolitionists simply stop here and state their intuitive conviction. People understandably balk at the suggestion that some heinous killer deserves their respect. Their understandable instinct is to dissociate themselves from such a killer, to regard her as not one of the same species as themselves. Yet members of the Supreme Court have consistently felt that the eighth amendment precludes us from allowing government to express this impulse. *See, e.g.,* Trop v. Dulles, 356 U.S. 86, 101 (1958) (denationalization as punishment "is a form of punishment more primitive than torture, for it . . . strips the citizen of his status in the national and international political community"). At the least, it must mean that we are to treat the worst criminal as a person, as one of ourselves, in spite of our revulsion and our temptation to cut her off.

If execution as punishment does fail the first-order test of respect for persons, I suspect it is because we are stepping in to deprive someone of a *future,* and there seems to be something very arrogant about this.

> The instinct of preservation of societies, and hence of individuals, requires . . . that individual responsibility be postulated and accepted. But . . . there never exists any total responsibility or, consequently, any absolute punishment or reward. . . . [T]he death penalty . . . simply usurps an exorbitant privilege by claiming to punish an always relative culpability by a definitive and irreparable punishment.

A. CAMUS, *supra* note 123, at 210, 221; *see* text accompanying notes 61–62 *supra.* In a parallel vein, Professor Murphy, *supra* note 61, argues that death "represents lost opportunity of a morally crucial kind." *Id.* at 242. Perhaps once in a rare while there could be an erstwhile human creature who forfeited the title of human being and could be exterminated. Even so, we cannot know what motivated her, what made her the way she is, though chances are some of the rest of us had some part in the process. *See* A. CAMUS, *supra* note 123, at 219. At any rate, any rationalization made on the basis of extremely rare cases cannot justify routine executions for murder. In his impassioned defense of execution, W. Berns argues that "the very awesomeness of condemning a man to death requires the punishment to be reserved for extraordinarily heinous crimes, but throughout most of modern history this has not been the case." W. BERNS, *supra* note 73, at 182.

through a political system, the second-order test of respect for persons is far more important. The first-order question is the wrong question to ask, because the government is not an ideal observer regarding people's moral deserts. The right question is whether we can allow execution to remain available in the political system given the risk of error, even if reserved for extremely rare cases.[125]

When making moral judgments, we must not omit the moral significance of the limitations of the world in which we must make them. Super due process is a moral rationale that takes into account the existence of a political system and its fallibility. We do not now have consensus about execution as punishment, in spite of resurgence of popular support for it (at least in the abstract).[126] One need look no further

---

125. The annals of the death penalty include "murderers" convicted on mistaken identification, "death-qualified" juries, and execution for crimes now not thought atrocious enough to warrant it. Its annals also include regretted actions during periods of political unrest, such as the execution of Sacco and Vanzetti, and the Rosenbergs. See Radin, supra note 5, at 1023–24 n. 137. See also Seidman, The Trial and Execution of Bruno Richard Hauptmann: Still Another Case that "Will Not Die," 66 GEO. L.J. 1(1977).

Sandra Lockett spent two years under sentence of death, which should give us pause, as it did Justice Marshall, who wrote: "That an Ohio trial court could impose the death penalty on petitioner on these facts, and that the Ohio Supreme Court on review could sustain it, casts strong doubt on the plurality's premise that appellate review in state systems is sufficient to avoid the wrongful and unfair imposition of this irrevocable penalty." 438 U.S. at 621 (Marshall, J., concurring in the judgment). One may speculate that the members of the Court voting for reversal in Lockett did believe that a moral error had been made; that this young woman who was merely an accomplice to a robbery committed by her older brother and a friend was simply not culpable enough to deserve death for her crime. So one may further speculate that had the sentencer "officially" considered these factors and still sentenced her to death, the Court might have endorsed some other theory to support reversal. See, e.g., note 5 supra (Justice White's proportionality theory), or the "Jackson" theory embraced by Justice Blackmun, 438 U.S. at 617–19 (Blackmun, J., concurring in part and concurring in the judgment), or defendant's various other fifth amendment, sixth amendment and due process claims, 438 U.S. at 595–96. Still in the face of substantial risk of moral error the Court allowed Florida to execute John Spenkelink, See Spenkelink v. Wainwright, 442 U.S. 1301 (1979). The execution was predicated on the aggravating circumstances that defendant's shooting of his traveling companion was "especially cruel, atrocious, and heinous and in connection with robbery of the victim to secure return of money claimed by [defendant]." Id. at 1304. See N.Y. Times, May 26, 1979, at 1, col. 6.

126. It is still fair to say America is deeply divided about the justifiability of execution. The support of 51% or even 60% evidences deep division. The dissenters are not a cult or a far-out minority but people in the mainstream of American life and government, including elected public officials and judges. Justice Marshall argued that enthusiasm for execution in the abstract would wane if people perceived how it operates in the concrete. Gregg v. Georgia, 428 U.S. at 232 (Marshall, J., dissenting); Furman v. Georgia, 408 U.S. at 361 (Marshall, J., concurring). Albert Camus had a similar view:

When the imagination sleeps, words are emptied of their meaning: a deaf population absentmindedly registers the condemnation of a man. But if people are shown the machine, made to touch the wood and steel and to hear the sound of a head falling, then public imagination, suddenly awakened, will repudiate both the vocabulary and the penalty.

A. CAMUS, supra note 123, at 177. Supporters of execution as a means of vindicating the moral order have had to face the fact that, if we believe in what we are doing, executions done in society's name should be witnessed by society. Thus, says Professor Berns: "[T]o impress upon the population the awesomeness of the moral order and the awful consequences of its breach, I think it is necessary that executions be public." W. BERNS, supra note 73, at 187. Professor Berns does not advocate that executions be televised, however, because not only should some viewers be spared, but also because television would make it a "vulgar spectacle." Id. at 188. He therefore concludes that on balance, executions should be witnessed by the members of the legislature. Newman, supra note 73, also opts against televised executions, for it would be a "concrete representation of the

than the Court's own decade of disarray. Nor do we have consensus on whether it can be validated by consensus, nor on what would constitute consensus if it could. To argue that execution nevertheless passes muster under the retributivist rights thesis would be to assert as moral truth for our society a proposition about which we are deeply divided. It is to risk a far greater wrong to the individuals upon whom it falls than the "wrong" that would be risked if execution were to be eliminated and some justifiable retribution were to be denied to society.

The issue is really whether we can accord due respect to *any* defendant sentenced to death in the context of a system that we know must wrongly kill some of them[127] although we do not know which. Thus it is allied to the equality issue at the core of super due process. In such a system we are in effect saying to each convicted defendant: "We are inflicting death upon you although we know there is some risk we are horribly wrong to do so, because a majority of us feel that it is right to inflict death upon people when their acts and character place them in a certain category, whose definition is also in dispute and whose members are not at the present time, we regret to say, unequivocally identifiable." Further, recall that at the beginning of this Article we assumed arguendo, as the Court has assumed in fact, that execution can pass the utilitarian test. Therefore, we are also saying to each convicted defendant: "Although we cannot prove it, a majority of us believe that by killing you, even if we understand we may be mistaken about your particular moral deserts, we will deter some other would-be killer and ensure against illegal mob violence. We are sorry, but we have to kill you for the good of society." This is treatment as a statistic, and it is treatment as a means to a social goal, but it is not treatment with "the degree of respect due the uniqueness of the individual."

---

punishment." He feels that the "symbolic aspects of punishment" are better reinforced through "the dramaturgical representation of punishments" and thus, "the best way to enhance the symbolic satisfaction of punishment is to dramatize, through fiction, what might go on in prisons and in other criminal punishments." Professor Newman further asserts that "punishment in secret is likely to enhance the mystery and drama of criminal punishment, to stimulate the imagination." *Id.* at 286.

127. "There is no perfect procedure. . . ." Lockett v. Ohio, 438 U.S. at 605.

PART III

ALTERNATIVES TO PUNISHMENT: REHABILITATION AND RESTITUTION

This section addresses an issue of practical urgency, an urgency underlined by the obvious fact that no sensible person could wholly approve of the present practices of criminal punishment that exist in our society. As prison riots have brought to light, most American prisons are inhuman pestholes that breed crime rather than reduce it. Animal brutalities from guards and fellow prisoners (for example, homosexual rapes) are the order of the day. Young persons, guilty perhaps of nothing more serious than marijuana possession, may be placed into a context where they are brutalized before they return to society, where they are alienated and become expert in sophisticated criminal techniques they have learned from older fellow prisoners. Only the extremely shortsighted could advocate more of the same as a solution to the growing problem of crime in our society, but alas, as usual, there is no poverty of shortsighted people in positions of influence and power.

For this reason, books such as Dr. Karl Menninger's widely read *The Crime of Punishment* (New York, 1968)—a brief preliminary study for which is contained in this collection—are in many ways welcome contributions to the "law and order" debate in American society. Menninger, an eminent psychiatrist, dramatically points up the failures and inhumanities of our present penal practices and persuasively advocates drastic reform. And for this much, all reasonable and decent people should surely be grateful to him. However, he goes beyond such negative criticism and advocates an alternative method of handling the crime problem, and his alternative method is, to say the very least, highly controversial.

Like a great many psychiatrists and social scientists, Menninger tends to regard criminal behavior as symptomatic of personality disorder. Thus he proposes that we drop our present practice of punishing criminals in prisons and indeed that we drop the whole complex business of the criminal law and criminal procedure. In his view, this wastes time and money, is inhuman, and fails to perform the important task of eliminating crime; for punishment, he claims, neither deters nor reforms people. Retribution, the only other possible justification left, can be rejected since it rests, according to Menninger, on an outdated and unscientific conception of personal responsibility or free will.

Since criminal behavior is really a kind of sickness, then, we should respond to such behavior therapeutically. Criminal behavior is to be *cured,* not punished. Instead of perpetuating the inhuman practice of confining people in prisons, we should treat and rehabilitate them in hospitals. When necessary, for their own good and ours, we may even employ preventive and indefinite detention. Since this confinement will be for therapy, and not for punishment, it will not be objectionable but will rather be a benefit to all concerned.

Although it sounds wonderful, it may be too good to be true. We should certainly humanize our present penal institutions and provide greatly increased opportunities for at least voluntary therapy. But should we abandon the criminal process entirely? Would it genuinely benefit even the criminal if we did so? At least in the criminal law a prisoner has some procedural protections contained in our Bill of Rights. But there is no therapeutic bill of rights, no developed concept of "cruel and unusual *therapy*" that might be used to block such procedures as electric shocks, lobotomies, and more sophisticated forms of psychosurgery, and certain drugs. Defective as the criminal process is, would it be obviously better to move toward what Nicholas Kittrie has called the "therapeutic state" in which psychiatrists have increased political power and discretionary control over the lives of citizens? (This has happened in the Soviet Union, and the increasing number of political dissidents there classified as "mentally ill" is disquieting.)

The readings open with Karl Menninger's essay "Therapy, Not Punishment," in which he argues that punishment is an ineffective and unscientific holdover from our unenlightened past. According to Menninger, we now have enough knowledge of human behavior both to understand social deviance and to cure it. We should, he argues, regard the criminal as a sick person who needs expert therapeutic help for rehabilitation. This will do the criminal good and will protect society.

There are, of course, reasons that one might be skeptical of Menninger's argument. On substantive grounds, one might well wonder if all criminals are really mentally ill. A criminal is simply someone who violates a criminal statute, as did such practitioners of civil disobedience as Gandhi and Martin Luther King, Jr. Do we really want to regard such persons as ill and seek to rehabilitate them? (The psychiatrist Thomas Szasz has argued that the whole idea of mental illness is a myth, a way of labeling people we don't like so that we can fail to take them seriously and even confine them without feeling guilty about what we are doing.) Also, is it really going to be possible to give criminal defendants (patients?) adequate due process guarantees in a largely therapeutic response to social deviance? Finally (as stressed by Herbert Morris in his "Persons and Punishment" in Part I), will we not lose some important concepts of human dignity and responsibility if we start to view human wrongdoing as a matter over which we have no control? These and other worries are raised in the selections by Allen and Wasserstrom in this section.[1]

If a therapeutic response to social deviance is really going to work as a way of controlling crime, it will almost certainly have to employ (as Menninger advocates) *preventive detention:* the confining of people on the basis, not of what they have in fact done, but of a *prediction* of what they are likely to do. Such a practice strikes most persons as intolerable, even bordering on totalitarianism. In his sensitive and provocative article, Ferdinand Schoeman makes a case that many of our reflex liberal objections to preventive detention can perhaps be met and that it may be hard to articulate a really good principled objection to the practice, just as it is difficult to articulate such objections to the analogous practice of quarantining persons who have dangerous communicable diseases.

Most theories of punishment treat crime as a threat to society or the criminal as owing some debt to society. (The state prosecutes and views itself as the injured party in criminal cases.) Many crimes, however, have *individual victims,* persons harmed by the criminal activity; sometimes their interests are forgotten in all the abstract talk about society or the state. Perhaps instead of punishment or in addition to punishment or as a kind of punishment, we should consider programs of *restitution,* whereby the criminal is forced, in so far as possible, to make the victim whole again. Such concerns are the focus of the article by Randy Barnett with which this anthology concludes.

---

1. Allen's essay is a classic statement of the skeptical case against the rehabilitative ideal. The forces pushing for criminal rehabilitation are now much smaller and quieter than when Allen wrote. Allen's case may have helped deprive the rehabilitative movement of its intellectual friends at a time when other social forces (fear of crime and the unwillingness of people to bear the huge expense of uncertain programs of rehabilitation) were moving a majority of citizens toward a hard-line "law and order" response to crime. The remaining friends of the rehabilitative ideal argue that it cannot be judged a failure because it never was given a fair test. For Allen's most recent reflections on the rehabilitative ideal see *The Decline of the Rehabilitative Ideal*, New Haven: Yale University Press, 1981.

Therapy, Not Punishment

Karl Menninger

Since ancient times criminal law and penology have been based upon what is called in psychology the pain-pleasure principle. There are many reasons for inflicting pain—to urge an animal to greater efforts, to retaliate for pain received, to frighten, or to indulge in idle amusement. Human beings, like all animals, tend to move away from pain and toward pleasure. Hence the way to control behavior is to reward what is "good" and punish what is "bad." This formula pervades our programs of child-rearing, education, and social control of behavior.

With this concept three out of four readers will no doubt concur.

"Why, of course," they will say. "Only common sense. Take me for example. I know the speed limit and the penalty. Usually I drive moderately because I don't want to get a ticket. One afternoon I was in a hurry; I had an appointment, I didn't heed the signs. I did what I knew was forbidden and I got caught and received the punishment I deserved. Fair enough. It taught me a lesson. Since then I drive more slowly in that area. And surely people are deterred from cheating on their income taxes, robbing

This article originally appeared under the title "Verdict Guilty, Now What?" in *Harper's Magazine*, August, 1959, pp. 60–64. Copyright ©1959 by *Harper's Magazine*. All rights reserved. Reprinted by special permission. Karl Menninger is a distinguished American psychiatrist and is the author of numerous books and articles, including *The Crime of Punishment* (New York: The Viking Press, 1968).

banks, and committing rape by the fear of punishment. Why, if we didn't have these crime road blocks we'd have chaos!"

This sounds reasonable enough and describes what most people think—*part of the time*. But upon reflection we all know that punishments and the threat of punishments do *not* deter *some* people from doing forbidden things. Some of them take a chance on not being caught, and this chance is a very good one, too, better than five to one for most crimes. Not even the fear of possible death, self-inflicted, deters some speedsters. Exceeding the speed limit is not really regarded as criminal behavior by most people, no matter how dangerous and self-destructive. It is the kind of a "crime" which respectable members of society commit and condone. This is not the case with rape, bank-robbing, check-forging, vandalism, and the multitude of offenses for which the prison penalty system primarily exists. And from these offenses the average citizen, including the reader, is deterred by quite different restraints. For most of us it is our conscience, our self-respect, and our wish for the good opinion of our neighbors which are the determining factors in controlling our impulses toward misbehavior.

Today it is no secret that our official, prison-threat theory of crime control is an utter failure. Criminologists have known this for years. When pocket-picking was punishable by hanging, in England, the crowds that gathered about the gallows to enjoy the spectacle of an execution were particularly likely to have their pockets picked by skillful operators who, to say the least, were not deterred by the exhibition of "justice." We have long known that the perpetrators of most offenses are never detected; of those detected, only a fraction are found guilty and still fewer serve a "sentence." Furthermore, we are quite certain now that of those who do receive the official punishment of the law, many become firmly committed thereby to a continuing life of crime and a continuing feud with law enforcement officers. Finding themselves ostracized from society and blacklisted by industry they stick with the crowd they have been introduced to in jail and try to play the game of life according to this set of rules. In this way society skillfully converts individuals of borderline self-control into loyal members of the underground fraternity.

The science of human behavior has gone far beyond the common sense rubrics which dictated the early legal statutes. We know now that one cannot describe rape or bank-robbing or income-tax fraud simply as pleasure. Nor, on the other hand, can we describe imprisonment merely as pain. Slapping the hand of a beloved child as he reaches to do a forbidden act is utterly different from the institutionalized process of official punishment. The offenders who are chucked into our county and state and federal prisons are not anyone's beloved children; they are usually unloved children, grown-up physically but still hungry for human concern which they never got or never get in normal ways. So they pursue it in abnormal ways—abnormal, that is, from *our* standpoint.

Why Our Crime Therapy Has Failed

What might deter the reader from conduct which his neighbors would not like does not necessarily deter the grown-up child of vastly different background. The latter's experiences may have conditioned him to believe that the chances of winning by undetected cheating are vastly greater than the probabilities of fair treatment and opportunity. He knows about the official threats and the social disapproval of such acts. He knows about the hazards and the risks. But despite all this "knowledge," he becomes involved in waves of discouragement or cupidity or excitement or resentment leading to episodes of social offensiveness.

These episodes may prove vastly expensive both to him and to society. But sometimes they will have an aura of success. Our periodicals have only recently described the wealth and prominence for a time of a man described as a murderer. Konrad Lorenz, the great psychiatrist and animal psychologist, has beautifully described in geese what he calls a "triumph reaction." It is sticking out of the chest and flapping of the wings after an encounter with a challenge. All of us have seen this primitive biological triumph reaction—in some roosters, for example, in some businessmen and athletes and others—*and* in some criminals.

In general, though, the gains and goals of the social offender are not those which most men seek. Most offenders whom we belabor are not very wise, not very smart, not even very "lucky." It is not the successful criminal upon whom we inflict our antiquated penal system. It is the unsuccessful criminal, the criminal who really doesn't know how to commit crimes, and who gets caught. Indeed, until he is caught and convicted a man is technically not even called a criminal. The clumsy, the desperate, the obscure, the friendless, the defective, the diseased—these men who commit crimes that do not come off—are bad actors, indeed. But they are not the professional criminals, many of whom occupy high places. In some instances the crime is the merest accident or incident or impulse, expressed under unbearable stress. More often the offender is a persistently perverse, lonely, and resentful individual who joins the only group to which he is eligible—the outcasts and the anti-social.

And what do we do with such offenders? After a solemn public ceremony we pronounce them enemies of the people, and consign them for arbitrary periods to institutional confinement on the basis of laws written many years ago. Here they languish until time has ground out so many weary months and years. Then with a planlessness and stupidity only surpassed by that of their original incarceration they are dumped back upon society, regardless of whether any change has taken place in them for the better and with every assurance that changes have taken place in them for the worse. Once more they enter the unequal tussle with society. Proscribed for employment by most concerns, they are expected to invent a new way to make a living and to survive without any further help from society.

Intelligent members of society are well aware that the present system is antiquated, expensive, and disappointing, and that we are wasting vast quantities of manpower through primitive methods of dealing with those who transgress the law. In 1917 the famous Wickersham report of the New York State Prison Survey Committee recommended the abolition of jails, the institution of diagnostic clearing houses or classification centers, the development of a diversified institutional system and treatment program, and the use of indeterminate sentences. *Forty-two years have passed.* How little progress we have made! In 1933 the American Psychiatric Association, the American Bar Association, and the American Medical Association officially and jointly recommended psychiatric service for every criminal and juvenile court to assist the court and prison and parole officers with all offenders.

That was twenty-six years ago! Have these recommendations been carried out anywhere in the United States? With few exceptions offenders continue to be dealt with according to old-time instructions, written by men now dead who knew nothing about the present offender, his past life, the misunderstandings accumulated by him, or the provocation given to him.

The sensible, scientific question is: What kind of treatment could be instituted that would deter him or be most likely to deter him? Some of these methods are well known. For some offenders who have the money or the skillful legal counsel or the good luck to face a wise judge go a different route from the prescribed routine. Instead of jail and deterioration, they get the sort of re-education and re-direction associated with psychiatric institutions and the psychiatric profession. Relatively few wealthy offenders get their "treatment" in jail. This does not mean that justice is to be bought, or bought off. But it does mean that some offenders have relatives and friends who *care* and who try to find the best possible solution to the problem of persistent misbehavior, which is NOT the good old jail-and-penitentiary and make-'em-sorry treatment. It is a reflection on the democratic ideals of our country that these better ways are so often—indeed, *usually*—denied to the poor, the friendless, and the ignorant.

Science Versus Tradition

If we were to follow scientific methods, the convicted offender would be detained indefinitely pending a decision as to whether and how and when to reintroduce him successfully into society. All the skill and knowledge of modern behavioral science would be used to examine his personality assets, his liabilities and potentialities, the environment from which he came, its effects upon him, and his effects upon it.

Having arrived at some diagnostic grasp of the offender's personality, those in charge can decide whether there is a chance that he can be redirected into a mutually satisfactory adaptation to the world. If so, the most suitable techniques in education, industrial training, group administration, and psychotherapy should be selectively applied. All this may be best done extramurally or intramurally. It may require maximum "security" or only minimum "security." If, in due time, perceptible change occurs, the process should be expedited by finding a suitable spot in society and industry for him, and getting him out of prison control and into civil status (with parole control) as quickly as possible.

The desirability of moving patients out of institutional control swiftly is something which we psychiatrists learned the hard way, and recently. Ten years ago, in the state hospital I know best, the average length of stay was five years; today it is three months. Ten years ago few patients were discharged under two years; today 90 per cent are discharged within the first year. Ten years ago the hospital was overcrowded; today it has eight times the turnover it used to have; there are empty beds and there is no waiting list.

But some patients do not respond to our efforts, and they have to remain in the hospital, or return to it promptly after a trial home visit. And if the *prisoner,* like some of the psychiatric patients, cannot be changed by genuine efforts to rehabilitate him, we must look *our* failure in the face, and provide for his indefinitely continued confinement, regardless of the technical reasons for it. This we owe society for its protection.

There will be some offenders about whom the most experienced are mistaken, both ways. And there will be some concerning whom no one knows what is best. There are many problems for research. But what I have outlined is, I believe, the program of modern penology, the program now being carried out in some degree in California and a few other states, and in some of the federal prisons.

This civilized program, which would save so much now wasted money, so much unused manpower, and so much injustice and suffering, is slow to spread. It is held back by many things—by the continued use of fixed sentences in many places; by unenlightened community attitudes toward the offender whom some want tortured; by the prevalent popular assumption that burying a frustrated individual in a hole for a short time will change his warped mind, and that when he is certainly worse, he should be released because his "time" has been served; by the persistent failure of the law to distinguish between crime as an accidental, incidental, explosive event, crime as a behavior pattern expressive of chronic unutterable rage and frustration, and crime as a business or elected way of life. Progress is further handicapped by the lack of interest in the subject on the part of lawyers, most of whom are proud to say that they are not concerned with criminal law. It is handicapped by the lack of interest on the part of members of my own profession. It is handicapped by the mutual distrust of lawyers and psychiatrists.

The infestation or devil-possession theory of mental disease is an outmoded, pre-medieval concept. Although largely abandoned by psychiatry, it steadfastly persists in the minds of many laymen, including, unfortunately, many lawyers.

On the other hand, most lawyers have no really clear idea of the way in which a psychiatrist functions or of the basic concepts to which he adheres. They cannot understand, for example, why there is no such thing (for psychiatrists) as "insanity." Most lawyers have no conception of the meaning or methods of psychiatric case study and diagnosis. They seem to think that psychiatrists can take a quick look at a suspect, listen to a few anecdotes about him, and thereupon be able to say, definitely, that the awful "it"—the dreadful miasma of madness, the loathsome affliction of "insanity"—is present or absent. Because we all like to please, some timid psychiatrists fall in with this fallacy of the lawyers and go through these preposterous antics.

As the Psychiatrist Sees It

It is true that almost any offender—like anyone else—when questioned for a short time, even by the most skillful psychiatrist, can make responses and display behavior patterns which will indicate that he is enough like the rest of us to be called "sane." But a barrage of questions is not a psychiatric examination. Modern scientific personality study depends upon various specialists—physical, clinical, and sociological as well as psychological. It takes into consideration not only static and presently observable factors, but dynamic and historical factors, and factors of environmental interaction and change. It also looks into the future for correction, re-education, and prevention.

Hence, the same individuals who appear so normal to superficial observation are frequently discovered in the course of prolonged, intensive scientific study to have tendencies regarded as "deviant," "peculiar," "unhealthy," "sick," "crazy," "senseless," "irrational," "insane."

But now you may ask, "Is it not possible to find such tendencies in any individual if one looks hard enough? And if this is so, if we are all a little crazy or potentially so, what is the essence of your psychiatric distinctions? Who is it that you want excused?"

And here is the crux of it all. We psychiatrists don't want *anyone* excused. In fact, psychiatrists are much more concerned about the protection of the public than are the lawyers. I repeat; psychiatrists don't want anyone excused, certainly not anyone who shows anti-social tendencies. We consider them all responsible, which lawyers do not. And we want the prisoner to take on that responsibility, or else deliver it to someone who will be concerned about the protection of society and about the prisoner, too. We don't want anyone excused, but neither do we want anyone stupidly disposed of, futilely detained, or prematurely released. We don't want them tortured, either sensationally with hot irons or quietly by long-continued and forced idleness. In the psychiatrist's mind nothing should be done in the name of punishment, though he is well aware that the offender may regard either the diagnostic procedure or the treatment or the detention incident to the treatment as punitive. But this is in *his* mind, not in the psychiatrist's mind. And in our opinion it should not be in the public's mind, because it is an illusion.

It is true that we psychiatrists consider that all people have potentialities for anti-social behavior. The law assumes this, too. Most of the time most people control their criminal impulses. But for various reasons and under all kinds of circumstances some individuals become increasingly disorganized or demoralized, and then they begin to be socially offensive. The man who does criminal things is less convincingly disorganized than the patient who "looks" sick, because the former more nearly resembles the rest of us, and seems to be indulging in acts that we have struggled with and controlled. So we get hot under the collar about the one and we call him "criminal" whereas we pityingly forgive the other and call him "lunatic." But a surgeon uses the same principles of surgery whether he is dealing with a "clean" case, say some cosmetic surgery on a face, or a "dirty" case which is foul-smelling and offensive. What we are after is results and the emotions of the operator must be under control. Words like "criminal" and "insane" have no place in the scientific vocabulary any more than pejorative adjectives like "vicious," "psycho-pathic," "bloodthirsty," etc. The need is to find all the *descriptive* adjectives that apply to the case, and this is a scientific job—not a popular exercise in name-calling. Nobody's insides are very beautiful; and in the cases that require social control there has been a great wound and some of the insides are showing.

Intelligent judges all over the country are increasingly surrendering the onerous responsibility of deciding in advance what a man's conduct will be in a prison and how rapidly his wicked impulses will evaporate there. With more use of the indeterminate sentence and the establishment of scientific diagnostic centers, we shall be in a position to make progress in the science of *treating* antisocial trends. Furthermore, we shall get away from the present legal smog that hangs over the prisons, which lets us detain with heartbreaking futility some prisoners fully rehabilitated while others, whom the prison officials know full well to be dangerous and unemployable, must be released, *against our judgment,* because a judge far away (who has by this time forgotten all about it) said that five years was enough. In my frequent visits to prisons I am always astonished at how rarely the judges who have prescribed the "treatment" come to see whether or not it is effective. What if doctors who sent their seriously ill patients to hospitals never called to see them!

The End of Taboo

As more states adopt diagnostic centers directed toward getting the prisoners *out* of jail and back to work, under modern, well-structured parole systems, the taboo on jail and prison, like that on state hospitals, will begin to diminish. Once it was a lifelong disgrace to have been in either. Lunatics, as they were cruelly called, were feared and avoided. Today only the ignorant retain this phobia. Cancer was then considered a *shameful* thing to have, and victims of it were afraid to mention it, or have it correctly treated, because they did not want to be disgraced. The time will come when offenders, much as we disapprove of their offenses, will no longer be unemployable untouchables.

To a physician discussing the wiser treatment of our fellow men it seems hardly necessary to add that under no circumstances should we kill them. It was never considered right for doctors to kill their patients, no matter how hopeless their condition. True, some patients in state institutions have undoubtedly been executed without benefit of sentence. They were a nuisance, expensive to keep and dangerous to release. Various people took it upon themselves to put an end to the matter, and I have even heard them boast of it. The Hitler regime had the same philosophy.

But in most civilized countries today we have a higher opinion of the rights of the individual and of the limits to the state's power. We know, too, that for the most part the death penalty is inflicted upon obscure, impoverished, defective, and friendless individuals. We know that it intimidates juries in their efforts to determine guilt without prejudice. We know that it is being eliminated in one state after another, most recently Delaware. We know that in practice it has almost disappeared—for over seven thousand capital crimes last year there were less than one hundred executions. But vast sums of money are still being spent—let us say wasted—in legal contests to determine whether or not an individual, even one known to have been mentally ill, is now healthy enough for the state to hang him. (I am informed that such a case has recently cost the State of California $400,000!)

Most of all, we know that no state employees—except perhaps some that ought to be patients themselves—want a job on the killing squad, and few wardens can stomach this piece of medievalism in their own prisons. For example, two officials I know recently quarreled because each wished to have the hanging of a prisoner carried out on the other's premises.

Capital punishment is, in my opinion, morally wrong. It has a bad effect on everyone, especially those involved in it. It gives a false sense of security to the public. It is vastly expensive. Worst of all it beclouds the entire issue of motivation in crime, which is so importantly relevant to the question of what to do for and with the criminal that will be most constructive to society as a whole. Punishing—and even killing— criminals may yield a kind of grim gratification; let us all admit that there are times when we are so shocked at the depredations of an offender that we persuade ourselves that this is a man the Creator didn't intend to create, and that we had better help correct the mistake. But playing God in this way has no conceivable moral or scientific justification.

Let us return in conclusion to the initial question: "Verdict guilty—now what?" My answer is that now we, the designated representatives of the society which has failed to integrate this man, which has failed him in some way, hurt him and been hurt by him, should take over. It is *our* move. And our move must be a constructive one, an intelligent one, a purposeful one—not a primitive, retaliatory, offensive move. We, the agents of society, must move to end the game of tit-for-tat and blow-for-blow in which the offender has foolishly and futilely engaged himself and us. We are not driven, as he is, to wild and impulsive actions. With knowledge comes power, and with power there is no need for the frightened vengeance of the old penology. In its place should go a quiet, dignified, therapeutic program for the rehabilitation of the disorganized one, if possible, the protection of society during his treatment period, and his guided return to useful citizenship, as soon as this can be effected.

Criminal Justice, Legal Values, and the Rehabilitative Ideal

Francis A. Allen

Although one is sometimes inclined to despair of any constructive changes in the administration of criminal justice, a glance at the history of the past half-century reveals a succession of the most significant developments. Thus, the last fifty years have seen the widespread acceptance of three legal inventions of great importance: the juvenile court, systems of probation and of parole. During the same period, under the inspiration of continental research and writing, scientific criminology became an established field of instruction and inquiry in American universities and in other research agencies. At the same time, psychiatry made its remarkable contributions to the theory of human behavior and, more specifically, of that form of human behavior described as criminal. These developments have been accompanied by nothing less than a revolution in public conceptions of the nature of crime and the criminal, and in public attitudes toward the proper treatment of the convicted offender.[1]

Reprinted with permission from the *Journal of Criminal Law, Criminology, and Police Science* 50 (1959), pp. 226–232. Copyright © 1959 by Northwestern University School of Law. The author is Professor of Law at the University of Michigan. His recent reflections on the ideas of this essay may be found in his *The Decline of the Rehabilitative Ideal*, New Haven: Yale University Press, 1981.

1. These developments have been surveyed in Allen, *Law and the Future: Criminal Law and Administration*, 51 Nw. L. Rev. 207, 207–208 (1956). See also Harno, *Some Significant Developments in Criminal Law and Procedure in the Last Century*, 42 J. Crim. L., C. and P. S. 427 (1951).

This history with its complex developments of thought, institutional behavior, and public attitudes must be approached gingerly; for in dealing with it we are in peril of committing the sin of oversimplification. Nevertheless, despite the presence of contradictions and paradox, it seems possible to detect one common element in much of this thought and activity which goes far to characterize the history we are considering. This common element or theme I shall describe, for want of a better phrase, as the rise of the rehabilitative ideal.

The rehabilitative ideal is itself a complex of ideas which, perhaps, defies completely precise statement. The essential points, however, can be articulated. It is assumed, first, that human behavior is the product of antecedent causes. These causes can be identified as part of the physical universe, and it is the obligation of the scientist to discover and to describe them with all possible exactitude. Knowledge of the antecedents of human behavior makes possible an approach to the scientific control of human behavior. Finally, and of primary significance for the purposes at hand, it is assumed that measures employed to treat the convicted offender should serve a therapeutic function, that such measures should be designed to effect changes in the behavior of the convicted person in the interests of his own happiness, health, and satisfaction and in the interest of social defense.

Although these ideas are capable of rather simple statement, they have provided the arena for some of the modern world's most acrimonious controversy. And the disagreements among those who adhere in general to these propositions have been hardly less intense than those prompted by the dissenters. This is true, in part, because these ideas possess a delusive simplicity. No idea is more pervaded with ambiguity than the notion of reform or rehabilitation. Assuming, for example, that we have the techniques to accomplish our ends of rehabilitation, are we striving to produce in the convicted offender something called "adjustment" to his social environment or is our objective something different from or more than this? By what scale of values do we determine the ends of therapy?[2]

These are intriguing questions, well worth extended consideration. But it is not my purpose to pursue them in this paper. Rather, I am concerned with describing some of the dilemmas and conflicts of values that have resulted from efforts to impose the rehabilitative ideal on the system of criminal justice. I know of no area in which a more effective demonstration can be made of the necessity for greater mutual understanding between the law and the behavioral disciplines.

There is, of course, nothing new in the notion of reform or rehabilitation of the offender as one objective of the penal process. This idea is given important emphasis, for example, in the thought of the medieval churchmen. The church's position, as described by Sir Francis Palgrave, was that punishment was not to be "thundered in vengeance for the satisfaction of the state, but imposed for the good of the offender: in order to afford the means of amendment and to lead the transgressor to repentance, and to mercy."[3] Even Jeremy Bentham, whose views modern criminology has often scorned

---

2. "We see that it is not easy to determine what we consider to be the sickness and what we consider to be the cure." Fromm, *Psychoanalysis and Religion* (1950) 73. See also the author's development of these points at 67–77.

3. Quoted in Dalzell, *Benefit of Clergy and Related Matters* (1955) 13.

and more often ignored, is found saying: "It is a great merit in a punishment to contribute to the *reformation of the offender,* not only through fear of being punished again, but by a change in his character and habits."[4] But this is far from saying that the modern expression of the rehabilitative ideal is not to be sharply distinguished from earlier expressions. The most important differences, I believe, are two. First, the modern statement of the rehabilitative ideal is accompanied by, and largely stems from, the development of scientific disciplines concerned with human behavior, a development not remotely approximated in earlier periods when notions of reform of the offender were advanced. Second, and of equal importance for the purposes at hand, in no other period has the rehabilitative ideal so completely dominated theoretical and scholarly inquiry, to such an extent that in some quarters it is almost assumed that matters of treatment and reform of the offender are the only questions worthy of serious attention in the whole field of criminal justice and corrections.

The Narrowing of Scientific Interests

This narrowing of interests prompted by the rise of the rehabilitative ideal during the past half-century should put us on our guard. No social institutions as complex as those involved in the administration of criminal justice serve a single function or purpose. Social institutions are multi-valued and multi-purposed. Values and purposes are likely on occasion to prove inconsistent and to produce internal conflict and tension. A theoretical orientation that evinces concern for only one or a limited number of purposes served by the institution must inevitably prove partial and unsatisfactory. In certain situations it may prove positively dangerous. This stress on the unfortunate consequences of the rise of the rehabilitative ideal need not involve failure to recognize the substantial benefits that have also accompanied its emergence. Its emphasis on the fundamental problems of human behavior, its numerous contributions to the decency of the criminal-law processes are of vital importance. But the limitations and dangers of modern trends of thought need clearly to be identified in the interest, among others, of the rehabilitative ideal, itself.

My first proposition is that the rise of the rehabilitative ideal has dictated what questions are to be investigated, with the result that many matters of equal or even greater importance have been ignored or cursorily examined. This tendency can be abundantly illustrated. Thus, the concentration of interest on the nature and needs of the criminal has resulted in a remarkable absence of interest in the nature of crime.

---

4. Bentham, *The Theory of Legislation* (Ogden, C. K., ed., 1931) 338–339. (Italics in the original.) But Bentham added:

> But when [the writers] come to speak about the means of preventing offenses, of rendering men better, of perfecting morals, their imagination grows warm, their hopes excited; one would supposed they were about to produce the great secret, and that the human race was going to receive a new form. It is because we have a more magnificent idea of objects in proportion as they are less familiar, and because the imagination has a loftier flight amid vague projects which have never been subjected to the limits of analysis.

Id. at 359.

This is, indeed, surprising, for on reflection it must be apparent that the question of what is a crime is logically the prior issue: how crime is defined determines in large measure who the criminal is who becomes eligible for treatment and therapy.[5] A related observation was made some years ago by Professor Karl Llewellyn, who has done as much as any man to develop sensible interdisciplinary inquiry involving law and the behavioral disciplines:[6] "When I was younger I used to hear smuggish assertions among my sociological friends, such as: 'I take the sociological, *not* the legal, approach to crime'; and I suspect an inquiring reporter could still hear much the same (perhaps with 'psychiatric' often substituted for 'sociological')—though it is surely somewhat obvious that when you take 'the legal' out, you also take out 'crime.'"[7] This disinterest in the definition of criminal behavior has afflicted the lawyers quite as much as the behavioral scientists. Even the criminal law scholar has tended, until recently, to assume that problems of procedure and treatment are the things that "really matter."[8] Only the issue of criminal responsibility as affected by mental disorder has attracted the consistent attention of the non-lawyer, and the literature reflecting this interest is not remarkable for its cogency or its wisdom. In general, the behavioral sciences have left other issues relevant to crime definition largely in default. There are a few exceptions. Dr. Hermann Mannheim, of the London School of Economics, has manifested intelligent interest in these matters.[9] The late Professor Edwin Sutherland's studies of "white-collar crime"[10] may also be mentioned, although, in my judgment, Professor Sutherland's efforts in this field are among the least perceptive and satisfactory of his many valuable contributions.[11]

The absence of wide-spread interest in these areas is not to be explained by any lack of challenging questions. Thus, what may be said of the relationships between legislative efforts to subject certain sorts of human behavior to penal regulation and the persistence of police corruption and abuse of power?[12] Studies of public attitudes toward other sorts of criminal legislation might provide valuable clues as to whether given regulatory objectives are more likely to be attained by the provision of criminal penalties or by other kinds of legal sanctions. It ought to be re-emphasized that the question, what sorts of behavior should be declared criminal, is one to which the behavioral sciences might contribute vital insights. This they have largely failed to do, and we are the poorer for it.

Another example of the narrowing of interests that has accompanied the rise of the

---

5. Cf. Hart, *The Aims of the Criminal Law,* 23 Law and Cont. Prob. 401 (1958).
6. See Llewellyn and Hoebel, *The Cheyenne Way* (1941). See also *Crime, Law and Social Science: A Symposium,* 34 Colum. L. Rev. 277 (1934).
7. *Law and the Social Sciences—Especially Sociology,* 62 Harv. L. Rev. 1286, 1287 (1949).
8. Allen, *op. cit. supra,* note 1, at 207–210.
9. See, especially, his *Criminal Justice and Social Reconstruction* (1946).
10. *White-Collar Crime* (1949). See also Clinard, *The Black Market* (1952).
11. Cf. Caldwell, *A Re-examination of the Concept of White-Collar Crime,* 22 Fed. Prob. 30 (March, 1958).
12. An interesting question of this kind is now being debated in England centering on the proposals for enhanced penalties for prostitution offenses made in the recently-issued Wolfenden Report. See Fairfield, *Notes on Prostitution,* 9 Brit. J. Delin. 164, 173 (1959). See also Allen, *The Borderland of the Criminal Law: Problems of "Socializing" Criminal Justice,* 32 Soc. Ser. Rev. 107, 110–111 (1958).

rehabilitative ideal is the lack of concern with the idea of deterrence—indeed the hostility evinced by many modern criminologists toward it. This, again, is a most surprising development.[13] It must surely be apparent that the criminal law has a general preventive function to perform in the interests of public order and of security of life, limb, and possessions. Indeed, there is reason to assert that the influence of criminal sanctions on the millions who never engage in serious criminality is of greater social importance than their impact on the hundreds of thousands who do. Certainly, the assumption of those who make our laws is that the denouncing of conduct as criminal and providing the means for the enforcement of the legislative prohibitions will generally have a tendency to prevent or minimize such behavior. Just what the precise mechanisms of deterrence are is not well understood. Perhaps it results, on occasion, from the naked threat of punishment. Perhaps, more frequently, it derives from a more subtle process wherein the mores and moral sense of the community are recruited to advance the attainment of the criminal law's objectives.[14] The point is that we know very little about these vital matters, and the resources of the behavioral sciences have rarely been employed to contribute knowledge and insight in their investigation. Not only have the criminologists displayed little interest in these matters, some have suggested that the whole idea of general prevention is invalid or worse. Thus, speaking of the deterrent theory of punishment, the authors of a leading textbook in criminology assert: "This is simply a derived rationalization of revenge. Though social revenge is the actual psychological basis of punishment today, the apologists for the punitive regime are likely to bring forward in their defense the more sophisticated, but equally futile, contention that punishment deters from [*sic*] crime."[15] We are thus confronted by a situation in which the dominance of the rehabilitative ideal not only diverts attention from many serious issues, but leads to a denial that these issues even exist.

Debasement of the Rehabilitative Ideal

Now permit me to turn to another sort of difficulty that has accompanied the rise of the rehabilitative ideal in the areas of corrections and criminal justice. It is a familiar observation that an idea once propagated and introduced into the active affairs of life undergoes changes. The real significance of an idea as it evolves in actual practice may be quite different from that intended by those who conceived it and gave it initial support. An idea tends to lead a life of its own; and modern history is full of the unintended consequences of seminal ideas. The application of the rehabilitative ideal to the institutions of criminal justice presents a striking example of such a development. My second proposition, then, is that the rehabilitative ideal has been debased in practice and that the consequences resulting from this debasement are serious and, at times, dangerous.

---

13. But see Andenaes, *General Prevention—Illusion or Reality?* 43 J. Crim. L., C. and P. S. 176 (1952).
14. This seems to be the assertion of Garafalo. See his *Criminology* (Millar trans. 1914) 241–242.
15. Barnes and Teeters, *New Horizons in Criminology* (2nd ed. 1954) 337. The context in which these statements appear also deserves attention.

This proposition may be supported, first, by the observation that, under the dominance of the rehabilitative ideal, the language of therapy is frequently employed, wittingly or unwittingly, to disguise the true state of affairs that prevails in our custodial institutions and at other points in the correctional process. Certain measures, like the sexual psychopath laws, have been advanced and supported as therapeutic in nature when, in fact, such a characterization seems highly dubious.[16] Too often the vocabulary of therapy has been exploited to serve a public-relations function. Recently, I visited an institution devoted to the diagnosis and treatment of disturbed children. The institution had been established with high hopes and, for once, with the enthusiastic support of the state legislature. Nevertheless, fifty minutes of an hour's lecture, delivered by a supervising psychiatrist before we toured the building, were devoted to custodial problems. This fixation on problems of custody was reflected in the institutional arrangements which included, under a properly euphemistic label, a cell for solitary confinement.[17] Even more disturbing was the tendency of the staff to justify these custodial measures in therapeutic terms. Perhaps on occasion the requirements of institutional security and treatment coincide. But the inducements to self-deception in such situations are strong and all too apparent. In short, the language of therapy has frequently provided a formidable obstacle to a realistic analysis of the conditions that confront us. And realism in considering these problems is the one quality that we require above all others.[18]

There is a second sort of unintended consequence that has resulted from the application of the rehabilitative ideal to the practical administration of criminal justice. Surprisingly enough, the rehabilitative ideal has often led to increased severity of penal measures. This tendency may be seen in the operation of the juvenile court. Although frequently condemned by the popular press as a device of leniency, the juvenile court, is authorized to intervene punitively in many situations in which the conduct, were it committed by an adult, would be wholly ignored by the law or would subject the adult to the mildest of sanctions. The tendency of proposals for wholly indeterminate sentences, a clearly identifiable fruit of the rehabilitative ideal,[19] is unmistakably in the direction of lengthened periods of imprisonment. A large variety of statutes authorizing what is called "civil" commitment of persons, but which, except for the reduced protections afforded the parties proceeded against, are essentially criminal in nature, provide for absolutely indeterminate periods of confinement. Experience has demonstrated that, in practice, there is a strong tendency for the rehabilitative ideal to serve purposes that are essentially incapacitative rather than therapeutic in character.[20]

---

16. See note 25, *infra*.

17. As I recall, it was referred to as the "quiet room." In another institution the boy was required to stand before a wall while a seventy pound fire hose was played on his back. This procedure went under the name of "hydrotherapy."

18. Cf. Wechsler, *Law, Morals and Psychiatry,* 18 Colum. L. School News 2, 4 (March 4, 1959): "The danger rather is that coercive regimes we would not sanction in the name of punishment or of correction will be sanctified in the name of therapy without providing the resources for a therapeutic operation."

19. Cf. Tappan, *Sentencing under the Model Penal Code,* 23 Law and Cont. Prob. 538, 530 (1958).

20. Cf. Hall, Jerome, *General Principles of Criminal Law* (1947) 551. And see Sellin, *The Protective Code: A Swedish Proposal* (1957) 9.

The Rehabilitative Ideal and Individual Liberty

The reference to the tendency of the rehabilitative ideal to encourage increasingly long periods of incarceration brings me to my final proposition. It is that the rise of the rehabilitative ideal has often been accompanied by attitudes and measures that conflict, sometimes seriously, with the values of individual liberty and volition. As I have already observed, the role of the behavioral sciences in the administration of criminal justice and in the areas of public policy lying on the borderland of the criminal law is one of obvious importance. But I suggest that, if the function of criminal justice is considered in its proper dimensions, it will be discovered that the most fundamental problems in these areas are not those of psychiatry, sociology, social case work, or social psychology. On the contrary, the most fundamental problems are those of political philosophy and political science. The administration of the criminal law presents to any community the most extreme issues of the proper relations of the individual citizen to state power. We are concerned here with the perennial issue of political authority: Under what circumstances is the state justified in bringing its force to bear on the individual human being? These issues, of course, are not confined to the criminal law, but it is in the area of penal regulation that they are most dramatically manifested. The criminal law, then, is located somewhere near the center of the political problem, as the history of the twentieth century abundantly reveals. It is no accident, after all, that the agencies of criminal justice and law enforcement are those first seized by an emerging totalitarian regime.[21] In short, a study of criminal justice is most fundamentally a study in the exercise of political power. No such study can properly avoid the problem of the abuse of power.

The obligation of containing power within the limits suggested by a community's political values has been considerably complicated by the rise of the rehabilitative ideal. For the problem today is one of regulating the exercise of power by men of good will, whose motivations are to help not to injure, and whose ambitions are quite different from those of the political adventurer so familiar to history. There is a tendency for such persons to claim immunity from the usual forms of restraint and to insist that professionalism and a devotion to science provide sufficient protections against unwarranted invasion of individual right. This attitude is subjected to mordant criticism by Aldous Huxley in his recent book, "Brave New World Revisited." Mr. Huxley observes: "There seems to be a touching belief among certain Ph.D's in sociology that Ph.D's in sociology will never be corrupted by power. Like Sir Galahad's, their strength is the strength of ten because their heart is pure—and their heart is pure because they are scientists and have taken six thousand hours of social studies."[22] I suspect that Mr. Huxley would be willing to extend his point to include professional groups other than the sociologists. There is one proposition which, if generally understood, would contribute more to clear thinking on these matters than any other. It is not a new insight. Seventy years ago the Italian criminologist Garafalo asserted: "The mere deprivation of liberty, however benign the administration of the place of confinement, is undeniably

---

21. This development in the case of Germany may be gleaned from Crankshaw, *Gestapo* (1956).
22. Huxley, *Brave New World Revisited* (1958) 34–35.

punishment."[23] This proposition may be rephrased as follows: Measures which subject individuals to the substantial and involuntary deprivation of their liberty are essentially punitive in character, and this reality is not altered by the facts that the motivations that prompt incarceration are to provide therapy or otherwise contribute to the person's well-being or reform. As such, these measures must be closely scrutinized to insure that power is being applied consistently with those values of the community that justify interferences with liberty for only the most clear and compelling reasons.

But the point I am making requires more specific and concrete application to be entirely meaningful. It should be pointed out, first, that the values of individual liberty may be imperiled by claims to knowledge and therapeutic technique that we, in fact, do not possess and by failure candidly to concede what we do not know. At times, practitioners of the behavioral sciences have been guilty of these faults. At other times, such errors have supplied the assumptions on which legislators, lawyers and lay people generally have proceeded. Ignorance, in itself, is not disgraceful so long as it is unavoidable. But when we rush to measures affecting human liberty and human dignity on the assumption that we know what we do not know or can do what we cannot do, then the problem of ignorance takes on a more sinister hue.[24] An illustration of these dangers is provided by the sexual psychopath laws, to which I return; for they epitomize admirably some of the worst tendencies of modern practice. These statutes authorize the indefinite incarceration of persons believed to be potentially dangerous in their sexual behavior. But can such persons be accurately identified without substantial danger of placing persons under restraint who, in fact, provide no serious danger to the community? Having once confined them, is there any body of knowledge that tells us how to treat and cure them? If so, as a practical matter, are facilities and therapy available for these purposes in the state institutions provided for the confinement of such persons?[25] Questions almost as serious can be raised as to a whole range of other measures. The laws providing for commitment of persons displaying the classic symptoms of psychosis and advanced mental disorder have proved a seductive analogy for other proposals. But does our knowledge of human behavior really justify the extension of these measures to provide for the indefinite commitment of persons otherwise afflicted? We who represent the disciplines that in some measure are concerned with the control of human behavior are required to act under weighty responsibilities. It is no paradox to assert that the real utility of scientific technique in the fields under discussion depends on an accurate realization of the limits of scientific knowledge.

There are other ways in which the modern tendencies of thought accompanying the rise of the rehabilitative ideal have imperiled the basic political values. The most important of these is the encouragement of procedural laxness and irregularity. It is my impression that there is greater awareness of these dangers today than at some other

23. *Op. cit. supra*, note 14, at 256.

24. I have developed these points in Allen, *op. cit. supra*, note 12, at 113–115.

25. Many competent observers have asserted that none of these inquiries can properly be answered in the affirmative. See, e.g., Sutherland, *The Sexual Psychopath Laws*, 40 J. Crim. L., C. and P. S. 543 (1950); Hacker and Frym, *The Sexual Psychopath Act in Practice: A Critical Discussion*, 43 Calif. L. Rev. 766 (1955). See also Tappen, *The Habitual Sex Offender* (Report of the New Jersey Commission) (1950).

times in the past, for which, if true, we perhaps have Mr. Hitler to thank. Our increased knowledge of the functioning of totalitarian regimes makes it more difficult to assert that the insistence on decent and orderly procedure represents simply a lawyer's quibble or devotion to outworn ritual. Nevertheless, in our courts of so-called "socialized justice" one may still observe, on occasion, a tendency to assume that, since the purpose of the proceeding is to "help" rather than to "punish," some lack of concern in establishing the charges against the person before the court may be justified. This position is self-defeating and otherwise indefensible. A child brought before the court has a right to demand, not only the benevolent concern of the tribunal, but justice. And one may rightly wonder as to the value of therapy purchased at the expense of justice. The essential point is that the issues of treatment and therapy be kept clearly distinct from the question of whether the person committed the acts which authorize the intervention of state power in the first instance. [26] This is a principle often violated. Thus, in some courts the judge is supplied a report on the offender by the psychiatric clinic before the judgment of guilt or acquittal is announced. Such reports, while they may be relevant to the defendant's need for therapy or confinement, ordinarily are wholly irrelevant to the issue of his guilt of the particular offense charged. Yet it asks too much of human nature to assume that the judge is never influenced on the issue of guilt or innocence by a strongly adverse psychiatric report.

Let me give one final illustration of the problems that have accompanied the rise of the rehabilitative ideal. Some time ago we encountered a man in his eighties incarcerated in a state institution. He had been confined for some thirty years under a statute calling for the automatic commitment of defendants acquitted on grounds of insanity in criminal trials. It was generally agreed by the institution's personnel that he was not then psychotic and probably had never been psychotic. The fact seemed to be that he had killed his wife while drunk. An elderly sister of the old man was able and willing to provide him with a home, and he was understandably eager to leave the institution. When we asked the director of the institution why the old man was not released, he gave two significant answers. In the first place, he said, the statute requires me to find that this inmate is no longer a danger to the community; this I cannot do, for he may kill again. And of course the director was right. However unlikely commission of homicide by such a man in his eighties might appear, the director could not be certain. But, as far as that goes, he also could not be certain about himself or about you or me. The second answer was equally interesting. The old man, he said, is better off here. To understand the full significance of this reply it is necessary to know something about the place of confinement. Although called a hospital, it was in fact a prison, and not at all a progressive prison. Nothing worthy of the name of therapy was provided and very little by way of recreational facilities.

This case points several morals. It illustrates, first, a failure of the law to deal adequately with the new requirements being placed upon it. The statute, as a condition to

---

26. A considerable literature has developed on these issues. See, e.g., Allen, *The Borderland of the Criminal Law: Problems of "Socializing" Criminal Justice,* 32 Soc. Ser. Rev. 107 (1958); Diana, *The Rights of Juvenile Delinquents: An Appraisal of Juvenile Court Proceedings,* 44 J. Crim. L., C. and P. S. 561 (1957); Paulsen, *Fairness to the Juvenile Offender,* 41 Minn. L. Rev. 547 (1957); Waite, *How Far Can Court Procedures Be Socialized without Impairing Individual Rights?* 12 J. Crim. L. and C. 430 (1921).

the release of the inmate, required the director of the institution virtually to warrant the future good behavior of the inmate, and, in so doing, made unrealistic and impossible demands on expert judgment. This might be remedied by the formulation of release criteria more consonant with actuality. Provisions for conditional release to test the inmate's reaction to the free community would considerably reduce the strain on administrative decision-making. But there is more here. Perhaps the case reflects that arrogance and insensitivity to human values to which men who have no reason to doubt their own motives appear peculiarly susceptible. [27]

Conclusion

In these remarks I have attempted to describe certain of the continuing problems and difficulties associated with what I have called the rise of the rehabilitative ideal. In so doing, I have not sought to cast doubt on the substantial benefits associated with that movement. It has exposed some of the most intractable problems of our time to the solvent properties of human intelligence. Moreover, the devotion to the ideal of empirical investigation provides the movement with a self-correcting mechanism of great importance, and justifies hopes for constructive future development.

Nevertheless, no intellectual movement produces only unmixed blessings. It has been suggested in these remarks that the ascendency of the rehabilitative ideal has, as one of its unfortunate consequences, diverted attention from other questions of great criminological importance. This has operated unfavorably to the full development of criminological science. Not only is this true, but the failure of many students and practitioners in the relevant areas to concern themselves with the full context of criminal justice has produced measures dangerous to basic political values and has, on occasion, encouraged the debasement of the rehabilitative ideal to produce results, unsupportable whether measured by the objectives of therapy or of corrections. The worst manifestations of these tendencies are undoubtedly deplored as sincerely by competent therapists as by other persons. But the occurrences are neither so infrequent nor so trivial that they can be safely ignored.

---

27. One further recent and remarkable example is provided by the case, In re Maddox, 351 Mich. 358, 88 N.W. 2d 470 (1958). Professor Wechsler, *op cit. supra,* note 18, at 4, describes the facts and holding as follows: "Only the other day, the Supreme Court of Michigan ordered the release of a prisoner in their State prison at Jackson, who had been transferred from the Ionia State Hospital to which he was committed as a psychopath. The ground of transfer, which was defended seriously by a State psychiatrist, was that the prisoner was 'adamant' in refusing to admit sexual deviation that was the basis of his commitment; and thus, in the psychiatrist's view, resistant to therapy! The Court's answer was, of course, that he had not been tried for an offense."

Problems with the Therapeutic
Approach to Criminality

Richard Wasserstrom

There is a view, held most prominently but by no means exclusively by persons in psychiatry, that we ought never punish persons who break the law and that we ought instead to do something much more like what we do when we treat someone who has a disease. According to this view, what we ought to do to all such persons is to do our best to bring it about that they can and will function in a satisfactory way within society. The functional equivalent to the treatment of a disease is the rehabilitation of an offender, and it is a rehabilitative system, not a punishment system, that we ought to have if we are to respond, even to criminals, in anything like a decent, morally defensible fashion.

Karl Menninger has put the proposal this way:

> If we were to follow scientific methods, the convicted offender would be detained indefinitely pending a decision as to whether and how to reintroduce him successfully into society. All the skill and knowledge of modern behavior science would be used to examine his personality assets, his liabilities and potentialities, the environment from which he came, its effects upon him, and his effects upon it.

Having arrived at some diagnostic grasp of the offender's personality, those in charge can decide whether there is a chance that he can be redirected into a mutually satisfactory adaptation to the world. If so, the most suitable techniques in education, industrial training, group administration, and psychotherapy should be selectively applied. All this may be best done extramurally or intramurally. It may require maximum "security" or only minimum "security." If, in due time, perceptible change occurs, the process should be expedited by finding a suitable spot in society and industry for him, and getting him out of prison control and into civil status (with parole control) as quickly as possible.[1]

It is important at the outset to see that there are two very different arguments which might underlie the claim that the functional equivalent of a system of treatment is desirable and in fact always ought to be preferred to a system of punishment.

The first argument fixes upon the desirability of such a system over one of punishment in virtue of the fact that, because no offenders are responsible for their actions, no offenders are ever justifiably punished. The second argument is directed towards establishing that such a system is better than one of punishment even if some or all offenders are responsible for their actions. A good deal of the confusion present in discussions of the virtues of a system of treatment results from a failure to get clear about these two arguments and to keep the two separate. The first is superficially the more attractive and ultimately the less plausible of the two. Each, though, requires its own explication and analysis.

One way in which the first argument often gets stated is in terms of the sickness of offenders. It is, so the argument begins, surely wrong to punish someone for something that he or she could not help, for something for which he or she was not responsible. No one can help being sick. No one ought, therefore, ever be punished for being sick. As the Supreme Court has observed: "Even one day in prison would be cruel and unusual punishment for the 'crime' of having a common cold."[2] Now, it happens to be the case that everyone who commits a crime is sick. Hence, it is surely wrong to punish anyone who commits a crime. What is more, when a response is appropriate, the appropriate response to sickness is treatment. For this reason what we ought to do is to treat offenders, not punish them.

One difficulty with this argument is that the relevance of sickness to the rightness or wrongness of the punishment of offenders is anything but obvious. Indeed, it appears that the conclusion depends upon a non sequitur just because we seldom, if ever, seek to punish people for being sick. Instead we punish them for actions they perform. On the surface, at least, it would seem that even if someone is sick, and even if the person cannot help being sick, this in no way implies that none of his or her actions could have been other than what it was. Thus, if the argument against ever punishing the guilty criminal is to be at all persuasive, it must be shown that for one reason or another, the sickness which afflicts all criminals must affect their actions in such a way that they are

---

1. Menninger, "Therapy Not Punishment," pp. 172 –179 of this book.
2. Robinson v. California, 370 U.S. 660 (1962).

thereby prevented ever from acting differently. Construed in this fashion, the argument is at least coherent and responsive. Unfortunately, there is now no reason to be persuaded by it.

It might be persuasive were there any reason to believe that all criminal acts were, for example, instances of compulsive behavior; if, that is, we thought it likely to be true that all criminals were in some obvious and distinguishable sense afflicted by or subjected to irresistible impulses which compelled them to break the law. For there are people who do seem to be subjected to irresistible impulses and who are thereby unable to keep themselves from, among other things, committing crimes. And it is surely troublesome if not clearly wrong to punish them for these actions. Thus, the kleptomaniac or the person who is truly already addicted to narcotics does seem to be suffering from something resembling a sickness and, moreover, to be suffering from something which makes it very difficult if not impossible for such a person to control the actions so compelled. Pity not blame seems appropriate, as does treatment rather than punishment.[3]

Now, the notion of compulsive behavior is not without difficulties of its own. How strong, for instance, does a compulsion have to be before it cannot be resisted? Would someone be a kleptomaniac only if such an individual would steal an object even though a policeman were known by the person to be present and observing every move? Is there anything more that is meant by compulsive behavior than the fact that it is behavior which is inexplicable or unaccountable in terms of the motives and purposes people generally have? More importantly, perhaps, why do we and why should we suppose that the apparently "motiveless" behavior must be the product of compulsions which are less resistible than those to which we all are at times subjected. As has been observed, ". . . it is by no means self-evident that [a wealthy] person's yearnings for value-less [items] are inevitably stronger or more nearly irresistible than the poor man's hunger for a square meal or for a pack of cigarettes."[4]

But while there are problems such as these, the more basic one is simply that there is no reason to believe that all criminal acts are instances of compulsive behavior. Even if there are persons who are victims of irresistible impulses, and even if we ought always to treat and never to punish such persons, it surely does not follow that everyone who commits a crime is doing a compulsive act. And because this is so, it cannot be claimed that all criminals ought to be exempted from punishment—treated instead—because they have a sickness of this sort.

It might be argued, though, that while compulsive behavior accounts only for some criminal acts, there are other sicknesses which account for the remainder. At this juncture the most ready candidate to absorb the remaining cases is that of insanity. The law, for example, has always been willing to concede that a person ought never be punished if the person was so sick or so constituted that he or she did not know the nature or quality of the act, or if this were known, that the person did not know that the act was wrong. And more recently, attempts have been made, sometimes successfully, to ex-

---

3. The Supreme Court has worried about this problem in, for example, the case of chronic alcoholism, in Powell v. Texas, 392 U.S. 514 (1968). The discussion in this and related cases is neither very clear nor very illuminating.

4. Barbara Wootton, *Social Science and Social Pathology* (London: G. Allen & Unwin, 1959), p. 235.

pand this exemption to include any person whose criminal action was substantially the product of mental defect or disease.[5]

Once again, though, the crucial point is not the formulation of the most appropriate test for insanity, but the fact that it is far from evident, even under the most "liberal" test imaginable, that it would be true that everyone who commits a crime would be found to be sick and would be found to have been afflicted with a sickness which in some sense rendered the action in question unavoidable. Given all of our present knowledge, there is simply every reason to suppose that some of the people who do commit crimes are neither subject to irresistible impulses, incapable of knowing what they are doing, nor suffering from some other definite mental disease. And, if this is so, then it is a mistake to suppose that the treatment of criminals is on this ground always to be preferred to their punishment.

There is, though, one final version of the claim that every criminal action is excusable on grounds of the sickness of the actor. And this version does succeed in bringing all the remaining instances of criminality, not otherwise excusable, within the category of sickness. It does so only by making the defining characteristic or symptom of mental illness the commission of an illegal act. All criminals, so this argument goes, who are not insane or subject to irresistible impulses are sociopaths—people afflicted with that mental illness which manifests itself exclusively through the commission of antisocial acts. This sickness, like any other sickness, should be treated rather than punished.

Once this stage of the discussion is reached, it is important to be aware of what has happened. In particular, there is no longer the evidentiary claim that all criminal acts are caused by some sickness. Instead there is the bare assertion that this must be so—an assertion, moreover, of a somewhat deceptive character. The illness which afflicts these criminals *is simply* the criminal behavior itself. The disease which is the reason for not punishing the action is identical with the action itself. At this point any attempt to substantiate or disprove the existence of a relationship between sickness and crime is ruled out of order. The presence of mental illnesses of these kinds cannot, therefore, be reasons for not punishing, or for anything else.

Thus, even if it is true that we ought never to punish and that we ought always to treat someone whose criminal action was unavoidable because the product of some mental or physical disease—even if we concede all this—it has yet to be demonstrated, without begging the question, that all persons who commit crimes are afflicted with some disease or sickness of this kind. And, therefore, if it is always wrong to punish people, or if it is always preferable to treat them, then an argument of a different sort must be forthcoming.

In general form that different argument is this: The legal system ought to abandon its attempts to assess responsibility and punish offenders and it ought instead to focus solely on the question of how most appropriately the legal system can deal with, i.e., rehabilitate if possible, the person presently before the court—not, however, because everyone is sick, but because no good comes from punishing even those who are responsible.

---

5. *See, e.g.,* Durham v. United States, 214 F. 2d 862 (D.C. Cir., 1954); United States v. Brawner, 471 F. 2d 969 (D.C. Cir., 1972); and Model Penal Code § 4.01.

One such proponent of this view is Lady Barbara Wootton. [6] Her position is an ostensibly simple one. What she calls for is the "elimination" of responsibility. The state of mind, or *mens rea,* of the actor at the time he or she committed the act in question is no longer to be determinative—in the way it now is—of how he or she shall be dealt with by society. Rather, she asserts, when someone has been accused of violating the law we ought to have a social mechanism that will ask and answer two distinct questions: Did the accused in fact do the act in question? If he or she did, given all that we know about this person (including his or her state of mind), what is the appropriate form of social response to him or her?

Lady Wootton's proposal is for a system of social control that is thoroughly forward-looking, and in this sense, rehabilitative in perspective. With the elimination of responsibility comes the elimination of the need by the legal system to distinguish any longer between wickedness and disease. And with the eradication of this distinction comes the substitution of a forward-looking, treatment system for the backward-looking, punitive system of criminal law.

The mental state or condition of the offender will continue to be important but in a different way. "Such conditions . . . become relevant, not to the question of determining the measure of culpability but to the choice of the treatment most likely to be effective in discouraging him from offending again. [7]

> [O]ne of the the most important consequences must be to obscure the present rigid distinction between the penal and the medical institution. . . . For purposes of convenience offenders for whom medical treatment is indicated will doubtless tend to be allocated to one building, and those for whom medicine has nothing to offer to another; but *the formal distinction between prison and hospital will become blurred, and, one may reasonably expect, eventually obliterated altogether. Both will be simply "places of safety" in which offenders receive the treatment which experience suggests is most likely to evoke the desired response.*[8]

Thus, on this view even if a person was responsible when he or she acted and blameworthy for having so acted, we still ought to behave toward him or her in roughly the same way that we behave toward someone who is sick—we ought, in other words, to do something very much like treating him or her. Why? Because this just makes more sense than punishment. The fact that he or she was responsible is simply not very relevant. It is wrong of course to punish people who are sick; but even with those who are well, the more humane and civilized approach is one that concerns itself solely with the question of how best to effect the most rapid and complete rehabilitation or "cure" of the offender. The argument is not that no one is responsible or blameworthy; instead, it is that these descriptions are simply irrelevant to what, on moral grounds, ought to be the only significant considerations, namely, what mode of behavior toward the offender is most apt to maximize the likelihood that he or she will not in the future commit those obnoxious or dangerous acts that are proscribed by the law. The only goal

---

6. Barbara Wootton, *Crime and the Criminal Law* (London: Stevens, 1963).
7. *Ibid.,* p. 77.
8. *Ibid.,* pp. 79–80 (emphasis added).

ought to be rehabilitation (in this extended sense of "rehabilitation") the only issue how to bring about the rehabilitation of the offender.

The moral good sense of this approach can be perceived most clearly, so the argument goes on, when we contrast this thoroughly forward-looking point of view with punishment. For if there is one thing which serves to differentiate any form of punishment from that of treatment, it is that punishment necessarily permits the possibility and even the desirability that punishment will be imposed upon an offender even though he or she is fully "cured"—even though there is no significant likelihood that he or she will behave improperly in the future. And, in every such case in which a person is punished—in every case in which the infliction of the punishment will help the offender not at all (and may in fact harm him or her immeasurably)—the act of punishment is, on moral grounds, seriously offensive. Even if it were true that some of the people who commit crimes are responsible and blameworthy, and even if it were the case that we had meaningful techniques at our disposal for distinguishing those who are responsible from those who are not—still, every time we inflict a punishment on someone who will not be benefited by it, we commit a seriously immoral act. This claim, or something like it, lies, I think, at the base of the case which can be made against the punishment even of the guilty. For it is true that any system of punishment does require that some people will be made to suffer even though the suffering will help them not at all. It is this which the analogue to a system of treatment, a rehabilitative system such as Lady Wootton's expressly prevents, and it is in virtue of this that such a system might be thought preferable.[9]

There are, I think, both practical and theoretical objections to a proposal such as this. The practical objections concern, first, the possibility that certain "effective" treatments may themselves be morally objectionable, and, second, the possibility that

---

9. There are some additional, more practical arguments that might be offered in support of such a proposal.

To begin with, by making irrelevant the question of whether the actor was responsible when he or she acted, the operation of the criminal law could be greatly simplified. More specifically, by "eliminating" the issue of responsibility we thereby necessarily eliminate the requirement that the law continue to attempt to make those terribly difficult judgments of legal responsibility which our system of punishment requires to be made. And, as a practical matter, at least, this is no small consideration. For surely there is no area in which the techniques of legal adjudication have functioned less satisfactorily than in that of determining the actor's legal responsibility as of the time he violated the law. The attempts to formulate and articulate satisfactory and meaningful criteria of responsibility; the struggles to develop and then isolate specialists who can meaningfully and impartially relate these criteria to the relevant medical concepts and evidence; and the difficulties encountered in requiring the traditional legal fact-finding mechanism—the jury—ultimately to resolve these issues—all of these bear impressive witness, it could plausibly be claimed, for the case for ceasing to make the effort.

In addition, it is no doubt fair to say that most people do not like to punish others. They may, indeed, have no objection to the punishment of others; but the actual task of inflicting and overseeing the infliction of an organized set of punishments is distasteful to most. It is all too easy, therefore, and all too typical, for society to entrust the administration of punishments to those who, if they do not actually enjoy it, at least do not find it unpleasant. Just as there is no necessary reason for punishments ever to be needlessly severe, so there is no necessary reason for those who are charged with the duty of punishing to be brutal or unkind. Nonetheless, it is simply a fact that it is difficult, if not impossible, to attract sensitive, kindly or compassionate persons to assume this charge. No such analogous problem, it might be argued, attends the call for treatment.

this way of viewing offenders may create a world in which we all become indifferent to the characteristics that distinguish those who are responsible from those who are not. The ease, for example, with which someone like Menninger tends to see the criminal not as an adult but as a "grown-up child"[10] says something about the ease with which a kind of paternalistic manipulativeness could readily pervade a system composed of "places of safety."[11]

These are, though, contingent rather than necessary worries. A system organized in accordance with this rehabilitative ideal could have a view that certain therapies were impermissible on moral grounds, just as it could also treat all of the persons involved with all of the respect they deserved as persons. Indeed, it is important when comparing and contrasting proposals for rehabilitative systems with punishment to make certain that the comparisons are of things that are comparable. There are abuses present in most if not all institutional therapeutic systems in existence today, but there are also abuses present in most if not all institutional penal systems in existence today. And the practical likelihood of the different abuses is certainly worth taking seriously in trying to evaluate the alternatives. What is not appropriate, however, is to contrast either an ideal of the sort proposed by Wootton or Menninger with an existing penal one, or an ideal, just penal system with an existing therapeutic one.[12]

These matters to one side, one of the chief theoretical objections to a proposal of the sort just described is that it ignores the whole question of general deterrence. Were we to have a system such as that envisioned by Lady Wootton or Menninger, we would ask one and only one question of each person who violated the law: What is the best, most efficacious thing to do to this individual to diminish substantially the likelihood that he or she will misbehave in this, or similar fashion, again? If there is nothing at all that need be done in order for us to be quite confident that he or she will not misbehave again (perhaps because the person is extremely contrite, or because we are convinced it was an impulsive, or otherwise unlikely-to-be-repeated act), then the logic of this system requires that the individual be released forthwith. For in this system it is the future conduct of the actor, and it alone, that is the only relevant consideration. There is simply no room within this way of thinking to take into account the achievement of general deterrence. H. L. A. Hart has put the matter this way in explaining why the *reform* (when any might be called for) of the prisoner cannot be the general justifying aim of a system of punishment.

---

10. "What might deter the reader from conduct which his neighbors would not like does not necessarily deter the grown-up child of vastly different background. . . .

"It is not the successful criminal upon whom we inflict our antiquated penal system. It is the unsuccessful criminal, the criminal who really doesn't know how to commit crimes and who gets caught. . . . The clumsy, the desperate, the obscure, the friendless, the defective, the diseased — these men who commit crimes that do not come off — are bad actors, indeed. But they are not the professional criminals, many of whom occupy high places." [Menninger, *op. cit., supra* note 12, pp. 134 –35.]

11. These are discussed persuasively and in detail by Morris in his important article, "Persons and Punishments," 52 *The Monist* 475 (1968), pp. 476 –90 [also pp. 24 –54 of this book].

12. I think that Morris at times indulges in an improper comparison of the two. *Ibid.*

The objection to assigning to Reform this place in punishment is not merely that punishment entails suffering and Reform does not; but that Reform is essentially a remedial step for which ex hypothesi there is an opportunity only at the point where the criminal law has failed in its primary task of securing society from the evil which breach of the law involves. Society is divisible at any moment into two classes (i) those who have actually broken a given law and (ii) those who have not yet broken it but may. *To take Reform as the dominant objective would be to forego the hope of influencing the second — and in relation to the more serious offences — numerically much greater class. We should thus subordinate the prevention of first offences to the prevention of recidivism.*[13]

A system of punishment will on this view find its justification in the fact that the announcement of penalties and their infliction upon those who break the laws induces others to obey the laws. The question why punish anyone at all *is* answered by Hart. We punish because we thereby deter potential offenders from becoming actual offenders. For Hart, the case for punishment as a general social practice or institution rests on the prevention of crime; it is not to be found either in the inherent appropriateness of punishing offenders or in the contingently "corrective" or rehabilitative powers of fines or imprisonments on some criminals.

Yet, despite appearances, the appeal to general deterrence is not as different as might be supposed from the appeal to a rehabilitative ideal. In both cases, the justification for doing something (or nothing) to the offender rests upon the good consequences that will ensue. General deterrence just as much as rehabilitation views what should be done to offenders as a question of *social control.* It is a way of inducing those who can control their behavior to regulate it in such a way that it will conform to the dictates of the law. The disagreement with those who focus upon rehabilitation is only over the question of whose behavioral modification justifies the imposition of deprivations upon the criminals. Proponents of general deterrence say it is the modification of the behavior of the noncriminals that matters; proponents of rehabilitation say it is the modification of the behavior of the criminals that is decisive. Thus, a view such as Hart's is less a justification of punishment than of a system of threats of punishment. For if the rest of society could be convinced that offenders would be made to undergo deprivations that persons would not wish to undergo we would accomplish all that the deterrent theory would have us achieve through our somewhat more visible applications of these deprivations to offenders. This is so because it is the belief that punishment will follow the commission of an offense that deters potential offenders. The actual punishment of persons is on this view necessary in order to keep the threat of punishment credible.

To put matters this way is to bring out the fact that the appeal to general deterrence, just as much as the appeal to rehabilitation, appears to justify a wholly forward-looking system of social control.

---

13. H. L. A. Hart, *The Concept of Law, op. cit. supra* note 6, p. 181 (emphasis added).

On Incapacitating the Dangerous

Ferdinand D. Schoeman

Given the extent and the intensity of public concern about violent crime, there is an ever increasing willingness to consider deterring and incapacitating potential offenders by means that until recently would have been summarily rejected as violative of respect for the rights and dignity of free and equal persons. Indeed, it is not just willingness to consider options that is expanding; it is actual practices, which include use of aversive conditioning, token economies, electrical, physical and chemical manipulation of the brain,[1] indeterminate sentencing, and criminal commitment of the legally innocent. What will be of concern in this paper is a variant of this last option. Specifically, the discussion will center on arguments both for and against civil preventive detention—the incapacitating of individuals thought to be dangerous—as a potentially legitimate means of promoting social protection.

Some opposition to the use of civil preventive detention to effect this end has focused

Reprinted from the *American Philosophical Quarterly*, vol. 16, no. 1 (1979) by permission of the publisher. Ferdinand D. Schoeman is a Professor of Philosophy at the University of South Carolina.
1. R. G. Spece, Jr., "Conditioning and Other Technologies Used to 'Treat?' 'Rehabilitate?' 'Demolish?' Prisoners and Mental Patients," *Southern California Law Review*, vol. 45 (1971), pp. 616–681, and *Individual Rights and the Federal Role in Behavior Modification* (Washington, 1974).

on the inadequacy of available predictive techniques for determining carefully enough who is dangerous. Other attacks have been directed at the vagueness of what is meant by the label "dangerous," or have stressed how inadequate present protections are for those civilly committed, whatever the rationale.[2] On the face of it, such particular objections seem directed to circumstances which appear in principle remediable, leaving open the possibility that under some future circumstances civil preventive detention of those deemed dangerous might be legitimate. Part I of this paper is devoted to an investigation of what such conditions might be.

Still other attacks on civil preventive detention have stemmed from more philosophical worries having to do with implications such a practice, however perfected, would have on our understanding of a person as an autonomous being deserving respect as well as on our appreciation of the role of the power—restraint aspect of the criminal law. Part II of this paper is devoted to gauging the moral weight of these more Olympian worries. A motif of the whole paper is a comparison of civil preventive detention with the presently accepted practice of quarantine, arguing that once certain conditions are met, it would not be consistent to countenance the use of quarantine and associated public health measures and reject civil preventive detention of the dangerous. The point of the paper then will not be to argue that civil preventive detention is not problematic, or that given available technology it is to be recommended. Rather, it is that assuming certain developments in both technology and law, no more serious problems arise in defending civil preventive detention, suitably qualified, than arise from the practice of quarantine as a measure for protecting public health. Civil preventive detention represents an assault on our notion of autonomous moral being only to the degree that quarantine does.

It is an important feature of gauging the legitimacy of the practice being considered here to be clear that the persons whose rights are to be transgressed for social protection need not be judged guilty of anything, need not be judged blameworthy, morally or legally, for any act they have committed. Furthermore, the reason such persons need not be thought blameworthy does not stem from any kind of general skepticism about the notions of praise or blame. Advocates of this practice may believe that those who commit crime are blameworthy and deserve punishment. The practice consists simply in incapacitating individuals predicted to be illegally violent, until such time as the potential for illegal violence diminishes to within tolerable levels. This practice of civil preventive detention involves restrictions on the liberty of persons who have not forfeited any rights by previous delinquent acts. For purposes of this paper, I shall include in the practice of civil preventive detention all interferences up to and including isolation of the dangerous person, with the presumption that the least restrictive means of accomplishing social protection is the maximum allowable under the practice.

---

2. Andrew von Hirsch, "Prediction of Criminal Conduct and Preventive Confinement of Convicted Persons," *Buffalo Law Review*, vol. 21 (1972), pp. 717–758 at Section 11, and "Civil Commitment of the Mentally Ill: Theories and Procedures," *Harvard Law Review*, vol. 79 (1966), pp. 1288–1298 at 1291.

I

As indicated, in this section I shall address the more practical and technical impediments to a morally legitimate system of preventive detention. Though, as I shall argue, some of the objections may prove decisive, I continue considering other objections and how a defender of civil preventive detention might be able to meet them. My justification for this procedure is first of all that we find out interesting things about our moral principles by continuing to address questions and press for answers. Second, since it could turn out that we are wrong in thinking that certain technical abilities are beyond human possibility, we should be prepared with contingency plans and contingency arguments just in case we find that we have been wrong. And third, as philosophers we might be interested in whether certain kinds of distinctions can be drawn, as well as whether theories can be defeated for certain kinds of reasons, even though we know that there may be practical objections which keep the issues from being pressing ones.

The first major source of opposition to civil preventive detention stems from skepticism about the adequacy of predictive techniques available or foreseeable on the basis of which mankind can be divided into two categories: the dangerous and the not-so-dangerous. The evidence on this predictability issue is reported to be as follows: There is no predictive technique available which does not include more false positives than true positives—which does not diagnose as future-guilty more persons who will not commit such crimes than persons who will. Furthermore, as one attempts to circumscribe a higher percentage of people who actually will commit crimes, the ratio of false positives to true positives increases.[3] (One does, after all, succeed in predicting all crimes that actually will be committed by claiming that everyone will commit every possible crime.)

It is worthwhile noting that some authorities on the issue of preventive detention treat this predictive problem as essentially the only problem with the practice, apparently conceding that if predictions improve sufficiently their opposition would vanish. No less an authority than Professor Alan Dershowitz expressed this view:

> What difference is there between imprisoning a man for past crimes on the basis of "statistical likelihood" and detaining him to prevent future crimes on the same kind of less-than-certain information? The important difference may not be one of principle; it may be, as Justice Holmes said all legal issues are, one of degree. The available evidence suggests that our system of determining past guilt results in the erroneous conviction of relatively few innocent people. . . . But the indications are that any system of predicting future crimes would result in a vastly larger number of erroneous confinements — that is, confinements of persons predicted to engage in violent crimes who would not, in fact, do so.[4]

There are actually numerous problems which arise in working out solutions to this predictive problem. How accurate need the predictive techniques be before we can act

---

3. A. R. Angel, E. D. Green, H. R. Kaufman, E. E. VanLoon, "Preventive Detention: An Empirical Analysis," *Harvard Civil Rights—Civil Liberties Law Review,* vol. 6 (1971), pp. 300–396 at 342.
4. Alan Dershowitz, "The Law of Dangerousness: Some Fictions About Predictions," *Journal of Legal Education,* vol. 23 (1970), pp. 24–47 at 31–32.

on their basis? How invasive can the probing into the lives and thoughts of individuals be in order to achieve acceptable levels of accuracy? On what basis can an individual be required to submit to testing, the result of which might include civil confinement of that individual?

Perhaps the easiest question to deal with is the one relating to the standard of accuracy. If, following Dershowitz's suggestion, prediction of crime can be made as accurate as trials by juries, then we seem to have the problem of standards solved. In the legacy of the criminal law, the maxim that better that ten guilty men go free than that one innocent person be punished can be used to supply either qualitative or quantitative assistance here. Qualitatively what is asserted is the importance of not interfering with a person unless one is justifiably very confident that he did the wrong attributed to him. Quantitatively what is asserted is that the accuracy rate must be 90% or better. It cannot be interpreted as saying that the worst thing in the world is to find an innocent person guilty, for that interpretation would preclude all procedures for determining guilt we mortals know.

For our purposes, one can set the accuracy threshold as high as one desires, even at 100%, since the issues we want to address arise almost independently of the level of accuracy achievable. For the issue to be addressed is whether it would be legitimate to preventively detain someone when there is *moral certainty* that without such detention that person will perform some dangerous criminal act. In light of this requirement, it cannot be maintained that civil preventive detention must rest on "mere probabilities" while criminal conviction and quarantine are based on knowledge.

It is worth mentioning in passing that this moral certainty accuracy threshold is considerably higher than we would require in cases of serious danger from diseases. Suppose that someone has smallpox, and that the chance of being contagious at all is 50 percent and that the chance of dying from contagion is 50 percent. Under these conditions we would, I think, unhesitantly insist on the enforced isolation of the carrier, until such time as he no longer posed a threat to others.

With the level of accuracy set, we can now focus on the second question: how invasive can the information gathering process be? Given that accurate predictions of many natural phenomena involve acquiring as much information of details as possible, it would be rather startling if accurate predictions about people did not involve most extensive probing into every facet of persons' personalities and surroundings, both physical and social. Since so much of how a person responds to a situation depends on how he perceives or misperceives it, and since social situations will depend not only on how one perceives but how all involved do, the prospect of making accurate predictions seems negligible. The problems of interaction and interpretation seem to complicate the task of predicting what people will do beyond the point at which it can seem worthwhile even trying. It appears that we introduce problems of invasion of privacy as a result of our scruples about the minimization of false positives.

Granting this problem, it appears that we can and morally must dispense with civil preventive detention, not on grounds that isolating an individual for the protection of others is unjust, but on grounds that the process of finding out that someone is dangerous is itself so invasive of privacy that we are not entitled even to make the investigation into the threat potential of our citizenry. For purposes of this paper I am willing to grant the point that predictive techniques require such wholesale invasions of privacy that efforts at achieving this information might be prohibited on that score alone, depending on the stakes, without any reference to the fact that the practice involves the detention of the innocent for the well-being of others. But then I want to go on to ask: If the information necessary for adequate predictions could be gathered or were available without invasion of privacy, would preventive detention then be legitimate? In the event that psychics could be used to predict what people would do, without paraphernalia like bugs or binoculars, and without interviews, would government use of their abilities be invasive of privacy? Is privacy invaded as a result of the means used for acquiring information or as a result of the state of knowing what another rightfully regards as his to conceal?[5]

How invasive can investigations be into the personal characteristics of individuals, and on what basis can such investigations be initiated? Besides the obvious point just made that the adequacy of data upon which to make predictions is directly proportional to the invasiveness of the means used to acquire it, another equally obvious point can be made. The fewer the number of people that can be legitimately screened, the smaller the percentage of would-be crime that can be arrested.

Again drawing attention to an analogy from public health, suppose that there is a deadly disease which spreads easily from carriers, who cannot contract the disease, to those who are susceptible. Next suppose that treatment for being a carrier requires months of confinement—a fact which affords people with a strong incentive not to undergo diagnostic test to discover whether they are indeed carriers. Finally suppose that 50,000 persons a year die from this disease. What would it be legitimate for the state to do in order to find and treat carriers of this disease, and thereby save 50,000 lives each year? In this context, I suspect that we would tend to demote in importance our concern over invasion of privacy, thinking that saving that many lives is so important as to be the decisive consideration. I am suggesting that under this circumstance mass mandatory screening would not seem out of the question, provided that such measures were prerequisite to preventing such an epidemic. If we may consider such measures for saving that many lives that otherwise would be lost because of disease, why not consider such measures to save that many lives otherwise lost because of fear, greed, jealousy, anger, love, etc.?

Some might be tempted to respond to this question by saying that it just is legitimate to isolate a person who is sick, something over which one has no control, but not for impending crime. But here the point must be made that even under quarantine, persons are not isolated because they are sick. Most sick persons are not quarantined. Persons quarantined are isolated *because they are dangerous to others,* the sickness being the cause of the danger. We shall return to this point of contention in Part II.

We must now ask ourselves, who can be screened and on what account? Using the strategy that we should try to stay within the bounds set by other acceptable social practices when setting limits on civil prevention detention, we shall not step beyond what the law seems to allow in cases of protecting the public health.

What we find in the area of public health law is that ". . .there are legally sanctioned

---

5. See *Olmstead vs U.S.,* 277 U.S. 438–474 (1927), Brandeis, J. dissenting.

compulsory examinations in which the subject may not be a willing participant because the examination primarily furthers the aim of public protection." [6] But still, with the exception of impending disaster, compulsory examination of individuals for communicable diseases must be based on more than mere suspicion. [7]

Two obvious questions arise in extrapolating this description of screening policy in the area of public health to screening for prevention of crime: What will count as reasonable grounds for examination, and when are situations dire enough to warrant loosening restrictions on barriers to screening? As suggested above, there is a certain parallel between epidemics and certain classes of crime—deadly consequences; similarities in terms of predictability and preventability via isolation may also emerge. Provided mass screening is thought legitimate in one case, why should it not be similarly conceived in the other?

The practice of preventive detention, to be justified, would not only have to be based on tests which had a very low rate of false positives, but would have to be administered on such a basis as to allow some rather significant reduction in the crime rate. Whether this can be done without overextensive invasion of privacy is something one can have grave doubts about. But the question here is: If effective screening can be done without unconscionable invasion of privacy, and if it could be shown that measures up to and including preventive detention would prevent high percentages of projected crimes, would such a practice of detaining the innocent but dangerous be legitimate? Would civil preventive detention be allowable provided our anxiety over the accuracy of predictions and over the invasiveness of screening could be calmed?

The next major line of criticism of practices of preventive detention focuses on the vagueness implicit in talk about detaining the "dangerous." Who will define what it is to be dangerous, and on what basis? Evidence from the field of civil commitment for the insane suggests widely varying practices, depending on not much more than the political and ethical biases of the examining doctors.[8] Such a disparity in the disposition of persons when based on individual value preferences rather than on clear standards represents the antithesis of a just system. On the other hand, there is no reason to think that the system of preventive detention which we have adumbrated thus far is differentially prey to this line of criticism. We can limit application of preventive measures to potential crimes which represent serious threat to life or bodily integrity, and we have specified already how accurate predictive devices must be before any interference is warranted, by indicating a moral certainty threshold.

There are, however, some related issues which must be addressed. Suppose that a person being tested for serious threat potential is found not to be dangerous, but is likely to violate a law of a less significant sort, like selling alcohol to minors. What should or can the government do with this information? Though it cannot detain the

6. Frank Grad, *Public Health Law Manual* (New York, 1970), p. 42.

7. Frank Grad, pp. 42–43.

8. Joseph Goldstein and Jay Katz, "Dangerousness and Mental Illness: Some Observations on the Decision to Release Persons Acquitted by Reason of Insanity," *Yale Law Journal*, vol. 70, pp. 225–239 at 235, and Alan Dershowitz, pp. 40, 41, and 43, and J. M. Livermore, D. P. Malmquist and P. E. Meehl, "On the Justification for Civil Commitment," *University of Pennsylvania Law Review*, vol. 117 (1968), pp. 75–96 at 81–82.

person to prevent such an act on the standards we have sketched, can it use this information to make eventual apprehension of the person inevitable by placing undercover officers in his bar? Can the government be asked, or expected and trusted not to give out information to businesses, which would have a great deal of interest in discovering whether potential employees are likely to embezzle, sell trade secrets, or do any of a large number of acts deleterious to the interests of the business?

In order to keep the practice of civil preventive detention a live option I shall distinguish between two types of tests. We shall distinguish between tests which indicate whether one specific crime type is likely and ones which give a read-out of a much more inclusive sort. Testing for dangerousness, we shall say, is only legitimate in case the tests devisable are of the specific sort and provide information only about behavior which is preventable according to the parameters already indicated.

The next major range of objections to systems of preventive detention, both civil and criminal, concentrates on issues falling under the heading of procedural safeguards. In this area of procedural safeguards, especially as it relates to civil commitment of the insane and the addicted, the fact that the infringements of liberties took place under a therapeutic rationale until recently blinded many people into thinking that talk of rights for such people interfered with acting on their behalf and in their interest.[9]

Recognizing the conflicts of interest involved in detention, we have not only demanded a very high level of predictive accuracy, but we here go on to recommend that the state supply those to be committed with resources to counteract state's expert testimony. Thus those in danger of being committed have a right to have the same accurate tests administered by non-state personnel, with differing results sufficient to preclude commitment.

There are other procedural safeguards which must be required. First of all, for those who are going to be committed, it has to be shown that nothing less invasive can be done feasibly. For instance, if a person "threatens" to seriously injure his child, supplying a guard or requiring counseling might do just as well as confining the parent. It is hard to conceive that for a high percentage of serious crimes such measures short of detention would not prove adequate.

What are the upper limits of confinement to prevent harm to others? Though it is not clear what the rationale would be for setting a limit, there is reason to require almost continual proof that the person confined is still dangerous. Here we find a similar situation to that of quarantine.

> The nature of quarantine as a species of physical confinement is borne out by the fact that the legality of keeping a person in quarantined premises, like the legality of other forms of detention, is tested by a *writ of habeas corpus.*[10]

What it is that has to be shown is that the likelihood of committing a certain kind of crime is still above the threshold mark, whatever it is. Once again the model of public

---

9. "Civil Commitment of Narcotics Addicts," *Yale Law Journal,* vol. 76 (1967), pp. 1160–1189 at 1181.
10. Frank Grad, pp. 47–48.

health serves us well. We should keep a person with a contagious and deadly disease confined for as long as it takes to eliminate or reduce significantly the possibility of contagion. Since this can involve potentially lifelong confinement in the case of some diseases, mere duration of confinement cannot serve to distinguish quarantine from preventive detention. Depending on how time-consuming and expensive retesting is, perhaps every day or every week those necessarily confined could be reexamined for signs of dangerousness. It would not be unreasonable to assume that for different kinds of crimes and for different kinds of persons schedules would eventually be available about minimum, maximum and average times required before detainees prove less likely to commit the acts feared. Such schedules could then serve as a basis for what counts as a reasonable interval between tests and what grounds would constitute a valid *habeas corpus* action.

What kind of compensation for losses should be available to those who are detained, their families and their business associates? How will it be possible for persons once detained not to have their reputations besmirched and their job prospects unaffected? I ask these questions not because the answers are readily available but because they focus on serious difficulties with the proposal here considered. The most consoling point that can be made is that since the action is civil and not criminal, there is no reason why almost all of one's normal activities could not be carried out, either in a place of safety or under some kind of supervision, or during hours or on occasions on which the predicted crime is unlikely to transpire. As Professor Lionel Frankel has said about civil commitment, requiring compensation for those detained would not only provide the state with an incentive to minimize the number of those committed as well as their period of detention, but it would "also serve to vindicate the compensated individual's dignity and status as a person" and "it would serve to affirm his continuing membership in a society as an individual before the law."[11]

II

Thus far in this paper we have considered three general problem areas for a system of preventive detention—problems with predicting, vagueness of standards of dangerousness, and inadequacy of procedural safeguards for persons civilly committed. We have shaped the practice when necessary to meet the major objections, elaborating a qualified version of civil preventive detention. On occasion the comparison has been made to the practices of quarantine and screening for contagious diseases to show the broad areas of similarity between measures designed to protect public health—measures which tend not to occasion much disagreement—and our practice of civil preventive detention.

But still someone might respond to the efforts so far made in favor of qualified preventive detention by saying: Besides the specific objections already mentioned, there is something more basic at stake in the issue of civil preventive detention. This more basic something has to do with our image of man as both autonomous and sacred, as entitled to a sphere of activity free from the interferences of others unless he intentionally interferes with another's sphere of freedom. To interfere preventively, this line of objection continues, even assuming the safeguards and provisions outlined, is to diminish the respect accorded to each individual's legitimate choices, to diminish one's sense of control over his own fate, and to impoverish the feeling for individual dignity protected by and encouraged through our present practices. The main issue that must be addressed is: does the very act of predicting and responding on the basis of a prediction to another person's behavior, when this response involves invoking nothing less than the police power of the state, violate something sacred in the human personality? Is it tantamount to denying that people are responsible? Does it involve seeing people as mere means to social ends? Does it presuppose a therapeutic and behavioristic, and not a moral and rights oriented, understanding of human activity? Is it an affront to human autonomy?[12]

Before responding to these challenges, it must be stressed that we are not saying about persons to be detained that they are as good as guilty and hence have no complaint against incapacitating efforts. Persons detained are detained not because they are guilty in any sense, but because they are dangerous—this danger being as real and as threatening if it results from free choice as if it results from involuntary spasm or microbe. But besides reiterating that the practice is to include numerous procedural safeguards, we emphasize that the practice in question involves no worse treatment of persons than does the practice of quarantine. In both practices persons are interfered with for the benefit of others.

Though civil preventive detention is not to be conceived as a cure for any disease—is not a therapeutic act—it does share with therapy several key features: both are imposed without any sense of moral outrage or resentment for those in its clutches, and the duration of detention is in both cases indeterminate. Perhaps it is thought that to deal with an individual's future conduct in this manner is tantamount to regarding his behavior in a medical-model and that such a perspective is what enervates our repeated claim that we are still looking on people as responsible. This allegation is made even more plausible by considering the perspective of a person about whom it is predicted that he will do some act unless detained in spite of his insistence that he won't, that he knows he won't, and that he is in the best position to know this, being the agent without whose intention the predicted behavior cannot take place. A person in this predicament will legitimately feel that his ability to control his conduct is questioned, if not denied outright. In the face of such a person's protests, our insistence that we are really still seeing him as free and responsible will surely seem disingenuous, if not self-deceptive.

So we have to show that we need not be denying a person's self-control just because we claim we have accurate predictive techniques which say he will do what he insists he won't. A number of alternatives present themselves. First of all, in disagreeing with a

---

12. Herbert Packer, *The Limits of the Criminal Sanction* (Stanford, 1968), pp. 74–77.

person about what he will do we might be saying that we know more about the circumstances than he does, our disagreement being attributed to his anticipation of circumstances different in significant ways from those he would actually confront. As an illustration of this, say we request of someone that he not use his telephone in the next few minutes to make a call. He responds saying that he will comply, at which point we know he is not going to adhere to his own decision. If we know that his wife will shortly run into the room and ask him to call the doctor quickly because their child stopped breathing, the person would have made a commitment he will not stick to. Here we shouldn't be tempted to think that the person couldn't control his behavior or that he wasn't acting as a responsible agent in acting in ways he just previously committed himself to avoiding.

Another way in which we might be successful in knowing more about what a person will do than the person himself knows is if we know more about how the agent will change than the agent himself does. If someone who just married maintained that he would never take an interest in pursuing extramarital relationships we might be skeptical, not on grounds that any such act is beyond the agent's control, but on the basis of our belief that the agent may not know very much about the natural history of human relationships, and hence is not in a favorable position to judge what he will eventually feel and what he will eventually find strong incentives for doing.

And finally, there are those cases in which we all act in ways we feel in cooler moments committed to avoiding. Though we usually do still want to regard ourselves as responsible for such behavior, it may well be predictable. And perhaps closely tied to such cases are those in which a person doesn't seem to lose control but still seems to be destined to act in ways he wants not to repeat. People who have bad eating, smoking, exercise or work habits fall into this category of persons who can be sincere in protesting that they will not do something which we have excellent inductive grounds for claiming that they will. Once again it would be probably too strong to say that they *cannot* act as they want, and hence are not responsible when they transgress their own resolutions. They just fail to muster the motivation at the crucial times or forget altogether that they are trying to do something different.

So without assuming compulsions or anything at all of a pathological nature, and without denying autonomy or choice to individuals, we can see how it is that we might come to discount people's own sincere assertions and resolutions about what they will do. Hence to make such predictions about people and deal with them on that basis does not necessarily involve us in changing our image of what it is to be a person, and does not force us to concede that we are implicitly using a medical model for interpreting people's behavior, for which issues of responsibility are inappropriate.

Of course some of the worries of those who oppose civil preventive detention are right on the mark: they worry that the basis of the preventive ideal involves denial of human dignity in the sense that it sanctions interfering with innocent people for the benefit of others. Though it is important for society not to coerce people for what they are, and we must all admit that, at times it *is* legitimate to coerce people though they have done nothing wrong. The issue cannot be over *whether* to coerce people in spite of no wrongdoing but over where to draw the line on thinking such coercion legitimate. We say this fully realizing that it involves considerably diminished capacity to avoid interferences of the state.[13] But it should be pointed out that, unlike quarantine, our practice of civil preventive detention is not invoked independent of a person's choices. It is after all, only because a person is likely to do what is proscribed or avoid what is required that confinement would be imposed. Still it is true in this case, as in the case of quarantine, that *given* a determination of future dangerousness to others there is little a person can then do to get himself reclassified.

One way of drawing this line as to when coercion prior to wrongdoing is justified is by distinguishing between controllable and uncontrollable harm, legitimizing preventive measures only in case the harm feared would be the product of some defective condition. Deference to autonomy and freedom from prior restraint would be accorded to those who can be thought responsible for their behavior—desirable or undesirable. Making civil preventive detention dependent upon the incapacity to make one's conduct conform to the law or to incapacities of any sort does enhance the scope of individual freedom and does underscore the significance of respecting people as ends in themselves. Recognizing a policy of restricting preventive detention to such conditions of incapacity would surely suffice to preclude restraint on the type of grounds being considered here. It *would* distinguish how we could legitimately respond to the threat posed by the criminally insane on the one hand, and how we could respond to the threat posed by the ordinary person. Where responsible choices are possible, there would be no prior restraint. Such restraint would be legitimized only in case responsible choices were impossible.[14]

The problem with this criterion for distinguishing legitimate from illegitimate detention is that it will not distinguish quarantine from the practice of preventive detention we are considering. Responsible choices are not impossible for those who are either afflicted with, or mere carriers of, deadly contagious diseases. The person quarantined is dangerous, not just because he is ill, but because he might do something independent of his illness which would constitute a danger to others, like contaminate food at a restaurant or supermarket. Thus, such a person's disease is not sufficient to cause harm, except when conjoined with his choices and his actions. So, attractive as the present criterion is, it does not draw the distinction where most would like it drawn, between communicable diseases and ordinary kinds of dangerous conduct.

Someone might respond by saying that the line can still be drawn between quarantine and preventive detention in the way just now adumbrated if sufficient notice is taken of the following contrast: while the person quarantined is dangerous because of his illness—something over which he has no control—the person preventively detained is dangerous because of his choices, something over which a person does have control. So while carriers of a deadly contagious disease cannot lead a normal life without harming others, the criminally dangerous person apparently can but chooses not to. Consequently, if the government treated both of these cases in the same way, even though choice entered into one case in a way it did not enter into the other, it would

---

13. Andrew von Hirsch, Sect. 11 and H. L. A. Hart, "Punishment and the Elimination of Responsibility," *Punishment and Responsibility* (Oxford, 1968) and Herbert Morris, "Persons and Punishment" *Monist*, vol. 52 (1968), pp. 475–501.
14. Lionel Frankel, pp. 247–250.

represent an assault on respect for choice and a cheapening of the consideration paid to autonomy.[15]

Though this development of the criterion is powerful, it won't succeed. While it is true that the contagious person may not intend to endanger those with whom he comes into contact, it is clearly not true that the only things we can be said to control are those things we intend to do. The blind man who drives may not intend to kill pedestrians, or even to endanger them. But we would not call his dangerousness behind the wheel uncontrollable. Obviously, he can avoid getting behind the wheel in the first place. Though the person quarantined is restricted much further than is the case with the blind man, the situation is analogous. For though the sick man is dangerous because of a condition out of his control, the amount of actual harm that results is within his control. Hence it is just as significant an affront to autonomy and just as serious a limitation of choice to quarantine the sick as to detain the potential murderer.

Another tack one might take in trying to detach the practice of quarantine from that of civil preventive detention from a moral perspective might involve noting that while quarantine is clearly a response to an emergency, civil preventive detention would represent an everyday affair. And, after all, acts we tolerate during catastrophic episodes can hardly serve as a model for how we generally ought to behave. The fact that triage may be right in the midst of battle does not warrant its practice during less stressful periods.

Several points deserve mentioning in response to this distinction between emergency and nonemergency circumstances. First of all it is not clear that if plagues or other contagious diseases were with us most of the time, we would abandon belief in the legitimacy of quarantine and mandatory screening. It is not obvious that our concern for civil liberties overrides our concern with public health. The next point to be made in response to the distinction between emergency and nonemergency situations is that the rarity of an event can in itself hardly qualify as a legitimate moral basis for making distinctions. What excuses or legitimizes triage is not its rarity but its military necessity, its role in national defense. If it were not necessary for national defense, the rarity of the instance in which it would be practiced would hardly be a point in its favor.

Of course it is true that quarantine would be imposed in times of serious social threat, but so would preventive detention, each possibly being justified on the ground that tens of thousands of persons will otherwise die or suffer severely. I fail to see why if x number of people die from one cause it is an emergency, while if the same number die from some different cause, it is not an emergency situation, assuming everything else is left constant.

One could always try the response that making certain concessions in rare cases results in fewer abrogations of rights than does the same concession applied to frequently recurring situations. But this response is self-defeating since still fewer rights-abrogations would result if the concessions were never made.

If there is something worse about civil preventive detention, qualified in the ways indicated in Part I, than there is about quarantine, not only have we failed to locate it, but

---

15. I am indebted to Professor Warner Wick for pressing this objection on my treatment of quarantine.

whatever it is that makes the distinction is nowhere to be found in the literature. Realizing this does not commit one to *actually* advocating civil preventive detention, for it must be remembered that there are grave practical and legal problems which keep our present world from being one in which the practice could be legitimized. In addition, the arguments throughout the paper relied on the reader's willingness to find quarantine morally acceptable. Those undisposed to think quarantine legitimate will find little in this paper to persuade them that preventive detention has virtues which outweigh its costs, even assuming the modifications in technology and law described above.[16]

---

16. I wish to express my appreciation to Professors Joseph Goldstein, Alan Goldman, Kenneth Kipnis, Denis Nolan, Patrick Hubbard, Warner Wick, William McAninch, Herbert Fingarette and Barry Loewer for helpful comments on earlier versions of this paper.

Restitution: A New Paradigm
of Criminal Justice

Randy E. Barnett

T his paper will analyze the breakdown of our system of criminal justice in terms of what Thomas Kuhn would describe as a crisis of an old paradigm— punishment. I propose that this crisis could be solved by the adoption of a new paradigm of criminal justice—restitution. The approach will be mainly theoretical, though at various points in the discussion the practical implications of the rival paradigms will also be considered. A fundamental contention will be that many, if not most, of our system's ills stem from errors in the underlying paradigm. Any attempt to correct these symptomatic debilities without a reexamination of the theoretical under-

Reprinted with permission from *Ethics*, vol. 87, no. 4, 1977. Copyright © 1977 by the University of Chicago. (Footnotes have been updated.) Randy E. Barnett is an Assistant Professor of Law at the Illinois Institute of Technology, Chicago—Kent College of Law.

[Author's note] This paper was made possible by a research fellowship from the Law and Liberty Project of the Institute for Humane Studies, Menlo Park, California. A somewhat expanded version of it appears in the book *Assessing the Criminal: Restitution, Retribution and the Legal Process*, ed. Randy E. Barnett and John Hagel (Cambridge, Mass: Ballinger Publishing Co. 1977). I respond to some objections to the view presented here and expand upon the analysis in "The Justice of Restitution," *American Journal of Jurisprudence* 25 (1980):117. Also, I wish to extend my appreciation to John V. Cody, Davis E. Keeler, Murray N. Rothbard, and Lloyd L. Weinreb for their invaluable criticism and comments. I am greatly in their debt and hope to be able at some future time to make suitable restitution.

pinnings is doomed to frustration and failure. Kuhn's theories deal with the problems of science. What made his proposal so startling was its attempt to analogize scientific development to social and political development. Here, I will simply reverse the process by applying Kuhn's framework of scientific change to social, or in this case, legal development.[1]

In the criminal justice system we are witnessing the death throes of an old and cumbersome paradigm, one that has dominated Western thought for more than 900 years. While this paper presents what is hoped to be a viable, though radical alternative, much would be accomplished by simply prompting the reader to reexamine the assumptions underlying the present system. Only if we are willing to look at our old problems in a new light do we stand a chance of solving them. This is our only hope, and our greatest challenge.

The Crisis in the Paradigm of Punishment

"Political revolutions are inaugurated by a growing sense, often restricted to a segment of the political community, that existing institutions have ceased adequately to meet the problems posed by an environment they have in part created. . . . In both political and scientific development the sense of malfunction that can lead to crisis is prerequisite to revolution."[2] Kuhn's description of the preconditions for scientific and political revolutions could accurately describe the current state of the criminal law. However, simply to recognize the existence of a crisis is not enough. We must look for its causes. The Kuhnian methodology suggests that we critically examine the paradigm of punishment itself.

The problems which the paradigm of punishment is supposed to solve are many and varied. A whole literature on the philosophy of punishment has arisen in an effort to justify or reject the institution of punishment. For our purposes the following definition

---

1. What immediately follows is a brief outline of Kuhn's theory. Those interested in the *defense* of that theory should refer to his book, *The Structure of Scientific Revolutions,* 2d ed., enl. (Chicago: University of Chicago Press, 1970). A paradigm is an achievement in a particular discipline which defines the legitimate problems and methods of research within that discipline. This achievement is sufficiently unprecedented to attract new adherents away from rival approaches while providing many unsolved questions for these new practitioners to solve. As the paradigm develops and matures, it reveals occasional inabilities to solve new problems and explain new data. As attempts are made to make the facts fit the paradigm, the theoretical apparatus gradually becomes bulky and awkward, like Ptolemaic astronomy. Dissatisfaction with the paradigm begins to grow. Why not simply discard the paradigm and find another which better fits the facts? Unfortunately, this is an arduous process. All the great authorities and teachers were raised with the current paradigm and see the world through it. All the texts and institutions are committed to it. Radical alternatives hold promise but are so untested as to make wary all but the bold. The establishment is loath to abandon its broad and intricate theory in favor of a new and largely unknown hypothesis. Gradually, however, as the authorities die off and the problems with the old paradigm increase, the "young turks" get a better hearing in both the journals and the classroom. In a remarkably rapid fashion, the old paradigm is discarded for the new. Anyone who still clings to it is now considered to be antiquated or eccentric and is simply read out of the profession. All research centers on the application of the new paradigm. Kuhn characterizes this overthrow of one paradigm by another as a revolution.

2. Ibid., p. 92.

from the *Encyclopedia of Philosophy* should suffice: "Characteristically punishment is unpleasant. It is inflicted on an offender because of an offense he has committed; it is deliberately imposed, not just the natural consequence of a person's action (like a hangover), and the unpleasantness is *essential* to it, not an accompaniment to some other treatment (like the pain of the dentist's drill)."[3]

Two types of arguments are commonly made in defense of punishment. The first is that punishment is an appropriate means to some justifiable end such as, for example, deterrence of crime. The second type of argument is that punishment is justified as an end in itself. On this view, whatever ill effects it might engender, punishment for its own sake is good.

The first type of argument might be called the *political* justification of punishment, for the end which justifies its use is one which a political order is presumably dedicated to serve: the maintenance of peaceful interactions between individuals and groups in a society. There are at least three ways that deliberate infliction of harm on an offender is said to be politically justified.

1. One motive for punishment, especially capital punishment and imprisonment, is the "intention to deprive offenders of the power of doing future mischief."[4] Although it is true that an offender cannot continue to harm society while incarcerated, a strategy of punishment based on disablement has several drawbacks.

Imprisonment is enormously expensive. This means that a double burden is placed on the innocent who must suffer the crime and, in addition, pay through taxation for the support of the offender and his family if they are forced onto welfare. Also, any benefit of imprisonment is temporary; eventually, most offenders will be released. If their outlook has not improved—and especially if it has worsened—the benefits of incarceration are obviously limited. Finally, when disablement is permanent, as with capital punishment or psychosurgery, it is this very permanence, in light of the possibility of error, which is frightening. For these reasons, "where disablement enters as an element into penal theories, it occupies, as a rule, a subordinate place and is looked upon as an object subsidiary to some other end which is regarded as paramount."[5]

2. Rehabilitiation of a criminal means a change in his mental *habitus* so that he will not offend again. It is unclear whether the so-called treatment model which views criminals as a doctor would view a patient is truly a "retributive" concept. Certainly it does not conform to the above definition characterizing punishment as deliberately and essentially unpleasant. It is an open question whether any end justifies the intentional, forceful manipulation of an individual's thought processes by anyone, much less the state. To say that an otherwise just system has incidentally rehabilitative effects which may be desirable is one thing, but it is quite another to argue that these effects themselves justify the system. The horrors to which such reasoning can lead are obvious from abundant examples in history and contemporary society.[6]

---

3. Stanley I. Benn, "Punishment," in *The Encyclopedia of Philosophy,* ed. Paul Edwards (New York: Macmillan Publishing Co., 1967), 7:29 (emphasis added).
4. Heinrich Oppenheimer, *The Rationale of Punishment* (London: University of London Press, 1913), p. 255.
5. Ibid.
6. See Thomas Szasz, *Law, Liberty and Psychiatry* (New York: Macmillan Co., 1963).

Rehabilitation as a reaction against the punishment paradigm will be considered below, but one aspect is particularly relevant to punishment as defined here. On this view, the visiting of unpleasantness itself will cause the offender to see the error of his ways; by having "justice" done him, the criminal will come to appreciate his error and will change his moral outlook. This end, best labeled "reformation," is speculative at best and counterfactual at worst. On the contrary, "it has been observed that, as a rule . . . ruthless punishments, far from mollifying men's ways, corrupt them and stir them to violence." [7]

3. The final justification to be treated here—deterrence—actually has two aspects. The first is the deterrent effect that past demonstrations of punishment have on the future conduct of others; the second is the effect that threats of future punishment have on the conduct of others. The distinction assumes importance when some advocates argue that future threats lose their deterrent effect when there is a lack of past demonstrations. Past punishment, then, serves as an educational tool. It is a substitute for or reinforcement of threats of future punishment.

As with the goals mentioned above, the empirical question of whether punishment has this effect is a disputed one.[8] I shall not attempt to resolve this question here, but will assume *arguendo* that punishment even as presently administered has some deterrent effect. It is the moral question which is disturbing. Can an argument from deterrence alone "justify" in any sense the infliction of pain on a criminal? It is particularly disquieting that the actual levying of punishment is done not for the criminal himself, but for the educational impact it will have on the community. The criminal act becomes the occasion of, but not the reason for, the punishment. In this way, the actual crime becomes little more than an excuse for punishing.

Surely this distorts the proper functioning of the judicial process. For if deterrence is the end it is unimportant whether the individual actually committed the crime. Since the public's perception of guilt is the prerequisite of the deterrent effect, all that is required for deterrence is that the individual is "proved" to have committed the crime. The actual occurrence would have no relevance except insofar as a truly guilty person is easier to prove guilty. The judicial process becomes, not a truth-seeking device, but solely a means to legitimate the use of force. To treat criminals as means to the ends of others in this way raises serious moral problems. This is not to argue that men may never use others as means but rather to question the use of force against the individual because of the effect such use will have on others. It was this that concerned del Vecchio when he stated that "the human person always bears in himself something sacred, and it is therefore not permissable to treat him merely as a means towards an end outside of himself."[9]

Finally, deterrence as the ultimate justification of punishment cannot rationally limit its use. It "provides *no* guidance until we're told *how much* commission of it is to be

7. Giorgio del Vecchio, "The Struggle against Crime," in *The Philosophy of Punishment*, ed. H. B. Acton (London: Macmillan Co., 1969), p. 199.

8. See, e.g., Samuel Yochelson and Stanton E. Samenow, *The Criminal Personality*, vol. 1, *A Profile for Change* (New York: Jason Aronson, Inc., 1976), pp. 411–16.

9. Del Vecchio, p. 199.

deterred."[10] Since there are always some who commit crimes, one can always argue for more punishment. Robert Nozick points out that there must be criteria by which one decides how much deterrence may be inflicted.[11] One is forced therefore to employ "higher" principles to evaluate the legitimacy of punishment.

It is not my thesis that deterrence, reformation, and disablement are undesirable goals. On the contrary, any criminal justice system should be critically examined to see if it is having these and other beneficial effects. The view advanced here is simply that these utilitarian benefits must be incidental to a just system; they cannot, alone or in combination, justify a criminal justice system. Something more is needed. There is another more antiquated strain of punishment theory which seeks to address this problem. The *moral* justifications of punishment view punishment as an end in itself. This approach has taken many forms.[12] On this view, whatever ill or beneficial results it might have, punishment of lawbreakers is good for its own sake. This proposition can be analyzed on several levels.

The most basic question is the truth of the claim itself. Some have argued that "the alleged absolute justice of repaying evil with evil (maintained by Kant and many other writers) is really an empty sophism. If we go back to the Christian moralists, we find that an evil is to be put right only by doing good."[13] This question is beyond the scope of this treatment. The subject has been extensively dealt with by those more knowledgeable than I.[14] The more relevant question is what such a view of punishment as a good can be said to imply for a system of criminal justice. Even assuming that it would be good if, in the nature of things, the wicked got their "come-uppance," what behavior does this moral fact justify? Does it justify the victim authoring the punishment of his offender? Does it justify the same action by the victim's family, his friends, his neighbors, the state? If so what punishment should be imposed and who should decide?

It might be argued that the natural punishment for the violation of natural rights is the deserved hatred and scorn of the community, the resultant ostracism, and the existential hell of *being* an evil person. The question then is not whether we have the right to inflict some "harm" or unpleasantness on a morally contemptible person — surely, we do; the question is not whether such a punishment is "good" — arguably, it is. The issue is whether the "virtue of some punishment" justifies the *forceful* imposition of unpleasantness on a *rights violator* as distinguished from the morally imperfect. Any *moral* theory of punishment must recognize and deal with this distinction. Finally, it must be established that the state is the legitimate author of punishment, a proposition which further assumes the moral and legal legitimacy of the state. To raise these issues is not to resolve them, but it would seem that the burden of proof is on those seeking to justify the use of force against the individual. Suffice it to say that I am skeptical of finding any theory which justifies the deliberate, forceful imposition of punishment within or without a system of criminal justice.

10. Robert Nozick, *Anarchy, State, and Utopia* (New York: Basic Books, 1974), p. 61.
11. Ibid., pp. 59–63.
12. For a concise summary, see Oppenheimer, p. 31.
13. Del Vecchio, p. 198.
14. See, e.g., Walter Kaufmann, *Without Guilt and Justice* (New York: Peter H. Wyden, Inc., 1973), esp. chap. 2.

The final consideration in dealing with punishment as an end in itself is the possibility that the current crisis in the criminal justice system is in fact a crisis of the paradigm of punishment. While this, if true, does not resolve the philosophical issues, it does cast doubt on the punishment paradigm's vitality as the motive force behind a system of criminal justice. Many advocates of punishment argue that its apparent practical failings exist because we are not punishing enough. All that is needed, they say, is a crackdown on criminals and those victims and witnesses who shun participation in the criminal justice system; the only problem with the paradigm of punishment is that we are not following it.[15] This response fails to consider *why* the system doggedly refuses to punish to the degree required to yield beneficial results and instead punishes in such a way as to yield harmful results. The answer may be that the paradigm of punishment is in eclipse, that the public lacks the requisite will to apply it in anything but the prevailing way.

Punishment, particularly state punishment is the descendant of the tradition which imparts religious and moral authority to the sovereign and, through him, the community. Such an authority is increasingly less credible in a secular world such as ours. Today there is an increasing desire to allow each individual to govern his own life as he sees fit provided he does not violate the rights of others. This desire is exemplified by current attitudes toward drug use, abortion, and pornography. Few argue that these things are good. It is only said that where there is no victim the state or community has no business meddling in the peaceful behavior of its citizens, however morally suspect it may be.[16]

Furthermore, if the paradigm of punishment is in a "crisis period" it is as much because of its practical drawbacks as the uncertainty of its moral status. The infliction of suffering on a criminal tends to cause a general feeling of sympathy for him. There is no rational connection between a term of imprisonment and the harm caused the victim. Since the prison term is supposed to be unpleasant, at least a part of the public comes to see the criminal as a victim, and the lack of rationality also causes the offender to feel victimized. This reaction is magnified by the knowledge that most crimes go unpunished and that even if the offender is caught the judicial process is long, arduous, and far removed from the criminal act. While this is obvious to most, it is perhaps less obvious that the punishment paradigm is largely at fault. The slow, ponderous nature of our system of justice is largely due to a fear of an unjust infliction of punishment on the innocent (or even the guilty). The more awful the sanction, the more elaborate need be the safeguards. The more the system is perceived as arbitrary and unfair, the more incentive there is for defendants and their counsel to thwart the truth-finding process. Acquittal becomes desirable at all costs. As the punitive aspect of a sanction is diminished, so too would be the perceived need for the procedural protections.

A system of punishment, furthermore, offers no incentive for the victim to involve himself in the criminal justice process other than to satisfy his feelings of duty or

---

15. See, e.g., "Crime: A Case for More Punishment," *Business Week* (September 15, 1975), pp. 92–97.

16. This problems is examined, though not ultimately resolved, by Edwin M. Schur in his book *Crimes without Victims—Deviant Behavior and Public Policy, Abortion, Homosexuality, and Drug Addiction* (Englewood Cliffs, N.J.: Prentice-Hall, Inc., 1965).

revenge. The victim stands to gain little if at all by the conviction and punishment of the person who caused his loss. This is true even of those systems discussed below which despense state compensation based on the victim's need. The system of justice itself imposes uncompensated costs by requiring a further loss of time and money by the victim and witnesses and by increasing the perceived risk of retaliation.

Finally, punishment which seeks to change an offender's moral outlook, or at least to scare him, can do nothing to provide him with the skills needed to survive in the outside world. In prison, he learns the advanced state of the criminal arts and vows not to repeat the mistake that led to his capture. The convict emerges better trained and highly motivated to continue a criminal career.

The crisis of the paradigm of punishment has at its roots the collapse of its twin pillars of support: its moral legitimacy and its practical efficacy. As Kaufmann concludes, "the faith in retributive justice is all but dead."[17]

Attempts to Salvage the Paradigm of Punishment

"All crises begin with the blurring of a paradigm and the consequent loosening of the rules for normal research."[18] And yet until a new paradigm is presented, authorities will cling to the old one, either ignoring the problem or salvaging the paradigm with ad hoc explanations and solutions. Why are paradigms never rejected outright? Why must there always be a new paradigm before the old one is abandoned? Kuhn does not explicitly discuss this, but R. A. Childs hypothesizes "that, as such, paradigms may serve the function of increasing man's sense of control over some aspect of reality, or some aspect of his own life. If this is so, then we would expect that a straightforward abandonment of a paradigm would threaten that sense of control."[19]

This psychological need for an explanation may in turn explain the many efforts to shore up the paradigm of punishment. The three attempts to be examined next have at their roots a perception of its fundamental errors, and at the same time they highlight three goals of any new paradigm of criminal justice.

1. Proportionate punishment. The king abandoned the composition system[20] for the system of punishment because punishment struck terror in the hearts of the people, and this served to inspire awe for the power of the king and state. But there was no rational connection between the seriousness of the crime and the gravity of the punishment and, therefore, no limit to the severity of punishment. Hideous tortures came to be employed: "But some of the men of the Enlightenment sought to counter

---

17. Kaufmann, p. 46.
18. Kuhn, p. 82.
19. R. A. Childs, "Liberty and the Paradigm of Statism," in *The Libertarian Alternative,* ed. Tibor Machan (Chicago: Nelson-Hall Co., 1974), p. 505.
20. Composition was the medieval version of a restitutionary system. For a fascinating outline of how such a system operated and how it came to be supplanted by state-authored punishment, see Stephen Schafer, *Compensation and Restitution to Victims of Crime,* 2d ed., enl. (Montclair, N.J.: Patterson Smith Publishing Corp., 1970); Richard E. Laster, "Criminal Restitution: A Survey of Its Past History and an Analysis of Its Present Usefulness," *University of Richmond Law Review* 5 (1970): 71–80; L. T. Hobhouse, *Morals in Evolution* (London: Chapman & Hall, 1951).

the inhumanity of their Christian predecessors with appeals to reason. They thought that retributive justice had a mathematical quality and that murder called for capital punishment in much the same way in which two plus two equals four." [21]

The appeal to proportionality was one of the early attempts to come to grips with deficiencies in the paradigm of punishment. It was doomed to failure, for there is no objective standard by which punishments can be proportioned to fit the crime. Punishment is incommensurate with crime. This solution is purely ad hoc and intuitive. We shall, however, find the *goal* of proportionate sentencing useful in the formation of a new paradigm.

2. Rehabilitation. It was noted earlier that the infliction of punishment tends to focus attention on the plight of the criminal. Possibly for this reason, the next humanitarian trend was to explore the proper treatment of criminals. Punishment failed to reform the criminal, and this led observers to inquire how the situation might be improved. Some felt that the sole end of the penal system was rehabilitation, so attention was turned to modifying the criminal's behavior (an obviously manipulative end). Emphasis was placed on education, job training, and discipline.

Unfortunately, the paradigm of punishment and the political realities of penal administration have all but won out. There is simply no incentive for prison authorities to educate and train. Their job is essentially political. They are judged by their ability to keep the prisoners within the walls and to keep incidents of violence within the prison to a minimum; as a result, discipline is the main concern. Furthermore, since he is sentenced to a fixed number of years (less time off for good behavior—so-called good time), there is no institutional incentive for the prisoner to improve himself apart from sheer boredom. Productive labor in prison is virtually nonexistent, with only obsolete equipment, if any, available. Except perhaps for license plates and other state needs, the prisoners produce nothing of value; the prisons make no profit and the workers are paid, if at all, far below market wages. They are unable to support themselves or their families. The state, meaning the innocent taxpayer, supports the prisoner, and frequently the families as well via welfare.

Rehabilitation has been a long-time goal of the penal system, but the political nature of government-run prisons and the dominance of the paradigm of punishment has inevitably prevented its achievement. Prisons remain detention centers, all too temporarily preventing crime by physically confining the criminals.

3. Victim compensation. It is natural that the brutalities resulting from the paradigm of punishment would get first attention from humanitarians and that the persons subjected to those practices would be next. Until recently, the victim of crime was the forgotten party. Within the last few years a whole new field has opened up called victimology. [22] With it has come a variety of proposals, justifications, and statutes. [23]

Certain features are common to virtually every compensation proposal: *(a)* Compensation for crimes would be dispensed by the state from tax revenue. *(b)* Compensa-

---

21. Kaufmann, p. 45.

22. For a brief definition of "victimology," see Emilo C. Viano, "Victimology: The Study of the Victim," *Victimology* 1 (1976): 1–7. For an extensive collection of papers on various aspects of victimology, see Emilo C. Viano, ed., *Victims and Society* (Washington, D.C.: Visage Press, 1976).

23. For a discussion and list of symposiums, journal articles, and statutes concerning victim compensation, see Steven Schafer, pp. 139–57, and appendix; see also Joe Hudson and Burt Galaway, eds., *Considering the Victim: Readings in Restitution and Victim Compensation* (Springfield, Ill.: Charles C. Thomas, 1975), esp. pp. 361–436.

tion is "a matter of grace" rather than an assumption by the state of legal responsibility for the criminal loss suffered by the victim. *(c)* Most proposals allow for aid only on a "need" or "hardship" basis. *(d)* Most are limited to some sort of crime of violence or the threat of force or violence. *(e)* None questions the paradigm of punishment.

The goal of these proposals and statutes is laudable. The victim *is* the forgotten man of crime. But the means proposed is the same tired formula: welfare to those in "need." In short, the innocent taxpayer repays the innocent victim (if the victim can prove he "needs" help) while the guilty offender is subjected to the sanction of punishment with all its failings. Like proportionate punishment and rehabilitation, the goal of victim compensation is a recognition of very real problems in our criminal justice system, and at the same time it ignores the source of these problems: our conception of crime as an offense against the state whose proper sanction is punishment. Until a viable, new paradigm is presented, *ad hoc* solutions like the ones discussed here are all that can be hoped for. And it is a vain hope indeed, for they attack the symptoms while neglecting the causes of the problem. What is needed is a new paradigm.

Outline of a New Paradigm

The idea of restitution is actually quite simple. It views crime as an offense by one individual against the rights of another. The victim has suffered a loss. Justice consists of the culpable offender making good the loss he has caused. It calls for a complete refocusing of our image of crime. Kuhn would call it a "shift of world-view." Where we once saw an offense against society, we now see an offense against an individual victim. In a way, it is a common sense view of crime. *The armed robber did not rob society; he robbed the victim.* His debt, therefore, is not to society; it is to the victim. There are really two types of restitution proposals: a system of "punitive" restitution and a "pure" restitutional system.

1. Punitive restitution. "Since rehabilitation was admitted to the aims of penal law two centuries ago, the number of penological aims has remained virtually constant. Restitution is waiting to come in."[24] Given this view, restitution should merely be added to the paradigm of punishment. Stephen Schafer outlines the proposal: "[Punitive] restitution, like punishment, must always be the subject of judicial consideration. Without exception it must be carried out by personal performance by the wrong-doer, and should even then be equally burdensome and just for all criminals, irrespective of their means, whether they be millionaires or labourers."[25]

   There are many ways by which such a goal might be reached. The offender might be forced to compensate the victim by his own work, either in prison or out. If it came out of his pocket or from the sale of his property this would compensate the victim, but it would not be sufficiently unpleasant for the offender. Another proposal would be that the fines be proportionate to the earning power of the criminal. Thus, "A poor man would pay in days of work, a rich man by an equal number of days' income or salary."[26] Herbert Spencer made a proposal along similar lines in his

---

24. Gerhard O. W. Mueller, "Compensation for Victims of Crime: Thought before Action," *Minnesota Law Review* 50 (1965): 221.

25. Schafer, p. 127.

26. Ibid.

excellent "Prison-Ethics," which is well worth examining.[27] Murray N. Rothbard and others have proposed a system of "double payments" in cases of criminal behavior.[28] While closer to pure restitution than other proposals, the "double damages" concept preserves a punitive aspect.

Punitive restitution is an attempt to gain the benefits of pure restitution, which will be considered shortly, while retaining the perceived advantages of the paradigm of punishment. Thus, the prisoner is still "sentenced" to some unpleasantness — prison labor or loss of X number of days' income. That the intention is to preserve the "hurt" is indicated by the hesitation to accept an out-of-pocket payment or sale of assets. This is considered too "easy" for the criminal and takes none of his time. The amount of payment is determined not by the *actual harm* but by the *ability of the offender to pay*. Of course, by retaining the paradigm of punishment this proposal involves many of the problems we raised earlier. In this sense it can be considered another attempt to salvage the old paradigm.

2. Pure restitution. "Recompense or restitution is scarcely a punishment as long as it is merely a matter of returning stolen goods or money. . . . The point is not that the offender deserves to suffer; it is rather that the offended party desires compensation."[29] This represents the complete overthrow of the paradigm of punishment. No longer would the deterrence, reformation, disablement, or rehabilitation of the criminal be the guiding principle of the judicial system. The attainment of these goals would be incidental to, and as a result of, reparations paid to the victim. No longer would the criminal deliberately be made to suffer for his mistake. Making good that mistake is all that would be required. What follows is a possible scenario of such a system.

When a crime occurred and a suspect was apprehended, a trial court would attempt to determine his guilt or innocence. If found guilty, the criminal would be sentenced to make restitution to the victim.[30] If a criminal is able to make restitution immediately, he may do so. This would discharge his liability. If he were unable to make restitution, but were found by the court to be trustworthy, he would be permitted to remain at his job (or find a new one) while paying restitution out of his future wages. This would entail a legal claim against future wages. Failure to pay could result in garnishment or a new type of confinement.

If it is found that the criminal is not trustworthy, or that he is unable to gain employment, he would be confined to an employment project.[31] This would be an industrial

---

27. Herbert Spencer, "Prison-Ethics," in *Essays: Scientific, Political and Speculative* (New York: D. Appleton & Co., 1907), 3:152–91.

28. Murray N. Rothbard, *The Ethics of Liberty* (Atlantic Highlands, N.J.: Humanities Press, 1982) pp. 85–95.

29. Kaufmann, p. 55.

30. The nature of judicial procedure best designed to carry out this task must be determined. For a brief discussion of some relevant considerations, see Laster, pp. 80–98; Burt Galaway and Joe Hudson, "Issues in the Correctional Implementation of Restitution to Victims of Crime," in *Considering the Victim*, pp. 351–60. Also to be dealt with is the proper standard of compensation. At least initially, the problem of how much payment constitutes restitution would be no different than similar considerations in tort law. This will be considered at greater length below.

31. Such a plan (with some significant differences) has been suggested by Kathleen J. Smith in *A Cure for Crime: The Case for the Self-determinate Prison Sentence* (London: Gerald, Duckworth & Co., 1965), pp. 13–29; see also Morris and Linda Tannehill, *The Market for Liberty* (Lansing, Mich.: Privately printed, 1970), pp. 44–108.

enterprise, preferably run by a private concern, which would produce actual goods or services. The level of security at each employment project would vary according to the behavior of the offenders. Since the costs would be lower, inmates at a lower-security project would receive higher wages. There is no reason why many workers could not be permitted to live with their families inside or outside the facility, depending, again, on the trustworthiness of the offender. Room and board would be deducted from the wages first, then a certain amount for restitution. Anything over that amount the worker could keep or apply toward further restitution, thus hastening his release. If a worker refused to work, he would be unable to pay for his maintenance, and therefore would not in principle be entitled to it. If he did not make restitution he could not be released. The exact arrangement which would best provide for high productivity, minimal security, and maximum incentive to work and repay the victim cannot be determined in advance. Experience is bound to yield some plans superior to others. In fact, the experimentation has already begun.[32]

While this might be the basic system, all sorts of refinements are conceivable, and certainly many more will be invented as needs arise. A few examples might be illuminating. With such a system of repayment, victim *crime insurance* would be more economically feasible than at present and highly desirable. The cost of awards would be offset by the insurance company's right to restitution in place of the victim (right of subrogation). The insurance company would be better suited to supervise the offender and mark his progress than would the victim. To obtain an earlier recovery, it could be expected to innovate so as to enable the worker to repay more quickly (and, as a result, be released that much sooner). The insurance companies might even underwrite the employment projects themselves as well as related industries which would employ the skilled worker after his release. Any successful effort on their part to reduce crime and recidivism would result in fewer claims and lower premiums. The benefit of this insurance scheme for the victim is immediate compensation, conditional on the victim's continued cooperation with the authorities for the arrest and conviction of the suspect. In addition, the centralization of victim claims would, arguably, lead to efficiencies which would permit the pooling of small claims against a common offender.

Another highly useful refinement would be *direct arbitration* between victim and criminal. This would serve as a sort of healthy substitute for plea bargaining. By allowing the guilty criminal to negotiate a reduced payment in return for a guilty plea, the victim (or his insurance company) would be saved the risk of an adverse finding at trial and any possible additional expense that might result. This would also allow an indigent criminal to substitute personal services for monetary payments if all parties agreed.

Arbitration is argued for by John M. Greacen, deputy director of the National Institute for Law Enforcement and Criminal Justice. He sees the possible advantages of such reform as the ". . .development of more creative dispositions for most criminal cases; for criminal victims the increased use of restitution, the knowledge that their interests were considered in the criminal process; and an increased satisfaction with the outcome; increased awareness in the part of the offender that his crime was committed

---

32. For a recent summary report, see Burt Galaway, "Restitution as an Integrative Punishment," in Barnett and Hagel, *Assessing the Criminal*, pp. 331–347.

against another human being, and not against society in general; increased possibility that the criminal process will cause the offender to acknowledge responsibility for his acts."[33] Greacen notes several places where such a system has been tried with great success, most notably Tucson, Arizona, and Columbus, Ohio.[34]

Something analogous to the medieval Irish system of *sureties* might be employed as well.[35] Such a system would allow a concerned person, group, or company to make restitution (provided the offender agrees to this). The worker might then be released in the custody of the surety. If the surety had made restitution, the offender would owe restitution to the surety who might enforce the whole claim or show mercy. Of course, the more violent and unreliable the offender, the more serious and costly the offense, the less likely it would be that anyone would take the risk. But for first offenders, good workers, or others that charitable interests found deserving (or perhaps unjustly convicted) this would provide an avenue of respite.

Restitution and Rights

These three possible refinements clearly illustrate the flexibility of a restitutional system. It may be less apparent that this flexibility is *inherent* to the restitutional paradigm. Restitution recognizes rights in the victim, and this is a principal source of its strength. The nature and limit of the victim's right to restitution at the same time defines the nature and limit of the criminal liability. In this way, the aggressive action of the criminal creates a *debt* to the victim. The recognition of rights and obligations make possible many innovative arrangements. Subrogation, arbitration, and suretyship are three examples mentioned above. They are possible because this right to compensation[36] is considered the property of the victim and can therefore be delegated, assigned, inherited, or bestowed. One could determine in advance who would acquire the right to any restitution which he himself might be unable to collect.

The natural owner of an unenforced death claim would be an insurance company that had insured the deceased. The suggestion has been made that a person might thus increase his personal safety by insuring with a company well known for tracking down those who injure its policy holders. In fact, the partial purpose of some insurance schemes might be to provide the funds with which to track down the malefactor. The insurance company, having paid the beneficiaries would "stand in their shoes." It would remain possible, of course, to simply assign or devise the right directly to the beneficiaries, but this would put the burden of enforcement on persons likely to be unsuited to the task.

---

33. John M. Greacen, "Arbitration: A Tool for Criminal Cases?" *Barrister* (Winter 1975), p. 53; see also Galaway and Hudson, pp. 352–55; "Conclusions and Recommendations, International Study Institute on Victimology, Bellagio, Italy, July 1–12, 1975," *Victimology* 1 (1976): 150–51; Ronald Goldfarb, *Jails: The Ultimate Ghetto* (Garden City, N.Y.: Anchor Press / Doubleday, 1976), p. 480.

34. Greacen, p. 53.

35. For a description of the Irish system, see Joseph R. Peden, "Property Rights in Medieval Ireland: Celtic Law versus Church and State," *Journal of Libertarian Studies* 1 (1977): 86.

36. Or, perhaps more accurately, the compensation itself.

If one accepts the Lockean trichotomy of property ownership,[37] that is, acquiring property via exchange, gifts, and *homesteading* (mixing one's labor with previously un-owned land or objects), the possibility arises that upon a person's wrongful death, in the absence of any heirs or assignees, his right to compensation becomes unowned property. The right could then be claimed (homesteaded) by anyone willing to go to the trouble of catching and prosecuting the criminal. Firms might specialize in this sort of activity, or large insurance companies might make the effort as a kind of "loss leader" for public relations purposes.

This does, however, lead to a potentially serious problem with the restitutional paradigm: what exactly constitutes "restitution"? What is the *standard* by which compensation is to be made? Earlier we asserted that any such problem facing the restitutional paradigm faces civil damage suits as well. The method by which this problem is dealt with in civil cases could be applied to restitution cases. But while this is certainly true, it may be that this problem has not been adequately handled in civil damage suits either.

Restitution in cases of crimes against property is a manageable problem. Modern contract and tort doctrines of restitution are adequate. The difficulty lies in cases of personal injury or death. How can you put a price on life or limb, pain or suffering? Is not any attempt to do so of necessity arbitrary? It must be admitted that a fully satisfactory solution to this problem is lacking, but it should also be stressed that this dilemma, though serious, has little impact on the bulk of our case in favor of a restitutional paradigm. It is possible that no paradigm of criminal justice can solve every problem, yet the restitutional approach remains far superior to the paradigm of punishment or any other conceivable rival.

This difficulty arises because certain property is unique and irreplaceable. As a result, it is impossible to approximate a "market" or "exchange" value expressed in monetary terms. Just as there is no rational relationship between a wrongfully taken life and ten years in prison, there is little relationship between that same life and $20,000. Still, the nature of this possibly insoluble puzzle reveals a restitutional approach theoretically superior to punishment. For it must be acknowledged that a real, tangible loss *has* occurred. The problem is only one of incommensurability. Restitution provides *some* tangible, albeit inadequate, compensation for personal injury. Punishment provides none at all.[38]

It might be objected that to establish some "pay scale" for personal injury is not only somewhat arbitrary but also a disguised reimplementation of punishment. Unable to accept the inevitable consequences of restitutional punishment, the argument continues, I have retreated to a pseudorestitutional award. Such a criticism is unfair. The true test in this instance is one of primacy of intentions. Is the purpose of a system to compensate victims for their losses (and perhaps, as a consequence, punish the criminals), or is its purpose to punish the criminals (and perhaps, as a consequence, compen-

---

37. For a brief explanation of this concept and several of its possible applications, see Murray N. Rothbard, "Justice and Property Rights," in *Property in a Humane Economy,* ed. Samuel L. Blumenfeld (La Salle, Ill.: Open Court Publishing Co., 1974), pp. 101–22.

38. That the "spiritual" satisfaction which punishment may or may not provide is to be recognized as a legitimate form of "compensation" is a claim retributionists must defend.

sate the victims for their losses)? The true ends of a criminal justice system will determine its nature. In short, arbitrariness *alone* does not imply a retributive motive. And while arbitrariness remains to some extent a problem for the restitutional paradigm, it is less of a problem for restitution than for punishment, since compensation has *some* rational relationship to damages and costs.

Advantages of a Restitutional System

1. The first and most obvious advantage is the assistance provided to victims of crime. They may have suffered an emotional, physical, or financial loss. Restitution would not change the fact that a possibly traumatic crime has occurred (just as the award of damages does not undo tortious conduct). Restitution, however, would make the resulting loss easier to bear for both victims and their families. At the same time, restitution would avoid a major pitfall of victim compensation/welfare plans: Since it is the criminal who must pay, the possibility of collusion between victim and criminal to collect "damages" from the state would be all but eliminated.
2. The possibility of receiving compensation would encourage victims to report crimes and to appear at trial. This is particularly true if there were a crime insurance scheme which contractually committed the policyholder to testify as a condition for payment, thus rendering unnecessary oppressive and potentially tyrannical subpoenas and contempt citations. Even the actual reporting of the crime to police is likely to be a prerequisite for compensation. Such a requirement in auto theft insurance policies has made car thefts the most fully reported crime in the United States. Furthermore, insurance companies which paid the claim would have a strong incentive to see that the criminal was apprehended and convicted. Their pressure and assistance would make the proper functioning of law enforcement officials all the more likely.
3. Psychologist Albert Eglash has long argued that restitution would aid in the rehabilitation of criminals. "Restitution is something an inmate does, not something done for or to him. . . . Being reparative, restitution can alleviate guilt and anxiety, which can otherwise precipitate further offenses."[39] Restitution, says Eglash, is an active effortful role on the part of the offender. It is socially constructive, thereby contributing to the offender's self-esteem. It is related to the offense and may thereby redirect the thoughts which motivated the offense. It is reparative, restorative, and may actually leave the situation better than it was before the crime, both for the criminal and victim.[40]
4. This is a genuinely "self-determinative" sentence.[41] The worker would know that the length of his confinement was in his own hands. The harder he worked, the faster he would make restitution. He would be the master of his fate and would have to face that responsibility. This would encourage useful, productive activity and instill a conception of reward for good behavior and hard work. Compare this with the cur-

---

39. Albert Eglash, "Creative Restitution: Some Suggestions for Prison Rehabilitation Programs," *American Journal of Correction* 40 (November–December 1958): 20.
40. Ibid.; see also Eglash's "Creative Restitution: A Broader Meaning for an Old Term," *Journal of Criminal Law and Criminology* 48 (1958): 619–22; Burt Galaway and Joe Hudson, "Restitution and Rehabilitation—Some Central Issues," *Crime and Delinquency* 18 (1972): 403–10.
41. Smith, pp. 13–29.

rent probationary system and "indeterminate sentencing" where the decision for release is made by the prison bureaucracy, based only (if fairly administered) on "good behavior"; that is, passive acquiescence to prison discipline. Also, the fact that the worker would be acquiring *marketable* skills rather than more skillful methods of crime should help to reduce the shocking rate of recidivism.

5. The savings to taxpayers would be enormous. No longer would the innocent tax-payer pay for the apprehension and internment of the guilty. The cost of arrest, trial, and internment would be borne by the criminal himself. In addition, since now-idle inmates would become productive workers (able, perhaps, to support their families), the entire economy would benefit from the increase in overall production.[42]

6. Crime would no longer pay. Criminals, particularly shrewd white-collar criminals, would know that they could not dispose of the proceeds of their crime, and if caught, simply serve time. They would have to make full restitution plus enforcement and legal costs, thereby greatly increasing the incentive to prosecute. While this would not eliminate such crime it would make it rougher on certain types of criminals, like bank and corporation officials, who harm many by their acts with a virtual assurance of lenient legal sanctions.[43] It might also encourage such criminals to keep the money around for a while so that, if caught, they could repay more easily. This would make a full recovery more likely.

A restitutional system of justice would benefit the victim, the criminal, and the taxpayer. The humanitarian goals of proportionate punishment, rehabilitation, and victim compensation are dealt with on a *fundamental* level making their achievement more likely. In short, the paradigm of restitution would benefit all but the entrenched penal bureaucracy and enhance justice at the same time. What then is there to stop us from overthrowing the paradigm of punishment and its penal system and putting in its place this more efficient, more humane, and more just system? The proponents of punishment and others have a few powerful counterarguments. It is to these we now turn.

Objections to Restitution

1. Practical criticisms of restitution. It might be objected that "crimes disturb and offend not only those who are directly their victim, but also the whole social or-der."[44] Because of this, society, that is, individuals other than the victim, deserves some satisfaction from the offender. Restitution, it is argued, will not satisfy the lust for revenge felt by the victim or the "community's sense of justice." This criticism appears to be overdrawn. Today most members of the community are mere spectators of the criminal justice system, and this is largely true even of the victim.[45] One major reform

---

42. An economist who favors restitution on efficiency grounds is Gary S. Becker, although he does not break with the paradigm of punishment. Those interested in a mathematical "cost-benefit" analysis should see his "Crime and Punishment," *Journal of Political Economy* 76 (1968): 169–217.
43. This point is also made by Minocher Jehangirji Sethna in his paper, "Treatment and Atone-ment for Crime," in *Victims and Society*, p. 538.
44. Del Vecchio, p. 198.
45. William F. McDonald, "Towards a Bicentennial Revolution in Criminal Justice: The Return

being urged presently is more victim involvement in the criminal justice process.[46] The restitution proposal would necessitate this involvement. And while the public generally takes the view that officials should be tougher on criminals, with "tougher" taken by nearly everyone to mean more severe in punishing, one must view this "social fact" in light of the lack of a known alternative. The real test of public sympathies would be to see which sanction people would choose: incarceration of the criminal for a given number of years or the criminal's being compelled to make restitution to the victim: While the public's choice is not clearly predictable, neither can it be assumed that it would reject restitution. There is some evidence to the contrary.[47]

This brings us to a second practical objection: that monetary sanctions are insufficient deterrents to crime. Again, this is something to be discovered, not something to be assumed. There are a number of reasons to believe that our *current* system of punishment does not adequately deter, and for the reasons discussed earlier an increase in the level of punishment is unlikely. In fact, many have argued that the deterrent value of sanctions has less to do with *severity* than with *certainty*,[48] and the preceding considerations indicate that law enforcement would be more certain under a restitutional system. In the final analysis, however, it is irrelevant to argue that more crimes may be committed if our proposal leaves the victim better off. It must be remembered: *Our goal is not the suppression of crime; it is doing justice to victims.*

---

of the Victim," *American Criminal Law Review* 13 (1976): 659; see also his paper "Notes on the Victim's Role in the Prosecutional and Dispositional Stages of the Criminal Justice Process" (paper presented at the Second International Symposium on Victimology, Boston, September 1976), and "The Role of the Victim in America," in Barnett and Hagel, *Assessing the Criminal*, pp. 295–305; Jack M. Kress, "The Role of the Victim at Sentencing" (paper presented at the Second International Symposium on Victimology, Boston, September 1976).

46. McDonald, pp. 669–73; Kress, pp. 11–15. Kress specifically analyzes restitution as a means for achieving victim involvement.

47. In two types of studies conducted for the Ventura County Board of Supervisors, Ventura, California, support for a restitutional program was indicated: "Both the citizen attitude survey and the Delphi goal-setting exercise revealed a strong concern for the *victim* as the 'forgotten man' of criminal justice. The Delphi panelists, in particular, emphasized the need for new kinds of criminal penalities in which the offender would be required to make restitution to his victim(s)" (*Development of a Model Criminal Justice System* [Santa Barbara, Calif.: Public Safety Systems, 1973], p. 85). The report recommends the implementing of a system of restitution. In the two cities mentioned earlier (Columbus and Tucson), support, at least by the parties involved, appeared strong. In the thousands of cases arbitrated by trained law students in Columbus, only 4 percent proceeded further up in the criminal system. In Tucson after one year the program has been successful in all but nine of 204 cases (with the cost of handling each case at $304 compared with $1,566 required to process the average felony case). General approval of restitution in lieu of punishment was indirectly referred to in the *Columbia Law Review's* oft-cited study, "Restitution and the Criminal Law": "[E]ven where the complainant can be persuaded to continue the criminal case, after having received private satisfaction, his apathy is often so pronounced and his demeanor so listless that he becomes an extremely weak witness. . . . Also the knowledge of actual restitution seems to greatly assuage the jury. Even the knowledge of the existence of a civil suit can lead the jury to recommend leniency or acquittal" (39 [1939]: 1189; see also n. 31). Restitution, it seems, is accepted and preferred by the average person. Early studies indicate that, when properly administered, even offenders perceive a restitutionary sanction as fair (William Marsella and Burt Galaway, "Study of the Perceived Fairness of Restitution as a Sanction for Juvenile Offenders" [paper presented to the Second International Symposium on Victimology, Boston, September 1976]).

48. Yochelson and Samenow, pp. 453–57.

A practical consideration which merits considerable future attention is the feasibility of the employment project proposal. A number of questions can be raised. At first blush, it seems naively optimistic to suppose that offenders will be able or willing to work at all, much less earn their keep and pay reparations as well. On the contrary, this argument continues, individuals turn to crime precisely because they lack the skills which the restitutional plan assumes they have. Even if these workers have the skills, but refuse to work, what could be done? Would not the use of force to compel compliance be tantamount to slavery? This criticism results in part from my attempt to sketch an "ideal" restitution system; that is, I have attempted to outline the type toward which every criminal justice system governed by the restitution paradigm should strive. This is not to say that every aspect of the hypothetical system would, upon implementation, function smoothly. Rather, such a system could only operate ideally once the paradigm had been fully accepted and substantially articulated.

With this in mind, one can advance several responses. First, the problem as usually posed assumes the offender to be highly irrational and possibly mentally unbalanced. There is no denying that some segment of the criminal population fits the former description.[49] What this approach neglects, however, is the possibility that many criminals are making rational choices within an irrational and unjust political system. Specifically I refer to the myriad laws and regulations which make it difficult for the unskilled or persons of transitory outlook[50] to find legal employment.[51] I refer also to the laws which deny legality to the types of services which are in particular demand in economically impoverished communities.[52] Is it "irrational" to choose to steal or rob when one is virtually foreclosed from the legal opportunity to do otherwise? Another possibility is that the criminal chooses crime not because of foreclosure, but because he enjoys and obtains satisfaction from a criminal way of life.[53] Though morally repugnant, this is hardly irrational.

Furthermore, it no longer can be denied that contact with the current criminal justice system is itself especially damaging among juveniles.[54] The offenders who are

---

49. For a discussion rejecting the usefulness of the latter description, see Szasz, pp. 91–146; for a recent study verifying Szasz's thesis, see Yochelson and Samenow, esp. pp. 227–35.

50. Edward C. Banfield put forth his controversial theory of time horizon in his book *The Unheavenly City* (Boston: Little, Brown & Co., 1970) and amplified it in *The Unheavenly City Revisited* (Boston: Little, Brown & Co., 1974), and most recently, "Present-orientedness and Crime," in Barnett and Hagel, *Assessing the Criminal,* pp. 143–162. For a critical, but favorable analysis of this approach, see Gerald P. O'Driscoll, Jr., "Professor Banfield on Time Horizon: What Has He Taught Us about Crime?" in Barnett and Hagel, *Assessing the Criminal,* pp. 143–162. A contrary, but ultimately compatible view is presented by Yochelson and Samenow, pp. 369–72.

51. For example, minimum wage laws, and so-called closed-shop union protectionist legislation.

52. For example, laws prohibiting gambling, prostitution, sale of drugs, "jitney" cab services, etc.

53. "It is not the environment that turns a man into a criminal. Rather it is a series of choices that he makes at a very early age. . . . [T]he criminal is not a victim of circumstances" (Yochelson and Samenow, pp. 247, 249). This is in essence the main conclusion of their research. (For a concise summary of their provocative book, see Joseph Boorkin, "The Criminal Personality," *Federal Bar Journal* 35 [1976]: 237–41.) In *The Criminal Personality,* vol. 2, *The Process of Change* (New York: Jason Aronson, Inc., 1977) they relate and examine the methods they have employed to change the criminal thought pattern. Of course, such an approach can itself be subject to abuse.

54. See, e.g., Edwin M. Schur, *Radical Noninterventionism, Rethinking the Delinquency Problem* (Englewood Cliffs, N.J.: Prentice-Hall, Inc., 1973).

hopelessly committed to criminal behavior are not usually the newcomers to crime but those who have had repeated exposure to the penal system. In Kuhn's words, "Existing institutions have ceased to meet the problems posed by an environment *they have in part created*."[55] While a restitutionary system might not change these hard-core offenders, it could, by the early implementation of sanctions perceived by the criminal to be just, break the vicious circle which in large part accounts for their existence.

Finally, if offenders could not or would not make restitution, then the logical and just result of their refusal would be confinement until they could or would. Such an outcome would be entirely in their hands. While this "solution" does not suggest who should justly pay for this confinement, the problem is not unique to a restitutionary system. In this and other areas of possible difficulty we must seek guidance from existing pilot programs as well as from the burgeoning research in this area and in victimology in general.

2. Distributionary criticisms of restitution. There remains one criticism of restitution which is the most obvious and the most difficult with which to deal. Simply stated, it takes the following form: "Doesn't this mean that rich people will be able to commit crimes with impunity if they can afford it? Isn't this unfair?" The *practical* aspect of this objection is that whatever deterrent effect restitution payments may have, they will be less for those most able to pay. The *moral* aspect is that whatever retributive or penal effect restitution payments may have they will be less for those who are well off. Some concept of equality of justice underlies both considerations.

Critics of restitution fail to realize that the "cost" of crime will be quite high. In addition to compensation for pain and suffering, the criminal must pay for the cost of his apprehension, the cost of the trial, and the legal expenditures of *both* sides. This should make even an unscrupulous wealthy person think twice about committing a crime. The response to this is that we cannot have it both ways. If the fines would be high enough to bother the rich, then they would be so high that a project worker would have no chance of earning that much and would, therefore, have no incentive to work at all. If, on the other hand, you lower the price of crime by ignoring all its costs, you fail to deter the rich or fully compensate the victim.

This is where the option of arbitration and victim crime insurance becomes of practical importance. If the victim is uninsured, he is unlikely to recover for all costs of a very severe crime from a poor, unskilled criminal, since even in an employment project the criminal might be unable to earn enough. If he had no hope of earning his release, he would have little incentive to work very hard beyond paying for his own maintenance. The victim would end up with less than if he had "settled" the case for the lesser amount which a project worker could reasonably be expected to earn. If, however, the victim had full-coverage criminal insurance, he would recover his damages in full, and the insurance company would absorb any disparity between full compensation and maximal employment project worker's output. This cost would be reflected in premium prices, enabling the insurance company which settled cases at an amount which increased the recovery from the criminal to offer the lowest rates. Eventually a "maximum" feasible fine for project workers would be determined based on these consider-

---

55. Kuhn, p. 92 (emphasis added).

ations. The "rich," on the other hand, would naturally have to pay in full. This arrangement would solve the practical problem, but it should not be thought of as an imperative of the restitutional paradigm.

The same procedure of varying the payments according to ability to pay would answer the moral considerations as well (that the rich are not hurt enough) and this is the prime motive behind *punitive* restitution proposals. However, we reject the moral consideration outright. The paradigm of restitution calls not for the (equal) hurting of criminals, but for restitution to victims. Any appeal to "inadequate suffering" is a reversion to the paradigm of punishment, and by varying the sanction for crimes of the same magnitude according to the economic status of the offender it reveals its own inequity. *Equality of justice means equal treatment of victims.* It should not matter to the victim if his attacker was rich or poor. His plight is the same regardless. Any reduction of criminal liability because of reduced earning power would be for practical, not moral, reasons.

Equality of justice derives from the fact that the rights of men should be equally enforced and respected. Restitution recognizes a victim's right to compensation for damages from the party responsible. Equality of justice, therefore, calls for equal enforcement of each victim's right to restitution. *Even if necessary or expedient, any lessening of payment to the victim because of the qualities of the criminal is a violation of that victim's rights and an inequality of justice.* Any such expedient settlement is only a recognition that an imperfect world may make possible only imperfect justice. As a practical matter, a restitutional standard gives victims an enormous incentive to pursue wealthy criminals since they can afford quick, full compensation. Contrast this with the present system where the preference given the wealthy is so prevalent that most victims simply assume that nothing will be done.

The paradigm of restitution, to reiterate, is neither a panacea for crime nor a blueprint for utopia. Panaceas and utopias are not for humankind. We must live in a less than perfect world with less than perfect people. Restitution opens the possibility of an improved and more just society. The old paradigm of punishment, even reformed, simply cannot offer this promise.

Other Considerations

Space does not permit a full examination of other less fundamental implications of such a system. I shall briefly consider five.

1. Civil versus criminal liability. If one accepts a restitutionary standard of justice, what sense does it make to distinguish between crime and tort, since both call for payment of damages? For most purposes I think the distinction collapses. Richard Epstein, in a series of brilliant articles, has articulated a theory of strict liability in tort.[56] His view is that since one party has caused another some harm and one of the

---

56. Richard A. Epstein, "A Theory of Strict Liability in Tort," *Journal of Legal Studies* 2 (1973): 151–204.

parties must bear the loss, justice demands that it falls on the party who caused the harm. He argues that intention is only relevant as a "third-stage" argument; that notwithstanding some fault on the part of the plaintiff (a second-stage argument), the defendant intended the harm and is therefore liable.[57] With a restitutional system I see no reason why Epstein's theory of tort liability could not incorporate criminal liability into a single "system of corrective justice that looks to the conduct, broadly defined, of the parties to the case with a view toward the protection of individual liberty and private property."[58]

There would, at least initially, be some differences, however. The calculation of damages under the restitutionary paradigm which includes cost of apprehension, cost of trial, and legal costs of both parties would be higher than tort law allows. A further distinction would be the power of enforcers to confine unreliable offenders to employment projects.[59]

2. Criminal responsibility and competency. Once a criminal sanction is based not on the offender's badness but on the nature and consequences of his acts, Thomas Szasz's proposal that the insanity plea be abolished makes a great deal of sense,[60] as does his argument that "all persons charged with offenses—except those grossly disabled—[are fit to stand trial and] should be tried."[61] On this view, Epstein's concept of fairness *as between the parties* is relevant. A restitution proceeding like a "lawsuit is always a comparative affair. The defendant's victory ensures the plaintiff's [or victim's] defeat. . . . Why should we prefer the injurer to his victim in a case where one may win and the other lose? . . . As a matter of fairness between the parties, the

---

57. Richard A. Epstein, "Intentional Harms," *Journal of Legal Studies* 3 (1975): 402–8; see also his article "Defenses and Subsequent Pleas in a System of Strict Liability," ibid., 3 (1974): 174–85.

58. Epstein, "Intentional Harms," p. 441. Epstein himself would disagree. In a recent article, also notable for its well-reasoned rejection of victim compensation / welfare schemes, "Crime and Tort: Old Wine in Old Bottles," in Barnett and Hagel, *Assessing the Criminal,* pp. 231–257, he draws an emphatic distinction between tort and criminal law. He rests this distinction on two characteristics of the criminal law: (*a*) that its function is to punish (and therefore *mens rea* is required and more stringent procedural safeguards are appropriate), and (*b*) since the defendant is prosecuted by the state, fairness as between the parties is not relevant. From these assumptions, Epstein reasons quite correctly that the two systems are inherently different. It should be obvious that a restitutionary paradigm undermines both assumptions. Gilbert M. Cantor in his article, "An End to Crime and Punishment" (*Shingle* 39 [May 1976]: 99–114), takes precisely this view, arguing that "the time has come to abolish the game of crime and punishment and to substitute a paradigm of restitution and responsibility. I urge that we assign (reassign, actually) to the civil law our societal response to the acts or behaviors we now label and treat as criminal. The goal is the *civilization* of our treatment of offenders. I use the word, 'civilization' here in its specific meaning: to bring offenders under the civil, rather than the criminal law; and in its larger meaning: to move in this area of endeavor from barbarism toward greater enlightenment and humanity" (p. 107; emphasis in original).

59. It would seem that the only way to account for these differences would be an appeal to the *mens rea* or badness of the criminal as opposed to the unintentional tortfeasor. Yet such an approach, it might be argued, is not available to a restitutionary system which considers the moral outlook of an offender to be irrelevant to the determination of the proper criminal sanction. A possible response is that this overstates the restitutionist claim. That a criminal's mental state does not justify punishment does not imply that it is not relevant to *any* aspect of the criminal justice process. It may well be that it is relevant to the consideration of methods by which one is justified in extracting what, on other grounds, is shown to be a proper sanction, that is, restitution.

60. Szasz, pp. 228–30.

61. Ibid., pp. 228–29. "The emphasis here is on gross disability: it should be readily apparent or easily explicable to a group of lay persons, like a jury" (p. 229). But even the qualification of gross disablement might be unjustified (see Yochelson and Samenow, pp. 227–35).

defendant should be required to treat the harms which he has inflicted upon another as though they were inflicted upon himself." [62]

3. Victimless crimes. The effect of restitutional standards on the legality of such crimes as prostitution, gambling, high interest loans, pornography, and drug use is intriguing. There has been no violation of individual rights, and consequently no damages and, therefore, no liability. While some may see this as a drawback, I believe it is a striking advantage of the restitutional standard of justice. So-called victimless crimes would in principle cease to be crimes. As a consequence, criminal elements would be denied a lucrative monopoly, and the price of these services would be drastically reduced. Without this enormous income, organized crime would be far less able to afford the "cost" of its nefarious activities than it is today.

4. Legal positivism. What is true for victimless crimes is true for the philosophy of legal positivism. On the positivist view, whatever the state (following all the correct political procedures) says is law, is law; hence, whatever the state makes a crime is a crime. A restitutional standard would hold the state to enforcing individual rights through the recovery of individual damages.

5. Legal process. Because the sanction for crime would no longer be punitive, the criminal process could explore less formal procedures for dispute settlement. Also, the voice of the victim would be added to the deliberations. One possible reform might be a three-tiered verdict: guilty, not proven, and not guilty. If found "guilty," the offender would pay all the costs mentioned above. If the charges are "not proven," then neither party would pay the other. If found "not guilty," the defendant would be reimbursed by the enforcement agency for his costs and inconvenience. This new interpretation of "not guilty" would reward those defendants who, after putting on a defense, convinced the trier of fact that they were innocent.

These and many other fascinating implications of restitution deserve a more thorough examination. As any new paradigm becomes accepted, it experiences what Kuhn calls a period of "normal research," a period characterized by continuous expansion and perfection of the new paradigm as well as a testing of its limits. The experimentation with restitutionary justice will, however, differ from the trial and error of the recent past since we will be guided by the principle that the purpose of our legal system is not to harm the guilty but to help the innocent—a principle which will above all restore our belief that our overriding commitment is to do justice.

---

62. Epstein, p. 398. In his article "Crime and Tort: Old Wine in Old Bottles," he takes exactly this approach with the insanity defense in tort law.

Suggestions for Further Reading

T he readings here are intended to provide students with an opportunity to increase the sophistication of their understanding of the issues explored in the present anthology. Thus some are more difficult than those contained in the text. Many will also lead the student into related areas of inquiry.

The Criminal Law and the Justification of Punishment

Andenaes, Johannes. *Punishment and Deterrence.* Ann Arbor: University of Michigan Press, 1974.

Fingarette, Herbert. "Punishment and Suffering," in *Proceedings at the American Philosophical Association* (1977).

Fletcher, George P. *Rethinking Criminal Law.* Boston: Little, Brown, 1978.

Gibbs, Jack P. *Crime, Punishment, and Deterrence.* New York: Elsevier, 1975.

Gross, Hyman. *A Theory of Criminal Justice.* Oxford: Oxford University Press, 1979.

Hampton, Jean. "The Moral Education Theory of Punishment," in *Philosophy and Public Affairs* 13 (3): 208–238 (Summer 1984).

Hart, H. L. A. *Punishment and Responsibility.* Oxford: Oxford University Press, 1968.

Kadish, Sanford H.; Stephen J. Schulhofer, and Monrad G. Paulsen, eds. *Criminal Law and Its Processes: Cases and Materials,* 4th ed. Boston: Little, Brown, 1983.

Moberly, Walter. *The Ethics of Punishment*. Hamden, Conn.: Shoestring Press, 1968.

Morris, Herbert. *On Guilt and Innocence*. Berkeley: University of California Press, 1976.

Murphy, Jeffrie G. *Retribution, Justice and Therapy: Essays in the Philosophy of Law*. Dordrecht, Netherlands: D. Reidel, 1979.

Murphy, Jeffrie G., and Jules L. Coleman. *The Philosophy of Law: An Introduction to Jurisprudence*. Totowa, N.J.: Rowman & Allanheld, 1984, chap. 3.

Nozick, Robert. "Retributive Punishment," in *Philosophical Explanations*. Cambridge: Harvard University Press, 1981, pp. 363–397.

Packer, Herbert. *The Limits of the Criminal Sanction*. Stanford, Ca.: Stanford University Press, 1968.

Pennock, J. Roland, and John W. Chapman, eds. *Nomos XXVII: Criminal Justice*. New York: New York University Press, 1984.

Zimring, Franklin E., and Gordon J. Hawkins. *Deterrence*. Chicago: University of Chicago Press, 1972.

Sentencing and the Death Penalty

Bedau, Hugo Adam, ed. *The Death Penalty in America*, 3d ed. Oxford: Oxford University Press, 1982. This book contains an excellent and extensive bibliography on the topic.

Gross, Hyman, and Andrew von Hirsch, eds. *Sentencing*. Oxford: Oxford University Press, 1981.

von Hirsch, Andrew. *Doing Justice: The Choice of Punishments*. New York: Hill & Wang, 1976.

Alternatives to Punishment (and the General Issues of Law and Psychiatry)

The books above by Hart, Morris, and Murphy contain essays relevant to this topic. See also the following:

Fingarette, Herbert. *The Meaning of Criminal Insanity*. Berkeley: University of California Press, 1972.

Kittrie, Nicholas N. *The Right to be Different: Deviance and Enforced Therapy*. Baltimore: Johns Hopkins University Press, 1971.

Moore, Michael S. *Law and Psychiatry: Rethinking the Relationship*. Cambridge: Cambridge University Press, 1984.

Szsaz, Thomas S. *The Myth of Mental Illness*. New York: Harper & Row, 1961.

———. *Psychiatric Justice*. New York: Macmillan, 1965.

Wexler, David B. *Mental Health Law: Major Issues*. New York: Plenum Press, 1981.